Generations and Politics

*A Panel Study of Young Adults
and Their Parents*

Generations and Politics

*A Panel Study of Young Adults
and Their Parents*

M. KENT JENNINGS AND RICHARD G. NIEMI

Princeton University Press
Princeton, New Jersey

Copyright © 1981 by Princeton University Press

Published by Princeton University Press, Princeton, New Jersey
In the United Kingdom: Princeton University Press, Guildford, Surrey

All Rights Reserved

Library of Congress Cataloging in Publication Data will be
found on the last printed page of this book

This book has been composed in linotype Caledonia

Clothbound editions of Princeton University Press books
are printed on acid-free paper, and binding materials are
chosen for strength and durability.

Printed in the United States of America by Princeton
University Press, Princeton, New Jersey

CONTENTS

LIST OF TABLES   vi
LIST OF FIGURES   viii
ACKNOWLEDGMENTS   xi

1   The Study of Persistence and Change   3

2   Persistence at the Individual Level: Involvement,
    Resources, and Participation   19

3   Persistence at the Individual Level: Political
    Preferences and Attitudes   48

4   The Dynamics of Family Transmission   76

5   Continuity and Change at the Aggregate Level:
    Involvement, Resources, and Participation   115

6   Continuity and Change at the Aggregate Level: Political
    Preferences and Attitudes   152

7   The Identification of Generations: Cohort versus Panel
    Change   190

8   The Prominence of Educational Stratification   230

9   Sex, Gender Roles, and the Challenge to Tradition   271

10 Race Comparisons in an Era of Change   306

11 Protest Behavior and Its Legacy   331

12 Conclusion: Interpretation of a Half-Empty Glass   380

    APPENDIX A   Data Sources   393
    APPENDIX B   Description of Basic Measures and Their
                 Distributions for Youths and Parents, 1965
                 and 1973   404
    INDEX   421

TABLE

2.1	References to Political Qualities of Good Citizen	27
2.2	Interest in Public Affairs	28
2.3	Local versus Cosmopolitan Focus of Political Interest	30
2.4	Frequency of Newspaper and Television Usage to Follow Public Affairs	31
2.5	Political Conversations in the Family	34
2.6	References to Active Political Qualities of Good Citizen	36
2.7	Internal Political Efficacy	37
2.8	Recognition and Understanding of Liberal-Conservative Dimension	38
2.9	Knowledge of Political Facts	40
2.10	Voting Turnout	42
3.1	Party Identification	50
3.2	Opinions on Public Policy Issues	56
3.3	Political Qualities Least Proud of as an American	63
3.4	Trust in Political Authorities	64
3.5	Summary Statistics on Evaluation of Sociopolitical Groups	66
3.6	Belief in Divinity of Bible	69
3.7	Frequency of Church Attendance	70
4.1	Parent-Youth Similarity in Television Viewing, 1965 and 1973	85
4.2	Parent-Youth Party Identification, 1973	91
4.3	Similarity between Parents' Attitudes in 1965 and Youths' Attitudes in 1973 on Different Issues	105
6.1	Real and Perceived Generation Gaps on Political Issues, 1973	162
7.1	Political Conversations with Family and Friends	224
7.2	Attributes of the Good Citizen	225
7.3	Qualities Least Proud of as an American	226
8.1	Stability and Change among Youths, by Education	240
8.2	Psychological Involvement in Politics, by Generation, Education, and Year	244
8.3	Political Resources, by Generation, Education, and Year	249
8.4	Opinions on Policy Issues, by Generation, Education, and Year	258
8.5	Nonpolitical Orientations, by Generation, Education, and Year	264
9.1	Psychological Involvement in Politics, by Generation, Sex, and Year	277
9.2	Political Resources, by Generation, Sex, and Year	281
9.3	Political Activity Index in 1973, by Generation and Sex	283
9.4	Partisanship and Voting, by Generation, Sex, and Year	284
9.5	Nonpolitical Orientations, by Generation, Sex, and Year	291

10.1   Psychological Involvement in Politics, by Generation, Race,
            and Year   311
10.2   Political Resources, by Generation, Race, and Year   314
10.3   Partisanship, by Generation, Race, and Year, and by Race and
            Education   319
10.4   Opinions on Policy Issues, by Generation, Race, and Year   321
10.5   Evaluations of Government, by Generation, Race, and Year   323
10.6   Evaluations of Sociopolitical Groups, by Generation, Race, and
            Year   325
10.7   Nonpolitical Orientations, by Generation, Race, and Year   328
11.1   Psychological Involvement and Political Resources among
            Protestors and Nonprotestors (College Graduates)   340
11.2   Comparison of Protestors and Nonprotestors, by Academic
            Milieu (College Graduates)   356
11.3   Effects of Protesting on Political Orientations, with Other
            Factors Controlled (College Graduates)   360
11.4   Self-Location on Public Policy Issues, by Level of Protest
            Activity (College Graduates)   366
11.5   Effects of Protest Activity Level, with Other Factors Controlled
            (Entire Youth Sample)   376
A.1   Summary of Field Work and Data Sources   394
A.2   Background Comparisons of Panel and Non-Panel Respondents
            from the 1965 Youth Survey   397
A.3   Sociopolitical Comparisons of Panel and Non-Panel
            Respondents from the 1965 Youth Survey   398
A.4   Comparisons of Partisan and Issue Positions of Panel and Non-
            Panel Respondents from the 1965 Youth Survey   399
A.5   Comparisons of Personal Interviews and Mass-Administered
            Questionnaires from Same Respondents, 1965 Youth   400
A.6   Selected Comparisons of Personal Interviews and Mailback
            Questionnaires, from 1973 Youth Survey   401
A.7   Comparisons of Indexes Based on Personal Interviews and
            Mailback Questionnaires from 1973 Youth   403

FIGURE

4.1 Psychological Involvement in Politics (Pair Similarity Over
     Time)   84
4.2 Political Resources (Pair Similarity Over Time)   86
4.3 Political Participation (Pair Similarity Over Time)   88
4.4 Partisanship and Voting (Pair Similarity Over Time)   90
4.5 Opinions on Public Policy Issues (Pair Similarity Over Time) 94
4.6 Evaluations of the Political System (Pair Similarity Over
     Time)   96
4.7 Evaluations of Sociopolitical Groupings (Pair Similarity Over
     Time)   97
4.8 Nonpolitical Orientations (Pair Similarity Over Time)   99
5.1 Models of Continuity and Change   119
5.2 References to Political Qualities of Good Citizen   125
5.3 Interest in Public Affairs   128
5.4 Mass Media Usage to Follow Public Affairs   130
5.5 Political Conversations in the Family   134
5.6 References to Active Political Qualities of Good Citizen   135
5.7 Internal Political Efficacy   137
5.8 Recognition and Understanding of Liberal-Conservative
     Dimension   140
5.9 Knowledge of Political Facts   143
5.10 Voting Turnout   148
5.11 Performance of Specific Political Activities   149
6.1 Party Identification   153
6.2 Republican Voting in Five Elections   155
6.3 Opinions on Public Policy Issues   158
6.4 References to Qualities Least Proud of as an American   168
6.5 Specific Objects Least Proud of as an American   170
6.6 Trust in Political Authorities   174
6.7 Faith and Confidence in Levels of Government   176
6.8 Mean Evaluation of Sociopolitical Groupings   178
6.9 Religious Beliefs and Practices   184
7.1 Models of Aggregate Continuity and Change   194
7.2 Models of Generational Effects   195
7.3 Interest in Public Affairs   200
7.4 Political Efficacy   204
7.5 Partisanship and Voting   206
7.6 Opinions on Public Policy Issues   208
7.7 Political Trust   212
7.8 Faith and Confidence in Levels of Government   216

7.9	Weekly Church Attendance	217
7.10	Interpersonal Trust	218
7.11	Personal Efficacy: Self-Confidence	220
8.1	Ratio of Active to Allegiant Descriptions of Good Citizen, by Years of Schooling	247
8.2	Voting Turnout by Years of Schooling	251
8.3	Performance of Specific Political Activities, by Years of Schooling	252
8.4	Proportion of Young Adults Favoring Republican Presidential Candidates, by Years of Schooling	256
10.1	Performance of Specific Political Activities, by Race	317
11.1	Timing of Protest Activities	334
11.2	Ratio of Active to Allegiant Descriptions of Good Citizen among Protestors and Nonprotestors (College Graduates)	342
11.3	Frequency of Other Political Activities among Protestors and Nonprotestors (College Graduates)	343
11.4	Party Identification among Protestors and Nonprotestors (College Graduates)	346
11.5	Preference for Republican Presidential Nominees among Protestors and Nonprotestors (College Graduates)	347
11.6	Opinions on Two Public Policy Issues among Protestors and Nonprotestors (College Graduates)	349
11.7	Levels of Civic Tolerance among Protestors and Nonprotestors (College Graduates)	350
11.8	Political Trust among Protestors and Nonprotestors (College Graduates)	352
11.9	Republican Preference in Presidential Elections, by Level of Protest Activity (College Graduates)	362
11.10	Evaluations of Political Groups, by Level of Protest Activity (College Graduates)	368
11.11	Groups with Too Little Influence, by Level of Protest Activity (College Graduates)	370

CARRYING out a large-scale longitudinal survey study requires the help of numerous individuals and no small degree of fortuitous circumstances. While the source of the fortuitous circumstances cannot be fixed, credit can be assigned to those who played especially important roles in the execution of our research. It has been a project of some magnitude and of long duration. We have undoubtedly tried the patience of those around us. The following commendations are but pale reflections of the appreciation we extend to them.

Several people at the University of Michigan's Institute for Social Research were of inestimable value. Warren Miller, Director of the Institute's Center for Political Studies, facilitated our undertaking in several ways—as he has with so many other scholars. John Scott, Tracy Berksman, and Carolann Baldiga provided energetic and often ingenious direction of the data-gathering phase. We are heavily indebted to the far-flung interviewing staff. They did a marvelous job of locating and then interviewing the respondents. Joan Scheffler guided the coding operation with her usual good judgment and patience.

The importance of skilled office staff in a project such as ours cannot be overemphasized. We were particularly fortunate in having Patricia Wancour and then Maureen Kozumplik as the project secretaries in Ann Arbor. Janice Brown and Donna French provided much-needed typing services in Rochester. The energy, dedication, and good humor of these individuals were remarkable.

A number of fine graduate students were closely associated with the project at various stages. We would like especially to thank Gregory B. Markus who, in time, also authored publications based on this study. Others include Joseph Alexander, Michael Denney, Samuel Evans, Roman Hedges, Ethel Klein, Bill McGee, David Newman, Virginia Sapiro, and Richard Smith. Their contributions and friendships were truly valued.

A study of this magnitude requires substantial financial and institutional support. Funding for the project came from the National Science Foundation and the Ford Foundation. Their support is gratefully acknowledged. Both of our universities have provided excellent physical facilities and a conducive intellectual environment. One of the authors, Jennings, benefited enormously from the facilities and services provided during his fellowship year at the Center for Advanced Study in the Behavioral Sciences.

As the project reached fruition in the form of this book, we profited from the helpful comments and encouragement of Fred I. Greenstein and Norval D. Glenn. At Princeton University Press, Sandy Thatcher once more proved to be a supportive editorial shepherd and Judith May rendered admirable service as our copy editor.

Portions of chapters 2 and 3 appeared previously in the *American Political Science Review* and portions of chapters 5 and 6 in the *British Journal of Political Science.*

Generations and Politics

*A Panel Study of Young Adults
and Their Parents*

CHAPTER ONE

The Study of Persistence and Change

CHANGE and continuity are inevitable partners and competitors in political life. Whether the object of attention is the international system, the nation-state, political groups, or the individual, it is essential to chart and understand the forces of change and continuity at work. These forces are often in a state of tension. Established patterns are customarily not easily displaced even in the face of consummate failure. Yet new ways of doing things, new perspectives, and new ideologies go searching for ostensible malfunctions in the political world. At the same time, these elements of conflict are often counterbalanced by complementarity. Old patterns rarely endure without alteration. Modification, adaptation, and more extreme change may even be essential for maintenance or survival. Similarly, of all proposed or possible changes, most go unrealized. Only occasionally are there drastic breaches with the past.

To say that change and continuity, and the tension between them, permeate political life is to state merely the beginning point for inquiry. How do we assess patterns of change and continuity? What constitutes meaningful change? Is strong continuity a hindrance or aid in developing and maintaining politically healthy systems and individuals? How much apparent change is actually spurious or idiosyncratic? What are the conditions fostering change and continuity among individuals and political systems? How are micro and macro levels of change and continuity interrelated? Are there cycles of changes? Is change inherently conflictual?

These large, cosmic questions can, in turn, be broken down into smaller, more specific ones. We can distinguish among the political objects of concern. For example, we might be interested in political bodies such as the nation-state, elite actors within those nations, the mass publics making up the populace, or elements of those mass publics. Although all of politics is in some respects one large cybernetic process, it is useful, indeed necessary, to study change and continuity among discrete parts involved in that process. In this book we focus on change and continuity among segments of the American mass public. But in doing so we shall not be unmindful of the connections to be made and the inferences to be drawn regarding the larger political systems of which these segments are a part.

3

THE NATURE OF THE STUDY

In approaching the question of change and continuity at the mass
public level we will utilize a set of materials that has its origins in
1965, at which time a national sample of high school seniors and their
parents was interviewed.[1] A follow-up study of these same individuals
was carried out in 1973, along with a fresh study of the high school
senior class of that year. These materials, spanning a dramatic eight-
year historical period, provide us with a unique opportunity to assess
change and continuity.

Individual and Aggregate Levels of Change

The study design allows for a multiplicity of analyses across generations, over the life course, and through time. An elementary yet fundamentally important distinction is that the data can be analyzed at
both the individual and aggregate levels. In the former case we take
advantage of the fact that we are dealing with the same set of individual respondents over time, thus giving us a panel of youths, a panel of
parents, and a panel of parent-youth pairs. In the latter case we capitalize upon the fact that we have similar observations of two distinct
biological generations across a substantial period of time. Although
both types of analysis use many of the same terms, and although it is
difficult to discuss one type without recourse to the other, their purposes and approaches are fundamentally different. Individual-level
analysis, as used here, concerns itself with the magnitudes of individual-level change and has only a secondary interest in the direction of
these movements. Aggregate analysis concerns itself with *net* change
and the directionality of these movements.

There are compelling reasons for employing both approaches whenever possible. For example, aggregate stability within a generation may
disguise enormous instability at the individual level; conversely, large
movement at the aggregate level may be a function of a minority undergoing exaggerated shifting. In analogous fashion, high rates of individual-level shifting may yield virtually no aggregate movement,
whereas relatively low rates of a unidirectional sort can generate quite
visible aggregate change. Utilizing both the individual- and aggregate-
level approaches provides us with a more comprehensive understanding of political dynamics.

Individual-level analysis is uniquely appropriate when addressing
the question of the durability of political attitudes and behaviors over

[1] The most complete report of the 1965 survey is M. Kent Jennings and Richard
G. Niemi, *The Political Character of Adolescence* (Princeton: Princeton University Press, 1974).

an individual's lifetime. Questions of persistence and change are fundamental to an understanding of how people cope with and relate to political phenomena. To what extent do adult political values and behaviors change in response to alterations in the political environment? In what way are these changes variable across differing attitudinal and behavioral domains? Does adult responsiveness reveal any consistent themes, such as greater change during the early years? Are certain kinds of individuals more likely to be unstable? Not only are these questions interesting in their own right, but from a system-level perspective, the answers to such questions have much to say about the potential for political conversion and mobilization in mass publics.

As developed in more detail subsequently (Chapter 2), there exists a variety of proposed models describing these patterns of durability. One pattern, which may be applicable to particular kinds of individuals or to particular types of political orientations, is that of lifelong openness. At the other extreme is a pattern that can be labeled lifelong persistence. Deviations from these idealized patterns, inspired in part by taking account of when people were born and where they are in their life cycles, have also been postulated. These models can best be explored, tested, and refined with repeated observations of the same individuals. We have the advantage in the present study of being able to compare two biologically linked generations as they have moved through the same historical time but through quite different life-stage time. Thus the models can be evaluated for the young adult and mid-life stages.

Valuable as the individual-level approach is, in the final analysis political leaders and lay persons alike deal in gross, averaged, grouped modes of thought. For scholars, too, indicators of the nation's political health are tracked over time by dealing with the national population and important subpopulations within the nation. While it is vitally important, for example, to know the causes and extent of individual changes associated with the marked decline in political trust over the past few years, the politically and substantively significant event is that it declined in the aggregate and especially so within some identifiable segments of the aggregate. We shall use the data in aggregate form to chart the net flows among both generations and to compare the relative distances between the two generations at both points in time. As explicated later (Chapter 5), theoretical models based on period effects, life-cycle effects, and generation effects will be employed to guide the interpretation of the aggregate analyses.[2]

[2] Individuals and to some extent entire disciplines prefer different terms for identical or almost identical concepts. Such is the case with certain terms we use throughout this book. We ordinarily use the terms "life-cycle" and "life-stage"

In the framework of our investigation, the aggregate approach takes on special significance in light of the presumed conflict between generations. If such conflict exists, it should be highly visible in our two sets of subjects, considering the ages represented and the time span embraced. The aggregate approach will also help untangle a different concern. Certain key groups, such as young, employed women, are often pictured as being in transition between old and new ways of thinking and behaving, both with respect to their immediate age-cohort predecessors and their lineage predecessors. The aggregate approach will help put in place the nature and magnitude of any such transitions, particularly so because we will also be able to draw on materials from the survey of the high school class of 1973.

Comparing the Two Generations

To illustrate the potential richness and complexities in carrying out our individual- and aggregate-level analyses, it is worth dwelling on the life course and historical corollaries of the two generations we have studied. First, and most obviously, there is a sharp difference in where they were in the life cycle. Three-fourths of the parents were between 40-54 years of age in 1965 and, inexorably, were between 48-62 by 1973. By definition, all had a child at least 25 or 26 years of age; a majority by 1973 had seen their last child through high school. A sizeable number were grandparents and a few were retired from work. In sharp contrast, even by 1973 one-fourth of the young adults had not married. Although a majority of those married had children, only a handful of the children were old enough to be in school. Home ownership was still rare, community roots remained rather fragile, and occupational endeavors were often new and uncertain.

Accompanying these dissimilarities are the differing political histories of the two generations. The parental generation came from homes where political memories extended back toward the turn of the century and where World War I was a salient event. All but a handful of the parents were born before the crash of 1929, and most were old enough to remember Franklin Roosevelt's first election and the agonies of the Great Depression. World War II touched them very personally. They nurtured their families during the cold war era, and they were well

---

effects to refer to changes associated with movement through the life span or the life course, as it is sometimes called. We prefer those designations to the more ambiguous and occasionally pejorative term, "aging effects." Our use of the term "generation effects" will generally parallel the meaning attached to "cohort effects" by some scholars, the distinction being that our generations are of the lineage type and do not represent birth cohorts per se. By period effects we usually mean the same thing as "historical effects." More discussion of these and related terms will be found especially in Chapters 2, 5, 7, and 11.

into middle age when the Great Society began to dissolve in riots and demonstrations.

The contrast offered by the political histories of their offspring is well known. All were born after the end of World War II and represent an early installment of the postwar baby boom. Most of them have but the dimmest recollection of Eisenhower's first election; Kennedy's 1960 victory is probably the first one recalled with any preciseness. They entered high school with the civil rights movement and about one-half left college in the midst of turmoil and discontent. They were in the epicenter of the student protest movement. All were touched either directly or indirectly by the Vietnam War.

In addition to being distinguished by current age and date of birth —and all that these two simple facts index—the two generations also differ on where the life course has taken them over the eight-year period covered by our observations. Whereas the personal lives of the parents underwent relatively little alteration (one of the major ones being the leave-taking of a child), the same was scarcely true of the young adults. The period between high school graduation and the mid-twenties is obviously one of major mobility, new endeavors, and role changes. Illustratively, all but one in ten no longer lived with their parents, about three in five had lived in at least two different localities, three-fourths had married, and one in ten of those marriages had already resulted in divorce or separation. The world of parenthood had been entered by 38% of these youths. Slightly over two-thirds had gone to college during the 1965-1973 period. One-half of the males had served in the military. Virtually all youths had entered the work force at some point, and as of 1973 four out of five were currently employed. Although some had held the same job during this period, the majority had either switched the locations of their jobs or their actual occupations. Finally, about three in four had voted in their first presidential election.

The time interval covered by the study also happens to embrace what has been called the most crucial age range for the creation of a distinctive, self-conscious political generation. There is nothing magic in these figures, but Karl Mannheim put the age span at 17-25.[3] Another scholar has recently built an elaborate biosocial rationale for 18-26 as the span wherein "political-cultural consciousness" takes firm hold and wherein, if the psychohistorical conditions are appropriate, a new political generation is born.[4] At a more general level, Erik Erikson's

---

[3] Karl Mannheim, "The Problem of Generations," English translation reprinted in Philip G. Altbach and Robert S. Laufer (eds.), The New Pilgrims (New York: David McKay, 1972).

[4] T. Allen Lambert, "Generations and Change: Toward a Theory of Generations as a Force in Historical Processes." Youth and Society, 4 (September 1972), 21-46.

work on identity crisis singles out late adolescence and early adulthood as a potentially important period for political character formation.[5] Overall, then, the life-stage changes experienced by the young
adults coupled with the dramatic historical occurrences touching their
lives, at a purportedly vulnerable time, help distinguish them from
their middle-aged parents.

Our initial study was couched very much in the political socialization genre. We focused on the high school seniors—on their political
attitudes and behaviors, on the role of various agents in formulating
these characteristics, and on important subpopulation variations. Parents were considered primarily in their role as agents of socialization.
Yet even in our earlier reporting we often used the parents as a foil
for interpreting the findings about their children. In particular, we
were often struck by high similarity between parents as a whole and
adolescents as a whole in the face of low to moderate agreement between pairs of parents and offspring. We also employed the parental
generation in an effort to draw inferences about life-cycle and generational processes.

For both theoretical and substantive reasons, the youth sample continued to occupy a somewhat more prominent role as we undertook
our longitudinal investigation. Young adulthood is customarily thought
of as a time of lability and receptivity. We therefore had caught the
young while still in the formative stages and could observe more clearly the unfolding of their political lives. Our particular youth generation
also lay dead center in the protest cohorts of the late 1960s, making it
a particularly attractive focus for our investigation.

Yet as we initiated our analysis it became clear that the parental
generation was not simply a mechanism by which we could "check" or
modify conclusions based on our analysis of the youth data—valuable
though that function is. Rather, the parental sample enabled us to take
a longer, more extensive sweep regarding life-course, generational,
and historical processes. Employing some analytic license, the parental sample gave us a vital extension rod. In addition, we grew to realize, along with an increasing number of other scholars,[6] that the so-
called middle years had been seriously neglected by most social scientists. Only recently has it been acknowledged that this is not necessarily a time of stasis, that for some individuals and with respect to
some aspects of life the period is ripe with discontinuities and depar-

[5] Erik H. Erikson, *Identity: Youth and Crisis* (New York: Norton, 1968).
[6] For example, Ronald P. Abeles and Matilda White Riley, "A Life-Course Perspective on the Later Years: Some Implications for Research," in Social Science
Research Council, *Annual Report, 1976-77* (New York: 1977), 1-16; and various
selections in Paul B. Baltes and K. Warner Schaie (eds.), *Life-Span Developmental Psychology: Personality and Socialization* (New York: Academic Press, 1973).

tures. As a result of these considerations, our presentation at most points will dwell about as much on the parental as on the youth generation, will draw comparisons between the two, and will occasionally introduce interpolations between the two.

In a number of ways, then, the setting and subjects of our inquiry exemplify the concept of transitions. The young adults represent most graphically a rate of high transition. In terms of life-stage development they were clearly more in transit than were their parents. It remains to be seen whether and how this higher rate of mobility is manifested in political fashion, though the leading hypothesis is one of a higher rate of change in that domain as well. But we have been alerted to the fact that development occurs over the entire life cycle, and so we must be mindful of movement within the parental generation also. The separate and combined movements of each generation as a whole may also lead to alterations in the relationships between the two. These transitions can be observed with respect to adjustments between parents and their own offspring as well as between middle-aged and young adults in general.

If only life-stage and generational transitions were occurring, matters would be complex enough. However, modern social, economic, and political orders seldom remain stationary for any prolonged period. Perhaps the upheavals and conflicts of the late 1960s and early 1970s cannot be neatly characterized as transitions. With hindsight, however, the case can be made that large-scale, long-lasting transitions were occurring, for example, in the form of the civil rights struggle, the women's movement, the changing role of the United States in world politics, and the erosion of confidence in public authorities and institutions. Life-stage and generational transitions are overlaid on, interact with, are sometimes dependent on, and occasionally inspire these macro-level transitions.

Content of the Study

In order to capitalize on the panel component of our design we will focus on those variables for which we have over-time observations. For the most part these are variables that have enjoyed wide currency in political research on the American public over the past two decades or so. Consequently, our findings can be nested within a broad range of other inquiries, especially since many of the measures employed are based on the identical questions used in other studies. By the same token, a somewhat smaller set of measures are virtual equivalents of those used in a number of political socialization studies of younger populations. At the same time, however, we will draw on a number of new indicators of phenomena for which we have only 1973 observations. Even a goodly number of these measures are drawn from instruments used in other inquiries, especially those of the University of Michigan's national election studies.

The traits of interest to us fall under six major rubrics, as follows:

1. Psychological involvement in politics and public affairs.
2. Political resources in terms of cognitive skills and motivational levels.
3. Political participation, defined as including electoral and nonelectoral domains, conventional and unconventional expressions.
4. Preferences and attitudes, emphasizing partisanship and issues of public policy.
5. Evaluations of actors and groups involved in the governmental process, focusing on political trust and affect toward sociopolitical groups.
6. Nonpolitical characteristics paralleling those in the political domain, specifically religious beliefs and behavior, trust in others, and self-esteem.

Although the rationale for employing these particular families of traits will be more fully developed in succeeding chapters, a couple of comments are in order about the nature of these variables. Taken together they cover many of the themes that have preoccupied students of political behavior for some time. One major thrust is represented by the trilogy of involvement, resources, and participation. Each of these components is important in its own right, for each references a key element in the normative view of how a representative and responsive system of government should function. But the three elements are also inextricably interrelated, sometimes leading and sometimes following one another, even though we are most accustomed to thinking of involvement and resources as being preconditions for participation per se. The acquisition, corollaries, durability, and flexibility of these qualities are questions of major concern, and we shall pursue them in our analysis.

Another major thrust in the recent research tradition has been directed toward the study of partisanship and voting on the one hand, and issue orientations and evaluations of governmental actors on the other. Indeed, the literature sometimes seems to be swamped by the efforts in the domain of partisanship and voting behavior. Yet it is clear that the pulse of American politics is most regularly and perhaps most consequentially registered in the electoral arena; and the halting changes in the party system have only made these topics more salient. By the same token, the topic of political evaluations has received an enormous amount of attention in an era of governmental crisis, and the controversy regarding attitudinal stability on matters of public policy is one of the preeminent ones in the study of mass publics. Finally, as we shall note at several points, our understanding of political phenomena is often enhanced by our study of the nonpolitical. It is for this reason that one of our clusters of variables is labeled "nonpolitical."

It would surely have been possible to concentrate on only one or two of the clusters listed. Numerous articles and books have been written about each, and we could have made a unique contribution by virtue of the materials at our disposal. A strategy of that sort would have led to an intensive analysis of a restricted set of political traits, probing in depth the properties of individual- and aggregate-level dynamics for the two generations. Especially in view of the great scholarly and popular interest in some of these topics—partisanship and participation, for example—it was tempting to adopt that strategy.

We have decided, instead, to paint with a broad brush. This decision was dictated by two major considerations. First, given our interest in developing and testing models of continuity and change, it seemed wiser to assess these models in their broad contours than to restrict ourselves to only one or two traits. While the latter approach would have given us a keener appreciation of the subtle processes at work, it also would have limited severely our capacity to generalize, to know whether the patterns uncovered were unique to particular clusters and single traits. A second consideration is that our report on the initial study carried out in 1965 had also been painted on a broad canvas. In the interests of achieving continuity with our own past intellectual predilections, and to invest these two reports with thematic continuity, we decided that the sweeping landscape rather than the detailed still life would be the appropriate genre.

STUDY PROCEDURES

A long-term panel investigation is heavily dependent on the success of the original inquiry. Our 1973 survey builds upon a complex research design and data collection carried out in the spring of 1965. Not all parts of that earlier investigation are relevant here. The key elements are a national sample of high school seniors, their parents, and the resulting familial pairs. To achieve a national probability sample of 1965 high school seniors, a selection of schools was first made with probability proportionate to size. About nine in ten of the schools selected agreed to take part in the study. Within schools systematic random samples were taken. Some 1,669 students were interviewed, an average number of 17 seniors per school; the response rate was over 99%. Interviews were taken with at least one parent (selected randomly) in 94% of the cases for a grand total of 1,562 parents and a like number of parent-child pairs. It is these two samples and the sample of pairs embedded therein that constitute the base for our panel. Properly speaking, the youth panel may be described as a probability sample of the high school senior class of 1965, as observed in 1965 and 1973. The parents and pairs become defined in terms of this basic definition of the youth sample.

Constructing the 1965-1973 Panels

In an effort to locate the original respondents eight years after the original study, we had some advantages and disadvantages when compared with other panel investigations. Our major disadvantage was that the addresses of the respondents had not been updated since 1965, with the partial exception of revised addresses garnered in 1967 for those respondents who had indicated they wanted a report on the study. Consequently, we had a gap of anywhere from 6½ to 8 years. On the other hand, we held a major advantage because of the parent-offspring nature of the original design. For the overwhelming majority of the 1973 respondents it was possible to use one member of the parent-offspring pair as a source of information about the location of the other. Due to the greater mobility of the young, the source of information was much more likely to be the parent.

A number of devices were used to locate one or the other member of the parent-child pairs. This included contacting the high schools from which the original samples had been drawn, using neighbors as informants about people who had moved, and using the services of the U.S. Post Office to forward mail and secure forwarding addresses. Once either the parent or offspring was personally contacted, the location of the other one was ascertained if, in fact, it had not already been obtained.[7] The diligence, ingenuity, and perseverance of the Survey Research Center's field staff were crucial in the tracking process. As indicated in Appendix A (Table A.1), we were extraordinarily successful in locating our original set of respondents. That over nine-tenths of the original panel was tracked is an impressive accomplishment, especially in view of the relatively long lapse between contacts and the fact that there was no central location for information about the sample.

---

[7] There were a few exceptions. One California father hoped that we would locate his "hippie" child because he had been unable to. (We did.) A few parents refused to tell us the whereabouts of their sons or daughters even though they personally would grant an interview and had no objection to our asking the offspring for one if we located them ourselves.

Having located the respondents, the next task was to secure information from them. On balance we were highly successful in that respect also. Field work was carried out in early 1973, with most of the materials being collected between January and March. Of the original 1,669 high school seniors, 80.8% ($N = 1,348$) agreed to take part in the follow-up; the comparable figure for the parents was 75.5% ($N = 1,179$). By any conventional standards these are extraordinarily high retention rates for samples of the mass public. For example, rates of retention typically run around 85% in the pre- and post-election surveys conducted by the University of Michigan's Center for Political Studies, and these interviews are separated by only a few weeks. Although illness, extended absence from home, or other reasons for unavailability were present, the greatest source of noncooperation was refusal. Discarding from the computational base those we were unable to locate, the refusal rate was 9% among the young and 13% among the parents.

Ideally, all of the respondents in the second wave would have been personally interviewed, as was the case in 1965. Great efforts were made in this respect by allowing the interviewers to leave their normal "beats," i.e., the primary sampling units (psu's) in which they are located, to interview respondents who were nearby. Nevertheless, a goodly number of our subjects, especially the young adults, were situated well beyond the economically feasible reach of our field staff. Rather than conveniently laying aside these individuals, and thus reducing the number of cases available for analysis as well as risking possible bias in the panel, we employed a mail questionnaire. This instrument contained all of the major closed-ended questions used in the interview schedule. To encourage the respondents' cooperation we offered a small monetary inducement. As it turned out, the rate of return was quite respectable (77% for youths, 64% for parents) and the quality of the data reasonably high. These questionnaire respondents comprise 17% of all the youth panelists, and 5% of the parent panelists. Selected comparisons between the mail and personal interview respondents are presented in Appendix A. There are surprisingly few differences between the two sets (Table A.3).

We were, then, singularly successful in keeping our panel intact over the eight-year period. Still, we must ask whether any bias was created by the attrition that occurred. Fortunately, the degree of bias is slight indeed. We performed a number of tests for each generation, where the test consisted of comparing the 1965 characteristics of those respondents who remained in the panel and those who did not. We used demographic and personal characteristics as well as strictly political ones. On the great majority of accounts there were no statistically or substantively meaningful differences between the two sets. This was especially so among the parents. Among the young adults the panel respondents were a bit more socially and economically privileged, politically conservative, and attentive (Table A.2). These modest differences combined with the high retention rates provide convincing evidence that the panel respondents reflect faithfully the composition of the original set of subjects.

In addition to sample attrition, a major peril involved in panel studies is contamination effects, i.e., having respondents' later reports affected by their participation in earlier phases of the study. Considering the eight-year lag between our two observations, it is extremely unlikely that contamination effects had any measurable impact on the observations that were recorded in 1973.[8] What evidence there is about panel effects of this type suggests that any such effects tend to decay rather quickly. Moreover, there was little of a dramatic nature attending the original data gathering. It would be a rare teenager or middle-aged parent who would alter his or her subsequent political character as a result of that single exposure to an interview in 1965.

An additional body of data used in the book is represented by the questionnaires administered to a large national sample of the high school graduates of 1973. Details about the collection of these data are given in Chapter 7.

Modifying the Instruments

A panel study, almost by definition, is constrained in terms of information to be elicited from the respondents subsequent to the initial observation. Much of what one is interested in pursuing has, for better or worse, been defined by the contents of the original data collection instruments. Queries dealing with continuity and change obviously demand repeated soundings based on the same or equivalent stimuli being supplied to the same respondents. Therefore, a major portion of the 1973 instruments was devoted to replicating questions developed in 1965. This included items falling into each of the major domains outlined earlier.

Despite the necessary emphasis on replication, a panel study that confined itself to repeated questions would surely be overlooking rich opportunities for uncovering dynamic elements, if not, in fact, falling

---

[8] However, it is not impossible. A respondent interviewed by one of us distinctly remembered being interviewed in high school because "I didn't know anything about politics." She reported that after an appointment for the interview was made, she asked her husband to give her a "crash" course on politics. Fortunately, he refused. Interestingly enough, she also "remembered" that we had interviewed her while she was in college, which, of course, we had not.

prey to the perils of slavish replication. At the very least, of course, some stimulus objects require modification. The most obvious example in our own study dealt with preferences regarding presidential candidates in the elections encompassed by our study periods. The cast of characters has changed but the question being addressed (partisan choice) remains in place. Beyond such obvious adjustments, it is also necessary to take account of a changing political environment. This is especially the case with respect to public policy issues. Although we were able to retain the same small set of questions first asked in 1965, it was apparent that a number of new and burning issues had entered the public domain across the eight-year span. Introducing some of these issues into the 1973 instrument made it possible, among other things, to examine the general continuity in attitudes about issues even when the specific content of those issues differed over time. Soundings on the new sets of issues also enabled us to treat the question of continuity in parent-child similarity at two different points in history and in the life cycles of the two generations.

In a quite different vein, we expended much effort in the 1973 wave reconstructing the political histories of the respondents in the interim between interviews. This enterprise was dictated in part by an interest in understanding the rate and process by which the young become inducted into adult modes of political participation. But we were also interested in investigating the degree to which the propensity for political participation is transmitted through the family, as well as in trying to make some assessments about the dependency of political action on location in the life stage. Given the historical circumstances marking the coming age of this cohort, we took especial note of unconventional versus conventional modes of participation. Since we have a host of information available from 1965 about the youths' participation in the organizational and governmental life of their high schools, we are also in a position to determine if there are parapolitical precursors of eventual political participation.

Another way in which the 1973 instrument was altered lay in the attention paid to personal life histories. Precisely in order to take advantage of the panel design, questions were asked about interim developments in the marital, parental, educational, occupational, geographical, and military phases of the respondents' lives. Because of their greater mobility in most of these dimensions, the young adults were asked about such developments in more detail than the parents. Armed with information about significant events marking their young adulthood years, we are in a position to assess the impact of these events on political matters. Although we have availed ourselves of only a portion of the rich analyses made possible by these life-history materials, it is clear that a panel study such as ours is greatly enhanced by their presence.

Modes of Analysis

By the standards of contemporary data analysis, the statistical manipulations through which we put our materials are modest. Only occasionally do we employ multivariate analysis in the conventional sense. Multiple regression, for example, is used primarily in Chapters 4, 9, 10, and 11. Instead we have relied mainly on rather simple descriptive statistics, bivariate relationships, and physical controls. Our decision to do so bears some comment.

One reason for this strategy is that we have elected to cover a very wide range of political characteristics. Indeed, virtually all of those treated in the earlier study and repeated in the 1973 undertaking are discussed. In addition, several variables developed only for 1973 are also analyzed. This strategy, in turn, was predicated upon—as suggested earlier—our desire to explore the many faces of persistence rather than to dissect one face. Almost necessarily this means a different analytic mode than if depth of understanding across a very narrow range of political traits had been our objective. For example, had we decided to focus on partisanship or on political resources, or even single topics within those domains, we would have employed a quite different set of statistical techniques inasmuch as a fuller understanding of the phenomena would have demanded more elaborated approaches.

Although this decision to paint with a broad stroke was the major factor in dictating our analytic modes, there were other considerations as well. By the nature of the study design, some variables are automatically built into or controlled for in the simpler forms of analysis we use. For example, studies dealing with continuity and change typically have to control statistically or physically for age. In our own case age was automatically controlled for and was for all practical purposes invariant in the youth generation; and even though more age variance was present in the parental generation, there was a high degree of clustering. It follows, then, that some crucial aspects of life-cycle and generational processes were, in effect, already being held constant in the analysis. By the same token, since the two generations represented members of the same original households, less attention had to be devoted to the possible contaminating effects of differential locational and socioeconomic properties. Illustratively, if some particular trait showed greater persistence among the young than among the middle-aged, we did not have to worry about whether that difference emerged because the social origins of the young lay in different environments than those represented contemporaneously by the parental generation.

Another reason for relying on relatively simple modes of analysis and presentation lies in the fact that "predictor" variables ordinarily absent from static design studies are often present in our panel design. Multivariate analyses of cross-sectional data often go to great lengths trying to account for the presence of this or that political trait, often employing predictor variables (e.g., education, occupation) that in fact follow temporally the incipient, if not, indeed, the crystallized version of the political trait being accounted for. Such analyses necessarily leave out any prior reading of the trait, and thus omit what is in all probability its "best" predictor. Of course our major objective, as noted above, is not to account for or predict variance in the 1973 soundings. If that were the case, we would have employed an altogether different strategy and would have circumscribed the range of political topics to be considered.[9]

What Is to Follow

We have divided our analyses into three major parts. In the next three chapters we concentrate on the individual as the unit of analysis. Chapters 2 and 3 give a broad view of change and continuity in political orientations at the individual level for each generation. Here the basic questions to be addressed concern comparisons over a variety of political orientations and across the two generations. Models of persistence and change at the micro level are developed and tested. Chapter 4 introduces the parent-offspring pair feature of the design. These pairs, which figured so prominently in our report of the 1965 investigation, are now used to assess the durability of and alterations in congruence between the political character of parents and that of their children. In essence, we are evaluating the family transmission model of political socialization.

Having established the parameters of persistence at the individual level, we then proceed to see how these individual-level changes are transformed into aggregate patterns. Chapters 5 and 6 are companions to Chapters 2 and 3, respectively, in that they treat at an aggregate

---

[9] A departure from our reports of the 1965 study is that the data are analyzed in their unweighted form. As described in *The Political Character of Adolescence* (Appendix), the samples had to be weighted due to imprecise information about the sampling frame. Technically the statistical results should be based on these weighted data. After extensive comparisons of analyses based on unweighted versus weighted data (respondents from the same school all have the same weight but weights vary across schools), we concluded that differences were almost invariably absent or trivial. For reasons of ease in analysis and presentation we decided to use the unweighted data.

level most of the political variables taken up in the earlier pair of chapters. A number of models are presented illustrating how life-cycle, generational, and period effects can be detected in the movement of the two generations over time. Special attention is devoted to the much-discussed topic of the generation gap. Chapter 7 adds an extra dimension by drawing on a survey of the high school senior class of 1973.

In Chapters 8 through 11 we treat population groupings of particular theoretical and substantive significance. Although several such groupings are available for analysis, we have focused on education, race, gender, and protest behavior as critical demarcators within the populace. Especially for the younger generation, these are groupings that have been the object of considerable discussion and research over the past decade or so. Controversy over the effects of higher education is a longstanding matter, and Chapter 8 focuses on that question with respect to political characteristics. The civil rights revolution beginning in the late 1950s and early 1960s has been said to have had a number of consequences for cross-generation and cross-race comparisons. Chapter 9 assesses the evidence regarding such consequences. Following in the wake of the civil rights movement was the womens' liberation movement, a phenomenon that gained great momentum during our study period. Chapter 10 makes comparisons based on gender and gender roles across the generations and across time. This chapter makes the greatest use of the details we accumulated regarding the marital, parental, and employment status of our subjects. One of the most distinguishing features of our young respondents is that they came of age during a period of rancorous conflict and a virtual epidemic of unconventional political behavior. Chapter 11 takes up the question of whether and how protestors and nonprotestors underwent differential changes during this time and whether protestors make up a distinctive subgroup within the youthful cohort. Finally, Chapter 12 presents an interpretive summary of the book.

CHAPTER TWO

Persistence at the Individual Level:
Involvement, Resources, and Participation

Iɴ this and the following chapter we focus on individual stability across the eight years encompassed by our study. Our attention is directed not so much to what kind of change occurred as to how much occurred and how it was distributed by generation and by subject matter. We begin the present chapter with a discussion of some prominent models of persistence, models that will guide our interpretation and understanding of the findings. Substantively, this chapter deals primarily with variables that attempt to index the individual's psychological involvement in the political sphere and the kinds of political skills and attributes upon which the individual can draw in relating to and participating in the political world. The topic of stability in rates of participation is also addressed, though more briefly due to the youthfulness of the filial generation.

MODELS OF PERSISTENCE

Following Sears,[1] we may think of four basic models of life-span persistence. First, there is the persistence of early socialization, or the *lifelong persistence* model. What is learned early is asserted to endure; resistance to change is asserted to increase as the individual becomes accustomed to and comfortable with a given set of orientations. In its extreme form this model posits that early learning is so powerful that even later developments in the content of political learning are laid on to and interpreted by the nature of early learning. An even more extreme version of this model maintains that the personality structure built up by the preschool child pretty much governs all subsequent

---

[1] David O. Sears, *Political Attitudes through the Life Cycle* (San Francisco: W. H. Freeman, forthcoming). Our thinking has been much influenced by this work and we draw freely on it throughout this and the following chapter. See also his "Political Socialization," in Fred I. Greenstein and Nelson W. Polsby (eds.), *The Handbook of Political Science*, Vol. II (Reading, Mass.: Addison-Wesley, 1975). For a similar conceptualization of the models to be used here see Roberta S. Sigel and Marilyn Brookes Hoskin, "Perspectives on Adult Political Socialization —Areas of Research," in Stanley Allen Renshon (ed.), *Handbook of Political Socialization* (New York: Free Press, 1977).

political development.[2] In its more limited form the model restricts itself to basic questions of attachment to the political system and to fundamental ideological predispositions.

At the opposite extreme is the *lifelong openness* model. This model
assumes little or no residues from pre-adult learning. The individual is
seen as being susceptible to changes in political orientations over the
entire life span. There are actually two major propositions involved in
the model. One is that individuals can change, that there are no inherent physiological or psychological properties, short of senescence,
which would prevent change. The other proposition is that individuals
do change. Both of these are empirical questions. If the answer to the
second is positive, then the answer to the first must also be positive.
But the reverse is not true. Simply because people can change over the
life span does not mean that they will. For the most part there do not
seem to be serious inherent limitations on learning over the life cycle;
therefore the model can be restricted to the proposition that lifelong
change does occur.[3]

Paradoxically, the lifelong openness model implies that individuals
are either very rational or very capricious. That is, they may change
their orientations as a conscious, deliberate reaction to alterations in
their personal or political environment. Or the intensity of their orientations may be so weak that perturbations may occur in an "uncon-
scious," willy-nilly fashion. In its more extreme form the model sweeps
across the full range of political beliefs and predispositions. In its more
limited form it applies to "issues of the day" and the more ephemeral
dimensions of political life.

Between the polar opposites of lifelong persistence and lifelong
openness stand two additional models which will, for present purposes,
be lumped together. The *life-cycle* model holds that while persistence
is the rule, certain orientations are very amenable to alteration at giv-
en life stages. As expounded by most writers in the field, the life-cycle

---

[2] For statements supporting this position see James C. Davies, "Political Socialization: From Womb to Childhood," in Renshon, *Handbook of Political Socialization*; Jeanne N. Knutson, "Prepolitical Ideologies: The Basis of Political Learning,"
in Richard G. Niemi and Associates, *The Politics of Future Citizens* (San Francisco: Jossey-Bass, 1974); Stanley Allen Renshon, "The Role of Personality Development in Political Socialization," and Norah Rosenau, "The Sources of Children's Political Concepts," both in David C. Schwartz and Sandra Kenyon
Schwartz (eds.), *New Directions in Political Socialization* (New York: Free Press,
1975).

[3] A vigorous stand is made on behalf of an (implied) openness model by Kenneth J. Gergen and Matthew Ullman, "Socialization and the Characterological
Basis of Political Activism," in Renshon, *Handbook of Political Socialization*. See
also Donald Searing, Gerald Wright, and George Rabinowitz, "The Primacy Principle: Attitude Change and Political Socialization," *British Journal of Political
Science*, 6 (January 1976), 83-113.

model has a directional component to it. However, there are dangers in assigning directionality. To illustrate, consider the argument about the tendency of young adults to veer toward political liberalism rather than conservatism. Instead of reflecting some sort of innate liberal propensity, this tendency may simply reflect the greater openness of youth to whatever social and political forces are at work. The disproportionate attractiveness for youth of conservative and right-wing charismatic leaders and movements (e.g., Hitlerism in Germany and Wallaceism in the United States) belies the thesis of inherent liberal tendencies among young people. A more balanced view is simply that individuals are particularly vulnerable to outside influences at certain life stages.

Stated in its extreme form the life-cycle model predicts a rather invariant staging of change across a variety of traits. In its more limited form the model simply says that the potential for and the actuality of change is greater at some stages than at others and that the range of affected orientations is narrow. But in either form it lays great weight on the reactivity of the individual to alterations in social circumstances, alterations which commonly, though not invariably, accompany the aging process.[4]

Another model lying between strong persistence and lifelong openness is the *generational* model. This model also posits strong persistence in general, but it allows for considerable new socialization and/ or resocialization with lasting effects during the formative, impressionable years. Unlike the life-cycle model, the generational one does not necessarily argue that change will occur. Especially in its stronger version, the generational model requires that powerful social and political movements be at work along with a resulting *Zeitgeist* that reflects the ideological content of these forces. The stronger version asserts substantial molding and remolding during late adolescence and young adulthood and an accompanying sharp breach with the preceding generation. A milder version argues for more gradual change and looks at

---

[4] Among the many works treating the intertwined concepts of the life cycle, generations, and historical periods are Matilda White Riley, Marilyn Johnson, Anne Foner et al., *Aging and Society*, Vol. III (New York: Russell Sage Foundation, 1972), especially Chapter 2, and a shorter version by Matilda White Riley, "Aging and Cohort Succession: Interpretations and Misinterpretations," *Public Opinion Quarterly*, 37 (Spring 1973), 35-49; Vern L. Bengtson and Neal E. Cutler, "Generations and Intergenerational Relations: Perspectives on Time, Age Groups, and Social Change," in Robert Binstock and Ethel Shanas (eds.), *The Handbook of Aging and Social Sciences* (New York: Van Nostrand Reinhold, 1976); and Norval D. Glenn, "Aging and Conservatism," *Annals of the American Academy of Political and Social Science*, 1515 (September 1974), 176-86. One of the best conceptual treatments of the life cycle in terms of our interests is Stanton Wheeler and Orville Brim, *Socialization After Childhood: Two Essays* (New York: Wiley, 1966).

the making of generations as a continual process lasting until adult-hood.[5]

Although the distinction between the life-cycle and generational models is a vital one, especially at the aggregate level, it is not of major concern here. Rather, we are primarily interested in establishing levels of stability and change at the individual level, and in seeing whether these levels can be accommodated by the lifelong persistence or life-long openness model, or something in between. Though we shall occasionally interpret change as being due to life-cycle or generational forces, the distinction between these latter two models is not critical for our task.

Evidence supporting any or all of these models is incomplete and at some points almost inchoate. The vast bulk of the literature limits itself to dealing with electoral behavior and public policy issues. Broader orientations and comparisons with nonpolitical attributes are scarcely touched. With the exception of recent cohort analysis and occasional isolated examples of panel studies, the literature boasts of little truly longitudinal analysis in an area that cries out for diachronic designs.[6] Somewhat fortuitously, the historical period and the samples embraced by our study provide an excellent opportunity to test, in part, the three models outlined above. Historically, the eight years comprised a national period of *Sturm und Drang*. If neither generation changed in the face of the volatile historical conditions, this would be highly supportive of the lifelong persistence model. Conversely, if both samples changed substantially, the inclusion of the parental generation would be strong evidence that openness to change is indeed lifelong.

The youth sample, aging from late adolescence to young adulthood, went through a life stage marked by the acquisition of new roles and statuses and initial entry into the "adult" world of politics, simultaneously experiencing intensive exposure to a distinctive political period.

[5] The milder version, with respect to post-World War II cohorts, is advanced by Ronald Inglehart, *The Silent Revolution: Changing Values and Political Styles among Western Publics* (Princeton, N.J.: Princeton University Press, 1977). The contemporary study of generational effects has been heavily influenced by Karl Mannheim (1928), "The Problem of Generations," English translation reprinted in Philip G. Altbach and Robert S. Laufer (eds.), *The New Pilgrims* (New York: David McKay, 1972).

[6] Some notable exceptions beginning at the pre-adult level include Theodore Newcomb et al., *Persistence and Change: Bennington College and Its Students After Twenty-Five Years* (New York: Wiley, 1967); Jack Block, *Lives Through Time* (Berkeley: Bancroft, 1971); Glen H. Elder, Jr., *Children of the Great Depression* (Chicago: University of Chicago Press, 1974); Hilde T. Himmelweit and Betty Swift, "Adolescent and Adult Authoritarianism Re-Examined: Its Organization and Stabilization over Time," *European Journal of Social Psychology*, 1 (No. 3, 1971), 357-84; and Andrew M. Greely and Joe L. Spaeth, "Political Change among College Alumni," *Sociology of Education*, 43 (April 1970), 106-13.

Thus both life-cycle and generational effects were potentially at high tide. The parents experienced far less change in their personal lives than did their offspring. Their social aging was relatively minor even though their chronological aging was exactly the same as that of their children. Thus if change is limited to the youth sample, the life-cycle/ generational model would be strongly supported.

It is obvious that with the parents in particular we cannot be sure to what extent we are catching the residues of pre-adult socialization versus young adulthood crystallization or even later developments. With respect to the filial generation we are closer in time to what is conventionally called the early or pre-adult learning stage. Yet even at that we do not know directly just how much the Time$_1$ findings in 1965 reflected the residues of earlier socialization. There is documented evidence of both change and stability among elementary and secondary school children.[7] Everything we know about individual development, however, suggests that earlier (pre-adult) profiles were more nearly approximated in the 1965 calibrations among the young than among their parents. Therefore, low to moderate stability among the young would suggest even lower persistence of *pre-adult* attributes among the parents, assuming we had such observations in hand.

We will use three summary measures of persistence and present in most instances the tabular materials upon which the summary measures rest. The simplest measure is the percentage of respondents falling on the main diagonal in a turnover table. We will call this the gross stability or persistence. Percentage figures are useful for parent-youth comparisons and are especially relevant when the response categories represent meaningful divisions of the population. The major defect of the measure is its dependence on the number of categories in the variable. Gross stability will be high or low depending on how finely the categories are divided. Fortunately, parent-youth comparisons are still valid because the questions and resulting variables are identical for both samples.

Correlations between the 1965 and 1973 responses will also be used. Correlations, especially the first one noted below, generally are less

[7] Some of the change is maturational and represents accretions in learning, but some of the apparent change is also simply measurement error, especially in terms of trying to uncover attributes that may simply not be present among younger children. See Robert D. Hess and Judith V. Torney, *The Development of Political Attitudes in Children* (Chicago: Aldine, 1967), Appendix A; Pauline Vaillancourt, "Stability of Children's Survey Responses," *Public Opinion Quarterly*, 38 (Fall 1973), 373-87; Vaillancourt and Niemi, "Children's Party Choices," and Roberta S. Sigel and Marilyn Brookes, "Becoming Critical about Politics," both in Niemi, *The Politics of Future Citizens*; Steven H. Chaffee, L. Scott Ward, and Leonard P. Tipton, "Mass Communication and Political Socialization," in Jack Dennis (ed.), *Socialization to Politics* (New York: Wiley, 1973).

sensitive to the number of response categories. This is an especially useful feature here because it allows more meaningful comparisons across different sorts of variables. In addition, correlations are sensitive to magnitudes of change rather than to the simple dichotomy of change or no change. Two rank-order correlations are reported—Kendall's τ_b and Goodman and Kruskal's γ. Our use of two such statistics follows Weisberg's suggestion that multiple measures, based on alternative models of a relationship, can yield more insight than one statistic.[8]

Given these various measures, what should be taken as indicative of greater or lesser persistence, and what should be taken as indicative of greater or lesser contrasts across the two generations? By presenting all three statistics, plus the tables upon which they are based, we make it possible to achieve an overall assessment. Yet some guidelines are necessary. In assessing persistence within each generation we will rely most on the τ_b correlation, partly because of its conservative nature and partly because we are more interested in questions of persistence as such rather than in differential persistence within categories of a variable. Somewhat arbitrarily, we will establish values around .30 or higher as demonstrating substantial persistence. An examination of some of the contingency tables generating values in the .30 range will show a pattern that, in percentage terms, would ordinarily be associated with at least moderately high persistence.[9] For occasional partic-

[8] Weisberg's prescription seems especially apropos here. We will find several instances in which these two measures yield very different values. The following table illustrates how this can happen:

		1973 Response		
		Yes	No	Total
1965	Yes	100%	0%	100%
Response				
	No	80%	20%	100%

In this instance τ_b will be considerably less than 1.0, the exact value depending on the marginals. This low to moderate correlation alerts us to the fact that 1965 responses are not an especially good predictor of 1973 responses; most individuals said "Yes" in 1973 regardless of their 1965 opinions. If we are looking for exact correspondence between 1965 and 1973, τ_b correctly tells us that that correspondence is not too high. But the response pattern represented in the table may make a great deal of sense. If there were strong period effects favoring the "Yes" response, this is exactly the kind of pattern we would expect to find. Gamma is especially sensitive to this type of change, and the perfect γ in the above table calls attention to this pattern in which change is concentrated in one 1965 response category. Thus the use of two statistics emphasizes the twin aspects of the table— the low predictability and the highly concentrated change. Reliance on only one statistic would not capture both elements. See Herbert F. Weisberg, "Models of Statistical Relationship," *American Political Science Review*, 68 (December 1974), 1638-55. See also Thomas P. Wilson, "Measures of Association for Bivariate Hypotheses," in Hubert M. Blalock, Jr. (ed.), *Measurement in the Social Sciences* (Chicago: Aldine, 1974).

[9] Our use of a criterion in the vicinity of .30 is in keeping with general practice

ular variables we will also emphasize the gross stability and the gamma correlation.

It is somewhat more difficult to establish what constitutes a meaningful difference in persistence levels across the two generations. Here the absolute percentages representing stability can be used more safely; let us say that a difference of at least 10% in the gross stability figures will constitute a difference worth talking about. Comparisons can also be made using the correlations. Again, we will rely primarily on the τ_b figures. The rule of thumb will be that cross-generational differences above the .10-.15 range will constitute a meaningful difference, with the understanding that such absolute differences in the higher correlation ranges carry more weight than those in the lower ranges. All such figures are to some extent arbitrary and depend in part upon one's theoretical objectives.

It should be pointed out that the results to be presented below are not an artifact of the differing educational attainments of the youths and parents. The youths, of course, are more educated than their parents. If stability were strongly related to education, then parent-youth contrasts would to some extent be a function of the education difference rather than being life-cycle or generational in origin. To check for this, the stability data reported below were also generated for each of three subgroups in the younger generation: those who had no college training, those who matriculated but did not receive a four-year degree, and those with at least a college degree. There are occasional differences in the stability figures, but there is no consistent pattern of greater or lesser stability in one group, as will be shown in Chapter 8.[10]

PSYCHOLOGICAL INVOLVEMENT IN POLITICS

The degree of attention paid to politics varies widely across individuals. Involvement of this sort is important because it tends to be related to more active forms of participation, to be a necessary though

---

in the literature. See, e.g., Edward N. Muller and Thomas O. Jukam, "On the Meaning of Political Support," *American Political Science Review*, 71 (December 1977), 1561-95, note 16. The .30 value may still seem low. But there are two major considerations to keep in mind. First is the fact that this is an eight-year panel. For almost any attitude and probably most nonattitudinal characteristics it is unreasonable to expect extremely high correlations such as .7 or .8 over this long a period. Second, there is the matter of question reliability. Many of the measures used by political scientists should in some way be corrected for unreliability. But so far there is little agreement about how best to do so or just what the magnitude of such correction factors should be.

[10] Our findings on this score coincide with those reported (with some surprise) for the 1956-58-60 election study panel. See Philip E. Converse, "Public Opinion and Voting Behavior," in Greenstein and Polsby, *Handbook of Political Science*, Vol. IV, 103-104.

not sufficient condition for higher forms of engagement. Involvement is typically assessed through questions ascertaining a person's general interest in public affairs and politics, the amount of attention devoted to politics through the mass media, and the frequency of political discourse. We follow that general strategy here, with a couple of additional measures.

Paying attention to politics is believed to have reasonably strong anchorings in early socialization, although the evidence on this point is conflicting.[11] Aside from acknowledging a gradual rise in interest with increasing age, much of the literature seems to assume constancy at the individual level. This would seem to be rather unlikely, for it does not allow for much individual development nor for the capacity of particular issues and candidates to arouse or dampen a concern with politics.

Our first approach to gauging the level of involvement is much more indirect than is usually the case. At each point in time the respondents were asked to give their descriptions of the idealized good citizen.[12] Over forty distinct categories were employed to code these characterizations. The mean number of codable descriptions was sizeable and relatively constant over time: 2.74 and 2.59 for the youths, 2.61 and 2.67 for the parents in 1965 and 1973, respectively. For analytical purposes the response categories have been grouped under a number of major rubrics.

One index of how salient politics was to our respondents is the frequency with which the good citizen was described in political terms. The good citizen may be many things—a moral, ethical person; a good, kind, considerate person; a good neighbor; and so forth. But the good citizen may also be described in terms of the individual's role in a democratic polity. To the degree that political roles dominate the normative depictions of the good citizen, we would say that a respondent sees a centrality of political matters over nonpolitical matters. Hence the higher the number of references to political roles, the greater the psychological involvement in politics.[13]

[11] Retrospective data (i.e., recall data about parents) indicate that more politically interested parents breed more politically interested offspring. But the correlation between parental self-reports and adolescent offspring self-reports is very weak. See M. Kent Jennings and Richard G. Niemi, *The Political Character of Adolescence* (Princeton, N.J.: Princeton University Press, 1974), Chapter 6; see also Chapter 4 of this present volume.

[12] With few exceptions the specific measures employed in this book are described in Appendix B. It should be pointed out that the combined measures used here are generally additive indexes rather than Guttman scales as in 1965. However, we have rescored the repeated measures so that all variables reported here are scored identically for 1965 and 1973.

[13] Partial validation of this proposition lies in the positive associations between this variable and other indicators of involvement.

Considering the open-ended nature of the stimulus and the wide variety of replies possible, the results suggest a moderate degree of persistence over time (Table 2.1). Although there is substantial shifting, those placing more emphasis on political qualities in 1965 were also more likely to do so in 1973. Nor is this simply a function of greater volubility among certain types of respondents. Controlling for the number of responses by forming ratios of political to nonpolitical references, for example, still resulted in roughly monotonic relationships across the eight years. Even with this extraordinarily "soft" indicator, then, there is evidence of continuity of psychological involvement in politics.

TABLE 2.1: References to Political Qualities of Good Citizen

Number of Mentions	1973				
	0	1	2	$\geqq 3$	Totals
1965					
0	Y[a] 26%	33	31	10	100% (70)
	P 36%	37	17	10	100% (242)
1	Y 13%	32	28	28	100% (231)
	P 18%	38	28	17	100% (350)
2	Y 11%	31	33	24	99% (464)
	P 10%	30	35	25	100% (321)
$\geqq 3$	Y 5%	27	32	36	100% (350)
	P 7%	29	30	34	100% (196)

	Y = .14		Y = .20		Y = 33%
τ_b		γ		gross stability[b]	
	P = .26		P = .35		P = 36%

[a] Y = Youth, P = Parent.
[b] Gross stability refers to the proportion of cases found on the main diagonal of the 1965-1973 turnover tables.

At the same time, stability in terms of the correlation coefficients is appreciably higher among parents than among youths. Here we have the first hint that greater crystallization will tend to characterize parents, or the middle-aged, as we shall also call them for the sake of variety. The percentage figures in the table reveal what lies behind the higher correlations. The monotonicity is more regular and the gradations more marked in the older generation. Having had a longer time in which to ponder the meaning of citizenship, the parents have apparently worked out a more stable definition than have their less experienced offspring.

If at least modest signs of continuity in psychological involvement can be discerned with this relatively cue-free stimulus, we should expect to see more dramatic results by using stimuli that have more pronounced cues and circumscribed response alternatives. Such is the case with the most general measure we have, which is simply the reported amount of attention paid to "what's going on in government." Continuity is significantly higher among both generations than it was for the preceding measure (Table 2.2). This statement applies to the correlations and the gross stability percentages (which happen to be comparable because each variable has four categories) and is also revealed by the pattern contained within the table. Although the cross-generational differences are small, they do indicate greater continuity among the parents.

TABLE 2.2: Interest in Public Affairs

Follow *Public Affairs*	Hardly at all		Only now and then	Some of the time	Most of the time	Totals
			1973			
1965						
Hardly	Y	17%	29	46	8	100% (24)
at all	P	28%	22	22	28	100% (86)
Only now	Y	9%	27	42	23	100% (177)
and then	P	9%	31	34	26	100% (152)
Some of	Y	3%	13	45	40	101% (581)
the time	P	3%	11	42	43	99% (355)
Most of	Y	1%	6	28	65	100% (565)
the time	P	1%	5	20	74	100% (58)

$$\tau_b \quad \begin{array}{c} Y = .32 \\ P = .39 \end{array} \qquad \gamma \quad \begin{array}{c} Y = .49 \\ P = .57 \end{array} \qquad \text{gross stability} \quad \begin{array}{c} Y = 50\% \\ P = 56\% \end{array}$$

The relatively high stability displayed here is comforting from a methodological point of view as well. One of the most common indicators of psychological involvement in politics is the type being used here. It is a simple measure and usually performs very well as a predictor of political participation. Indeed, we used it rather extensively in analyzing the first wave of the study. Yet it is nothing more than a subjective self-appraisal offered by an individual. It has few if any concrete referents. It is, therefore, reassuring to note that even with this relative lack of concreteness the stimulus elicits a strong degree of continuity over time.

Another indicator of psychological involvement distinguishes among the objects of attention. People are drawn differentially toward certain domains of politics. One way of dividing these domains is by the scope of affairs—international, national, state, and local. Rank orderings applied to these four levels were "unfolded" to create a cosmopolitanism scale. Comparing positions on this scale across years demonstrates the degree to which the panel members maintained stable objects of attention.[14]

Our expectation here should be conditioned by the results attached to the question about the general salience of politics, where we found a moderately high level of continuity even though the texture of politics in 1973 was very different from 1965. But the referent in that instance was simply government in general. Diminutions of interest in one substantive or geopolitical domain could be counterbalanced by gains in others. To the extent that people remain generally sensitive or insensitive to public affairs, these shifts in focus would not affect the stability of general interest in politics.

In the present case, however, we are specifying particular domains of politics. Short-term effects can be operative, so that what is happening at a particular level of government may be all-absorbing at the time of the interview, only to have faded a few weeks or months afterward. For example, there may be a local- or state-level scandal. Longer-term effects can also be operative in the sense that the changing life space of the individual may have made some levels of government more salient in 1973 versus eight years earlier. Our expectations, then, would be that continuity on the *focus* of political interest would be lower than on the overall *level* of interest.

These expectations are fulfilled, though much more so for the young than the middle-aged. Indeed, the persistence among the latter is not strikingly lower than it is for the more general indicator of political interest. Although the gross stability in focus of interest is almost identical for both generations, the relative stability as represented by the correlations is considerably higher among parents (Table 2.3). There was much more in the way of extreme shifting among the young, especially those toward the less cosmopolitan end in 1965. Fresh confrontations with the realities of the various domains undoubtedly played a part in the greater volatility of the young. On the other hand, parents were by no means immune to change. While there is undoubtedly some capriciousness in their orderings, it seems likely that perceived alterations in the political world (e.g., increased cynicism about

14 This technique is described in M. Kent Jennings, "Pre-Adult Orientations to Multiple Levels of Government," *Midwest Journal of Political Science*, 9 (August 1967), 291-317.

TABLE 2.3: Local versus Cosmopolitan Focus of Political Interest

Cosmopol- itanism		Least 1	2	3	4	5	6	Most 7	Totals
					1973				
1965									
Least 1	Y	13%	13	13	18	8	18	16	99% (38)
	P	25%	29	11	14	14	3	4	100% (72)
2	Y	18%	26	6	24	12	6	9	101% (34)
	P	19%	27	21	13	14	6		100% (63)
3	Y	6%	8	13	32	17	17	8	101% (53)
	P	13%	20	15	30	13	8	1	100% (78)
4	Y	5%	6	10	26	21	26	7	101% (188)
	P	8%	11	12	34	16	14	4	99% (189)
5	Y	4%	4	8	21	19	21	12	99% (183)
	P	10%	4	8	32	24	20	3	101% (147)
6	Y	3%	4	4	19	16	47	8	101% (369)
	P	2%	4	6	20	21	34	12	99% (171)
Most 7	Y	3%	1	4	16	17	44	15	100% (221)
	P	3%	3	7	22	12	34	17	98% (58)

$$Y = .21 \qquad\qquad Y = .26 \qquad\qquad Y = 28\%$$
$$\tau_b \qquad\qquad\qquad \gamma \qquad\qquad\qquad \text{gross stability}$$
$$P = .36 \qquad\qquad P = .43 \qquad\qquad P = 28\%$$

the role of the federal government) as well as changes in their own circumstances (e.g., children finishing their schooling) had substantial effects on the relative salience of various governmental levels.

More concrete measures of psychological involvement take the form of responses to questions about exposure to public affairs via the mass media of newspapers, magazines, television, and radio. The cross-generation comparisons are very similar to those for the measure of general salience. Table 2.4 details the results for the two most widely used media, newspapers and television. Similar patterns prevail for magazine and radio usage.[15] Parental persistence ranges from moderate to high, and it is substantially higher than youth persistence on all save radio usage.

Beyond this general picture, the pattern seems to be one of a fairly large core of dedicated users, and in the case of radio and magazines a core of nonusers, along with considerable fluctuation in use by the

[15] For magazines the summary figures for the young are $\tau_b = .27$, $\gamma = .44$, gross stability = 55%; for the parents, .42, .68, and 65%. For radio the figures for the young are .11, .15, and 37%; for the parents, .23, .36, and 46%.

TABLE 2.4: Frequency of Newspaper and Television Usage
to Follow Public Affairs

		1973			
Read Papers	Not at all[a]	3-4 times a month	2-3 times a week	Almost daily	Totals
1965					
Not at all[a]	Y 35%	6	24	34	99% (204)
	P 56%	8	17	19	100% (192)
3-4 times a month	Y 21%	11	36	32	100% (81)
	P 36%	12	17	36	100% (42)
2-3 times a week	Y 19%	9	32	39	99% (434)
	P 25%	5	29	41	100% (189)
Almost daily	Y 9%	7	23	61	100% (616)
	P 8%	2	12	78	100% (744)

$$Y = .24 \qquad Y = .34 \qquad Y = 45\%$$
$$\tau_b \qquad \gamma \qquad \text{gross stability}$$
$$P = .47 \qquad P = .67 \qquad P = 63\%$$

		1973			
Watch TV	Not at all[a]	3-4 times a month	2-3 times a week	Almost daily	Totals
1965					
Not at all[a]	Y 17%	16	21	46	100% (191)
	P 30%	9	18	43	100% (114)
3-4 times a month	Y 14%	16	24	46	100% (225)
	P 11%	14	24	50	99% (107)
2-3 times a week	Y 9%	12	21	58	100% (421)
	P 13%	9	21	58	101% (221)
Almost daily	Y 7%	7	19	66	99% (499)
	P 4%	5	14	77	100% (721)

$$Y = .15 \qquad Y = .23 \qquad Y = 36\%$$
$$\tau_b \qquad \gamma \qquad \text{gross stability}$$
$$P = .26 \qquad P = .43 \qquad P = 55\%$$

[a] Includes a small number of respondents who said "a few times a year."

remaining individuals. Consider newspaper reading, for example.
Among the younger generation, a clear majority of "almost daily" users
in 1965 still read newspapers that frequently in 1973. At the other end,
half of the youths who did not listen to radio news in 1965 had not
begun to use it eight years later. In each case the figures for parents
show even more stability.

Along with this stable core, however, are frequent changes among those who use the media intermittently, and large changes among the minority who go against the trend—relying on radio and magazines or not using television and newspapers. The fluctuations among intermittent users are probably the least important. Some of these ostensible changes simply reflect unreliability in the questions. Moreover, it is probably the case that for a host of idiosyncratic reasons, people sometimes alter their behavior slightly, say from reading newspapers five or six times a week to only two or three times a week; unless these changes are uniformly in one direction, they are of little consequence. But the changes by those bucking the trend are often substantial. For example, of those who did not follow politics in the newspapers in 1965, nearly a fifth of the parents and fully a third of the youths said they read newspapers almost daily in 1973. Comparable increases in television usage were even sharper. For radio and magazines, it was the declines among 1965 users that reached these levels.

These results suggest a surprising amount of circulation between frequent and infrequent usage. Taking the results at face value, from about 10% to 25% of respondents in the case of television and newspapers, and about 25% to 35% in the case of magazines and radio, shifted from very high to very low use or vice versa. Moreover, we assume that numerous ups and downs in usage occurred but were not tapped by the two interviews.

Rather high degrees of circulation are also apparent in the turnover tables dealing with the main medium relied upon for news. In accord with our previous findings, gross stability is higher among parents than offspring, 54% versus 45%. That means, however, that close to one-half of each generation purportedly changed its mind about which of the media—papers, magazines, television, or radio—was most utilized. In both generations the least turnover occurred among those stressing television in 1965. Approximately two-thirds of those originally citing television continued to do so eight years later. Newspaper fans were the next most faithful, with one-half of the parents and two-fifths of the youth holding steady. Those relying most on radio and magazines were the least stable, with less than a third in each generation continuing to select those media later on. Not surprisingly, television tended to be the big winner among those who switched their choices. This was especially true among the young.[16]

Perhaps the most acute indicator of psychological involvement in

[16] An analysis of static and over-time linkages between media behavior and other political attributes in the youth panel is presented by Steven H. Chaffee, et. al., "Mass Communication in Political Socialization," in Renshon, *Handbook of Political Socialization*. The positive relationship of the print media usage to other forms of involvement, resources, and activity is especially noted.

politics is the frequency with which people talk to others about political matters. Use of the electronic and printed media is, after all, a rather passive mode of involvement. One is taking in and observing without necessarily reflecting on and discussing the content and meaning of what is being consumed. In the very act of verbalizing a thought about politics, that thought comes to have more substance and form. The thought also becomes vulnerable to challenge and modification as well as support and reinforcement. Political discourse is probably the penultimate step in the chain leading toward manifest political action designed to affect political outcomes. Indeed, it is sometimes difficult to distinguish between interchanges that are primarily private conversations with no specific targets in mind versus those where the goal is to achieve a more manifestly political outcome beyond the immediate setting.

People typically report talking more about politics with family than with nonfamily members, partly because politics is one of those sensitive subjects that, like religion, is often avoided when one is uncertain about the status of the personal relationships at hand. In both 1965 and 1973 we asked the parents how often they talked with their spouses about ". . . any kind of public affairs and politics, that is, anything having to do with local, state, national or international affairs." For the two-thirds of the youth sample which was married by 1973 the same question could be asked. But questions about spouses could not, of course, be used in 1965. What we use as the surrogate is the youths' reported frequency of discussion with members of their families. Among other things, the presence of a different referent in 1965 means that there were more targets of opportunity for the young in 1965, since the number of family members was nearly always greater than the N of one represented by a spouse. The difference also means we must be cautious in comparing the youth and parental stability figures.

Bearing this caveat in mind, we can turn to the results presented in Table 2.5. Considering first the parents, it is apparent that persistence was high. Conjugal patterns seem to develop such that some couples spend a good deal of time talking about politics (relative to others) whereas others scarcely ever broach the topic. If nothing else, stability of this sort probably makes for a more harmonious, predictable married life. It is worth noting that persistence in conversational frequency approaches that for newspaper readership (see Table 2.4), despite the fact that the latter has a much more concrete empirical referent—calendar frequencies versus the more subjective categories used for assessing frequency of political talk.

Of quite a piece with our findings on media behavior, we find that the young show more volatility in terms of political talk also. Obvi-

TABLE 2.5: Political Conversations in the Family[a]

		1973			
	Never	Not very often	Pretty often	Very often	Totals
1965					
Never	Y 26%	39	29	6	100% (183)
	P 48%	33	15	5	101% (139)
Not very often	Y 21%	40	33	7	101% (43)
	P 15%	45	32	7	99% (247)
Pretty often	Y 9%	40	42	9	100% (323)
	P 8%	21	52	19	100% (293)
Very often	Y 9%	22	48	22	101% (293)
	P 9%	15	34	43	101% (196)

$$Y = .25 \qquad\qquad Y = .37 \qquad\qquad Y = 32\%$$
$$\tau_b \qquad\qquad\qquad \gamma \qquad\qquad \text{gross}$$
$$P = .41 \qquad\qquad P = .54 \qquad \text{stability} \quad P = 47\%$$

[a] For parents the referent is the respondent's spouse in each year; for youths the referent is family members in 1965 and spouse in 1973.

ously this lower level, while not feeble by any means, could be the result of using two different stimuli, one the family of orientation, the other the family of procreation. Yet in one sense that is precisely the point. An inevitable part of the maturation process for most young adults is taking leave of their parents and sibs and establishing their own domicile. The definition of family changes. It is this life-cycle development that makes the young more vulnerable to alteration in the mode and frequency of intimate political discourse. By contrast, most parents had the same familial setting in 1965 as 1973, save for the exiting of at least one offspring.

POLITICAL RESOURCES

What a person brings to the political arena has much to do with eventual participation and the probability of obtaining successful outcomes. For example, people who feel efficacious participate more than do those who feel ineffectual. People with an ability to understand and manipulate political symbols have more say in what happens than do those with little capacity on that count, *ceteris paribus*. Resources can be tangible and structural (e.g., wealth), rather than sociopsychological in nature. Here we content ourselves with the latter. We will employ four indicators of political resources: sense of civic obligation, political efficacy, understanding of political ideology, and political knowledge.

To what degree should we expect these resources to remain stable over the life span? Given their known association with social class there should be at least moderate persistence, because social class does not ordinarily change radically over the life span. The resources examined here would also seem to reflect states of mind and habits that are integral to the political personality. On the other hand, resources can rise and fall depending upon their use, how important they are to the individual, and the ease with which they can be acquired. Taking into account the social and political aging of the young generation in particular, we might well expect considerable turnover in resources.

The first resource to be examined, sense of civic obligation, is our most oblique indicator. It will be recalled from the previous section that one way of denoting psychological involvement in politics lay in observing the degree to which the good citizen equaled the political citizen in the eyes of our two generations. Political virtues fell into two distinct subgroups, however. On the one hand were those stressing political allegiance—obeying laws, being loyal, honoring the country, paying taxes, and the like. A second set of responses stressed the more active, participant component of the political repertory—being interested in and paying attention to politics, taking an active role, voting, taking part in campaigns, and a great variety of intensive and specific forms of participation.

The corollaries and implications of these two themes are different. Following the usage of those who developed a specific measure some years ago, we may think of the second theme as imposing a sense of civic obligation or citizen duty on an individual.[17] It is a prescription that one ought to behave in a participant fashion rather than (or in addition to) a passive fashion. As such it constitutes a motivation or resource that should prompt people to engage in political action. It can serve as a norm (in much the same way as efficacy does) that impels one toward the political thicket. It is in this more indirect fashion that the sense of civic duty is here called a political resource.[18]

How stable is this commodity? Again, we should bear in mind the open-ended nature of the stimulus being used. Respondents were under no compunction to describe the good citizen in political terms in general, nor in activist political terms in particular. With that backdrop, it is not too surprising that the measures of persistence are, by

---

[17] Angus Campbell, Gerald Gurin, and Warren E. Miller, *The Voter Decides* (Evanston, Ill.: Row, Peterson, 1954), 194-99.

[18] It is reassuring that this measure has a modestly strong relationship to the other indicators of resources used here and to the political activity index presented in the next section.

conventional standards, rather moderate (Table 2.6). That they are as substantial as they are testifies to the fundamental role of civic obligation in the vast repertory of citizen roles. Commitment to a sense of duty is by no means ephemeral, even when tapped in such an indirect manner.

TABLE 2.6: References to Active Political Qualities of Good Citizen

Number of Mentions	1973				
	0	1	2	≥ 3	Totals
1965					
0	Y 44%	31	18	8	101% (250)
	P 61%	25	10	3	99% (473)
1	Y 32%	32	25	11	100% (402)
	P 43%	33	19	4	99% (329)
2	Y 27%	27	29	16	99% (332)
	P 33%	35	20	11	99% (233)
≥ 3	Y 16%	33	33	18	100% (131)
	P 24%	28	30	18	100% (74)

$$\tau_b \quad Y = .17 \quad\quad \gamma \quad Y = .23 \quad\quad \text{gross stability} \quad Y = 32\%$$
$$P = .25 \quad\quad P = .36 \quad\quad P = 41\%$$

It is instructive that as we move from measures of psychological involvement to political resources we see an emergence of the same gross pattern according to generation. On all counts the middle-aged have greater stability than do the young. Contributing in part to that greater persistence is the fact that parents who deemphasized participant roles in 1965 tended to stick by that declaration to a greater extent than did the youths. To the extent that a sense of civic duty constitutes a resource that can be engaged, it is likely to be a more permanent feature in the middle years.

The second resource to be examined, political efficacy, refers to the feeling that one can have some control over the political environment, that there are various ways in which the individual can cope with that environment. It has been demonstrated that the standard four items in the Michigan political efficacy scale actually decompose into two dimensions.[19] One can be called "external efficacy" because it alludes

[19] George I. Balch, "Multiple Indicators in Survey Research: The Concept 'Sense of Efficacy'," *Political Methodology*, 1 (Spring 1974), 1-44. This also proved to be true, though not as clearly so, with our 1973 data.

more to properties of the system, and the other "internal efficacy" because it alludes more to properties inhering within the individual. The two items for which we have over-time data for both samples are of the internal variety. Responses to these two items have been combined to form an index.

In Table 2.7 we observe a rather characteristic pattern—higher gross stability and rank order correlations among the parents than among the young adults. Within both generations, however, the least efficacious of 1965 tended to remain more stable than did the highly efficacious. Considering the great strains over the period of time, it is perhaps surprising that persistence remained as high as it did.

TABLE 2.7: Internal Political Efficacy

		1973		
	Low	Medium	High	Totals
1965				
Low	Y 47%	43	10	100% (284)
	P 69%	27	4	100% (449)
Medium	Y 28%	51	21	100% (627)
	P 37%	50	12	99% (458)
High	Y 13%	49	38	100% (417)
	P 21%	41	38	100% (244)

$$\tau_b \quad \begin{array}{l} Y = .28 \\ P = .39 \end{array} \qquad \gamma \quad \begin{array}{l} Y = .44 \\ P = .58 \end{array} \qquad \text{gross stability} \quad \begin{array}{l} Y = 46\% \\ P = 55\% \end{array}$$

The two other indicators of political resources deal more with the individual's comprehension and understanding of the political system. In contrast to most other measures used in this study, they have a very heavy component of cognition. First is a measure capturing the respondent's political sophistication about the ideological cast of the party system. Given that parties are an integral part of the American political process, an ability to see the ideological divisions between the parties presumably puts one in a better (or at least different) position to evaluate what is happening, to make "rational" decisions, and to take adversarial roles. Additionally, the particular measure employed has been shown to be useful in cross-age comparisons.[20]

[20] Philip E. Converse, "The Nature of Belief Systems in Mass Publics," in David Apter (ed.), *Ideology and Discontent* (New York: Free Press, 1964); and Jennings and Niemi, *Political Character of Adolescence*, Chapter 4.

There is a strong expectation of weaker persistence among the young, primarily as a result of change in one direction. Although their understanding of the political parties apparently increases rapidly during the high school years, they are still less sophisticated than older adults. Recognition of traditional party images should grow quickly as they move into the electorate. Parental recognition and understanding, by contrast, should remain more stable. Particular aspects of party ideology no doubt rise and fall in prominence, but overall characterizations of the parties are unlikely to change rapidly. The strong cognitive component of the measure should result in at least reasonably high persistence for both generations.

In some ways the expectations are handsomely met (Table 2.8). Parents exhibited greater persistence than their offspring, and the continuity for both generations is strong enough to document more than incidental persistence. Ideological sophistication is not ephemeral. Nev-

TABLE 2.8: Recognition and Understanding of
Liberal-Conservative Dimension

| | | None | | | | Broad | |
		1	2	3	4	5	Totals
1965							
None 1	Y	38%	9	14	15	23	99% (429)
	P	51%	7	15	18	9	100% (352)
2	Y	18%	5	18	20	39	100% (164)
	P	29%	7	13	36	15	100% (134)
3	Y	28%	4	25	16	27	100% (127)
	P	32%	1	25	31	10	99% (105)
4	Y	7%	4	7	34	48	100% (98)
	P	16%	3	7	53	21	100% (291)
Broad 5	Y	6%	2	11	28	53	100% (265)
	P	9%	2	8	30	51	100% (190)

$$\tau_b \quad \begin{array}{l} Y = .29 \\ P = .39 \end{array} \qquad \gamma \quad \begin{array}{l} Y = .39 \\ P = .50 \end{array} \qquad \text{gross stability} \quad \begin{array}{l} Y = 35\% \\ P = 43\% \end{array}$$

Definitions of the categories are: 1. No apparent recognition of terms (does not know if parties differ in liberal-conservative terms and does not know if anybody else sees them as differing); 2. Recognition and an attempt at matching but inability to give any meaning for terms; 3. Recognition but some error in matching; 4. Recognition and proper matching but a narrow definition of terms (like "spend-save"); 5. Recognition and proper matching of the labels (liberal, conservative), meaning, and party, and a broad understanding of the terms liberal and conservative.

ertheless, one might have expected greater stability among the parents, especially assuming a lifelong persistence model. At the extreme ends of the scale continuity is rather strong, but toward the middle the picture is more ambiguous and far from perfectly monotonic. It would be difficult to argue that the relative ideological positioning of the two parties had altered substantially in an objective sense over the eight-year period. From a subjective viewpoint changes may have occurred; the discontinuity displayed by many parents could stem from such subjective appraisals.

As for the young adults, there was even less persistence, as expected. The tabular configuration is also more ragged than in the case of the parents. Especially impressive is the heavy influx from the least sophisticated of 1965 into the ranks of the most sophisticated of 1973, as evidenced by the first two rows of Table 2.8. Just how fixed the perceptions of the young will remain is problematic in view of the evidence of considerable shifting among the middle-aged.

Our final indicator of resources provides a dramatic contrast even though it, too, is a more cognitively based measure than most others used. We wished to have some way of indexing the amount of information possessed about contemporary political history and about the technical operations of government. Such an index would help characterize people according to the amount of information they could bring to bear on political participation and decision-making. The questions we used dealt with matters over which there is no factual dispute, as might, for example, be the case on the party differences measure just discussed. Six such questions were asked at both points in time. Our expectations are for high persistence. We would not expect serious losses in information since all the questions deal with more than transitory phenomena. Individuals tend, if anything, to enlarge rather than decrease their storehouse of information, with the possible exception of rote learning and ad hoc acquisition. What might contribute more to instability would be gains in information. Because they are newer to the adult world the young should exhibit less stability. This would follow from their gaining more factual information about contemporary political history while forgetting some of the textbook lessons acquired in their civics classes.

Looking first at the additive index combining the six questions, we find extraordinarily high persistence in each generation (Table 2.9). Indeed, the youths' τ_b correlation is the highest instance of political stability to be reported here, and that for the parents is exceeded only by the fractionally higher mark for party identification. In passing, it is worth noting that the gross stability figures are very similar to those for recognizing party differences, despite the fact that the latter has

TABLE 2.9: Knowledge of Political Facts

Number Correct		0	1	2	3	4	5	6	Totals
					1973				
1965									
0	Y	22%	13	35	26			4	100% (23)
	P	43%	29	14	7	7			100% (14)
1	Y	4%	34	31	21	8	1	1	100% (77)
	P	5%	22	52	12	8			99% (40)
2	Y	2%	12	26	41	15	3		99% (177)
	P	4%	13	49	29	4	1		100% (142)
3	Y		3	21	37	27	9	3	100% (254)
	P		2	18	52	21	5	2	100% (291)
4	Y		1	9	24	30	21	15	100% (240)
	P			5	19	47	24	4	99% (269)
5	Y			4	9	30	34	23	100% (183)
	P			1	11	20	42	26	100% (183)
6	Y		1	2	5	6	23	64	101% (128)
	P		1	1	4	7	27	61	101% (130)

τ_b Y = .56 γ Y = .67   gross stability   Y = 36%

P = .66   P = .79   P = 48%

two fewer categories contributing to the turnover matrix. Yet the rank-order correlations for the knowledge measure are much higher. Only slight shifts to adjacent categories took place versus the more severe movements on the party measure. On balance, factual inventories are relatively invariant.

An analysis of the individual items making up the index reveals the same kind of findings as for the index as a whole. In each instance the persistence is high and the parents hold the edge. But results for the individual items do convey additional insights into the dynamics of information gain and loss. In 1965 almost all youths and parents knew the names of the state governors; most knew that Germany had concentration camps during World War II. Over the next eight years few individuals forgot these facts. It is perhaps surprising at first to see how many of those uninformed in 1965 had acquired the information by 1973. But on questions on which knowledge is so widespread and which are in the news as frequently as these, the answers are easy to pick up if one has somehow avoided them previously. And sensibly, the governor's name is the most frequently learned, with the historical information trailing well behind.

The turnover for a question inquiring which country was ruled by Marshal Tito is also in line with our expectations. This piece of information was less widely distributed than that for the previous two items, and accordingly, more people forgot it after 1965 and fewer of the uninformed acquired it. Slightly more of the uninformed youths than parents learned Tito's identity, perhaps because contemporary politics took on more meaning for them as adults.

The other three items contain mild surprises. A high number of youths were uninformed in 1965 about Franklin Roosevelt's political affiliation. The absence of this information in 1965, together with the rate at which it was acquired later, supports the view that knowledge of partisan politics is still being learned as individuals enter the adult world. Significantly, though, more youths than parents also forgot this information over the eight years between interviews, helping maintain a generational difference regarding a figure very familiar to parents but of only historical significance to the youths.

Facts about governmental operations show more turnover than expected, at least as indexed by correct answers to questions about a Senator's term of office and the number of Supreme Court justices. Considerable backsliding was apparent among the young adults as predicted, but nearly as many informed parents also failed to retain the information. Those initially uninformed also learned at what seem to be high rates, considering the absence of formal schooling or other efforts to teach technical facts and figures. This is especially the case for the question about the Senate term of office, since the Senate in general was not subject to as much attention as was the Supreme Court in this time period.

Despite these varying patterns across the six separate items, the overall conclusion must be that persistence is remarkably high in this domain. Simply in terms of the gross stability, the range for the individual items was from 69% to 89% for the youths and from 79% to 91% for the parents. And while stability was somewhat higher among people who had correct information in 1965, the level was not radically lower among those who were ill-informed in 1965.

POLITICAL PARTICIPATION

A logical next step in our presentation would be to move from psychological involvement and political resources into political action. It makes little sense, however, to talk about persistence of political participation when the youth sample was simply too young to have had much opportunity or legal right to take part in political action in 1965. Nevertheless, it will be possible to offer one example—that of voting —to illustrate the patterns one might expect to find had full materials been available for both generations. More complete materials dealing with other modes of participation are available for the parents, and some surrogate indicators are also available for the youths.

It has been concluded that voting (and nonvoting) in national elections tends to become a habit over time, although just how long it takes the habit to form is uncertain. Moreover, the declining rates of turnout in recent years suggest that a smaller proportion of the populace is becoming addicted. There seems to be a cadre of voters, one of nonvoters, and a third composed of episodic voters. By taking our respondents' reports of their voting behavior in the 1968 and 1972 presidential elections we can arrive at a first approximation as to how habitual voting has become in the entering compared with the established electorate.

Considering first the parents, it is clear that continuity is high (Table 2.10). The exact agreement figure (gross stability) is one of the highest to be found for dichotomous variables in our inquiry, and the rank-order correlations are very large. Contributing to the extremely high stability are the high rates of turnout in each election. Although stability is by no means meager among the youths, turnout is considerably more variable among them than among their parents. Many of the nonvoting youths in 1968 subsequently turned out in 1972, while parental nonvoters largely remained inactive. Large majorities of voters in 1968 went to the polls again in 1972, but the drop-off was slightly greater among the young. These results combined to make gross stability much lower among the young. Fully one-third failed to vote in

TABLE 2.10: Voting Turnout

	1972		
	Voted	Did not vote	Totals
1968			
Voted	Y 82%	18	100% (708)
	P 90%	10	100% (1019)
Did not	Y 58%	42	100% (465)
vote	P 19%	81	100% (129)
	Y = .27 τ_b	Y = .54 γ	Y = 66% gross stability
	P = .59	P = .95	P = 89%

one of the first two presidential elections for which they were eligible to register.

The age at which voting was first possible was related to turnout levels in an interesting way. Those who were twenty-one in 1968 turned out at a 60% rate in that year and at a 72% rate in 1972. Those who were first eligible in 1972 turned out at a rate of 69%, only three percentage points below the "experienced" group. Age per se, rather than the number of opportunities, was the more dominant factor determining turnout levels. A probable explanation for this is that those of our respondents who were twenty-one in 1968 had just recently become so, whereas those first eligible in 1972 had long since passed that threshold. Becoming cognizant of the electoral opportunities and engaging in the necessary procedures of registration had a relatively brief time to be realized for these first eligible in 1968.

By adding other reports on electoral performance we can provide further confirmation of middle-aged stability and youthful stuttering. For each generation we have the turnout in the 1970 off-year election and for the parental generation we have the reported turnout for the 1964 presidential contest (drawn from the 1965 interviews). These can be combined with 1968 and 1972 reports to form a correlation matrix, as shown below. Figures without parentheses are τ_b values; those within parentheses are γ values.

	Parents			
Youths	1964	1968	1970	1972
1964		.51 (.91)	.44 (.83)	.45 (.84)
1968	x		.61 (.97)	.59 (.95)
1970	x	.45 (.78)		.60 (.92)
1972	x	.27 (.54)	.35 (.72)	

The large differences between the τ_b and γ correlations arise from the overwhelming tendency of voters in one election to vote in a succeeding one versus the more variable behavior among the nonvoters. These kinds of configurations generate especially high γ correlations and convey important information. Regardless of which statistic is considered, however, parental stability was far higher than youth stability across matching pairs of elections. It is also patent that parental stability over a period covering three presidential elections was rather high in an absolute sense. The contrast between the two generations is precisely what one would expect given the seasoned versus immature histories of the two. The new voters are entering the electorate in a halting, uneven fashion and have had relatively few trials in order to become habituated one way or the other.

If voting is an apt example, we would be inclined to extend our generalizations about growth and persistence to other forms of participation also. The observed pattern may well be true of activity related to national election campaigns, but if one considers a host of other, more specific, modes and domains of participation the extension may not apply with equal strength. Taking part in nonconventional activities, for example, is more common among the young and may never be repeated later in life.[21] Similarly, being involved in educational politics is very much a function of where one is in the life cycle.[22] Of course, it may be that the protestors of yesterday become the electoral gladiators of today, and that the school activists turn to other domains once their children leave school. In this respect there would be continuity of a broad sort.

Exploratory work with the parental respondents demonstrates that broad persistence of this kind is, indeed, very common. A number of questions were asked in 1973 about political activities during the previous eight years. These activities included trying to influence the votes of others, attending political rallies, wearing buttons or using stickers, making financial donations, performing other electoral activities, contacting public officials, writing letters to editors, engaging in protests or demonstrations, and working with others to solve community problems. The frequencies of such activities, along with the exercise of four voting opportunities, were summed to yield a political activity index ranging from 0-13; for present purposes the index was trichotomized into low (0-2 acts), medium (3-5), and high (6-13) categories.[23]

Location on this activity index can be compared with a number of measures based on the 1965 interviews. For example, participation in school affairs as of 1965 is positively related to the activity index ($\tau_b = .19$, $\gamma = .35$). Similarly the degree of participation in the high

[21] Klaus R. Allerbeck, M. Kent Jennings, and Leopold Rosenmayr, "Generations and Families: Political Action," in Samuel H. Barnes, Max Kaase, et al., *Political Action: Mass Participation in Five Western Democracies* (Beverly Hills: Sage, 1979).

[22] M. Kent Jennings, "Another Look at the Life Cycle and Political Participation," *American Journal of Political Science*, 23 (November 1979), 755-71.

[23] A fuller treatment of the activity index and its constituent parts is given in Paul Allen Beck and M. Kent Jennings, "Political Periods and Political Participation," *American Political Science Review*, 73 (September 1979), 737-50.

school PTA is also associated with activism later on ($\tau_b = .18, \gamma = .30$). Taking a broader form of political endeavor as the point of comparison strengthens the over-time correspondence. The more parents reported taking part in community affairs as of 1965, the higher their overall activity was: $\tau_b = .28, \gamma = .51$. Even when using rather disparate indicators of participation, we find moderate to strong relationships between activity levels in the more distant and more recent past.

If we encounter persistence when the domains and modes are incongruent, we should find even higher persistence by looking at more comparable behavior. Parents in 1965 were asked if they had ever performed the various electoral activities listed above during the previous ten years. The frequencies were summed to provide an additive index. This index is similar to the one developed in 1973 except that the latter is more inclusive.[24] What we are doing, then, is comparing two activity indexes, one based on (roughly speaking) the 1956-1965 period and the other on the 1966-1972 period.

Cross-tabulating the two demonstrates the profound tendency for participation levels to be perpetuated over time among mature adults. Illustratively, of those who were low participants of the earlier period (those performing no acts), some 60% were also in the low category in the later period, compared with 28% in the middle category, and only 11% in the high category. By contrast, of those who were high participants (three or more acts) in 1965, only 3% were in the low category later on, compared with 19% in the middle category, and an astounding 78% in the high category. Of course, there are plentiful examples of individuals who accelerated or decelerated their levels of political activity. But the dominant picture is one of strong stability in participation levels, as witnessed by the summary statistics of $\tau_b = .48$ and $\gamma = .64$. These are impressive figures because they indicate, when extrapolated to other segments of the adult population, that the habit of participation does become ingrained by the middle years, that the ingress and egress into the participant strata is *relatively* limited within a particular cohort. They also suggest that the engine of political change is fueled partly by changing attitudes, values, and goals among the participating strata in addition to the energy supplied by population replacement and the episodic participants.

Although it is not possible to carry out the same sort of analysis for the youth sample, surrogate measures from the 1965 interviews can be employed. These provide weak to moderate evidence for the carryover of prepolitical participation and attitudes from the late adolescent

[24] The earlier index is described in *The Student-Parent Socialization Study Codebook* (Ann Arbor: Inter-University Consortium for Political and Social Research, 1971, 1977).

years to actual political participation in the young adult years, with the latter being designated by an activity index built in the same fashion as that for the parents. Illustratively, the level of interest expressed in politics and public affairs in 1965 is related to later activity levels ($\tau_b = .19$, $\gamma = .30$). Similarly, the anticipated level of participation as an adult is related to the actual level reported subsequently ($\tau_b = .19$, $\gamma = .32$). The frequency of political conversations with family members and with friends is also associated with later performance: $\tau_b = .17$, $\gamma = .25$ for family members and .11 and .17 for friends.

There has been considerable speculation about how participation in high-school politics and organizational life bears on participation in the "real" world of politics. There is some modest support for the argument that participation in the prepolitical world of high-school government is a training ground for later involvement. Using a six-point index based on the number of activities and offices held during high school, one can see, at the extremes, a clear association between the two domains. Of those scoring zero on the high school activities index, 51% also scored low on the political activity index, 36% scored medium, and only 12% scored high. At the other end, of those engaging in five or more activities, 19% scored low whereas 40% scored medium, and 41% scored high. However, the overall correlation between the two indexes is modest ($\tau_b = .17$ and $\gamma = .23$).

This relatively weak correspondence between adolescent prepolitical and adult political activity on the one hand, and the robust correspondence of adult political activity over time among mature adults indicates that political participation is *sui generis*, that there are few, if any, solid experiential precursors in the pre-adult years to account for the adult-level political activism. By the same token, once the individual undergoes a number of trials or opportunities for participation during the early part of his or her adult life, a pattern *tends* to become set.[25]

In terms of our models, the results would support a lifelong persistence interpretation, where lifelong was restricted to the adult years. Despite the relatively weak to moderate association between prepolitical activities and predispositions versus subsequent political activity on the part of the youths, it would be erroneous to conclude that lifelong openness characterizes political participation. Rather, the unfolding of the life cycle presents young adults with the opportunity for a form of participation that simply did not exist previously. With no directly comparable previous behavior conditioning them, the youths

[25] Subsequent analysis utilizing causal modeling ascribes a more elevated role for the impact of high-school activity. See Paul Allen Beck and M. Kent Jennings, "Pathways to Participation," paper presented at the annual meeting of the American Political Science Association, Washington, D.C., September 1980.

are more susceptible to life-cycle factors, the nature of the opportunity structures, and a variety of chance elements. Barring unanticipated generational effects, the presence of stability among the parents leads us to expect the young adults to emerge eventually with participation persistence levels not dissimilar to those of the preceding generation.

In this chapter we have dealt almost exclusively with variables that have little in the way of affect or controversy attached to them. While individuals differ in their degree of psychological involvement and political resources, these are not matters that divide the populace. They are basically in the cognitive and behavioral realms, being reflections of individual capacities and motivations. We have observed modest to very strong evidence of persistence among both generations, with the elder having consistently higher stability. But what if we consider variables in the affective and evaluative realms? Do any of the models (openness, persistence, or life-cycle/generational effects) characterize political attitudes, preferences, and evaluations? And does the pattern of stronger stability continue to mark the middle-aged more so than the younger adults? The following chapter turns to an examination of these questions.

CHAPTER THREE

Persistence at the Individual Level:
Political Preferences and Attitudes

In this chapter we will take up several types of variables that have rested at the heart of the controversy about the stability of political orientations. We begin with partisanship, move on to issues of public policy, and then to evaluations applied to actors in the governmental process. In an effort to draw larger generalizations about stability over time and across generations we shall also introduce a number of non-political dimensions. Finally, we shall provide an overall summary and evaluation of the materials covered in this and the preceding chapter.

PARTISANSHIP AND ELECTORAL BEHAVIOR

One of the strongest arguments traditionally used to support the lifelong persistence model is the durability of party identification and voting behavior. Despite obvious fluctuations at the individual and aggregate levels, the constancy of these attributes stands well ahead of most other political characteristics for which there are diachronic data. Much of the early literature in political socialization focused on the development of party identification in the pre-adult years with the implicit assumption of relatively high carryover into adulthood. Coupled with the emphasis on the emergence of diffuse support for the political system, the findings on partisanship supplied strong evidence in favor of the lifelong persistence model.

Until recently partisanship was viewed as highly rigid among older adults. Among young adults some change was anticipated, but primarily in the direction of increasing strength of identification with one's preferred party. Recent studies, however, have questioned both of these conclusions.[1] Party identification may be stable compared to many other orientations, but it is far from unchanging. And it seems clear that strength of identification has not been increasing with age since the downturn in partisanship began in the mid-1960s.[2]

[1] Richard G. Niemi and Herbert F. Weisberg, "Is Party Identification Stable?" in Niemi and Weisberg (eds.), *Controversies in American Voting Behavior* (San Francisco: W. H. Freeman, 1976).

[2] There is considerable controversy about whether partisanship increased with age prior to the mid-1960s. Among others see Philip E. Converse, *The Dynamics*

The data from our panel (Table 3.1) add to this revised view of partisan stability while at the same time re-emphasizing the comparative persistence of partisanship.[3] Most impressive is the weakening rather than strengthening ties of the youth generation, a point to be emphasized on the basis of aggregate shifts. But also impressive is the sheer amount of turnover among the young. Roughly 40% changed their basic response (i.e., Democrat, Independent, or Republican), and this figure applies whether we define Independents as pure Independents and leaners together or as only those who decline to express any party leanings.

These data make it clear that the partisan feelings of young adults can frequently be altered—at least to such an extent that they regard themselves as Independents. But they also show only a small number of youth actually switching party allegiance, with about 9% moving from a strong or weak Democratic position to a strong or weak Republican position, or vice versa. Yet it seems to us that the particular form of malleability shown here came about in response to the dominant forces during this period, and that during times of strong partisan pressures young adults would presumably change partisanship quite freely.

The row percentages in the lower panel of Table 3.1 provide an important perspective on this point. Change among 1965 Democrats could easily occur in response to historical pressure toward feelings of independence; the small number of Democratic-Republican switches would suggest strong resistance to actual partisan shifts. But changes by 1965 Republicans, and especially Independents, cannot be so easily explained. Over one in seven Republicans had switched to a Democratic position by 1973—and almost one in four, if leaners are considered partisan. Still more significant, a third of the 1965 Independents became partisan despite the overall trend toward independence. These changes suggest that not only are young adults open to the call for independence, but that they are also quite capable of switching to a partisan position and even from one party to another. If historical

---

of Party Support (Beverly Hills: Sage, 1976) and Paul Abramson, "Developing Party Identification: A Further Examination of Life Cycle, Generational, and Period Effects," American Journal of Political Science, 23 (February 1979), 78-96.

[3] The entries in Table 3.1 depart very slightly from an earlier report due to the fact that mailback respondents had no "Independent-leaner" option, thus inflating the "pure Independent" category when these data were merged with those based on personal interviews. When the sevenfold scale is used in this volume, the mailback respondents are eliminated from the analysis. For the earlier report see M. Kent Jennings and Richard G. Niemi, "The Persistence of Political Orientations: An Over-Time Analysis of Two Generations," British Journal of Political Science, 8 (July 1978), 333-63.

TABLE 3.1: Party Identification[a]

1965		Strong Democrat	Weak Democrat	Indep. Democrat	Indep.	Indep. Republican	Weak Republican	Strong Republican	Totals	
Strong Democrat	Y	23%	39	21	5	7	5	—	100%	(193)
	P	52%	37	7	1	1	3	—	101%	(270)
Weak Democrat	Y	9%	46	18	10	8	7	2	100%	(260)
	P	17%	60	6	4	5	6	2	102%	(248)
Independent Democrat	Y	7%	21	29	21	12	7	4	101%	(164)
	P	8%	29	36	17	5	4	2	101%	(107)
Independent	Y	4%	11	20	32	17	13	2	99%	(151)
	P	1%	8	16	45	13	14	2	99%	(106)
Independent Republican	Y	0%	7	18	24	28	17	6	100%	(88)
	P	2%	2	9	6	34	36	11	100%	(64)
Weak Republican	Y	3%	10	13	14	23	28	10	101%	(158)
	P	3%	3	4	8	6	55	21	100%	(157)
Strong Republican	Y	7%	12	6	8	15	21	31	100%	(89)
	P	4%	1	—	4	5	28	58	100%	(131)

τ_b $Y = .40$ $P = .68$ γ $Y = .47$ $P = .78$ gross stability $Y = 32\%$ $P = 52\%$

TABLE 3.1 (cont.)

1965		Democrats	Independents	Republicans	Totals
Democrats	Y	59%	34	6	99% (539)
	P	82%	12	5	99% (537)
Independents	Y	18%	65	16	99% (480)
	P	20%	62	19	101% (295)
Republicans	Y	15%	39	46	100% (302)
	P	5%	15	80	100% (308)
		Y = .43	Y = .63	Y = 58%	
	τ_b	P = .71	γ P = .89	gross stability P = 76%	

[a] The 7 × 7 figures exclude the mailback respondents.

forces are in a largely partisan rather than unaligned direction, we would expect considerable shifting of new adults in the direction of those pressures.

It should be also stressed that persistence of party identification (in terms of the τ_b correlation) among the young is exceeded only by that for political knowledge and, as seen below, several pairs of votes. By absolute standards the stability is impressive. Nevertheless, the malleability of young adults is emphasized by the greater stability of the parents. Though even in the older generation there was some movement in and out of the Independent category, the parents' partisanship fluctuated far less than that of their offspring. Movement out of the partisan categories was especially infrequent. Indeed, the absolute degree of continuity based on a trichotomy of Democrats, Independents, and Republicans is as high as one is likely to find on any political variable where there are divisions within the populace. Similarly, the τ_b correlation is one of the two highest encountered in our analysis, surpassed only by that for the 1970 versus 1972 congressional votes.[4] For this generation change in the middle years among Democrats and Republicans is infrequent.

The greater malleability of young adults is also apparent in their voting behavior, but with an interesting twist. Though the youths were ineligible to vote in 1964 and some were still too young in 1968, preferences or actual votes were obtained for the 1964, 1968, and 1972 presidential contests. As expected, preference for the same party's candidate in all three elections was less frequent among offspring than among parents. However, the difference was only 10% (43% versus 53%). Consequently, differences between the generations in terms of consistent candidate preferences were less than differences in terms of consistent party identification.

Equally interesting is a comparison of stability between 1964 and 1968 with that between 1968 and 1972. The percentages preferring the same party (considering Wallace a third party) are as follows:

	1964-1968	1968-1972
Y	55%	69%
P	66%	74%

In both pairs of years parents were more stable, but the cross-generational difference in the second period is only half that of the first pe-

[4] Significantly, the stability level is almost identical to that found in the election study panel of the late 1950s. Philip E. Converse, "The Nature of Belief Systems in Mass Publics," in David Apter (ed.), *Ideology and Discontent* (New York: Free Press, 1964), 240. It is also very similar to that found in a subsequent panel —see note 9.

riod. If these results generalize at all, they suggest a rapid decline in change proneness very early in adulthood, though the decline in a relative one that allows for fairly large amounts of change later in life.

A parsimonious way of demonstrating both the short-range and long-range character of voting preference stability is to array the various interrelationships in a correlation matrix. For comparative purposes we can also add the reported vote in the 1970 and 1972 congressional elections. The results are as follows, the τ_b and γ coefficients being distinguished by parentheses around the latter. (P = presidential preferences, C = congressional preferences.)

		Parents			
	64-P	68-P	72-P	70-C	72-C
Youths					
64-P		.43	.37	.49	.44
		(.75)	(.82)	(.81)	(.76)
68-P	.31		.51	.43	.40
	(.58)		(.78)	(.62)	(.60)
72-P	.22	.46		.48	.50
	(.50)	(.70)		(.84)	(.86)
70-C	.18	.35	.40		.75
	(.37)	(.56)	(.73)		(.96)
72-C	.20	.35	.48	.71	
	(.41)	(.54)	(.83)	(.95)	

In contrast to the results on voting turnout presented in the preceding chapter, the results on voting preferences produce relatively small differences between the stability levels of the two generations. Not surprisingly, the most visible disparities involve the 1964 election, with the parental correlations all being substantially higher than those for the young adults. Of course the young were not eligible to participate in that election and they expressed their preferences in the absence of any prior voting experience. For parents the 1964 election was but another in a long series. The correlations including the 1964 election are, with the exception of the 1970-1972 congressional pair, in much the same vicinity as the other combinations.

Aside from the understandable 1964 departures, the two generations look remarkably similar. Young voters appear to reach a fairly quick crystallization in voting preference, at least to a level of stability equal to that of veteran voters. Significantly, for both generations the strongest association lies in the pair of congressional elections, where the short-term forces of presidential candidate appeal and overriding national issues are not as compelling. Young voters apparently adopt very quickly the norms of supporting the same congressional party and/or the incumbent. Bearing in mind the limited voting histories of the younger generation, it appears that moderate to high persistence characterizes the direction of the vote over time and that this firmness sets in rather quickly.

OPINIONS ON PUBLIC POLICY ISSUES

A good deal of the controversy surrounding the question of aging and persistence has been generated by the findings about opinions on issues of the day. Just as the work in party identification tends to be used to support the lifelong persistence model, that on popular issues tends to be used to support either a lifelong openness model or, in a quite different vein, a model which posits exceedingly weak attitudinal consistency and structuring over time. The instability observed in one of the few national-level panel studies led to the conclusion that positions taken on what seemed to be major issues of the day were often capricious and filled with "noise," so much so that at the extremes they were characterized as being "nonattitudes."[5] If that were universally so, then the ostensible residues of pre-adult socialization would be weak indeed. In recent years, however, the "nonattitudes" argument has been challenged and a vigorous debate has ensued.[6]

One complication in studying opinions about public issues is that the attitude objects may change instead of or in addition to the object evaluators.[7] Two examples will help clarify the distinction. A mass of evidence indicates that white Americans are now more positively dis-

[5] Ibid., and Philip E. Converse, "Attitudes and Non-Attitudes: Continuation of a Dialogue," in Edward R. Tufte (ed.), *The Quantitative Analysis of Social Problems* (Reading: Mass.: Addison-Wesley, 1970).

[6] Norman H. Nie, with Kristi Andersen, "Mass Belief Systems Revisited: Political Change and Attitude Structure," *Journal of Politics*, 36 (August 1974), 549-91; James Stimson, "Belief Systems: Constraint, Complexity, and the 1972 Election," *American Journal of Political Science*, 19 (August 1975), 393-418; Christopher H. Achen, "Mass Political Attitudes and the Survey Response," *American Political Science Review*, 69 (December 1975), 1218-31; Philip E. Converse, "Public Opinion and Voting Behavior," in Fred I. Greenstein and Nelson W. Polsby (eds.), *Handbook of Political Science*, Vol. IV (Reading, Mass.: Addison-Wesley, 1975); W. Lance Bennett, "The Growth of Knowledge in Mass Belief Studies: An Epistemological Critique," *American Journal of Political Science*, 21 (August 1977), 465-500; and a number of studies analyzing the consequences of changes in question wording. For the latter see, inter alia, George F. Bishop, Alfred J. Tuchfarber, Robert W. Oldenick, and Stephen E. Bennett, "Questions about Question Wording . . . ," *American Journal of Political Science*, 23 (February 1979), 187-92, and the sources cited therein.

[7] Again we are indebted to David Sears, *Political Attitudes through the Life Cycle* (San Francisco: W. H. Freeman, forthcoming), Chapter 12.

posed toward blacks than they were two decades ago. One interpretation is that white attitudes have changed while the attitude object—
blacks—has remained stable. Yet it is very apparent that changes have
occurred among blacks during this period. So the apparent change in
white attitudes might reflect a change in blacks instead of or in addition to alterations in underlying white attitudes. Another example is
that of American public opinion regarding other nations of the world.
Within the space of a generation Americans have moved from a point
of hostility toward World War II enemies to a point where these same
countries are among the most admired. It is clear that the attitude object, country, has changed dramatically. Attitudes toward the kinds of
actions associated with earlier negative affect toward these countries
would presumably be rather stable. Thus what might be interpreted
as great instability of attitudes toward an object could actually disguise persistence in attitudes toward particular object traits.

Although the political significance of object-inspired attitudinal
shifts such as those just discussed is great, the analytic distinction between object-inspired and actor-inspired change is vital. If it is the
object that is changing, then modifications in the object's behavior
would be expected to engender corresponding shifts at the actor level
and depressed over-time consistency. On the other hand, if it is the
actors who are changing (via other mechanisms) then changes in the
actors' evaluations would most likely be unrelated to alterations in the
objects. More importantly, our appraisal of the actors' observed changes
would be quite different. In the short run it may make little difference which explanation is correct: one wants to know, for example,
whether whites are becoming more tolerant and whether Americans
feel more positive toward former enemies. But the difference is pivotal. We must, therefore, be especially careful in interpreting ostensibly
low continuity, and should not be too hasty in proclaiming "nonattitudes."

Even though we have come to expect opinions on specific issues to
show considerable fluctuation over time, cross-generational differences in rates or types of fluctuation should also be found. As high
school seniors, the younger generation reported opinions just as frequently as did their parents. Yet greater instability among young
adults might well be expected on the grounds that their attitudes were
less firmly based and that their opinions would be subject to considerable strain as they gradually came in contact with a wider environment.

Responses to four issue questions are available for the over-time
analysis. The results (Table 3.2) conform in a general way to the expectation of considerable instability and of greater instability among

the young, though we will emphasize the opposite point of view in each case. An important point to make at the outset, however, is that the distance between issue stability and partisan stability is considerable, especially for the older generation. Indeed, the absolute values of the issue correlations among the latter and the distance between those values and that for party identification are extraordinarily similar to those prevailing in the cross-sectional panel study of the late 1950s.[8] Although the parent sample is scarcely a microcosm of the general adult population—and given its higher level of political activism

TABLE 3.2: Opinions on Public Policy Issues

3.2a School Related Issues

School Integration			1973		
		Pro	Depends	Con	Totals
1965					
Pro	Y	54%	15	32	101% (798)
	P	58%	14	29	101% (550)
Depends	Y	46%	19	34	99% (110)
	P	32%	28	40	100% (114)
Con	Y	34%	17	49	100% (253)
	P	22%	13	65	100% (286)

$$Y = .15 \quad\quad Y = .24 \quad\quad Y = 49\%$$
$$\tau_b \quad\quad\quad \gamma \quad\quad\quad \text{gross}$$
$$P = .32 \quad\quad P = .51 \quad\quad \text{stability} \quad P = 56\%$$

School Prayers			1973		
		Con	Depends	Pro	Totals
1965					
Con	Y	59%	5	36	100% (282)
	P	59%	3	38	100% (149)
Depends	Y	31%	8	62	101% (39)
	P	21%	8	70	99% (47)
Pro	Y	21%	2	78	101% (708)
	P	7%	1	92	100% (815)

$$Y = .37 \quad\quad Y = .65 \quad\quad Y = 70\%$$
$$\tau_b \quad\quad\quad \gamma \quad\quad\quad \text{gross}$$
$$P = .49 \quad\quad P = .84 \quad\quad \text{stability} \quad P = 83\%$$

[8] Converse, "Nature of Belief Systems," 238-41.

TABLE 3.2 (cont.)

3.2b Civil Liberties Issues

Communist Holding Office		1973 Pro	Con	Totals
1965				
Pro	Y	81%	19	100% (488)
	P	71%	29	100% (335)
Con	Y	47%	53	100% (837)
	P	30%	70	100% (796)

$$Y = .34 \qquad Y = .66 \qquad Y = 63\%$$
$$\tau_b \qquad\qquad \gamma \qquad\qquad \text{gross stability}$$
$$P = .38 \qquad P = .70 \qquad P = 70\%$$

Anti-Church Speeches		1973 Pro	Con	Totals
1965				
Pro	Y	95%	5	100% (1168)
	P	83%	17	100% (866)
Con	Y	86%	14	100% (174)
	P	54%	46	100% (290)

$$Y = .12 \qquad Y = .51 \qquad Y = 84\%$$
$$\tau_b \qquad\qquad \gamma \qquad\qquad \text{gross stability}$$
$$P = .29 \qquad P = .61 \qquad P = 74\%$$

we would expect somewhat higher stability—the parallelism across the two studies nevertheless suggests that the nature of over-time stability has not altered appreciably.[9] Adding weight to this conclusion is the fact that the longer time span covered by our own observations would tend to cancel out any advantage the parental sample might have compared with a straight cross-section of adults.

Let us now take a closer look at the findings for each policy issue. Consider first the overall amount and type of change. Whether one observes the contingency table entries or the summary measure it is obvious that many individuals gave different responses in 1965 and 1973. Moreover, the number of switches increases if we incorporate individ-

[9] Of course the Center for Political Studies 1972-74-76 election study panel will provide the ultimate comparison with the earlier panel. A first report confirms our speculation. See Philip E. Converse and Gregory B. Markus, "Plus Ça Change . . .: The New CPS Election Study Panel," *American Political Science Review*, 73 (March 1979), 32-49.

uals with no opinion. The school prayer and school integration questions were prefaced by asking whether the respondent had "been interested enough in this to favor one side over the other." As many as 23% (youths on school prayers) had no opinion in 1965, 1973, or both.[10] Including these respondents lowers the percentage with a stable, substantive answer to 43% and 46% of the youths and parents, respectively, on the school integration question, and to 54% and 72% on the school prayers question. Presumably, if the other two questions had included such a preface, similar results would have occurred. Clearly, then, a fair amount of instability exists, and some unknown portion of it undoubtedly rests in respondent capriciousness.

Three considerations, however, caution against overemphasizing the instability. First, with the exception of the younger generation's performance on the school integration issue the over-time continuity would have to be considered at least moderately high. (The very low τ_b on the speech issue will be discussed shortly.) Indeed, the correlations compare on the whole rather favorably with those for variables taken up in the preceding chapter, though certainly not with political knowledge or party identification. Over eight turbulent years, from about 50% to 85% of the respondents evinced no net change of mind on these four issues, albeit some of these nonchangers are so classified by chance alone.

Second, and perhaps more important, is the type of change that occurred. Shifts transpired primarily in one direction. The most extreme case of this is the younger generation's attitude toward the legitimacy of speeches against churches. The τ_b correlation is low, reflecting the fact that individuals' 1965 responses poorly differentiated their 1973 responses. Yet extraordinarily few of those originally supporting such speeches switched their positions, whereas a very large shift occurred among those originally opposed, as indicated by the large γ coefficient. To a great extent this pattern characterizes several of the individual turnover tables, with the school integration issue being the chief exception. The importance of this observation is that it strongly suggests that individuals were reacting to societal moods rather than simply answering randomly—as would be implied by a "nonattitudes" interpretation.

A third consideration brings us back to the subject of change in the object rather than change in the actor and is directly relevant to the issue of the federal government's role in integrating the schools. For each generation the τ_b correlations are lowest on this issue—with the understandable exception of the free speech topic. The γ correlations and the gross stability percentages stand alone as showing the least con-

---

[10] This includes a small percentage which said it had an opinion but could not say which it favored.

tinuity. Since the aggregate shift was toward favoring a reduced federal role in achieving integration, as will be discussed in Chapter 6, it might be thought that change was largely unidirectional. But Table 3.2a reveals that about as many of the "con" respondents in 1965 switched to a "pro" position in 1973 as vice versa. Because there were so many more favorable than opposed respondents in 1965 the net aggregate shift was in the "anti" direction. Certainly for those who really (as opposed to randomly) switched from "pro" to "con," the explanation would seem to lie largely in the intrusion of the busing issue. Thus the attitude object, integration, had come to take on a different meaning, or to have additional elements attached to it since 1965. It is more difficult to apply the same reasoning to those who went from "con" to "pro," although it is instructive that far fewer of the parents than of the youths made such a switch. Perhaps in this instance, aside from the random change, the bulk came from people who now saw integration as a desirable goal which could be achieved only by a strong federal role, busing or not. But the overall point is that changes in the object probably lie at the base of much of the observed attitude instability.

A nice contrast is provided by the other school-related issue, that of the legitimacy of prayers in schools. Although occasional legal cases arose over the eight years, in general the time period was marked by relative quiet on this subject. New elements were essentially lacking. Thus the attitude object would appear to have changed considerably less than on the integration issue, and the greater persistence becomes more explicable.

Generational differences in persistence conform to expectations and to the pattern laid down with respect to other types of orientations. On three of the four issues all measures are lower for the young than for the middle-aged, and the skewed 1965 distribution among the young on the speech issue largely explains their higher gross stability. The latter is the only instance out of all findings presented in this volume (relating the same 1965-1973 variables) in which *any* measure of persistence is higher for the young adults than for their parents.

On balance, the assumption that more plasticity on issues of the day will be found in young adults is validated, although the possibility that this could be a generational rather than life-cycle phenomenon should not be ruled out. At the same time, these cross-generational differences should not be exaggerated. Attitudes of older adults seem to be somewhat more resistant to change than those of young adults, but it would be misleading to conclude that the former are rigid in their views or immune to contemporary political trends. Even on issues on which there are intergenerational cleavages in terms of mean tendencies (such as the school prayers and free speech issues), older as well as younger adults are quite capable of shifting their sentiments.

Strong secular trends can have the effect of reducing over-time persistence and, in the process, blurring or reducing the attitudinal distinctions previously existing. Such was clearly the case with respect to integration of the schools, where the secular movement was very much in a "conservative" direction between 1965 and 1973. If it is assumed that some attitude objects do (or might) change over time, then another approach to the question of persistence is to compare attitude objects that are nominally different but are judged to be equivalent in meaning across time. If, for example, a particular set of issues defines the liberal-conservative split at one point in time but another set does so at a subsequent point in time, then the appropriate strategy is to compare the correspondence on these sets in order to demonstrate the stability of a liberal versus conservative outlook. Determining exactly what constitutes equivalency is the great obstacle in this procedure. Limitations in the 1965 data prevent a full-fledged attack of this sort, but a limited exercise is possible.

The civil rights issue was the issue domain, par excellence, during the mid-1960s, before the Vietnam War and spin-off topics were fully ushered in. And the federal government's role in integrating the schools was a rich embodiment of that issue. Comparisons were made between stances on that issue, as of 1965, and on the following half dozen seven-point scales,[11] as of 1973: protecting the rights of the accused versus stopping crime regardless of their rights; government helping minority groups versus minority groups helping themselves; making use of marijuana legal versus setting penalties higher; busing to achieve integration versus keeping children in neighborhood schools; having equal roles for men and women versus women's place being in the home; and having extremely liberal versus extremely conservative views. In addition, the two issues of whether the police treat some people worse than others and whether the United States should have entered the Vietnam War were put to the respondents, and these were likewise related to respondents' stances on the school integration question. While these eight issues by no means exhaust the issue agenda as of the early 1970s, they obviously do include many of the most prominent and controversial topics.

One way of summing up the findings is to say that in no instance are the correlations between 1965 position on integration and 1973

[11] The seven-point scale format posed two alternative positions anchoring the ends of a scale presented to the respondents. They were then asked to locate themselves (and other groups or individuals) on one of the seven locations. An option of "haven't thought about it" was offered, with the result that some respondents did not locate themselves.

position on various issues as high as the correlations between 1965 and 1973 integration stands. This holds true for both generations and to about the same degree. In some instances there is greater "continuity" among the young, while in others it is greater among the middle-aged; but these are trivial differences in a sea of modest correlations to begin with. Admittedly, all of the correlations have the correct signs, and in two or three cases they reach the .2 to .3 range for the γ coefficient. Even these stronger relationships, however, scarcely lead one to say that the holders of the liberal (or conservative) view on a key issue of the 1960s were likely to occupy the same relative positions on key issues of the early 1970s.

Because integration was such a powerful and unique type of issue, we performed the same analysis for the other three issues addressed above and for the affect felt toward blacks as registered on the feeling thermometer.[12] Some of the resulting correlations ran higher than did those emerging from the integration issue, but only in a couple of instances did the γ coefficient exceed .30. In evaluating these results it must be remembered that for most of the issues in 1973, and for two of them in 1965, prefatory questions were asked to screen out those respondents who considered themselves uninterested or uninformed about the topic. Thus the amount of random position-taking should have been minimized.

The implication of these findings is that the boundary lines of liberalism-conservatism are extremely permeable as one moves through life and across issues. That the parents were no more predictable in their views than their offspring suggests that life experience, itself, is no sure guide to the consistent allocation of individuals to the liberal or conservative side of a given issue. On the other hand, the fact that the young adults were no more predictable than their parents shows that even substantially higher levels of education and coming of age during a time of political heat are no guarantees to what the analyst would define as issue consistency over time. It has been known for some time that issue publics are remarkably diverse, and that even during the recent period of apparently high "issue constraint" there were large numbers of people holding seemingly conflicting views at a single point in time. What we have demonstrated here, for two distinct generations, is that the longitudinal picture is also muddy, that the liberals on yesterday's issue are not necessarily the liberals on today's.

12 The thermometer technique consisted of a card running from 0°-100°. Respondents were informed that 0° represented cold, unfavorable feelings and 100° represented warm, favorable feelings, with 50° representing the midpoint between warm and cold feelings. "Don't know" responses were coded in a separate category.

EVALUATIONS OF GOVERNMENT AND SOCIOPOLITICAL GROUPS

Another domain in which changes among attitude holders must be weighed very carefully against changes in the attitude objects is that of the evaluations accorded political actors and groups. It was rather widely believed until a few years ago that such evaluations had substantial durability. With hindsight it is clear that one of the reasons for this conclusion was that research had been conducted during a relatively quiescent period. Since there was not a great deal of questioning of the status quo and since group attachments appeared to be anchored in early learning, it was not unnatural to come to that conclusion. Beginning as early as the civil rights and free speech movements, hitting stride with the antiwar and urban unrest period, and perhaps culminating with the Watergate revelations, the grounds for such conclusions became increasingly weak. Great changes in the aggregate have been observed with respect to evaluations made of both public and private sector actors.[13] Nor have all of these been in a downward direction, though that has certainly been the modal pattern. At a superficial level, then, it would seem obvious that openness rather than rigidity characterizes these orientations. We shall comment directly on this point as we take up our findings.

We begin with a side attack on the question. During the course of the interviews, the respondents were asked to describe those things they were least proud of as Americans. Taking the two soundings together, over seventy separate categories were used to code the responses. One way of reducing this sheer volume and variety is to group the responses according to major themes. For example, some responses fell into a moral, ethical, and religious dimension, others into social problems, others into race relations, others into political institutions and processes, and so forth. As will become forcefully apparent in Chapter 6, the relative emphasis given various themes changed dramatically across the eight years. Of concern to us at present, however, is the degree of individual stability in portraying these national images. Specifically, we are interested in the degree to which explicitly political failings were consistently cited by our two generations. Are political and governmental shortcomings a relatively constant component of national attributes, or do the vicissitudes of political life and the changes in one's personal life act to make such attributions relatively unstable?

Cross-tabulating the frequency of mentions in 1965 against those of 1973 reveals that the continuity is modest at best, so modest among the young as to be scarcely visible (Table 3.3). But even among the parents, with their traditional edge over the young, the persistence is

[13] Arthur H. Miller, "Political Issues and Trust in Government: 1964-1970," *American Political Science Review*, 68 (September 1974), 951-72.

TABLE 3.3: Political Qualities Least Proud of as an American

Number of Mentions		1973			
		0	1	≥ 2	Totals
1965					
0	Y	31%	45	24	100% (731)
	P	42%	40	18	100% (720)
1	Y	26%	44	30	100% (299)
	P	27%	45	29	101% (283)
≥ 2	Y	28%	45	27	100% (75)
	P	17%	49	34	100% (88)

$$\begin{array}{ccc} Y = .06 & Y = .10 & Y = 34\% \\ \tau_b & \gamma & \text{gross} \\ P = .17 & P = .29 & \text{stability} \quad P = 41\% \end{array}$$

weak. Within both generations, significant proportions moved from voicing no disapproval of political matters into citing one or more topics; but there was almost as much movement in the opposite direction in a proportional sense. What is disguised by the proportions in the table, of course, are the numbers upon which they are based. Thus the shifting of those with no mention in 1965 is much more significant at the aggregate level than is the comparable shifting among those with two or more mentions simply because the base N is nine to ten times larger in the former category. Disregarding that aspect, however, it is clear that there is a relative openness and lack of rigidity about characterizing American society. Given the conflicts that raged during the eight-year span, it is not surprising that we should observe this relative lack of persistence. One would be inclined to attribute the instability to changes in the object much more than to changes in the individual, especially since each generation exhibited such modest continuity.

As noted, this mode of attacking the question of continuity in the evaluation of governmental institutions is rather indirect, partly because it allows the individual to construct a characterization unprompted by any direct cues about politics. Moreover, there is likely to be a certain degree of grasping for whatever answers come into one's mind when such global open-ended questions are asked. Our next indicator suffers from neither of these liabilities, but results based on it tend to support those from the open-ended queries.[14]

[14] Moreover, there is a moderately strong positive correlation between the index constructed from the open-ended responses and the other indicators of government evaluation.

One of the most talked about phenomena in contemporary American politics is the level of trust accorded officials of the national government. The decline in trust beginning around 1964 is by now a familiar story. We employed the five standard Michigan items in building an index of political trust for the two years.

At the individual level the degree of persistence is quite modest for each generation (Table 3.4). Although the typical pattern of greater continuity among parents is present, the τ_b correlations are among the lowest observed for the political variables examined here. Thus the likelihood of changing one's level of trust in the actions and motivations of government officials, though slightly diminished in the middle years, appears to remain substantial over a large portion of the life span. We have argued elsewhere that entry into adulthood and the political aging that accompanies it are likely to bring about rather rapid shifts in political trust. The data bear that out with a vengeance. What we were less prepared for was the widespread discontinuity among the middle-aged. In the absence of compelling data or theories pointing toward life-cycle or generation-induced change at that stage of the life cycle, we would argue that the changes were inspired by

TABLE 3.4: Trust in Political Authorities

			1973					
	Low					High		
	1	2	3	4	5	6	Totals
1965							
Low 1	Y 24%	44	28		4		100% (25)
	P 31%	35	21	5	6	1	99% (99)
2	Y 18%	45	19	10	8	1	101% (74)
	P 26%	31	29	9	5	1	101% (160)
3	Y 21%	32	25	6	14	2	100% (144)
	P 17%	29	26	15	13		100% (205)
4	Y 12%	37	29	7	12	3	100% (174)
	P 20%	25	24	13	15	3	100% (143)
5	Y 13%	26	25	12	21	3	100% (532)
	P 12%	18	28	16	23	4	101% (404)
High 6	Y 10%	18	28	14	26	4	100% (270)
	P 6%	13	19	14	30	17	99% (99)

τ_b Y = .18 P = .27 γ Y = .23 P = .34   gross stability Y = 17% P = 23%

modifications in the attitude object rather than changing affect toward a constant entity.

Such an argument does not mean that attitudes did not change in the ordinary, everyday meaning of the term. By most standards the lack of persistence lends support to the lifelong openness model. But a change induced by general receptivity or by life-cycle/generational effects is fundamentally different than one inspired by modifications in the attitude object. When the secular forces are pushing disproportionately in one direction, as was the case between 1965 and 1973, it is much more reasonable to attribute micro-level instability to a changing attitude object. If the government officials of 1973 had been seen in the same light as they were in 1965, it is doubtful that instability would have been so rampant. Of course this argument does not override the counterargument that the mass public was flexible enough in its attitudinal structure to permit changes in the attitude object to work their will on expressions of trust.

While political trust in the national government underwent a spectacular movement between 1965 and 1973, change in the relative trust accorded the three levels of government was also substantial. Youths and parents were asked which level of government—national, state, or local—they most preferred, and which they least preferred. For present purposes this is treated as a dichotomous measure, national government being one category and state and local being collapsed into a non-national category. Our reasoning here is that most of the dynamics at work during this period were overwhelmingly related to the national government as an object of attention. Conceived in this way, the relevant summary statistics show relatively little persistence among youths: $\tau_b = .13$, $\gamma = .32$, gross stability = 55%. There was considerably more continuity among parents: $\tau_b = .29$, $\gamma = .54$, gross stability = 64%. As anticipated, the major source of the instability among both generations was the movement of those who had expressed most faith and confidence in the national government as of 1965. This differential movement is reflected in the substantially higher γ coefficients.

Lack of persistence would be even greater if we incorporated into one measure all the information generated by the question sequence. For example, in 1965, almost none of the young adults or parents said they had faith in no level of government, whereas close to 5% in each generation proclaimed that sentiment in 1973. In 1965 only about 1% expressed equal confidence in all three levels; eight years later about 10% felt that way. Perhaps in more tranquil times greater individual stability would be found. During this period the relative trust afforded the various governments seems to have been influenced very heavily by the momentous happenings at the national level. That the impact of these events was felt more heavily by the young than by the middle-aged is very much in keeping with the life-cycle/generational model of persistence.

Another set of objects for which we have over-time evaluations are eight sociopolitical groupings. To the degree that politics comes to be interpreted and reflected by large collectivities, changing evaluations of them serve to index important shifts in public opinion. For example, at the aggregate level the filial generation registered noticeable declines in its assessments of big business and labor unions over the eight-year period, thereby suggesting growing disenchantment with both of these traditional rivals. Ratings of the groupings were obtained through the "feeling thermometer" technique; the higher the temperature recorded the more positive the evaluation.

At the individual level the common pattern emerges (Table 3.5). With the exception of the tie on ratings of Southerners, parents maintained greater stability than did their offspring. The differences range from the trivial to the more significant, as in the instance of Protestants, labor unions, and big business. While all of the parent correlations are reasonably healthy, the same is not true among the young adults. Only one of the τ_b correlations is above .30, and three sink below .20. Whether because of life-cycle or generational processes, the young were considerably less stable.

TABLE 3.5: Summary Statistics on Evaluation of Sociopolitical Groups

	Youths			Parents		
	τ_b	γ	Gross stability[a]	τ_b	γ	Gross stability[a]
Southerners	.32	.39	56%	.32	.39	59%
Catholics	.28	.35	56%	.36	.44	61%
Blacks	.25	.30	54%	.30	.36	61%
Whites	.24	.33	54%	.26	.35	66%
Jews	.23	.31	61%	.32	.40	63%
Protestants	.19	.24	52%	.31	.41	71%
Labor unions	.17	.21	50%	.42	.50	58%
Big business	.14	.17	42%	.29	.34	55%

[a] These figures are based on the main diagonal plus the ones on either side of the diagonal in a 10×10 matrix. Corresponding percentages taking only the main diagonal cells are. for youths - 25%, 28%, 23%, 26%, 35%, 28%, 20%, and 17%; for parents - 28%, 32%, 26%, 32%, 34%, 36%, 29%, and 26%.

Although the persistence exhibited by the middle-aged is substantial, one might wonder why it is not even higher, especially for the more politically and physically visible groups such as big business, labor unions, and blacks. It is unfortunate that soundings were not taken about the political parties, qua groups. Certainly if party identification is taken as the surrogate for the evaluation of party as a group (as Converse seemed to do several years ago),[15] then there is a dramatic difference between the stability of party evaluations versus other group evaluations. On the other hand, it may be that the feeling thermometer is too blunt an instrument to capture sensitive judgments about these more general groups compared with the evaluations made of prominent political personalities and more crisply defined political groups. Yet another possible explanation is that the societal vicissitudes during the era we covered resulted in more than the "normal" amount of instability.

An examination of the matrices underlying these correlations suggests one major reason for the cross-generational differences. For six of the groups the young moved in almost massive proportions to the middle or 50° position on the thermometer. So great was the movement that over a third placed each of these groups at 50°. A corresponding move was scarcely visible among the middle-aged. For the two groups where this movement did not occur, labor unions and big business, there were strong unidirectional shifts among the young who had rated them highly in 1965. Both of these kinds of changing evaluations lowered persistence levels among the younger generation. A consideration of what lay behind these trends among the young will be taken up in Chapter 6.

An interesting substantive consequence to be observed is that the greatest generation gap in persistence levels, as measured by the correlation coefficients, occurred with respect to the two most specific groups—labor unions and big business. All of the other groups are much more inclusive, are not characterized by occupational labeling, and are less clearly "interest groups." It seems likely, and the results are supportive, that a more experienced segment of the populace such as parents would have a more stable image of these entities than would individuals just coming of age. For the latter, big business and labor are more likely to be abstractions encountered in civics books and newspapers than organizations and personalities whose actions might have some direct bearing on their lives. But by the time the young reach their mid-twenties these images would have acquired more substance, thus resulting in alterations in their 1965 ratings. For the parents, of course, big business and labor unions would have been more permanent fixtures in their lives for some time.

[15] Converse, "The Nature of Belief Systems," 239-41, and note 35.

NONPOLITICAL CHARACTERISTICS

Whatever may be the degree of persistence with respect to political attributes, it would be extremely helpful to have comparative materials from nonpolitical domains. Only in that way can we determine if the political is unique. And in terms of the larger question of persistence at the micro level, only by drawing comparisons can we begin to generalize about persistence phenomena. Our data are not extensive, but they are varied enough to offer some reference points by which to to gauge the results found in the political domain.

Religion is often mentioned in the same breath with politics as an arena which is controversial and which also has deep-seated roots in pre-adulthood. A commitment to a particular religion or denomination is held to be as strong or stronger than a commitment to a political party. The results from our panel are fully of a piece with this appraisal. Movement across the broad religious groupings was relatively rare over the eight-year period. Dividing the groupings into Catholic, Protestant, Jewish, other, and none, we find that 81% of the young and 94% of the middle-aged remained stable. (The lower figure for the young is largely a consequence of a movement toward the "none" position.) These are extraordinarily high proportions. Lifelong persistence of basic religious loyalties appears to be the overwhelming mode.

But these five major categories can disguise internal shifting within the many-splendored denominational alternatives of American Protestantism. Therefore, stability figures were calculated on the full range of preferences, letting each specific preference stand alone. Over forty such designations were expressed. Not surprisingly, gross stability declines under this procedure, the new figures being 62% for the young and 84% for the middle-aged. Continuity is still high by any conventional standards, but now not quite so monumental, especially among the young.

It is instructive to compare these latter figures with those for party identification. The fair comparison here is the broad three-way grouping of Republicans, Independents, and Democrats, since the more elaborate seven-way classification also taps the intensity of the preference. Among the young the two rates of stability are exceedingly close, 62% for religion and 58% for partisanship. Among the parents the difference is only slightly greater, 84% versus 76%. Both domains, then, exhibit high continuity and both show the characteristic pattern of lower stability in young adulthood. It is quite unlikely that any other social attribute of a nonascriptive type would reach the heights of religion in terms of stability. By that standard, the persistence of party identification is impressive indeed. Moreover, that persistence occurred during an historical period marked by exceptionally heavy strain on the party system.

We have two other measures tapping religious orientations. Although there are no direct parallels for them in the political arena, they will nevertheless serve to locate the political within the larger set of orientations. First is an attitudinal measure ascertaining the individual's belief about the divine nature of the Bible. By most criteria stability is high here also (Table 3.6). The correlations are among the very highest encountered in our attitudinal data, and probably represent the upper range of attitudinal continuities to be found in general populations. Given the absence of similar unchanging attitude objects in the political realm, it is difficult to draw comparisons. However, it is probably no accident that the public issue with the highest overtime attitudinal stability was that of the legitimacy of prayers in school. Here we have a commingling of the political and religious. Religiously tinged political issues have great salience, as even a casual recall of American political history reveals.

TABLE 3.6: Belief in Divinity of Bible

		1973		
	Not divine; of little relevance	Contains human error	God's Word	Totals
1965				
Not divine;	Y 61%	37	2	100% (57)
of little relevance	P 61%	26	13	100% (54)
Contains	Y 15%	73	12	100% (640)
human error	P 10%	72	18	100% (453)
God's Word	Y 5%	44	51	100% (570)
	P 3%	23	75	101% (608)

$$\begin{array}{cccc} & Y = .44 & Y = .72 & Y = 62\% \\ \tau_b & & \gamma & \text{gross} \\ & P = .56 & P = .81 & \text{stability} \quad P = 73\% \end{array}$$

A final indicator of religious orientation is the frequency of church attendance. Surprisingly enough, this behavioral measure was less stable among the young, and no more so among the middle-aged, than was the attitudinal measure of belief in the Bible (Table 3.7). Turnover among the young was dramatically higher than among parents, in large part a function of the drastically reduced rates of church attendance. Perhaps the most comparable political data at our disposal

TABLE 3.7: Frequency of Church Attendance

| | | 1973 | | | |
	Never	Few times per year	1-2 times per month	Weekly	Totals
1965					
Never	Y 59%	23	9	9	100% (22)
	P 40%	43	11	6	100% (63)
Few times per year	Y 36%	47	7	11	101% (150)
	P 21%	57	12	10	100% (269)
1-2 times per month	Y 18%	53	18	12	101% (198)
	P 6%	36	31	27	100% (182)
Weekly	Y 10%	34	16	40	100% (753)
	P 3%	10	11	76	100% (586)

$$\tau_b \quad \begin{matrix} Y = .32 \\ P = .58 \end{matrix} \qquad \gamma \quad \begin{matrix} Y = .51 \\ P = .76 \end{matrix} \qquad \text{gross stability} \quad \begin{matrix} Y = 37\% \\ P = 62\% \end{matrix}$$

are the reported frequencies of following politics through the mass media. The correlations all run lower than for church attendance, though with the exception of radio listening not drastically so. Direct comparisons of gross stability can be made with the two leading media of television and newspapers since they are also four-category variables, as is church attendance. In this comparison political continuity remained as high ($\pm 8\%$) as did religious continuity. To the extent that the measures are comparable, habits of spectator politics are nearly as fixed as those of "spectator" religion, and flux is much greater among the young in both domains.

Three additional nonpolitical orientations are available for further comparisons. These are social-psychological attributes and are often referred to as personality characteristics. One is something of an analogue to political trust in that it deals with interpersonal trust,[16] the degree of trust which people are willing to invest in each other. Over-

[16] It is rather widely believed that trust in people forms the basis of trust in government or is at least linked to it. Robert E. Lane, *Political Life* (Glencoe, Ill.: Free Press, 1959), 164. The empirical evidence is only moderately supportive, however. See, e.g., Richard L. Cole, "Toward a Model of Political Trust: A Causal Analysis," *American Journal of Political Science*, 19 (February 1975), 63-80. Working with the present set of data, Markus found in a multivariate analysis that our measure of personal trust did have a modest relationship to political trust in both samples and at both points in time. See Gregory Blake Markus, "Continuity, Change and the Political Self: A Model of Political Socialization" (unpublished Ph.D. thesis, University of Michigan, 1975), Chapter 6.

time associations among the young were $\tau_b = .27$, $\gamma = .36$, and gross stability $= 40\%$. Corresponding associations among parents were .42, .57, and 49%. It is not without significance that the recurrent pattern of less continuity among the young asserts itself here as well as in the political and religious realms. Also significant is the greater stability of interpersonal trust than political trust (cf. Table 3.4). The reasons are not hard to divine. Whereas the attitude object, governmental actors, changed dramatically over the years, people in general may be presumed to have changed much less. And whereas the evaluation of governmental actors depends in part on the changing composition of the object vis-à-vis the evaluator (e.g., the partisan similarity between the two), that would not apply in the case of such abstractions as "most people."

Standing in partial contrast to the trust comparisons are those involving efficacy. Two indexes of personal efficacy were constructed, one referring to opinion strength and one referring to self-confidence.[17] The statistics for opinion strength were, for youths $\tau_b = .20$, $\gamma = .26$, and gross stability $= 28\%$; for parents the statistics were .37, .45, and 32%. Corresponding figures for the self-confidence measure were .23, .32, and 35% among the young, and .34, .44, and 36% among the middle-aged. Again we are struck by the demonstrably more stable orientations among the middle-aged in a strictly nonpolitical domain. As the evidence accumulates, it is clear that a configuration of greater instability applies to the young in virtually all domains, a theme to which we return in the conclusion.[18]

What distinguishes the efficacy findings from those on trust is that political efficacy has just as great a persistence in both generations as

[17] Personal efficacy is also often assumed to have a political analogue. See Lane, *Political Life*, 149. Again, the evidence of a tie-in between the personal and political dimensions tends to be modest, though positive, in the empirical attempts that have been made to show the linkage. Stanley A. Renshon, "Personality and Family Dynamics in the Political Socialization Process," *American Journal of Political Science*, 19 (February 1975), 63-80; Edward Carmines, "Self Esteem, Political Salience, and Political Involvement," paper presented at the annual meeting of the Midwest Political Science Association, Chicago, April 1973. However, Markus found little or no relationship between the measure labeled "self-confidence" and the index of internal political efficacy. Markus, "Continuity, Change, and the Political Self," Chapter 6.

[18] One of the few studies that includes repeated personality assessments between adolescence and young adulthood produced over-time correlations in much the same range as those found in our filial generation and lower than those found in the parental generation. Cited in Kenneth J. Gergen and Matthew Ullman, "Socialization and a Characterological Basis of Political Activism," in Stanley Allen Renshon (ed.), *Handbook of Political Socialization* (New York: Free Press, 1977), p. 438. The parent study from which this finding is drawn is the well-known work by Jerome Kagan and Howard Moss, *From Birth to Maturity* (New York: Wiley, 1962).

does personal efficacy. One might well expect a personality attribute such as personal efficacy to be relatively more enduring. After all, the individual's self-image begins to develop very early in life and tends to be reinforced as the child matures. On the other hand, our indicators of personal efficacy are rather "soft," and also probably fail to capture, as would more intensive methods, the core elements of the trait. At the same time, the political efficacy measure has the advantage of being content-specific. In general, observed continuity will be greater the more specific the referent.

We close with one final example from the nonpolitical realm, one that is quite apt for the youth cohort in particular. Partly as a matter of idle sociological curiosity, we asked both samples in 1965 what they thought about the character of contemporary teenagers, whether they were worse, about the same, or better than they used to be. Because coming to terms with succeeding cohorts is one of the conflicts facing young adults, we thought it worthwhile to repeat the question in 1973. Although the comparison of the over-time marginals is most enlightening (see Chapter 6), the stability figures are also worth noting. Since they have recently made the critical transition from teenager to young adult, we might well expect greater instability among the youths. The inevitable comparison for them would be 1973 vintage teenagers and the 1965 vintage. Regardless of whether they think teenagers have improved, worsened, or stayed the same, the youths are more likely to have altered their views in some respects. Being much more distant from their own teen years, and having witnessed the passage of several cohorts, the parents should have a more stable fix on the nature of teenagers or at least have more fixed views about the evolving nature of teenagers in American society.

As with the other nonpolitical dimensions, so too with this one: parents are more stable than young adults. For parents the relevant figures are $\tau_b = .25$, $\gamma = .44$, and exact agreement $= 58\%$. Corresponding figures for the filial generation are .07, .12, and 46%. (It should be noted that the high proportion of each sample asserting that teenagers are about the same as before severely constrains the magnitudes of the correlations.) What is especially charming about this example is that it is drawn from a domain not only having little or nothing to do with politics, but also one that has special relevance for the young adults. Teenagers as attitude objects have an immediacy and concreteness that do not necessarily characterize all of our other attitude objects. From that perspective, it is reassuring to witness the same pattern of lesser stability among the young as was found for the other nonpolitical measures.

The upshot of looking at these nonpolitical attributes is that the patterns observed in the political realm have their parallels in the nonpolitical. Modest to substantial persistence prevails, though elements of continuing openness are present even among the middle-aged. Change among young adults is moderately to substantially more frequent than it is among the middle aged. Deep-seated tendencies in both the political and nonpolitical domains render some orientations relatively impervious to alteration. Thus the political world is not unique.

Conclusion

Having surveyed the results of our over-time study of these two generations, what sorts of conclusions can we arrive at in terms of the models of persistence introduced at the outset? Two or three general patterns stand out.

First, adult political orientations are far from eminently stable commodities. Qualifications can, of course, be added. Rates of turnover vary widely from one orientation to another; movement sometimes takes place within narrow limits; and some of the apparent turnover is due to measurement error induced by question unreliability. Nevertheless—and leaving aside momentarily the question of respondent unreliability—enough discontinuity was observed to suggest that adults must change and rechange a number of times throughout their adult lives. Surely two interviews eight years apart do not capture all of the motion taking place over that period of time. Yet, even the amounts of instability reflected by these two soundings warrant the conclusion that turnover on most political orientations touches most of the population—or some of the population multiple times—during the adult life span. From this perspective, there is much to be said for the lifelong openness model.

Of course it is difficult to sift out real change from the spurious change flowing from measurement unreliability. The latter is properly conceived of as not just a matter of item unreliability (the reduction of which would ordinarily yield higher stability rates), but also of the interaction between properties of the item *and* the individual respondent.[19] Lack of crystallization and weak cognitive structuring undoubtedly contribute to lowered levels of apparent persistence among respondents who nevertheless render replies in the interview setting. Consequently, the apparent "openness" to change is contaminated by the presence of some individuals in given domains who are not under-

[19] Converse, "Attitudes and Non-Attitudes."

going real change. A full-fledged attack on the question of real versus spurious change is beyond the task of this inquiry, especially given the lack of more than two-wave data.

On the other hand, there were several indications of authenticity in the observed changes. That the movements were often real rather than spurious can be seen in comparing two of the measures of stability and in looking at the contingency tables upon which they are based. The γ correlations were often considerably higher than the τ_b correlations, thereby suggesting a particular kind of change—one in which the flow in one direction was demonstrably greater than that in the other direction. Particularly when conforming to known period effects, as in the case of cynicism, or to life-cycle effects, as in increasing electoral turnout, these flows demonstrate reasonable and predictable reactions to political events and life-cycle processes rather than random fluctuations.

The persistence exhibited across the eight-year span was rather remarkable for a number of orientations, especially in the parental generation. Adding strength to this observation are the fact that any measurement error due to question unreliability results in underestimates of the true persistence and the fact that alterations in the attitude objects themselves would usually lead to decreased levels of measured persistence. Subjectivity also enters in here, because what may strike one analyst as rather mediocre signs of persistence may strike another as handsome, especially in view of the many dimensions of the measurement problem. Thus, while we would emphasize the apparent openness to change, there is no gainsaying the evidence of lifelong persistence. What is perhaps most crucial in resolving the conflicting interpretations supplied by the two models is that we were able, by and large, to argue why the strong persistence or the lifelong openness models seemed to apply in particular instances.

A second major conclusion is that discontinuities occurred more frequently in early than in later adulthood. Almost invariably, by any measure, there was less stability among the young than among their parents. To this extent theories that describe young adulthood as a time of structuring and restructuring of the political self are supported. Similarly, the theories of "hardening" associated with the middle years receive support. But we must be careful in so arguing, for it is possible to take the position that this particular younger generation is simply less stable or that this particular parental generation is more stable.[20]

[20] A strong argument for making a scrupulous attempt to rule out possible generational effects before adopting the maturational, life-cycle explanation in instances of this type is forwarded by Neal E. Cutler, "Political Socialization Research as Generational Analysis: The Cohort versus the Lineage Approach," in

It will require much scrutiny of key subgroups within each generation to resolve the matter, and even then we will not be able to speak of other historical periods.

One set of findings, however, speaks very much in favor of the life-cycle explanation. As we have stressed, less persistence characterzied the filial generation across all the various political topics covered here, attitudinal and nonattitudinal. It would be difficult to argue that generational effects alone could be the source of lower youth persistence across all of these domains. Even more convincing are the results from the nonpolitical orientations introduced. Even allowing that the lesser persistence in the religious realm might be part of some generational phenomenon (and there is a decided unidirectional shift), that would still leave standing the lesser persistence on the three social-psychological orientations. Finally, as we had occasion to observe at some points in our discussion, movement among the young was by no means always one-sided, a necessary condition for wholesale generational effects. All of these arguments can be applied, *mutatis mutandis*, to the presence of greater continuity in the parental generation.[21] Only if one simply maintained that this particular young generation was more changeable in *all* respects than the preceding one could the life-cycle explanation be cast aside.

In sum, it would be unwise to conclude that the evidence presented here supports only one of the several possible models of lifelong political development.[22] The persistence of pre-adult socialization (which here means the end of high school) is supported in that stability is high in some domains and change is often confined to narrow limits. A life-cycle modification model is surely borne out in that many of the observations we made are consistent with what is known about changes in the lives of young adults and with youth-parent differences. And the degree of change among the middle-aged certainly points to some degree of lifelong openness.

Renshon (ed.), *Handbook of Political Socialization*. For an elegant attempt designed to sort out these twin possibilities see Kenneth D. Bailey, "Continuity and Change in Children's Attitudes toward the President," paper presented at the annual meeting of the Southern Political Science Association, Atlanta, November 1976.

[21] The question of over-time stability should not be confused with the question of constraint or interconnectedness among political traits at a particular point in time. It has been demonstrated with the 1965 data that coherence was usually as high among the youths as among the parents. Sandra Kenyon Schwartz, "The Validity of Adolescents' Political Responses," *Youth and Society*, 8 (March 1977), 212-44. We found basically the same sorts of cross-generational similarities when we replicated her analysis with the 1973 data.

[22] An ambitious effort to assess many of the processes involved via the use of simultaneous equation models applied to this set of data in Markus, "Continuity, Change, and the Political Self," Chapters 5-7.

CHAPTER FOUR

The Dynamics of
Family Transmission

Our earlier work with the 1965 wave concentrated heavily on the parent-offspring pairs generated by the study design. In part we used these pairs to explore generational differences and life-cycle development. But the main way in which we used the pair data was to analyze intensively the place of the family as an agent of socialization. Because of the presence of information on other sources of socialization we were also able to assess the relative place of parents vis-à-vis other agents. And because we had a subsample containing information for both mother and father we were able to talk about the relative place of each parent and to size up the socialization consequences of politically homogeneous versus heterogeneous parents.

At the time our initial research was launched it was widely believed that the family was the dominant socialization agent. Although our research left the role of the family quite strong relative to the other agents examined, both the direct and indirect effects of the family appeared to be markedly lower and more variable than had been assumed.[1] Approaching the results primarily from a social learning perspective, we found that moderate to strong correlations between parental and offspring orientations were the exception rather than the rule. True, there were certain circumstances, such as having homogeneous parents, which typically increased the correspondence between parent and child. Similarly, there were certain kinds of orientations, especially those that were very salient, concrete, and frequently reinforced, which were more likely to be reproduced by the offspring. Nevertheless, a major conclusion reached was that the process of socialization is so complex and dependent upon unique individual capacities and histories as to weaken the bonds of direct transmission from parent to child.

Subsequent research has done little to alter this conclusion. A secondary analysis of data gathered by Yankelovich in 1969 from a national sample of pairs (youths aged 17-23) uncovered mostly modest

[1] For a summary of the "agent" literature, see Paul Allen Beck, "The Role of Agents in Political Socialization," in Stanley Allen Renshon (ed.), *Handbook of Political Socialization* (New York: Free Press, 1977).

correlations between parental and offspring attitudes and goals.[2] Two local, well-designed studies both reported lineage correspondence in the ranges observed in our 1965 research for similar variables. One emphasized the importance of object-salience in leading to stronger pair concordance. The second found, in addition to even more modest pair correlations, that parents were nevertheless more influential in shaping adolescent orientations than were peers.[3] Another inquiry managed to gather three-generation data. In addition to finding modest pair correspondence between the two younger generations on indicators of broad social values, the study also uncovered less grandparent-grandchild correspondence on these values than we had in dealing with partisanship.[4] Finally, results in non-American settings are not at all dissimilar to those obtained in the United States.[5]

Although these and other studies have in general supported the findings of moderate to low dyadic concordance,[6] they have shared a short-

[2] Richard G. Niemi, R. Danforth Ross, and Joseph Alexander, "The Similarity of Political Values of Parents and College-Age Youths," *Public Opinion Quarterly*, 42 (Winter 1978), 503-20.

[3] Kent L. Tedin, "The Influence of Parents on the Political Attitudes of Adolescents," *American Political Science Review*, 68 (December 1974), 1579-92; Bruce Campbell, "A Theoretical Approach to Peer Influence in Adolescent Socialization," *American Journal of Political Science*, 24 (May 1980), 324-44.

[4] Vern L. Bengtson, "Generation and Family Effects in Value Socialization," *American Sociological Review*, 40 (June 1975), 358-71. Three-generation results for our study are reported in Paul Allen Beck and M. Kent Jennings, "Parents as 'Middle Persons' in Political Socialization," *Journal of Politics*, 37 (February 1975), 83-107.

[5] Akira Kubota and Robert E. Ward, "Family Influence and Politicization in Japan," *Comparative Political Studies*, 3 (July 1970), 11-46; Joseph Massey, *Youth and Politics in Japan* (Lexington, Mass.: Lexington Books, 1976); M. Kent Jennings, Klaus R. Allerbeck, and Leopold Rosenmayr, "Generations and Families: General Orientations and Political Satisfaction," and Allerbeck, Jennings, and Rosenmayr, "Generations and Families: Political Action," in Samuel H. Barnes, Max Kaase et al., *Political Action: Mass Participation in Five Western Democracies* (Beverly Hills: Sage, 1979); Gunnel Gustafsson, "Environmental Influence on Political Learning," in Richard G. Niemi and Associates, *The Politics of Future Citizens* (San Francisco: Jossey-Bass, 1974).

[6] A contrary view, employing a multiple indicator and concept reliability approach to analyze our 1965 data, has been advanced by Russell J. Dalton, "Reassessing Parental Socialization: Indicator Unreliability versus Generational Transfer," *American Political Science Review*, 74 (June 1980), 421-31. Although this is a most useful corrective, it does not necessarily undermine our major contentions and those of others. In the first place, many of our results rest, in fact, on multiple indicators of what we take to be the underlying construct (e.g., political trust and political knowledge and sophistication). Second, indicator unreliability approaches make a variety of important assumptions about error terms which are not fully testable. Violations of these assumptions generate problematic consequences. Third, it is uncertain just how expansive one can be in aggregating variables and still remain faithful to specific concepts of interest. Fourth, the application of such techniques does not necessarily alter the over-time patterns we will report, even if it alters results at any single time point. Finally, Dalton's approach has some

coming common to our earlier work, viz., the lack of longitudinal materials tracing the development of presumed parental impact on offspring. Virtually all of the reported research has dealt with adolescent-parent pairs and at only one point in time. Little is known about the relationships prior to and ancillary to that stage. Concordance may wax and wane depending upon stages in the development of the child,[7] particular types of orientations, alterations in the family structure, changes in the life space of the parents, and so forth.

With our materials we cannot, of course, retreat in time to explore pair relationships prior to adolescence. We can, however, move ahead in time to explore the intriguing question of the shape of pair similarity as the young moved through their first eight years beyond high school. By all accounts the high point of parental molding by both direct and indirect means was probably ending when we first sampled the youths as high school seniors, if, indeed, it had not already ended some years earlier. Thus our findings about the low to moderate correspondence between parent and child at that point lead us to suspect strongly that eight years later, as young adults, the offspring will be very imperfect replicas of their parents.

The question is not as simple as it might appear, however.[8] Parents as well as youths are changing, as we have seen in previous chapters. This leads to multiple ways of approaching the question of pair similarity. First, we can compare similarity in 1965 with similarity in 1973. This will answer the question of whether high school seniors or young adults are more like their parents, realizing that the parents themselves

---

parallels with that of studying genotypic as opposed to phenotypic continuity. Our own approach might be characterized as more phenotypic (trait-specific) whereas the approach taken by Dalton leans more toward the genotypic. Continuities of the latter type will almost necessarily be stronger. For discussions of the two classes with respect to individual-level continuity of personality characteristics see Jerome Kagan, "The Three Faces of Continuity in Human Development," in David A. Goslin (ed.), *Handbook of Socialization Theory and Research* (Chicago: Rand McNally, 1968), and Norman Livson, "Developmental Dimensions of Personality: A Life-Span Formulation," in Paul B. Baltes and K. Warner Schaie (eds.), *Life-Span Developmental Psychology* (New York: Academic Press, 1973).

[7] This point is developed in Robert Weissberg and Richard Joslyn, "Methodological Appropriateness in Political Socialization Research," in Renshon, *Handbook of Political Socialization*, pp. 47-53.

[8] Lest there be any confusion, it should be emphasized that we are talking about agreement between individual youths and their parents in this chapter and not about agreement between parents and youths as a whole (dealt with in Chapters 5 and 6). Although the distinction is obvious, the difference between pair and group correspondence has not always been explicitly dealt with. See R. W. Connell, "Political Socialization in the American Family: The Evidence Re-Examined," *Public Opinion Quarterly*, 36 (Fall 1972), 323-33, and M. Kent Jennings, "Analyzing Parent-Child Pairs in Cross-National Survey Research," *European Journal of Political Research*, 5 (June 1977), 179-97.

may be different at the two points in time. Second, we can consider how similar young adults are to what their parents were like eight years earlier. If young adults are coming to resemble their parents as parents were at that point in time, this measure of similarity will be higher than that based on current parental attributes. But there is still another possibility. Youths may influence parents in the direction of their (i.e., the youths') earlier positions. Hence parental responses may be more similar to those rendered at an earlier time by their own children. This suggests that we consider the correspondence between 1973 parent orientations and 1965 offspring orientations.

We can best represent these four parent-youth linkages with a simple figure which will serve as the basic paradigm for the first part of this chapter:

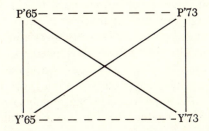

Our strategy will be to look at bivariate statistics for each of these links in some detail, since they provide the most direct evidence about the pattern of pair similarity over time.

As compelling as the evidence from this analysis is, however, there are several additional ways of testing lineage correspondence. One is to consider concordance on measures employed for the first time in 1973, with particular attention to similarity regarding issues and personalities that gained prominence subsequent to the first panel wave. It may be—as suggested by the familiar adage about one's parents becoming smarter as one ages—that offspring begin to reflect parental attitudes and behavior only after they actually enter the adult world of politics and confront contemporary events and personalities. We test for this possibility in the second part of the chapter.

Another important consideration is the type of parent characteristic that best predicts offspring attributes. Most work on parent-youth correspondence assumes that identical characteristics—e.g., survey responses to the identical question—yield the best predictions. But this may not be the case, for a variety of reasons.[9] We will test here one other important possibility. Do attitudes of parents in 1965 in one area

[9] For a useful discussion of this point, see Weissberg and Joslyn, "Methodological Appropriateness."

influence the later attitudes of their offspring in another area? That is, do parents' attitudes on contemporary issues while their child is a high school senior predict their offspring's responses to nominally different but functionally equivalent stimuli in later years? If so, our view of family influence needs to be drastically altered. This concern is also taken up in the second part of the chapter.

Finally, it may be that pair correspondence patterns as a whole do not adequately reflect the degree of shifting and stability at the level of individual pairs. Consequently, we need to investigate the continuity of individual pair correspondence over time. We will analyze the persistence of parent-offspring agreement patterns and also take up the question of why some pairs grow closer over time while others move further apart.

Two important methodological points must be clarified before proceeding. First, though our basic paradigm is precisely that used in one form of cross-lagged panel analysis (two-variable, two-wave), we shall not rely specifically on methods developed for that approach.[10] We are not suggesting that this paradigm is a closed causal system; specifically, the typically greater change among youths than parents between 1965 and 1973 suggests additional influences on the younger generation. Nonetheless, we feel that conclusions about student-parent concordance can be safely drawn, and some more tentative judgments about mutual influence can be made.

The other methodological point concerns the way in which we measure parent-youth agreement. We will present both the correlation (τ_b) between parent and offspring responses and the percentage of parent-youth pairs in agreement (perfect or near-perfect as noted in each case). This helps circumvent the very real problem that covariation in parent and youth responses, which is tapped by correlations, may vary substantially from absolute agreement, which is measured by percentage agreement scores.[11] In the past we have relied most heavily on correlations and have defended their use as appropriate.[12] However, inasmuch as our chief concern here is on change over time in agreement levels, and since the number of response categories for a given question remains unchanged from 1965 to 1973, comparisons of percentage agreement scores within one diagram are more appropriate than usual. Therefore, reference to these percentages will provide extra support for our interpretation of changes in parent-youth similar-

[10] For a discussion of the assumptions and methods underlying two-variable, two-wave panel analysis, see Richard D. Shingles, "Causal Inference in Cross-Lagged Panel Analysis," *Political Methodology*, 3 (Number 1, 1976), 95-133.

[11] Weissberg and Joslyn, "Methodological Appropriateness," 58-65.

[12] Niemi, Ross, and Alexander, "Similarity of Political Values."

ity. Nevertheless, as in the past, we will refer most often to the correlations.

Changes in Pair Similarity, 1965-1973

When first studying the question of intergenerational transmission, we predicted a general decline in parent-youth similarity as offspring reach adulthood.[13] Our reasoning was simply that as young people leave their parents' home, parental influence is likely to decline along with the decline in proximity and the increasing presence of nonfamily forces. But a number of countervailing possibilities must be entertained. Life-cycle processes might suggest increasing lineage similarity. For example, adolescents often go through a period in which independence from parents' ideas is valued for its own sake. As this period passes they might revert back to the political profiles of their parents, and concordance would rise. This seems unlikely to us, partly because greater parent-child similarity has not been found prior to adolescence.[14] Still, it is a possibility that deserves consideration. Fortunately, the fact that the youths are 25-26 years old means that they are well beyond adolescence. If this process of returning to or freshly manifesting parental orientations exists, we should see it in this age group.

Another life-cycle argument is that young people become more like their parents simply because they begin taking on adult characteristics as they move into the adult world. Weissberg and Joslyn point out that developmental patterns over the life cycle mean that "even a child who eventually will be identical to an adult will not be like that adult until adulthood. Thus to search for close similarity (as opposed to different positions on the same developmental path) between, say, a 10-year-old and a 35-year-old is to bias the results toward very modest relationships at best."[15] Comparisons of young with older adults will not entirely overcome this problem, since the young people might change still more by the time they reach their parents' current age. But if a significant life-cycle pattern exists, some increased similarity due to these "sleeper effects"[16] should be apparent here—either between

[13] M. Kent Jennings and Richard G. Niemi, "The Transmission of Political Values from Parent to Child," *American Political Science Review*, 62 (March 1968), 171.

[14] Connell, "Political Socialization in the American Family"; Jack Dennis, "Political Learning in Childhood and Adolescence: A Study of Fifth, Eighth, and Eleventh Graders in Milwaukee, Wisconsin," Technical Report No. 98, Wisconsin Research and Development Center for Cognitive Learning, Madison, 1969, 31.

[15] Weissberg and Joslyn, "Methodological Appropriateness," 50-51.

[16] Developmental psychologists use this term to denote the later or delayed manifestation of a characteristic, the conditioning or learning of which occurred in a substantially earlier time; the context must be right for the behavior to be

youths and parents in 1973 or between youths in 1973 and parents as of eight years earlier.

Of course, life-cycle development of this sort might lead to increasing similarity of the generations as a whole without resulting in greater lineage congruence. One of the standard findings in the recent literature is that generational correspondence is unevenly related to pair correspondence.[17] For this reason we shall pay close attention to the relationship between aggregate and pair similarity, referring as necessary to material to be covered in detail in Chapters 5 and 6. We shall also have occasion to show just how the two kinds of similarity can take quite divergent paths.

Still another possible change in pair similarity, to which we have already alluded, may result if young people influence their parents. Young people may take strong stands on certain matters and try to convert their parents rather than change their own attitudes. If this "reverse socialization" occurs, it seems particularly likely on orientations where there are generational differences and on which youths' opinions are strongly held and probably highly skewed as well. If on such issues enough of the young held on to their positions as of 1965 and proselytized their parents in the interim, pair correspondence would rise by 1973. This might manifest itself in the $P'73 \times Y'73$ link or in the $Y'65 \times P'73$ link.

Given the usual assumptions about the asymetrical process of socialization within the family, there has been virtually no research on the possibility of reverse socialization. Nevertheless, it has been widely speculated that the incidence of such processes increases during times of turmoil and secular change, as during the recent protest period. Moreover, there is some evidence from the 1965 wave of the present study that adolescents can serve at least as transmission belts of information and affect about political objects.[18] Therefore, while we do not anticipate strong currents running in this direction, it is another possibility that needs to be considered.

With these considerations as a backdrop, let us turn to the results. In assessing the results in this section it must be borne in mind that

---

elicited. See Jerome Kagan and Howard Moss, *From Birth to Maturity* (New York: Wiley, 1962).

[17] Tedin, "Influence of Parents"; Jennings, "Analyzing Parent-Child Pairs"; Massey, *Youth and Politics in Japan*, especially Chapter 7; Niemi, Ross, and Alexander, "Similarity of Political Values"; and M. Kent Jennings, "The Variable Nature of Generational Conflict: Some Examples from West Germany," *Comparative Political Studies*, 9 (July 1976), 171-88.

[18] M. Kent Jennings, "Discontent with Schools: Some Implications for Political Socialization and Behavior," *Youth and Society*, 7 (September 1975), 49-68.

they reflect the concordance of parent-child pairs as a whole. They do not necessarily reflect the continuities and discontinuities of individual pairs over time. Illustratively, identical correlations for the P'65 × Y'65 and P'73 × Y'73 links do not necessarily mean that agreement between individual pairs was identical at both points in time. "Individual-level" analysis of the pairs is taken up in the final two sections of this chapter.

Psychological Involvement in Politics

Our first look at parent-offspring pair similarity over time is contained in Figure 4.1.[19] What is most impressive about these initial results is how little change is apparent. Certainly there is no indication here that youths are more like their parents as young adults than as high school seniors. This is true whether we interpret that to mean similarity to parents in 1973 or in 1965.

These results are also impressive because of net aggregate shifts that transpired over time. The clear tendency in the aggregate movement on these items was for heightened similarity between parents and offspring in 1973 compared to 1965 (Chapter 5). In several instances— the good citizen, cosmopolitanism, television viewing—the convergence was striking, and in no case was there more than a minor divergence. While we know that there is no automatic carryover from the aggregate level to that of lineage pairs, or vice versa, we might expect the growing aggregate similarity to be reflected in at least slightly higher parent-offspring concordance. Why this was not the case calls for some explanation, since it is a result that will recur with some frequency.

In explicating the connection between aggregate and lineage correspondence, another phenomenon can also be clarified. For most of the items in Figure 4.1, the correlations and percentage agreement scores show similar movements. It is at first a bit disturbing that these two measures can ever move in opposite directions. But it is not hard to see why this can occur, and the differences are usually small enough to be of no consequence. In the case of television viewing, however, as well as in some later instances, a relatively large decline in the parent-youth correlation exists alongside a reasonably healthy increase in the number of parent-youth pairs actually agreeing.

Inspection of the parent-youth cross-tabulations for television viewing habits (Table 4.1) makes clear just what happened over the years

[19] In Figures 4.1-4.8, correlations for P'65 × Y'65 differ slightly from those previously published because they are based only on respondents in both waves of the panel.

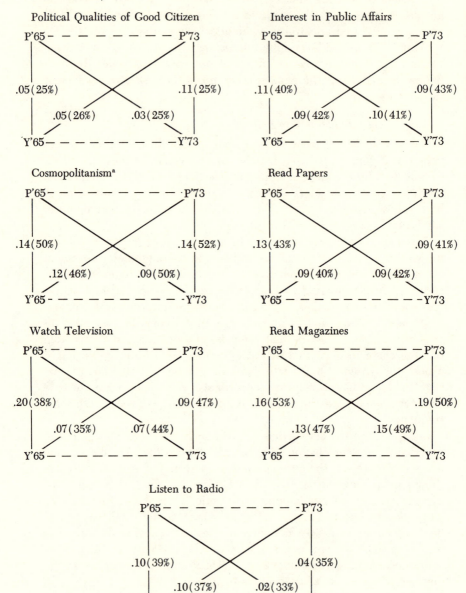

FIGURE 4.1: Psychological Involvement in Politics (Pair Similarity Over Time)

Political Qualities of Good Citizen

P'65 – – – – – – – – P'73

.05(25%)   .11(25%)

.05(26%)   .03(25%)

Y'65 – – – – – – – – – Y'73

Interest in Public Affairs

P'65 – – – – – – – – – P'73

.11(40%)   .09(43%)

.09(42%)   .10(41%)

Y'65 – – – – – – – – – Y'73

Cosmopolitanism[a]

P'65 – – – – – – – – – P'73

.14(50%)   .14(52%)

.12(46%)   .09(50%)

Y'65 – – – – – – – – – Y'73

Read Papers

P'65 – – – – – – – – – P'73

.13(43%)   .09(41%)

.09(40%)   .09(42%)

Y'65 – – – – – – – – – Y'73

Watch Television

P'65 – – – – – – – – – P'73

.20(38%)   .09(47%)

.07(35%)   .07(44%)

Y'65 – – – – – – – – – Y'73

Read Magazines

P'65 – – – – – – – – – P'73

.16(53%)   .19(50%)

.13(47%)   .15(49%)

Y'65 – – – – – – – – – Y'73

Listen to Radio

P'65 – – – – – – – – – P'73

.10(39%)   .04(35%)

.10(37%)   .02(33%)

Y'65 – – – – – – – – – Y'73

[a] Percentage figure includes near-perfect agreement (i.e., includes differences of one category).

TABLE 4.1: Parent-Youth Similarity in Television Viewing, 1965 and 1973

1965	Parents				1973	Parents			
	1[a]	2	3	4		1	2	3	4
Youths					Youths				
1	30%	21%	15%	11%	1	15%	10%	9%	9%
2	17	21	23	13	2	16	22	12	10
3	31	35	34	32	3	21	20	24	20
4	23	24	28	44	4	48	47	54	61
Totals	101%	101%	100%	100%	Totals	100%	99%	99%	100%
	(101)	(97)	(200)	(649)		(92)	(76)	(176)	(713)

[a]1 = A few times a year or not at all; 2 = 3-4 times a month; 3 = 2-3 times a week; 4 = almost daily.

since 1965 and shows how variations in different kinds of agreement come about. As high school seniors, the large group of youths whose parents were frequent viewers watched considerably less television than their parents, so much so that youths as a whole watched with much less regularity. Yet parents' habits moderately differentiated adolescent viewing levels. These two features explain the moderate pair correlation (.20) coexisting with a low level of aggregate similarity. Eight years later, the young people had increased their viewing time appreciably across all categories of parental viewing. Thus, in the aggregate, they watched television almost as much as their parents. But the increase in viewing was especially great in families in which parents saw little television. Hence, in 1973 parental viewing habits provided little differentiation among the youths; consequently, the pair correlation was low (.09). Less similarity between infrequent parent viewers and their offspring meant greater similarity between parents and youths as a whole. If there was less similarity between infrequent parent viewers and their offspring, why does the percentage agreement score rise? The decrease in pair correspondence among infrequent parent viewers was more than made up for by the increase in agreement among the large set of frequent parent viewers (cf. the "4-4" cells in Table 4.1).

This detailed examination of parent-youth similarity for television viewing suggests some of the complexity involved in trying to understand fully the movement of parent-youth agreement over time. Still, television viewing was somewhat extreme, especially in the degree of divergence between the correlation and percentage scores. Overall, the results so far suggest rather clearly that there is no increase in lineage agreement as young people move into the first decade of adult life.

Political Resources

Pair similarity of political resources is unusual in that no declines are observed between 1965 and 1973 in either the correlational or percentage measures (Figure 4.2). Nor are there always declines in the cross-lagged linkages. The increases in similarity are nominal, to be sure. But it is the only area, aside from voting turnout, in which no declines are observed.

FIGURE 4.2: Political Resources (Pair Similarity Over Time)

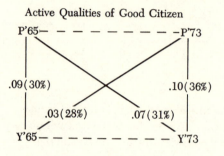

Active Qualities of Good Citizen

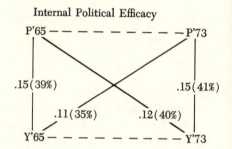

Internal Political Efficacy

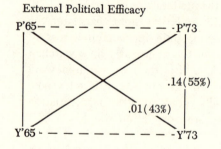

External Political Efficacy

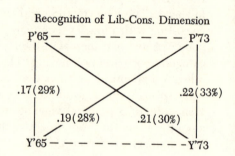

Recognition of Lib-Cons. Dimension

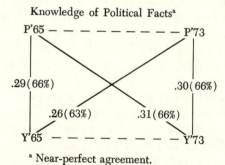

Knowledge of Political Facts[a]

[a] Near-perfect agreement.

At least a partial explanation for this result surely lies in the nature of two of the measures. Because of the objective quality of the indicators used, the staying power of parental influence on their children's propensity to acquire and retain knowledge would seem to be of a different character from influence on attitudes. One might move away from parents' partisan or policy preferences after learning more about politics or coming under the sway of other influences, but it makes no sense to reject factual information which is known to one's parents. Thus, as children leave their parents' home, there is little reason to expect the correlation between parent and youth knowledge to decline; indeed, it is essentially the same in both years.

Recognition of the liberal-conservative dimension and of its various interpretations likewise has a knowledge component to it. While placement of the political parties on the dimension is not free of subjective assessments, there is common enough agreement about it that one is not so likely to reject a parent's understanding of it. More generally, the sensitivity to such matters and the intellectual capacity to deal with them are likely to have dyadic persistence.

Knowledge of political parties is also distinctive because of the degree to which it increases after completion of high school. Hence this may very well be an example of low parent-child continuity in adolescence being attributable to immaturity in the development of the younger generation. As one would expect if this explanation is correct, the increase in agreement in 1973 came about because of a substantial decline in the number of "sophisticated parent-unaware offspring" pairs. It is especially significant, then, that on a highly cognitive measure for which there is considerable post-adolescent development, parent-offspring agreement rose only marginally. Life-cycle development may keep parent-offspring similarity from declining, but it does not appear to create substantial leaps in concordance.

Finally, it should be noted that the aggregate similarity of the two generations is unrelated to the movement of the pair statistics. Parents and youths in the aggregate grew significantly closer in their levels of knowledge, youths surpassed parents measurably in their awareness of the liberal-conservative dimension, and there was no change on the remaining two items (Chapter 5). Though there is some overlap in the forces underlying aggregate and pair similarity, there is much that is not common to the two processes as well.

A prime argument about the effects of familial political socialization is that a predisposition toward political activity tends to be inherited. Children coming from politically active and involved families are assumed to be more likely to become active and involved themselves. This argument had its most recent popular exposition in the claim that

the leading wedge of student activists in the 1960s came from politically active families. Our modest findings with respect to psychological involvement and even the stronger ones with regard to political
resources should lead us to temper these expectations. On the other
hand, overt participation is in many respects the most critical test; because it requires that extra effort, we might find that familial similarity
holds up better here than in the other domains.

Upon inspection, however, pair similarity in participation turns out
to be in the same general range as it is for involvement and resources.
Unfortunately, we have over-time data on only one measure of political
participation—turnout in the elections of 1968, 1970, and 1972 (Figure
4.3). Pair concordance remained relatively low for the off-year election
of 1970. Between 1968 and 1972, parent-youth agreement rose by a
small, but probably a meaningful amount. The reason for the modest
upswing lies in the relationship of voting turnout to education. In 1968
the youth turnout was low, as is typical of first time voters (see Chapter 6). This meant that in groups with high parental turnout—e.g.,

FIGURE 4.3: Political Participation (Pair Similarity Over Time)

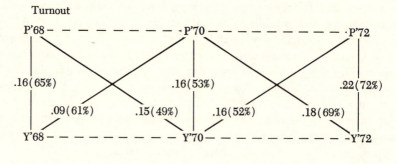

Turnout

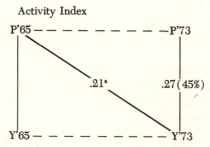

Activity Index

[a] Based on the 1965 parental activity scale (5 categories) and the 1973 youth
activity index (3 categories). Absolute agreement cannot be calculated because
the number of categories differs and the measures differ in some respects.

well-educated parents—agreement was in fact very limited. (The τ_b was actually negative, but this figure is dependent on very few non-voting college-educated parents.) As turnout among the young rose in the next presidential election, it brought about marginally greater agreement between well-educated parent voters and their offspring ($\tau_b = .14$ among college-educated parents). This increase is largely responsible for the slightly greater parent-youth correspondence in 1972. Significantly, since the gap in turnout between older and younger adults is closed rather slowly, this particular statistic may rise a bit more as the offspring mature further.

It should be highlighted that the turnout questions tap parent-youth agreement for different years than do almost all of the other items. In 1968 the offspring were mostly 20-21 years old, and naturally were 22-23 two years later and 24-25 two years after that. (The 1968 comparison necessarily excludes 20-year-olds.) While too much significance should not be placed on any single activity, it is noteworthy that the absolute levels of parent-youth agreement for each measurement are not out of line with those for other attributes. Insofar as this evidence is representative, parent-offspring concordance was not significantly different throughout our eight-year panel than it was at the end points.

The absolute level of agreement in 1972 is important in another way as well. Even if our above reasoning is correct and intergenerational concordance increases slightly in future elections, parent-offspring correspondence will still only be moderate. Insofar as turnout is indeed a critical test, family similarity is not overwhelming at any time in late adolescence and throughout the period into the mid-20's and beyond.

Also shown in Figure 4.3 is the similarity of overall participation levels. While the 1973 measures are drawn from the 1973 interviews, they are based on recall of activities carried on over the entire eight-year period of the panel. Hence it gives additional support to the conclusion that parent-youth similarity did not fluctuate widely over the panel period. The absolute level of concordance is likewise supportive of our general knowledge of parent-youth agreement levels. Although the 1965 parental activity index is restricted to electoral behavior, it may be used to establish the degree to which parental activity during a child's upbringing has a subsequent effect. As expected, the relationship is positive, but clearly not strong enough to say that activism is predominantly hereditary.

Partisanship and Voting

It would be difficult to exaggerate the importance of the findings about the transmission of party identification for constructing theories about the family's role in political socialization. Based initially on recall data about parents' party preferences, these findings were subsequently verified, though in attenuated form, by matching the self-reports of parents and their offspring. The relatively high degree of lineage correspondence has served not only as a basis for speculation about the relative stability of the American party system, but also about the overwhelming place of parents in molding the political character of their offspring. Our initial report of the 1965 observations, however, did much to show the special character of party identification; its salient, concrete, and reinforced qualities made it an especially apt candidate for successful transmission.

Despite this prominence of party identification, the most dramatic change in dyadic agreement over the course of our panel occurred in partisanship and presidential candidate preference (Figure 4.4). Rath-

FIGURE 4.4: Partisanship and Voting (Pair Similarity Over Time)

Party Identification[a]

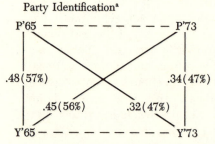

.48(57%)   .34(47%)

.45(56%)   .32(47%)

[a] Percentages are based on the threefold classification.

Presidential Preference[b]

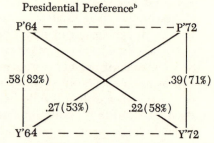

.58(82%)   .39(71%)

.27(53%)   .22(58%)

[b] Results for intermediate elections are presented in the text.

er unexpectedly in both cases, the decline in presidential preference was the greatest of all we observed and that for partisanship was fourth highest among the more than 30 measures. While these items still yield the highest pair correlations of any in 1973, they are now only marginally above those for several other attributes (political knowledge, attitude toward the Bible, and church attendance). In absolute terms, agreement must be regarded as only moderate.[20]

[20] It has been asserted by some that even the high level of lineage congruity in the domain of partisanship sprang from commonalities in the environment shared by both parents and offspring—rather than being a function of parent to child transmission. A multivariate analysis of the data used here has demonstrated that any effects of socioeconomic status and race, two of the frequently cited common influences, are in fact funneled through the parent-child linkage. This proved true at both time points. See Gregory Blake Markus, "Continuity, Change and the Political Self: A Model of Political Socialization," (unpublished Ph.D. dissertation, University of Michigan, 1975), Chapter 3.

The full array of 1973 partisanship responses is shown in Table 4.2. As in 1965, few young people took a partisan position opposite that of their parents. Due primarily to the sharp rise in the number of Independents among youths, however, the percentage disagreeing (using the three-way classification) now constituted an absolute majority of the pairs (53%). But it should not be thought that parent-youth disagreement exists solely because of partisan parents whose children have taken up the currently-popular Independent label. Reminiscent of the individual turnover figures (Chapter 3), almost half of the offspring of Independent (as of 1973) parents referred to themselves as partisans.

TABLE 4.2: Parent-Youth Party Identification, 1973

Youths	Strong Dem.	Weak Dem.	Ind. Dem.	Ind.	Ind. Rep.	Weak Rep.	Strong Rep.	Total
			Parents					
Strong Dem.	4.0%	2.6	1.1	.1	.1	.8	.1	8.9
Weak Dem.	5.4	10.1	2.4	2.3	1.1	3.0	1.0	25.2
	(22.1)[a]			(7.0)		(4.9)		(34.1)
Ind. Dem.	3.7	6.2	2.6	1.3	1.1	2.9	1.9	19.8
Ind.	1.8	3.8	1.3	2.9	2.0	1.9	1.3	15.1
Ind. Rep.	1.2	2.3	.8	1.7	1.1	4.1	2.5	13.7
	(19.1)			(14.9)		(14.6)		(48.6)
Weak Rep.	1.0	1.3	.7	1.1	1.0	4.2	2.9	12.1
Strong Rep.	.1	.6	.1	.2	.5	1.2	2.5	5.3
	(3.0)			(3.6)		(10.8)		(17.4)
Total	17.1	27.0	9.1	9.6	6.8	18.1	12.2	100.0%
	(44.1)			(25.5)		(30.3)		(834)

$\tau_b = .35$

[a] The 3 × 3 table is given by the numbers in parentheses; they are (within rounding error) the sum of the numbers just above them. The percentage base for this table is the number of pairs wherein both parents and offspring were personally interviewed.

One might still conclude from the partisanship data alone that the younger generation was attracted to the label "Independent" but would vote the same way as their parents. One might also hypothesize that if there were a resurgence of support for the two parties, the young people would be drawn back to the party supported by their parents. This is where the significance of the presidential preference figures becomes apparent. Not only were young people moving away from their parents' partisan tendencies, they veered away from their parents' candidate preferences as well. The younger generation might some day gravitate toward new or existing parties; but there is little reason to expect the movement to be heavily in the direction of their parents' party.

The voting results are even more striking if we add data (based on recall questions) on presidential voting in 1968 and on congressional voting in 1970 and 1972. Congruence declined steadily from 1964 on, whether measured by pair correlations or percentage agreement:[21]

	1964	1968	1970	1972
President	.58	.52		.39
	82%	76%		71%
Congress			.42	.33
			71%	67%

While a majority of parents and offspring still voted the same way in 1972, similarity was steadily eroding. When we remember that 50% agreement would result entirely by chance, the percenatge still agreeing in 1972 seems particularly unimpressive. Thus, even with regard to the presidential vote, the most visible single political act for most people, congruence was substantially reduced less than a decade after the young people had reached adulthood. Nor can this result be explained by a generational cleavage forced by the particular circumstances of the 1972 election. In the aggregate parents and youths were only a few percentage points further apart in their preferences in 1972 than they had been in the 1960s, and the difference was identical to that in 1970.

The data on candidate preferences in 1968 and 1970 lend added support to our contention that there was little or no cyclical variation in concordance throughout the entire panel period. Especially in regard to partisanship, turnout, and candidate preferences, it is likely that there was a slow but steady erosion in pair agreement. Though we have no sure way of knowing what happens later on in life, there is little to suggest that similarity will increase substantially in subsequent years. More likely is a leveling off at low to moderate resemblance, with mild fluctuations depending on circumstances.

Nor does it seem likely that there will be meaningful increases in agreement with what parents were like when the offspring were still at home. The link showing the partisan similarity between parents in

[21] For presidential years voters and preferences of nonvoters are used. For congressional years preferences of nonvoters were not obtained.

1965 and youths in 1973 is even lower than the contemporary 1973 link. In the case of candidate preferences, short-term forces make it likely that lagged correlations are relatively small on the average. This is indeed true for the P'64 × Y'72 link.

Finally, the partisanship and voting comparisons should lay to rest the notion that transmission of these characteristics is somehow different from that of other attributes. Some researchers—perhaps as a consequence of our own emphasis in describing the 1965 results[22]—have argued that the transmission of partisanship is inherently different from the transfer of other political attitudes. The fact that similarity of partisanship and candidate preferences declines to levels approximating those of several other attributes suggests that while the former may be more salient than other political orientations, there is no inherent reason for transmission to be successful in one area and unsuccessful in all of the others.[23]

Opinions on Public Policy Issues

We have longitudinal data on parent-youth concordance for only four public policy issues. Yet these four issues show at least three distinct patterns of change. The summary pair correlations and percentage scores in Figure 4.5 show these differences quite clearly. On one issue, school prayers, there was a small decline in agreement, the pair correlation dropping by .05. In contrast, the "communist" and "speeches" issues show an upswing in the parent-youth correlations; in the latter case percentage agreement also rises. Finally, on the school integration question there is a precipitous decline in agreement by either measure.

The variety of changes is made clearer, however, by an inspection of the tables underlying the summary statistics. First, the school prayer issue shows no more change in the detailed view than in the summary scores. Agreement levels with pro-prayer parents are identical in 1965 and 1973; the same is true of anti-prayer parents. And the number of pairs in each cell of the parent-youth cross tabulation is nearly identical in the two years.

On the other three issues there were moderate to strong changes over time in the levels of agreement with parents holding particular views. For example, on the school integration question, a large majority (83%) of the offspring of pro-integration parents adopted their parent's position in 1965. By 1973 this proportion had dropped to 59%. Since there was almost no change in agreement with anti-integration

---

[22] Jennings and Niemi, "The Transmission of Political Values."

[23] This point is also supported by Tedin's analysis. See Tedin, "Influence of Parents."

Figure 4.5: Opinions on Public Policy Issues (Pair Similarity
Over Time)

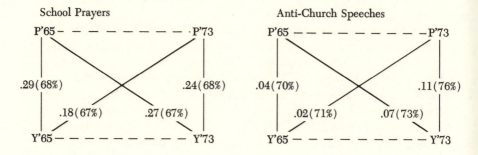

School Prayers

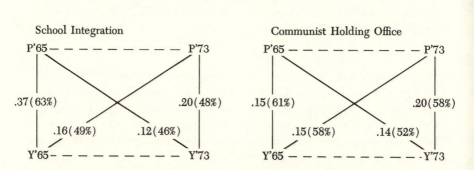

School Integration

parents, overall agreement dropped substantially. On the "communist" question, there was also a large decline in parent-youth agreement among one group of parents. Those opposed to the proposition found 66% of their children agreeing in 1965, but only 48% agreeing eight years later. In this case, however, agreement went up by an even larger amount (49% to 71%) among parents who were favorable. This led to a small increase in the overall correlation. A similar though less extreme shift took place on the anti-church speeches issue. These shifting levels also meant that there were large changes on all three issues in the way pairs were distributed in the parent-youth cross tabulation.

To make matters still more complicated, there was a negative relationship between aggregate changes and pair concordance. The integration issue was the one policy item on which aggregate agreement rose (Chapter 6). Yet it was on this issue that pair agreement declined precipitously. The communist and free speech issues showed increasing gaps between the generations at the aggregate level, but pair agreement rose. (There was little aggregate or pair change on the school prayers issue.) More than ever, then, what happens at the level of the parent-offspring pairs cannot be assumed to coincide with aggregate-level movements.

The amount of variability on these four issues along with the negative relationship between the aggregate and pair levels suggests that the policy area is one of the most difficult in which to generalize. The patterns of change for both generations at the individual and aggregate levels are sufficiently varied, and the starting points sufficiently diverse, that the contours of change at the level of parent-youth pairs seem for the moment rather unpredictable. What is clear, however, is that there is no uniform increase in parent-youth agreement levels as young people move out of the "rebellious" adolescent years.

Evaluations of Government and Sociopolitical Groups

Evaluations of virtually all government-related phenomena underwent rapid if not dramatic changes during the period covered by our panel. At an aggregate level (Chapter 6), both younger and older generations were much more critical of American society, especially of its political qualities. The trust accorded government by both generations fell at a dizzying pace. And among the young, there was a substantial shift in confidence away from the national government and toward state and local governments. All of this, of course, was based on considerable shifting of individuals.

In spite of these maneuvers at the aggregate and individual levels, one can make a strong case for expecting increases in parent-offspring pair correspondence. Two measures in particular were prime candidates for the claim that low parent-adolescent correlations were attributable to immature development of political attitudes among teenagers. Because of the apparent declines in political trust from childhood on into adulthood, high school seniors would not be expected to have the same level of trust as their parents. While it seems unlikely that this would seriously affect the *correlation* between parent and youth pairs, *percentage agreement scores* might remain low until the offspring reached adult age. This hypothesized pattern is an intriguing possibility, but in fact parent-youth pairs agreed less by either measure in 1973 than in 1965 (Figure 4.6). Moreover, the declines were quite substantial as measured against the attitudes and behaviors already covered, especially when one takes into account the initially low correspondence in 1965.

A similar situation holds for confidence in varying levels of government. The aggregate alterations were quite predictable from changes in the life cycle as one moves from adolescence into adulthood, and an increase in parent-youth agreement would not have been surpris-

FIGURE 4.6: Evaluations of the Political System (Pair Similarity Over Time)

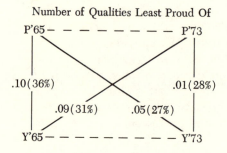

Number of Qualities Least Proud Of

P'65 – – – – – – – – P'73

.10(36%)   .01(28%)

.09(31%)   .05(27%)

Y'65 – – – – – – – – – Y'73

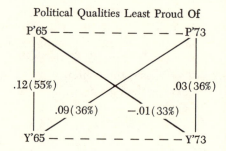

Political Qualities Least Proud Of

P'65 – – – – – – – – – P'73

.12(55%)   .03(36%)

.09(36%)   –.01(33%)

Y'65 – – – – – – – – – Y'73

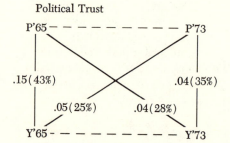

Political Trust

P'65 – – – – – – – – – P'73

.15(43%)   .04(35%)

.05(25%)   .04(28%)

Y'65 – – – – – – – – – Y'73

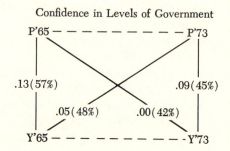

Confidence in Levels of Government

P'65 – – – – – – – – – P'73

.13(57%)   .09(45%)

.05(48%)   .00(42%)

Y'65 – – – – – – – – – Y'73

ing. Yet again, pair concordance declined both in correlational and percentage agreement terms.

A parallel argument based on post-high school development could probably be made for the group thermometer ratings, although we are less sure of life-cycle changes in such ratings. We will note in Chapter 6 that young people much more often in 1973 than in 1965 chose the neutral, 50° reading. We attribute this to growing sophistication and involvement, which led to less stereotyped reactions to group labels. While again there is no automatic effect of this change on the pair correlations, the earlier stereotyped views might have held down agreement levels in 1965. Thus, while parents' and youths' mean ratings differed by more in 1973 than in 1965, pair correspondence, particularly correlations, might well increase. Yet agreement figures dropped below their 1965 levels on most group ratings over the period of the panel (Figure 4.7). If normal developmental processes have any uplifting effect on parent-youth concordance, they are overwhelmed here by forces in the other direction.

In fairness to the developmental argument, we should re-emphasize the distinction between pair correlations and aggregate comparisons.

FIGURE 4.7: Evaluations of Sociopolitical Groupings (Pair Similarity Over Time)

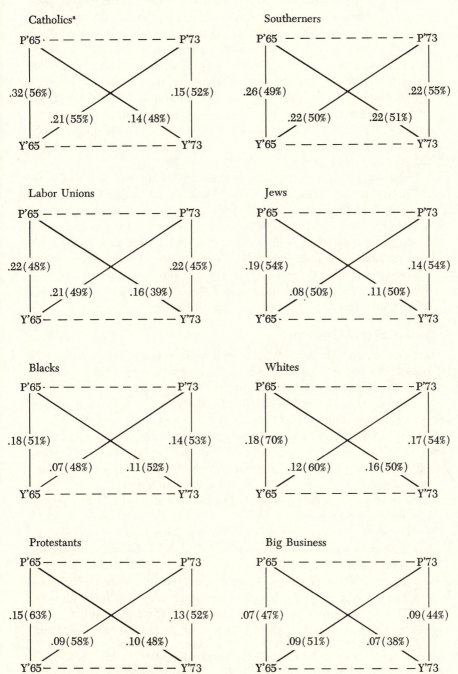

Catholics[a]

P'65 — — — — — — — — — P'73

.32(56%)   .15(52%)

.21(55%)   .14(48%)

Y'65 — — — — — — — — Y'73

Southerners

P'65 — — — — — — — — P'73

.26(49%)   .22(55%)

.22(50%)   .22(51%)

Y'65 — — — — — — — — Y'73

Labor Unions

P'65 — — — — — — — — — P'73

.22(48%)   .22(45%)

.21(49%)   .16(39%)

Y'65 — — — — — — — — Y'73

Jews

P'65 — — — — — — — — P'73

.19(54%)   .14(54%)

.08(50%)   .11(50%)

Y'65 — — — — — — — — Y'73

Blacks

P'65 — — — — — — — — P'73

.18(51%)   .14(53%)

.07(48%)   .11(52%)

Y'65 — — — — — — — — Y'73

Whites

P'65 — — — — — — — — P'73

.18(70%)   .17(54%)

.12(60%)   .16(50%)

Y'65 — — — — — — — — Y'73

Protestants

P'65 — — — — — — — — — P'73

.15(63%)   .13(52%)

.09(58%)   .10(48%)

Y'65 — — — — — — — — Y'73

Big Business

P'65 — — — — — — — — P'73

.07(47%)   .09(44%)

.09(51%)   .07(38%)

Y'65 — — — — — — — — Y'73

[a] Percentage figures include near-perfect agreement.

For both political trust and judgments about governmental levels, parents and young adults showed markedly greater aggregate agreement than had parents and high school seniors (Chapter 6), just as one would predict on the basis of a developmental model. But this predictable increase in aggregate similarity did not boost pair concordance, even in the percentage agreement scores. Conversely, mean parent and youth values on the thermometer ratings differed more in 1973 than in 1965, which also seems consistent with developmental changes. But parent-youth correlations did not always drop by a correspondingly large amount, and percentage agreement remained the same or rose for three of the eight groups.

Taken together, these results provide convincing evidence that typical life-cycle development in the post-adolescent period does not invariably lead to greater parent-youth concordance. Earlier there did appear to be one such case of increasing intergenerational agreement (voting turnout) and possibly one case in which the agreement level was maintained because of life-cycle alterations (recognition of the liberal-conservative dimension). In general, however, there is no clear upward path in parent-offspring agreement rates even when youthful development continues into the adult life cycle.

Nonpolitical Orientations

In analyzing the 1965 data, as well as in previous chapters in this book, we have noted a similarity between expressions of partisan and religious affiliations. The similarity of these two domains carries over to pair correspondence. The decline in parent-youth agreement on specific denominational affiliation cannot be measured in correlational terms, but the drop in percentage agreement indicates as large a decline in lineage correspondence as was that for party identification (Figure 4.8).[24] Given the extremely high stability of parental affiliations (84% with the set of finely coded denominations), much of the decline in pair correspondence is in this case attributable to changes in youthful attachments.

The other two measures in the religious domain also reveal declining pair correspondence between 1965 and 1973. Church attendance is unusual in that there is often a fall-off in late adolescence and young adulthood which is recouped in later years.[25] If this pattern characterizes the generation of 1965 seniors, we speculate that the amount of agreement will rise somewhat as the young adults age still further. But in their appraisal of the Bible and in their nominal affiliations,

[24] Even if we use the broad classification into Protestant, Catholic, Jew, other, and none, parent-youth concordance dropped 14% (92% to 78%).
[25] See Chapter 7, footnote 11.

FIGURE 4.8: Nonpolitical Orientations (Pair Similarity Over Time)

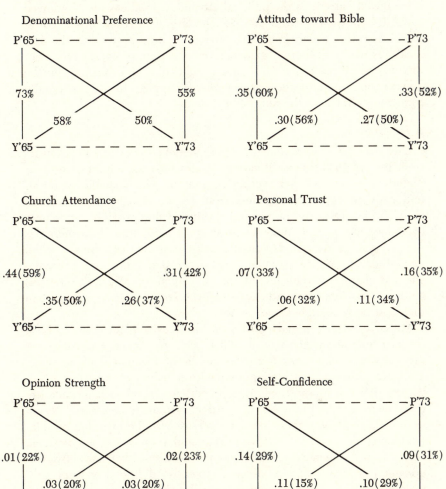

Denominational Preference

P'65 – – – – – – – – P'73

73%   55%

58%   50%

Y'65 – – – – – – – – – – Y'73

Attitude toward Bible

P'65 – – – – – – – – – P'73

.35(60%)   .33(52%)

.30(56%)   .27(50%)

Y'65 – – – – – – – – – Y'73

Church Attendance

P'65 – – – – – – – – – P'73

.44(59%)   .31(42%)

.35(50%)   .26(37%)

Y'65 – – – – – – – – – Y'73

Personal Trust

P'65 – – – – – – – – – P'73

.07(33%)   .16(35%)

.06(32%)   .11(34%)

Y'65 – – – – – – – – – Y'73

Opinion Strength

P'65 – – – – – – – – – P'73

.01(22%)   .02(23%)

.03(20%)   .03(20%)

Y'65 – – – – – – – – – Y'73

Self-Confidence

P'65 – – – – – – – – – P'73

.14(29%)   .09(31%)

.11(15%)   .10(29%)

Y'65 – – – – – – – – – Y'73

we would anticipate no reversal of the downward trend occurring between 1965 and 1973.

Personal trust continues to behave rather differently from political trust. Whereas the latter showed a large decline in pair correspondence, agreement on personal trust increased by a larger amount than any other variable. The two personal efficacy measures show no clear pattern. On neither measure was change very great, especially when it is noted that percentage agreement increased slightly on both measures even though the correlation declined on one of them.

In an overall way, the results for nonpolitical orientations show the same mixed pattern as the political attributes. Declines overshadowed gains in both quantity and size. Yet the largest increase in pair correspondence also occurred in this domain. Thus, even with the few measures we have, there is evidence that the path of agreement is not uniform on all matters outside of the political realm. Neither, on the other hand, does lineage correspondence appear to vary markedly from the political to the nonpolitical area.

A SUMMARY

Our detailed look at lineage correspondence over the eight years from 1965 to 1973 showed a variety of movements, including one area (political resources) plus voting turnout in which similarity rather uniformly increased. Nonetheless, from a more global perspective, the most striking result is the general decline in parent-youth agreement over the panel period. Whether measured by the number of increases (11) versus decreases (21) in similarity (with 3 ties), by the small magnitude of the increases compared to the size of declines, or by the average change in the correlations (a decline of .034), the general tendency was for young adults to be even less like their parents than they had been as high school seniors.

Moreover, as we noted earlier, the declines did not seem to be a function of the specific age at which we interviewed the youths. A few retrospective figures from the middle of the panel period were, aside from turnout, very congruent with a model of progressive decay in pair correspondence. Except perhaps on church attendance, there seemed to be little reason to expect systematic increases later on in life, although both increases and decreases can be expected on relatively volatile matters such as presidential preferences and specific policy issues. Specifically, there was no indication that normal developmental processes from adolescence to early adulthood or from early to later adulthood result in increases over the moderate to low pair correspondence observed originally in 1965.

Nor were the young becoming similar to what their parents were like in 1965 or parents becoming similar to their offspring in 1965. The P'65 × Y'73 link is consistently lower than the P'65 × Y'65 link. Moreover, the drop-off between these two links is most often greater than the drop between P'65 × Y'65 and P'73 × Y'73. What appears to have happened is that period effects, working in similar directions on parents and youths, kept contemporary similarity from falling precipitously. But in the P'65 × Y'73 comparison period effects have changed the younger generation while the older, of course, remains constant. Consequently, this link is especially weak. Similarly, the Y'65 × P'73 link also shows a consistent decline from initial pair similarity.[26] More-over, in a path analysis treating several of the same variables ad-dressed here, Markus found statistical evidence for reverse socializa-tion only with respect to partisan identification and the issues touching on tolerance of nonconformity.[27] Influence on the older generation by the young, while an exciting possibility, finds little support in these data.

Further analysis of the data presented thus far lends additional sup-port to these conclusions. There are no hidden factors that would sug-gest strong family influence but which are not picked up by the statistics presented in Figures 4.1-4.8. For example, if a parent and youth were identical in both 1965 and 1973, but both changed their positions in the same direction in the intervening years, this would not generally raise the pair correlation, but it would suggest the possibility of parent, youth, or mutual influence. A search was made for such cases on a limited basis. Though a few were found, they do not occur frequently. For example, of those pairs who agreed on their party identification in the two years, in only 10% of the cases (or 3% of all cases) had both members of the pair changed their partisan outlook in the same direc-tion. In a similar fashion, if one examines just parents and youths who differed in 1965 or just those pairs in which one member changed over the eight-year period, the evidence uniformly shows more movement away from parents than toward them. Thus, however the data are analyzed, the global picture is one of a small, but widespread decline in parent-youth similarity over the eight-year period.

These declines mean that the absolute levels of lineage congruence in 1973 are even lower than the customarily low to moderate levels observed in 1965. Most noticeable from this perspective in the dramatic drop in agreement levels for partisanship and candidate preference. As noted earlier, the 1973 pair correlation for partisanship is above sev-eral other correlations by the barest of margins. Aside from partisan-ship and voting, the other 1973 correlations further attest to the mod-est degree of lineage similarity on political attitudes and behavior. The highest parent-youth correlations are for nonpolitical matters—the di-vinity of the Bible and church attendance. Next highest is that for

[26] In looking for reverse socialization, it seems most relevant to compare the Y'65 × P'73 and P'65 × Y'65 links rather than the Y'65 × P'73 and P'65 × Y'73 links (which would be the focus of a cross-lagged panel analysis). The Y'65 × P'73 link, on average, is marginally greater than the P'65 × Y'73 link. This is probably due solely to the fact that parents as a whole changed less than youths, and does not indicate reverse socialization whereby youths influence their parents. As noted, whatever parental change did take place made parents less like their children in either year.

[27] Markus, "Continuity, Change, and the Political Self," Chapter 3.

political knowledge, which is conceptually quite distinct from opinions and actions. All the other correlations are .24 or below despite the diversity of measures employed. Even the more salient, concrete issues, which showed relatively high correlations in 1965, are now hardly distinguishable from other attributes.

This leveling off of agreement rates came about because the decline in similarity was particularly evident among the variables for which there was most agreement in 1965. Of the measures on which the 1965 correlation was .30 or greater, all showed a decline, and the average drop was nearly .14. Of the correlations below .30, nearly half rose or showed no change at all, and the average change was a minuscule −.001. While statistically this is suggestive of regression effects, substantively it suggests that a kind of plateau is being reached at which pair similarity is modestly positive. Parents and their offspring are surely not the antitheses of one another, but concordance is not marked either.

Altogether, the 1965 data along with the panel results make a strong case for only a moderate degree of sustained parental impact in the late adolescent years and a slight but widespread decline in that impact during young adulthood—a decline which sometimes occurs in the face of increasing generational similarity. Life-cycle factors often influence young people to be like the preceding generation of adults, but based on the analysis in this chapter it is clear that they do not necessarily increase lineage similarity.

PAIR SIMILARITY IN 1973: NEW MEASURES

The results so far offer strong evidence of a declining degree of parent-offspring similarity as young people move into the adult years. Yet a number of interesting questions remain, three of which can be addressed with measures newly introduced in 1973. The first such question is the degree of similarity on issues that gained prominence after 1965—that is, after the young people had attained adulthood and many had moved out of their parents' homes. Of course a parental imprint should not be completely absent from young adults, even for issues that are of recent vintage. If the family as an agent of socialization means anything, it should mean the inculcation of predispositions and states of readiness that enable the maturing individual to confront new stimuli in patterned ways. Yet the expanding world of the young adult coupled with the customary physical separation of parent and child probably means that pair correspondence is low on all of these new measures.

Questions about a large set of new issues, groups, and personalities were introduced for the first time into the 1973 interview. Some of these referred to issues that simply did not exist as matters of public discussion in 1965 (e.g., whether marijuana should be legalized, male-female equality). Others called for "thermometer" ratings of groups, such as radical students, which were not relevant political actors in 1965. Thermometer ratings were also obtained for newly prominent individuals such as Ralph Nader and Gloria Steinem. Still other questions called for judgments about whether recently visible groups, such as television commentators and people on welfare, had "too much influence," "just about the right amount of influence," or "too little influence."

Pair correlations for these items resoundingly confirm our expectations of low parent-youth correspondence. Though a complete analysis of these data will be left for elsewhere, the overall landscape is clearly summarized by statistics for the items mentioned above: marijuana, .24; sex equality, .15; radical students, .12; Nader, .13; Steinem, .07; television commentators, .08; people on welfare, .13. Even the highest of these correlations can be regarded as moderate at best.

Moreover, there are methodological and substantive factors that make these results even more meaningful. Issue positions were tapped by "seven-point scales," designed to measure attitudes more finely and more reliably than agree-disagree items. This improvement in measurement should, if anything, inflate the parent-youth correlations at least marginally. Yet the correlations are low. In addition, cases were eliminated from the base (for the seven-point scale comparisons) if either the parent or youth was not placed on the scale. This includes those who said they had no interest in a topic and were therefore not asked what their position was. Thus, agreement among *all* pairs is even lower than the correlations indicate.

The nature of the attitudinal questions would also lead one to expect higher agreement in at least some instances. The Vietnam War, for example, was so salient and emotional that strong traces of family-inspired perspectives should be observed. And while there is a moderate generational difference of opinion on how the war was handled, there is virtually no aggregate difference about getting involved in Vietnam in the first place. Yet parent-youth pairs did not see eye to eye on either of these questions (correlations of .13 and .12). Similarly, other seven-point scales were about issues of considerable visibility and importance, but congruence remained low.

The second question that can be addressed with data just from the 1973 wave concerns the possibility that the 1965 results were a product of a limited variety of indicators as well as of measurement techniques that have since been improved. This possibility can be checked by observing pair similarity on items that were newly introduced in 1973 but referred to individuals or issues of longstanding prominence and concern. For example, representative correlations based on thermometer scores were .28 for Richard Nixon and .15 for the Democrats. Similarly, there was a correlation of .14, using the seven-point scale format, on whether the government should provide jobs for everyone. On the group power judgments, groups with a long history of political involvement, such as Catholics and farmers, yielded equally low pair correlations (.09 and .14, respectively). Even if we assume that these correlations have declined a bit from what they were in 1965, none of the results is out of line with our original observations. Moderate to low parent-youth agreement in 1965 was apparently not an artifact of methods or choice of topics.

Finally, new measures from 1973 allow us to check a third hypothesis: that there is a kind of general similarity in parent-youth attitudes that is somehow not apparent on specific issues. In analyzing the 1965 wave, we suggested that "parents influence children through their entire attitude structure rather than simply via their opinion on isolated issues."[28] However, at that time we lacked the data to test this notion adequately.

One important improvement in the 1973 interview that sheds light on this question was the introduction of a general liberal-conservative measure. This was a seven-point scale on which individuals were asked to place themselves along a dimension ranging from extremely liberal to extremely conservative. If relative placement on the overall political spectrum is transferred between generations despite disagreements about specific issues, the pair correlation for this single indicator should be quite high. The results—even when limited to the two-thirds of the pairs in which both members placed themselves on the scale—permit no such interpretation. The correlation is .21, only a shade higher than that for most specific issues and, of course, well below even the 1973 correlation on party identification.

There is, however, another way in which parents' attitudes might be reflected in their children's attitudes without high parent-offspring correlations of the type we have examined so far. This could occur through an indirect, lagged process. Parental attitudes on issues at an earlier point in time could partially determine young people's views on other, related issues at a subsequent date. Thus, for example, one might anticipate that parents' views on the "communist" question

[28] M. Kent Jennings and Richard Niemi, *The Political Character of Adolescence* (Princeton: Princeton University Press, 1974), 86-87.

would correlate well with their children's attitudes on the rights of the accused. Or one might look for a moderate correlation between parents' attitudes on the matter of school prayers and their children's views on the legalization of marijuana. And so on.

Correlations of this sort are given in Table 4.3 for all four issues tapped in 1965 and a variety of issues included only in 1973. None of the correlations reaches .20. And apart from liberal-conservative self-placement, none of the correlations is even as high as .11. The idea is therefore untenable that parents' influence in this less direct fashion accounts for a large amount of the variation in their children's attitudes. Overall, parent-offspring comparisons drawing on the new measures in the 1973 wave support our conclusion that parental influence is none too strong.

TABLE 4.3: Similarity between Parents' Attitudes in 1965 and
Youths' Attitudes in 1973 on Different Issues

Youths' Attitudes 1973	Parents' Attitudes 1965			
	Anti-Church speeches (pro)[a]	Communist holding office (pro)	School prayers (anti)	School integration (pro)
Protect rights of accused	.03	.07	.07	.06
Government should help minorities	.07	.10	.06	.09
Legalize marijuana	.10	.10	.10	.09
Police treat all people the same	.00	.04	.03	.03
Women should have equal role with men	.06	.06	.07	.04
Should have stayed out of Vietnam	.06	.05	−.02	.03
Liberal views (cons-lib self-placement)	.12	.10	.09	.17

[a] Directionality is indicated so that the sign of the correlation can be interpreted. All of the youth measures are scored from conservative to liberal.

THE PERSISTENCE OF WITHIN-FAMILY CONCORDANCE

In looking at the parent-offspring pairs at two points in time we witnessed a widespread though often temperate decline in dyadic congruence. But this was the overall, aggregate movement. The tendency toward declines could be made up of slight shifts among most pairs, sharp departures among some pairs, or some combination of the two. In addition, shifts working in opposite directions among pairs might be commonplace. Virtually the same overall pair correlations in 1965 and 1973 could mask much shifting in the congruence of particular pairs. Alternatively, even very low similarity at each point in time could be associated with relatively stable levels of within-family proximity over time. Another way of approaching the question of socialization outcomes, then, is to ask: what is the persistence or continuity of concordance over time? Do the more congruent pairs of 1965 remain the more congruent ones of 1973; do the more noncongruent pairs of 1965 remain the more noncongruent ones of 1973? Are the patterns of parent-child correspondence laid down by late adolescence—whether weak or strong—replicated in young adulthood?

To answer these questions we must relate individual pair similarity in 1965 with that in 1973. Our procedure was straightforward. We employed the results of pair cross-tabulations in each year to generate agreement scores. Cells on the main diagonals represented perfect agreement and were coded "0" to represent no disagreement. With each succeeding set of diagonals on each side of the main diagonal the amount of disagreement between parent and offspring was obviously increasing. (For religious affiliation this assumption is not met, and hence it is excluded from the analysis.) Cases lying in these cells were given progressively higher scores, "1" for one step off the main diagonal, "2" for two steps off, and so forth. Thus two sets of agreement scores were generated, one for 1965 and one for 1973. These scores were then cross-tabulated so that the rank-order similarity of agreement levels over time could be observed. The higher the correlation the more stable was the relationship between parent and child. As a minimal condition of persistence the signs should, of course, be positive.

At one level the results suggest that agreement patterns within families do tend to persist. On all but a few of the variables examined the correlations were positive. Pairs tending toward agreement in 1965 did likewise in 1973; pairs tending toward disagreement in 1965 also did likewise in 1973. The clear exception is the index of political trust. As we saw, there was a tremendous amount of individual- and aggregate-level change on this dimension among both generations, but especially so among the younger. If there had been a prime candidate for a reversal in pair agreement, it might well have been political trust. For virtually all of the other orientations, however, the results at least meet the minimal criterion for persistence.

Having made that point, we must immediately add that the magnitudes of the relationships scarcely support an interpretation of strong continuity. The τ_b correlations range from .01 to .23 with corresponding gammas of .01 to .44. These results are tempered somewhat by two considerations. First, whatever measurement error exists in each measure is multiplied by our procedures. We have employed observations of two samples at two widely separated points in time. When these are combined into the type of "super" measure used here, the opportunities for errors derivative of measurement quality are large indeed. Thus the persistence figures would seem to be extremely conservative estimates.

A second qualification is that there is some asymmetry in terms of the deviations from the 1965 agreement scores. Typically, those pairs in higher congruence in 1965 were more likely to remain stable than were those pairs in lower congruence. That is, the more disagreement there was between parent and child in 1965 the more unstable was that relationship over time. It proved more difficult for pairs to remain at the extreme of dissonance than at the extreme of consonance. Although these results are in part statistical artifacts,[29] they do help specify the conditions under which persistence will be greater.

Still, the overall pattern is one of modest persistence at best. Continuity was especially weak on the group ratings, with the highest being .10 for Jews and with five of the eight correlations being less than .05. It is probably no accident that one of the highest showings of continuity came in the area of political information. As noted earlier, this is one of the more stable political qualities at the individual level, and it was one of the few not to show a decline among pairs taken as a whole.

What is perhaps more significant is that the other three outcomes above the level of .20 all have a religious component. Opinions on the issue of school prayers, on the right to make speeches opposing religion, and on the divine nature of the Bible are deeply imbued with tradition and emotion. Family patterns seem more likely to be sustained in this highly charged arena than in others. Nor are these results a consequence of uniformly high and unchanging pair similarity at the overall level, since these three issues embody a variety of configurations when 1965 and 1973 pair correlations are examined (see Figures 4.5 and 4.8). Rather, religion seems to add a special dimension, in some instances helping to keep agreeing pairs in harmony and in others helping to keep disagreeing pairs at odds. By comparison, few issues could match that of school integration for controversial and emotional content. Yet there is virtually no persistence in within-family agreement patterns on that volatile issue.

With the few exceptions noted, the major message emerging is that the persistence of within-family concordance is modest indeed. By inference, the source of whatever stability exists at the level of parent-

---

[29] This is because pairs at both points in time tended to cluster toward the diagonal cells so that the proportion of strongly congruent pairs outweighed by a large margin the proportion of strongly noncongruent pairs. When the agreement scores are cross-tabulated, it is inevitable that by chance alone a sizeable proportion of the cases will be in the strongly congruent cells.

child pairs as a whole is comprised only in part, over and above chance, of the same actual pairs. A few illustrations are in order.

Although the concordance for party identification remains one of the highest observed in 1973, there was a substantial decline from 1965 to 1973. The leading hypothesis is that many desertions occurred among the more congruent pairs whereas the less congruent pairs remained less congruent. Or, from the standpoint of the destination year, 1973, the more congruent pairs had their origins overwhelmingly among similar pairs in 1965. Yet the persistence of agreement patterns over time is but .17, a positive association, but one leaving much room for diverse turnover patterns among the pairs.

In fact, substantial numbers who were in partisan agreement in 1965 found themselves at odds in 1973, and vice versa. For simplicity's sake let us use the proportions in absolute agreement as the reference points. Of the 272 cases in perfect agreement in 1973 (using the seven-way partisan break), some 42% came from pairs also having perfect agreement in 1965; but 25% came from pairs disagreeing by two or more steps off the main diagonal. At the other extreme, of the 227 pairs disagreeing by as much as three steps in 1973, some 26% of them actually came from a state of complete harmony in 1965. As these figures suggest, the independent and often cross-cutting movements of parent and child can lead to considerable turnover in pair proximity while at the same time leaving the end state—1973 concordance—moderately high.

Another example of internal shifting occurs with respect to recognition and understanding of party differences. In this instance there was a small rise in pair concordance over time, from .17 to .22. The persistence of agreement patterns, however, was even lower than that for party identification (.09). Again working from the destination perspective of 1973, it is instructive to observe the turnover in pair alignment. Of the 262 cases in perfect agreement in 1973, some 41% originated from an identical state in 1965, but some 39% came from pairs that had disagreed by two or more steps in 1965. By the same token, of the 314 pairs disagreeing by two or more steps in 1973, a total of 27% had seen eye to eye eight years earlier.

Finally, we may consider the example of internal political efficacy, an orientation for which pair correspondence was low at both points in time and for which continuity of agreement patterns was virtually identical to that for party identification. Although 43% of the 419 agreeing pairs of 1973 had also agreed in 1965, 57% had disagreed (mostly by one step because of a small number of response categories). Of the few pairs disagreeing by two or more steps in 1973, 28% had agreed perfectly eight years earlier. It is clear, then, that parent-offspring agreement represents a mosaic of movement to and fro within family dyads. Pair similarity in 1965 is typically a poor predictor of similarity in 1973.

SOURCES OF CHANGING SIMILARITY

The previous section demonstrated that many individual pairs became more similar during the eight-year period while others became less similar and still others retained the same distances. Some portion of this ebbing and flowing is surely a product of random fluctuations on the part of one or both partners in the dyads. But it is also likely that some portion reflects a genuine drawing to or away from each other. On what basis might we account for the increasing agreement versus disagreement? Several important kinds of explanatory variables immediately come to mind, suggesting the need for a multivariate model including all of them.

Perhaps the most obvious factors are those which affect the kinds of opinions that young people come in contact with. If parents remain a chief source of political opinion and discussion, one might expect a stable or perhaps even increasing level of agreement with them. In contrast, young people whose contacts are almost exclusively outside their parents' home, and are with individuals likely to hold conflicting opinions, could be expected increasingly to have attitudes that are independent of their parents' viewpoints.

To assess the importance of these factors we utilized three variables. The first is simply how often the young people see their parents. This varies all the way from youths who live with their parents (12%) to youths who see them 2-3 times a year (10%) or less (7%). If the amount of contact with parents makes a difference in parent-youth similarity, the considerable variation in the number of times parents and children see each other should be a powerful explanatory variable. A second variable affecting opinion sources is whether or not the young person is married. The high level of affect involved in marriage and the frequency of interaction between spouses suggests that marriage may be an important factor tending to lower similarity with parents. The third variable helps capture the *kinds* of contacts made by a young person. Whatever the sources of "educational" differences (see Chapter 8), there is no gainsaying that people with varying levels of education frequently differ in their political orientations. Thus it seems reasonable that a person who has considerably more or less education than his or her parent would come in contact with ideas and opinions somewhat at variance with those of the parent. For this purpose we constructed a variable from the cross-classification of parent-youth education levels. At the one extreme were parent-youth pairs in which both had achieved the same education level, while at the opposite end were pairs in which one respondent was much more highly educated.[30]

A second kind of factor that might alter youth-parent similarity is relative political involvement. Where either parent or youth has participated much more than the other, their attitudes might well diverge because of varying amounts and sources of political information and influence. To some extent, of course, there is a simultaneity problem. Greater participation might be a result of divergent attitudes rather than a cause of disagreement. But since none of the youths could participate much until after high school, their developing participation levels as young adults might well have drawn them closer to or further from parental attitudes. To measure participation levels we constructed a nine-point index for youths and an identical index for parents, where the index value is a count of the number of types of participation.[31] Relative participation was then determined by comparing parent and youth scores, with 0 representing equal participation levels and 9 representing the extreme of differing degrees of involvement. Most scores were in the 0-3 range, with 16% of the pairs having scores of 4 or more.

A third type of factor which might predict changes in similarity is affect between parents and offspring. Though closeness of parent and youth did not have a consistent impact on similarity in 1965, the obviousness of the connection—that parents and youths who get along better will remain more like each other—suggests that we should consider it here. For this purpose youths' 1965 and 1973 reports of closeness to parent were combined in an additive fashion.[32]

A fourth consideration was whether the parent's age would affect growing similarity and dissimilarity. Quite simply, if parents and youths were further apart in age, would dissimilarity tend to grow as the youths reached adulthood? Finally, we considered the possibility that the sources of changing similarity would be different for white versus minority group members and for males versus females. There was some indication in 1965 that transmission rates varied somewhat be-

[30] Since all youths, by design, had a high school education, the "most discrepant" category consisted only of youths much more highly educated than their parents. For each of the two intermediate categories, either respondent could be the more educated.

[31] The measure is identical to that described in Chapter 2, except for the exclusion of the voting items.

[32] Separate questions were asked about the mother and father. The form was, "How close would you say you are to your mother—very close, pretty close, or not very close?" The question used to build the index was the one for the parent who was interviewed.

tween sons and daughters and between blacks and whites for given orientations.[33] Here the hypothesis has no particular direction except *perhaps* for females. Altogether, then, we have eight predictors of increasing (decreasing) similarity.

In order to assess the importance of these eight predictors we constructed a measure for each orientation showing the strength *and* the direction of the change in concordance over time. Our procedures began with the basic sorts of tables used for generating persistence of agreement patterns. The cross-tabulation of agreement scores from 1965 and 1973 produced square matrices whose main diagonals represented no change in agreement level over time—regardless of whether that level reflected perfect concordance, discordance, or some value in between. Entries on one side of the diagonal then represented instances where the pairs became more alike, while those on the other side stood for those which became less alike. The further away from the diagonal, the more extreme was the increase or decrease in similarity. For each orientation, then, we arranged all pairs on a continuum stretching from those with greatly heightened levels of dissimilarity on one end to those with greatly heightened levels of similarity on the other, with those undergoing no change occupying the midpoint of the continuum.

Each of the eight predictor variables was used as an independent variable in a regression equation where the dependent variable was the change in concordance between 1965 and 1973. Where the differences between parents and youths could not be very great, such as for dichotomous policy items, the dependent variable had only three categories. Students could become more like their parents over the eight-year period, maintain the same degree of similarity, or become less like their parents. Where greater degrees of similarity and dissimilarity were apparent, such as on political trust, the dependent variable had more categories, ranging from a relatively large increase to a relatively large decrease in similarity.

Bivariate relationships between each of the independent and dependent variables were examined for nonlinear functional forms. For example, there might exist no *linear* relationship between frequency of seeing parents and increasing or decreasing similarity, yet those who see their parents less than once or twice a month might all be drifting away from parental views while those in more frequent contact are all increasing their agreement with parents. No consistent nonlinear patterns were found, so that a linear regression did not seem to distort the form of the relationships. Since the possible impact of race and sex

[33] Jennings and Niemi, *Political Character of Adolescence*, 44, 158.

involved interaction effects—i.e., the effect of other variables in the equation might vary by race and sex—regressions were run for all respondents with race and sex included as predictors. Then for selected dependent variables, regressions were rerun for males and females and for whites and minority group members separately.

Despite the straightforward and seemingly obvious connections between the independent variables and changes in pair similarity, the regression results make it clear that the sources of changing similarity do not lie in the types of factors considered. Typically, the proportion of variance explained was extraordinarily low—on the order of two or three percent—and the regression coefficients were mostly not significant despite the large sample size, and varied in magnitude and in their sign.[34]

The lack of predictive power of these factors is of considerable interest. For one thing, it bears closely on a popular explanation given for the decline in pair similarity, viz., that the decline is due to the decreased interaction between parents and offspring after high school graduation. The present results cast doubt on this explanation because we found virtually the same patterns of rising and falling similarity even when comparing young people who continue to live with their parents with those who see their parents very infrequently.

Reconciliation of our results with the declining interaction theory may lie in the recognition that there is a psychological leave-taking that may override physical arrangements. Physical propinquity alone does not suffice for maintaining high congruence. Even if interaction and affect remain high, the emerging young adult is almost inevitably exposed to additional learning sources. Interaction with peers and other adults becomes politically salient and important to young adults even though they continue to interact frequently with parents. In addition, the processes of self-development, the working out of a unique personality, act to temper the political hold of parents even among young adults in close proximity to them.

Changes in similarity apparently have little, if anything, to do with direct influence of parents on youths or vice versa. We conjecture that whatever direct influence exists has largely been felt by the end of high school. Little family influence will take effect subsequently, regardless of the extent of interaction, relative amounts of education, and so on. Whatever changes do occur in similarity may be purely an artifact of other factors that happen to push youths and their parents in similar or opposite directions.

---

[34] For blacks, the R^2's were larger, but the small N meant that they were still not significant.

CONCLUSION

In concluding Chapter 3 we emphasized the degree to which there is lifelong openness to changes in political attitudes and behavior. The results in this chapter reinforce that view, although it is impossible to gauge the degree to which the role of the family is the cause of life-long openness and to what degree it is an effect of it. But whatever the causal relationship, the generally declining lineage similarity suggests a further weakening of parental influence from the surprisingly modest levels observed when the youths were high school seniors.

In many respects these results might have been anticipated. But the pervasiveness of the decline in youth-parent concordance was not: the correlations representing agreement on repeated measurements rarely increased more than marginally, and a substantial majority declined; the decline was evident throughout the family pairs, and could not be attributed only to those where the offspring were emotionally estranged from their parents, or physically separated from their parents, or socially or geographically distant, and so on; and there was no indication that all of this was due to temporary factors, and that a later reversal of the declining similarity is to be expected.

Similarly, the results for the nonpanel measures suggest waning parental influence on a broad scale. Agreement on new issues, groups, and personalities was uniformly low; new measures of longstanding concerns yielded no greater intergenerational agreement; similarity on an overall liberal-conservative dimension was modest; and there was little support for the notion of generalized, nonspecific parental influence. Though these measures by themselves do not speak to the issue of change, they are perfectly consistent with the model of declining influence suggested by the panel data.

Altogether, then, it is unlikely that what we have observed is an artifact of the particular circumstances of our study. If low or declining similarity were limited to a small subset of the political orientations, conclusions about parental influence would vary widely depending on what kinds of attitudes or behaviors one considered. Or if little or declining similarity were observed only for young people widely separated from their parents, only for young people disaffected from their parents, and so on, the results might be quite different from one segment of the population to another. But none of this was the case.

It is always possible that the results might be different for other historical periods. Just as differences between younger and older adults might be due to life-cycle or to generational factors, so too these *lineage* patterns could be the result of life-cycle processes or of historical circumstances at the time of the study. But the modest parent-youth concordance in our study and others, and the post-high-school decline shown here, are both so widespread that their sources probably lie in general processes of maturation rather than in anything peculiar to the 1960s and 1970s. A life-cycle rather than a generational explanation seems most appropriate.

CHAPTER FIVE

Continuity and Change at the Aggregate Level: Involvement, Resources, and Participation

OUR focus in the three previous chapters has been at the individual level. One of the great advantages of the panel design is that it permits exactly the sort of comparisons that we have made of the same individuals and parent-child pairs over a period of time, thereby enhancing our understanding of how political life unfolds across time, generations, and the life cycle. Any good understanding of these processes must ultimately be able to draw on what is occurring at the micro level. From another perspective, though, it is vital to know the net results of the stabilities and instabilities characterizing individuals over time. What is crucial from this viewpoint is not so much the degree of persistence at the individual level but, rather, the net flows, the aggregate profile. Obviously, the more perceptive observer also wants to know whether the composition accounting for the profile has changed or remained the same—whether, for example, liberals and conservatives have the same make-up across a given time interval. Still, the gross distributions are of burning interest. In the next three chapters we accommodate this interest by moving away from persistence at the individual level to examine the amount and direction of change at the aggregate level.

At the height of the student movement in the United States it was being freely predicted that an unbridgeable gulf was forming between the generations. Differences over political ends and especially over the means to reach those ends reached epidemic proportions. The defensive reaction of the middle-aged "establishment" seemed merely to speed the progress of the widening chasm.[1] Nor were the differences confined strictly to the ranks of hard-core college radicals, as the movement branched out to include a wide array of sympathetic supporters on the campuses. Some observers also saw strong signs of generational

---

[1] In addition to the more spectacular evidence of generational cleavage, a good deal of survey data was offered. Perhaps the best known, partly because of its three-part showing on CBS television, was Daniel Yankelovich, Inc., *Generations Apart* (New York: Columbia Broadcasting System, 1969).

change among working-class youth.[2] And at a more general level the counterculture seemed likely to diffuse into all segments of the rising generation, thereby helping to create and sustain a sociopolitical cleavage between the generations.[3]

With the softening of young voices and the alteration of the public agenda, the predictions of *politically* conflicted generations have diminished. The failure of the McGovern campaign in 1972 to realize fully the youth vote potential, visibly expanded by the franchise extension, was seen by many as the swan song of the youth movement and age-based politics. What had appeared to be unresolvable conflict a few years previously now seemed to be more like tolerable tension. If vivid differences in life styles marked the generations, these differences did not appear to have their sequels in the political sphere.

Of course, some observers never regarded the intergenerational differences as constituting what came to be called the generation gap.[4] The apparent cleavage was said to be an illusion, a function of the vociferous few, something which would dissolve as the young passed through another life stage, or as a phenomenon not really very different from past illustrations of age-graded conflict. On the other hand, other observers maintain that the gap still exists, that basically different kinds of political orientations and frameworks have been adopted by the young, and that the youthful cohorts baptized into politics from the mid-1960s onward constitute a new political generation.[5] Still others argue that there has been selective continuity and change, that in some respects the rising generation has evolved a different set of preferences and modes of behavior, but that in other respects it echoes very faithfully the generation of its parents.

Complicating even more these divergent perspectives is the possibility that older generations may be in a state of flux also. While a good deal of the social science literature, especially in the area of political socialization, held until quite recently that change is relatively

[2] For example, Milton Mankoff and Richard Flacks, "The Changing Social Base of the American Student Movement," *The Annals*, 395 (May 1971), 54-69; and Richard Flacks, "On the New Working Class and Strategies for Social Change," *Social Policy*, 1 (March-April 1971), 7-15.

[3] Two of the most visible exponents of this view were Theodore Rozak, *The Making of the Counter Culture* (Garden City, N.Y.: Doubleday, 1969), and Charles A. Reich, *The Greening of America* (New York: Random House, 1970).

[4] A very useful discussion of different interpretations of the generation gap, from which the following discussion borrows, is Vern L. Bengtson, "The Generation Gap: A Review and Theology of Social Psychological Perspectives," *Youth and Society*, 2 (September 1970), 7-32.

[5] Part of that interest centered on what would happen to the activists of the period. For suggestive evidence that there is carryover of ideology to later years, see James M. Fendrich, "Activists Ten Years Later: A Test of Generational Unit Continuity," *Journal of Social Issues*, 30 (No. 3, 1974), 95-118, and Chapter 11 in this volume.

rare after adolescence, we saw in Chapters 2 and 3 that change and instability are by no means confined to the young. At the aggregate level, cross-sectional evidence suggests that older people were not immune to the same forces affecting the young in the recent past,[6] and that they were not completely impervious to the lessons which the young were trying to broadcast. The more dramatic forms of youthful expression may simply have overshadowed movements which were also at work among older people.

Of obvious utility in trying to sort out these conflicting views on change and continuity are the longitudinal materials at our command. With them we will be able to state what the parental and filial generations were like both before and after the onset of a radically changed political climate beginning around the mid-1960s. At the simplest level this will help resolve the question of the absolute and relative size of the so-called generation gap at different points in time, thereby shedding light on propositions about age-based political cleavages and on hypotheses about the changing political character of the American citizenry. More fundamentally, however, such materials will enable us to go beyond the generation-gap formulation. In particular, we can (1) specify the domains of continuity and change; (2) detect the residues of the historical period as it affected each generation; (3) establish the degree to which place in the life cycle prompted change and continuity; and (4) define those political traits which promise to constitute more or less permanent schisms between the generations.

In the present chapter we begin by introducing various pictorial models that will serve as guidelines in helping us evaluate patterns of change and continuity revealed by the data. We then use these models to explore materials focusing on psychological involvement in politics, political resources, and—to a lesser extent—political participation. Chapter 6 will then be devoted to political preferences and attitudes, as well as illustrative nonpolitical orientations. A conclusion dealing with the two chapters as a whole comes at the end of Chapter 6. In many respects these two chapters are the aggregate analogues of the individual-level analysis contained in Chapters 2 and 3.

MODELS OF CONTINUITY AND CHANGE

In comparing generations with each other and with themselves over time, we must be alert to four types of phenomena: (1) continuity over time; and discontinuity as a function of (2) life-cycle effects, (3)

6 Warren E. Miller and Teresa E. Levitin, *Leadership and Change* (Cambridge, Mass.: Winthrop, 1976); and Norman H. Nie, Sidney Verba, and John R. Petrocik, *The Changing American Voter* (Cambridge, Mass.: Harvard University Press, 1976).

generational effects, and (4) period effects.[7] Some of these terms were employed in Chapters 2 and 3 and we must distinguish their usage as applied to aggregate versus individual-level analysis. It will be helpful to sketch in diagrammatic terms some configurations that would describe these various processes at work among our two generations.

Figure 5.1a, for example, depicts a near-perfect continuity model. It represents continuity in two senses. First, there is little or no difference between the generations at either point in time. There is neither a real nor a spurious generation gap. Continuity is represented in the time dimension also. Both generations occupy the same position at both points in time. As we have already stressed, this perfect continuity at the aggregate level implies nothing with certainty about continuity—or persistence, as we called the phenomenon in previous chapters—at the individual level. We have examples in our data of substantial individual-level change yielding aggregate continuity as well as discontinuity.

In talking about life-cycle effects at the individual level we restricted ourselves to the concept that individuals are more open, receptive, or vulnerable to change at some points in the life span than at others. We ruled out of our discussion, for the most part, questions about the direction of change and whether such change acted to bring the two generations into closer or more distant alignment. Now, however, we want to address ourselves more explicitly to the twin considerations of directionality and its consequences for intergenerational juxtapositioning.

Life-cycle effects are often interpreted as movements by the young which, as they pass through time, bring them into line with the older generation when it occupied that age bracket. This interpretation rests on the assumption that certain kinds of change are endemic to the life course. These changes stem from shifting responsibilities, opportunities, and needs which accompany the aging process. Many of the changes are held to transpire as people move through young adulthood and into the middle years. But life-cycle effects may also be a function of movements among older people which would increase, or conceivably decrease, the distance between them and the young. A conventional life-cycle effects model is shown in Figure 5.1b, in which the filial generation moves toward the older one, and in which change in the older generation has stopped. Implicit here is the assumption

[7] A comprehensive treatment of these topics is found in Matilda White Riley, Marilyn Johnson, Anne Foner et al., *Aging and Society*, Vol. III (New York: Russell Sage Foundation, 1972). See especially Chapter 2, and a shorter version by Matilda White Riley, "Aging and Cohort Succession: Interpretations and Misinterpretations," *Public Opinion Quarterly*, 37 (Spring 1973), 35-49.

FIGURE 5.1: Models of Continuity and Change

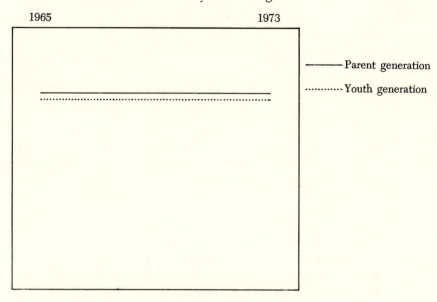

1965   1973

———— Parent generation

·········· Youth generation

(a) Continuity: generations remain the same over time, absolutely and relative to each other

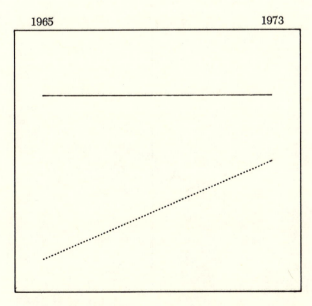

1965   1973

(b) Life-cycle effects: younger generation converges with older as it ages

FIGURE 5.1 (cont.)

1965   1973

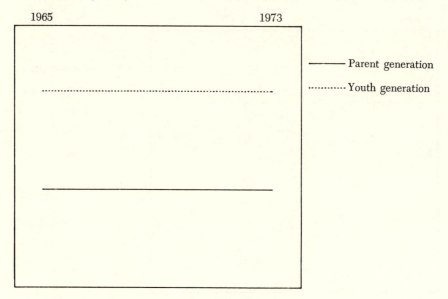

——— Parent generation

··········· Youth generation

(c) Generation effects: generations begin apart and remain so over time

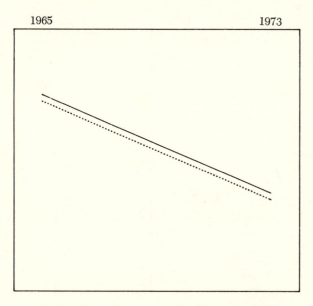

(d) Period effects: generations begin the same and move
congruently over time

FIGURE 5.1 (cont.)

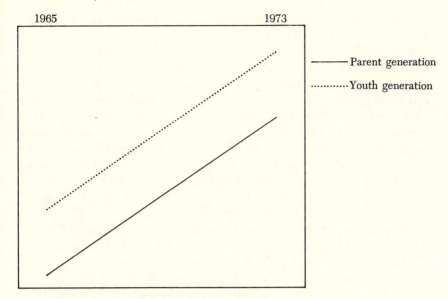

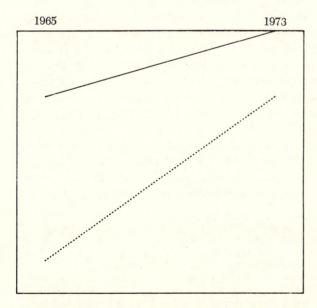

1965   1973

——— Parent generation

···········Youth generation

(e) Hybrid generation-period effects: generations begin
apart and move in same direction at equal rates

1965   1973

(f) Hybrid life-cycle-period effects: generations begin
apart and move in same direction; younger moves much
more rapidly as result of place in life cycle

that subsequent shifting by the young generation would serve to bring it even closer to the older one.

As with life-cycle effects, so too with generational effects. At the individual level we lumped together these two dynamics as intermediate points between a model of lifelong persistence on the one hand and lifelong openness on the other. We were simply concerned with whether there were effects, whatever the directional component involved, that fitted neither of the two contrasting models of persistence versus openness. More commonly, however, generational effects are of interest for what they say about the political complexion or disposition of birth cohorts. Hence the terms "depression generation," the "silent generation," and the "student protest generation" convey a sense of discontinuity with the past and, often, with the future as well.

An ideal type of generational difference model is shown in Figure 5.1c. Here the two stand apart in 1965 and maintain that division in 1973. Sustained cleavages of this order are what people usually have in mind when speaking of a *true* generation gap. Generation effects derive from birth cohorts undergoing a shared community of experiences under roughly similar circumstances at pivotal, impressionable points (usually before mature adulthood) in the life cycle. Differential experiences within a generation can lead to generation-units.[8]

The third major indicator of discontinuity is displayed in its ideal form in Figure 5.1d. Period effects work their will on each generation, reflecting the important events and trends of the time. They are often referred to as *Zeitgeist* effects. True period effects have a roughly common impact on all or most segments of society. Illustratively, certain elements of a war, an economic depression, a unique regime, a technological innovation, or mass cultural movement leave their mark on the entire society, even though other elements touch population segments in unique ways.

It would be difficult to interpret Figure 5.1d in any way other than period effects, given the great life-cycle and experiential differences between the two generations. Of course period effects, like the other processes, are not usually so easily identified in the real world. Rather,

[8] The classic formulation of the generational concept remains that of Karl Mannheim, "The Problem of Generations," English translation reprinted in Philip G. Altbach and Robert S. Laufer (eds.), *The New Pilgrims* (New York: David McKay, 1972). On student movements in particular see Lewis S. Feuer, *The Conflict of Generations* (New York: Basic Books, 1969). Herbert Hyman anticipates some current analytic problems in *Political Socialization* (Glencoe: Free Press, 1959), Chapter 6. One of the best empirical applications of the political generation concept is David Butler and Donald Stokes, *Political Change in Britain* (New York: St. Martins, 1969). For a provocative cross-national application see Ronald Inglehart, *The Silent Revolution: Changing Values and Political Styles among Western Publics* (Princeton: Princeton University Press, 1977).

the three factors of age, date of birth, and historical period often work simultaneously and in varying combinations. One very likely illustration of this is contained in Figure 5.1e, which depicts a hybrid generation-period effects model. The gap between the generations in 1965 remains in 1973, but each generation has moved at a corresponding rate over time.

Another hybrid model, life-cycle plus period effects, is demonstrated in Figure 5.1f. In this instance the generations are set apart in 1965 and both move with the times. But the younger generation, because of its still impressionable years, changes more rapidly and begins to converge with the older.

One can imagine other patterns based on complex relationships between aging, generations, and periods. For example, curvilinear life-cycle development would add to the array of patterns we might expect to find, thereby adding to the difficulty of interpreting changes observed in the real world. Even some of the relatively "clean" models already presented are susceptible to alternative interpretations. One must take into account substance and theory in assessing over-time patterns, especially given the statistical intractability occasioned by the multicollinearity involved in the age, date of birth, and historical era triad.[9] Nonetheless, the models and processes we have outlined are among the most prominent patterns to be expected and will at least serve as points of departure.

A relevant point here is that generational discontinuities are no less real simply because there are compositional factors "explaining" them. Rather than being derivative of "shared communities of experiences," the deviance of a generation may simply be due to a change in its composition, say by race and ethnicity, migration, skill level, educational attainment, or selective mortality.[10] It is often conjectured, for example, that differences between young and old arise because the young are much better educated. Controlling for education washes out the generation gulf. Such explanations no more reduce the age cleav-

[9] There is a growing and controversial literature in the area. See especially Karen Mason Oppenheim et al., "Some Methodological Issues in Cohort Analysis of Archival Data," *American Sociological Review*, 38 (April 1973), 242-58; Norval D. Glenn, "Cohort Analysts' Futile Quest: Statistical Attempts to Separate Age, Period and Cohort Effects," *American Sociological Review*, 41 (October 1976), 900-904. On the importance of using "side information" in interpreting results in cohort analysis, see Philip E. Converse, *The Dynamics of Party Support* (Beverly Hills, Calif.: Sage, 1976), Chapter 1.

[10] Although this explanation seems simple enough, the reality is more complicated. For example, there is the question of whether certain compositional factors, education being a prominent one, have the same equivalency of measurement over time. This is one of the drawbacks to standardization as a statistical way of checking for compositional effects.

age as such than do those which say that the young will become more like the old in due time. Clearly, we want to know whether the generational cleavage is temporary or permanent and whether it rests on a true difference in "communities of shared experiences" or has different bases. But in terms of some vital functions of the system the point is whether different generations are more alike or unalike, regardless of the reasons.

Although we will deal with subpopulations in subsequent chapters, we have taken into account at this stage the most obvious compositional difference between the two generations, viz., educational attainment. For most of the analysis to follow we have examined the results for those with high school diplomas, those with some college, and those with at least a college degree. There are some absolutely large attitudinal and behavioral differences across the three groups, not only in 1973 *after* most of the educational achievements, but in 1965 as well, *before* the achievements. We shall report on many of these differences and their movements across time in Chapter 8.

For the present, however, the central point is that the three educational subgroups tended to move in tandem between 1965 and 1973. Thus regardless of whether the drift was down, up, or stable, the direction of the drift tended to be very much the same for all three. This being the case, most of what we report below concerning the young generation (in terms of direction at least) is not a function of one subgroup performing at odds with another nor of wildly disproportionate contributions from the college educated. While not completely solving the composition problem by any means, these results do tell us that when we observe what appear to be either generational, life-cycle, or period effects, we can be reasonably sure that all three educational strata are sharing in these processes.

PSYCHOLOGICAL INVOLVEMENT IN POLITICS

At each point in time the respondents were asked to describe the idealized good citizen (see Chapter 2). One indicator of how salient politics is to the respondents is the frequency with which a political theme is expressed. Presumably, the more often an individual stresses the political qualities of the good citizen, the more salient politics is to that person and the greater the psychological involvement. By this standard the younger generation was more psychologically attuned to politics at both time points. Figure 5.2 shows the mean number of references to political qualities. Although the edge declined in 1973, the young were still the more inclined to see the good citizen in political

FIGURE 5.2: References to Political Qualities of Good Citizen

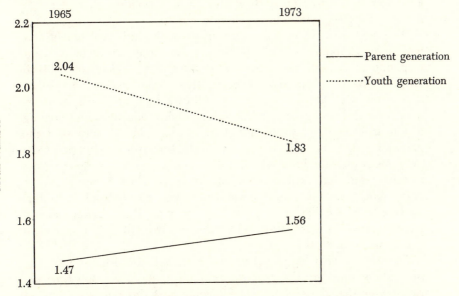

terms. Another way of demonstrating the prominence of political themes in a more standardized fashion is to compute the ratio of political references to nonpolitical references. For the young these ratios were 2.91 and 2.41 in 1965 and 1973, respectively; corresponding figures for the parents were 1.29 and 1.41. Clearly the young emphasized political aspects to a much greater extent than did the middle-aged. Thus the centrality of politics would seem to be greater.

At first glance one is inclined to see the persistence of these differences over time as a demonstration of the generational model. Yet two factors caution us against such an interpretation. In the first place, the differences narrow considerably, partly as a function of a small increment among the parents but more significantly as a result of a sizable decrement among the youth. If the young adult years witness the crystallization of political identity, then the differences should have been maintained or even strengthened. Second, as we noted in our report on the first wave, the gist of both formal and informal citizenship training in the pre-adult years is very much politically laden. The prescriptive norms involve the citizen in relation to the *political* community. As one enters the adult world, the difficulty of living up to these prescriptions becomes more obvious on the one hand, and the importance of other personal attributes for making life livable rises on the other. While it may well be that the younger cohort will continue to put more

stress on the political dimension than does its predecessor, the noticeable drop in the absolute and relative place of political characteristics
is fully of a piece with a life-cycle interpretation.

We now turn to several measures of psychological involvement that
were more explicitly political in terms of the stimulus presented to our
respondents. As will be demonstrated shortly, the *objects* of political
interest change substantially over relatively short periods of the life
cycle. But what about the *level* of political interest? It has been argued that the young generation—being highly educated and coming
of age in exceptionally politicized times—has already surpassed the
parental generation in its concern with the body politic. Judging from
previous adult data, however, overall political interest appears to grow
at a moderate rate well into the middle years. There is some controversy about whether it tails off among the very old.[11] If political interest rises with age, both the parent and young adult generations should
have changed to reasonably similar degrees over the eight-year span
covered by our study.

That this is what happened can be observed from Figure 5.3a. The
percentages indicate the proportion of respondents at each time period saying that they follow what is going on in government "most of
the time." In interpreting this result it is essential that we have been
able to draw upon previous data about life-cycle development, because the parallel lines of change could be interpreted as indicative
of period effects. Here we have an instance, however, in which life-
cycle effects do not occur solely among young adults, but continue
throughout most if not all of adult life. Thus a pattern that might reflect period effects is more likely to be a result of normal life-cycle
changes. While the young adults have nearly reached the level of interest expressed by their parents in 1965, we expect that they will surpass this level by the time they reach a comparable age because of
their greater education.

If it is true that the general salience of public affairs changes only
modestly but at the same rate for the two generations, the same is
clearly not true for the salience of particular arenas of politics. The relative emphasis placed on the various levels of international, national,
state, and local affairs has been conceptualized as representing one's
degree of cosmopolitanism or its mirror image, localism. Working with

---

[11] Recent work indicates that the widely perceived disengagement of older
people is in part an artifact of socioeconomic composition. See Norval D. Glenn,
"Aging, Disengagement, and Opinionation," *Public Opinion Quarterly*, 33 (Spring
1969), 17-33; Norval Glenn and Michael Grimes, "Aging, Voting, and Political
Interest," *American Sociological Review*, 33 (August 1969), 563-75; and Sidney
Verba and Norman Nie, *Participation in America* (New York: Harper and Row,
1972), Chapter 9.

the seven-point scale emerging from the rankings applied to these levels, it is apparent that both generations, but especially the filial one, became somewhat less cosmopolitan over time. With "7" standing for the most cosmopolitan position and "1" for the least, the mean youth scores declined from 5.24 to 4.88, while the parents had a smaller drop of 4.30 to 4.08. Due to the manner in which the scale is constructed, these comparative scores understate a critical shift among the youths.

A better grasp of the dynamics can be obtained by examining the rankings applied to the specific levels of international and local politics. Figure 5.3b shows the proportions selecting international affairs as the domain to which they pay most (first rank) attention. It is obvious that the salience of international politics has declined rather drastically among the young. Since there was only a slight movement among the older generation, we may rule out large-scale period effects.

Is there something peculiar about this generation which causes the precipitous drop, or is this restriction of scope a normal life-course development? A generational interpretation is suspect, because this young generation has been more exposed to international stimuli, including travel, than any previous one. Rather, the explanation probably lies in life-cycle change, as the press of other domains becomes the political reality with which adults must deal. Sitting in the high school classroom, the romance and intrigue of the international scene hold great attraction. But in the "adult world," there are more localized institutions, officials, and forms which must be dealt with; and news must be monitored which has more potential for personal consequence. The pattern displayed here also fits cross-sectional data from national surveys taken in 1966 and 1968. The sizeable dip thus seems to be very much a function of life-course development.[12]

If the young as high school seniors were heavily oriented to international affairs as their first loyalty, they were equally oriented to local affairs as their last (fourth rank) domain of interest. Figure 5.3c reveals that parents held steady, but their offspring showed a modest drop in placing local affairs as their least favored domain. As young adults begin to settle into a community and feel its impact on their lives, they begin a slow gravitation toward the local arena. That the gap between the young and old still persists, though narrowed, suggests that further penetration into the life cycle will be necessary before they achieve union with the parental generation.

[12] Data from 1966 are presented in M. Kent Jennings and Richard G. Niemi, *The Political Character of Adolescence* (Princeton: Princeton University Press, 1974). A period effect may have accelerated the movement in the young cohort, however. Disengagement from Vietnam and the rise of pressing domestic issues are secular forces which probably contributed disproportionately to the declining internationalism of the current young.

FIGURE 5.3: Interest in Public Affairs

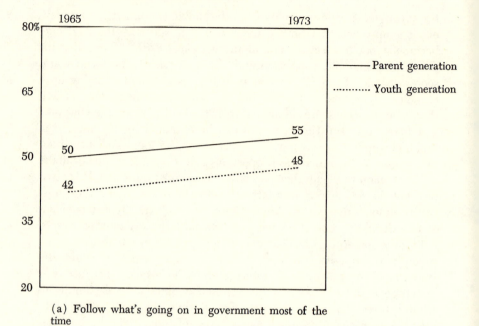

(a) Follow what's going on in government most of the time

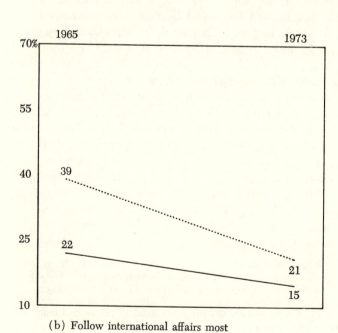

(b) Follow international affairs most

Figure 5.3 (cont.)

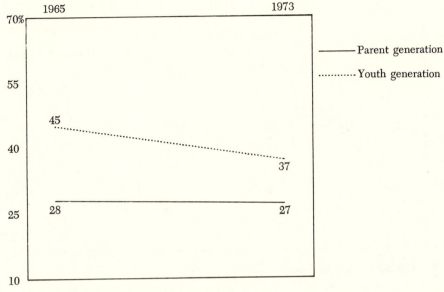

(c) Follow local affairs least

Now let us move to another set of rather general measures, this time assessing media behavior in regard to politics. Here the problem is complicated by long-term trends in media usage, as we shall see in a moment. First, judging solely from previous cross-sectional data, we would expect television viewing to rise considerably among the younger adults. In contrast, use of radio and magazines could be expected to increase little, if any. Expectations about newspaper reading are more complicated in that cohort analysis has shown that readership begins to increase around the age of twenty-five,[13] or almost the precise age of our young adults in 1973. This anticipated upsurge may not yet be visible among our respondents. Superimposed on these life-cycle expectations, however, are probable long-term changes in media usage. These seem to be working primarily in the direction of increasing reliance on television and decreasing reliance on radio and, to some extent, newspapers.

Data on usage of all four media are presented in Figure 5.4. As expected, television viewing rises dramatically in the filial generation. Altered patterns of daily time use and something as simple as having

[13] James Danowski and Neal E. Cutler, "Political Information, Mass Media Use in Early Adulthood, and Political Socialization: Seeking Clarity through Cohort Curves," in Paul M. Hirsch, Peter V. Miller, and F. Gerald Kline (eds.), *Strategies for Communication Research* (Beverly Hills: Sage, 1977).

FIGURE 5.4: Mass Media Usage to Follow Public Affairs

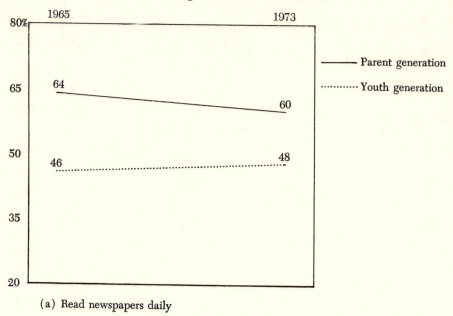

———— Parent generation

·············· Youth generation

(a) Read newspapers daily

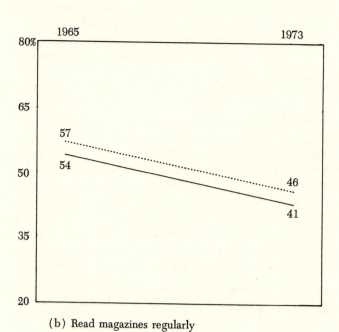

(b) Read magazines regularly

FIGURE 5.4 (cont.)

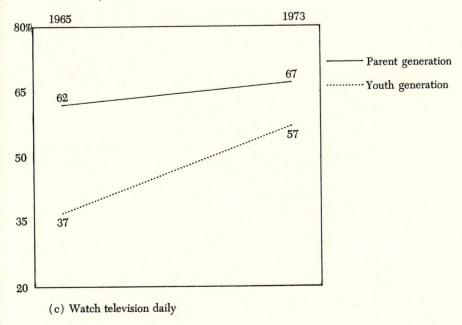

(c) Watch television daily

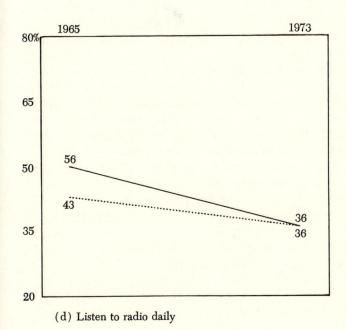

(d) Listen to radio daily

one's own television set are life-stage developments related to the
sharp gain for television watching. Hence the first generation raised
on television assumes its rightful place. Newspaper readership is almost constant over this eight-year period and remains well below
parental levels. Long-term trends are at work here since even within
the parental generation there is a modest movement away from newspaper readership and toward television viewing.

The declines in magazine reading and in radio listening are perhaps
as anticipated, but they suggest still further the increasing reliance
being placed on television. While magazine readership was quite high
among the seniors in 1965, there was still room for marginal advances
to achieve parental levels at that time (taking into account the greater
education of the young). But instead of gaining, the young adults decreased their use of magazines at a rate virtually identical with that of
the parents. The decrease in radio usage is perhaps less surprising, but
no less significant. Certainly the radio was no longer the primary
source of political news even by 1965, but the level of usage was still
quite high, perhaps due in large part to captured audiences such as
car drivers and to news coverage picked up as an incidental part of
entertainment listening. For whatever reason, however, it is clear that
minimum levels of radio usage for political news had not been reached
by 1965.

Overall, the rise in the use of television to keep informed about public affairs, coupled with a fall or no gain for other media, describe a
strong period effect. The continued lag in newspaper usage by the
younger generation also suggests a generation effect, and the increased
use of television a life-cycle effect.

The secular trends affecting media usage are also reflected in the
data describing main media relied upon for following public affairs.
Between 1965 and 1973 the reliance on magazines dropped from 19%
to 12% among the young and from 12% to 7% among parents. Small decreases also occurred with respect to radio. At the same time, television as the prime source of news rose from 46% to 52% among the youths
and from 43% to 53% among the middle-aged. The nearly identical
movement across the two generations illustrates the universality of the
deeper penetration of television as the key medium. In addition, the
small variations between the generations in terms of directional shifts
worked to bring them even closer together by 1973 than they had been
eight years earlier. The best example of this is in the reliance on newspapers. In 1965 the two generations were separated by nine percentage
points, with parents placing more emphasis than their offspring on the
papers (32% to 23%). By 1973, as a result of slight shifts in opposing
directions, only three percentage points separated the two; the paren-

tal figure was 30%, the youth figure 27%. Taking into account both the absolute and main reliance indicators of media usage shows that increasing convergence, rather than divergence, characterizes the generational pattern.

We argued in Chapter 2 that an even more acute indicator of psychological involvement than media consumption is the frequency of political discourse with family and friends. At the individual level we found that the stability of political conversation frequency within the family was substantially higher for parents than for young adults, though even among the latter there was clear evidence of continuity. Contributing in part to the lower stability among the young was the fact that the referent changed from members of their family of orientation in 1965 to their spouses in 1973, whereas spouses remained as the constant referent for the parent respondents. We concluded that it was this change in life stage that prompted lower stability of politically oriented talk.

If we turn to the aggregate picture, it is clear that this life-stage change resulted in a strong unidirectional shift. While in 1965 over four-fifths of the young reported frequent conversation with other family members, in 1973 only slightly over half reported such conversations with their spouses. What is especially impressive here is that the filial figure is virtually identical with that of the parental generation, and that the latter changed not a whit across the eight years. Nor is the 1973 parallelism between the generations a demonstrable artifact of differential marriage rates among the young according to prior levels of psychological involvement. There is no relationship between conversation frequency as of 1965 and whether one was married by 1973.

According to the configuration of Figure 5.5, a life-cycle model would seem to fit the data exceedingly well. But is it reasonable to equate talking with members of one's family at one point in time with talking with one's spouse at another point in time? In an absolute sense, the answer is no. Not only are there more members in a family than one, but the relationship between spouses is different from that between adolescents and their parents or sibs. From another perspective, though, there is a functional equivalence between the two sets of talking partners. At each time point the referent is the respondent's most immediate family, the family that one is closest to. (Given the ages of our young adults, none of them had children old enough for very serious political conversations.) If political discourse within the available family is the yardstick, the sharp drop depicted in Figure 5.5 is a real one. Even leaving that point aside would do nothing to erase the fact that by their mid-twenties, and very early in their marriages, the young

Figure 5.5: Political Conversations in the Family[a]

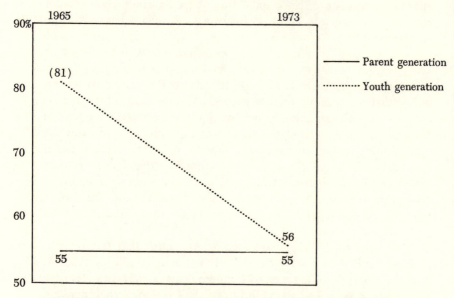

[a] For parents the referent in each year is the respondent's spouse; for youths the referent is family members in 1965 and spouse in 1973.

adults had reached a level of discourse on a par with that of their elders. It seems likely, especially in view of the great stability shown by the parents, that this plateau will remain in place for some time.

On balance, young adulthood is a time of considerable fluctuation with respect to psychological involvement in politics. The substantial shifting among the young suggests that the residues of earlier socialization are far from impervious to either life-cycle or, less likely in this case, generational impacts. By the same token, the middle years are a period of relative stability, although in an absolute sense a great number of parents exhibited variability also.

POLITICAL RESOURCES

At the individual level we found the persistence of political resources to vary all the way from modest proportions in the relatively soft domain of participatory norms to very strong ones in the domain of hard, political facts. Similarly, we will find at the aggregate level instances approaching high continuity among one or both generations, as well as examples of rather sharp discontinuity. Again, we will discuss four types of political resources: sense of citizen duty, political efficacy, conceptual sophistication, and political knowledge.

It will be recalled that there were two political themes prevalent in the portrayal of the good citizen, one called allegiant and the other participant. We were struck by the degree to which the high school seniors of 1965 emphasized the participant mode, what we called in Chapter 2 the sense of citizen duty or civic obligation. Ordinarily one would feel that people stressing this mode over the allegiant mode as a prescriptive norm would be more predisposed to take an active part in politics. Previously we speculated that the young would de-emphasize the active mode as they moved into young adulthood simply because of the realization that the idealized, active citizen was a difficult model to live up to on a day-to-day basis.[14]

In absolute terms we were correct. As Figure 5.6 reveals, the proportion referring to active roles declined modestly, as it did in the parental generation also. Nevertheless, the young remained well ahead

FIGURE 5.6: References to Active Political Qualities of Good Citizen

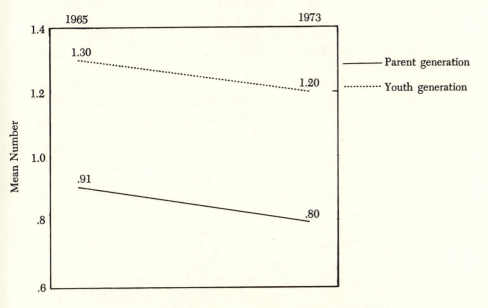

in this emphasis. It is certainly possible to interpret these figures as life-cycle rather than generational by conceiving of the two generations as "rolling cohorts." That is, since the parents had aged by eight years and since the young had also, we in effect have four different age groups. The monotonically decreasing entries for the participant

[14] Jennings and Niemi, *Political Character of Adolescence*, Chapter 10.

mode (1.3, 1.2, .91, and .80) could be seen as a life-stage development analogous to the development noted in political interest.[15]

Another piece of evidence steers us away from such a perspective. We had fully expected the allegiant responses to rise among the young, as an offset against the anticipated fall in civic duty emphasis. Yet this did not happen. Quite to the contrary, there was a slight fall from .73 to .62. Moreover, there was a visible rise in allegiant descriptions among the older generation, the mean numbers being .54 and .74. The upshot of the cross-cutting movement is that an initial youth advantage was transformed into a parental one. How are we to account for this reversal? The answer would seem to lie very much in the experiencing of and reactions to the various protest movements and turbulence of the period. The parental reaction was in part to see these events as a rejection of the system, with the recommended antidote being a call for more loyalty and obedience to law, i.e., basically a law-and-order response. Hence the parents actually began to lay heavier stress on allegiant behaviors. By contrast, the youths apparently saw the perils of allegiance, especially of a blind sort. As other portions of the 1973 interviews reveal, they were both much more active in the protest movements and more sympathetic with those who were. What we are proposing, then, is a rather complicated generational impact statement.

With one additional operation we can indicate the relative place of the participant role within the two generations. Ratios showing the occurrence of participant to allegiant references were calculated. For the young the ratio was 1.78 in 1965, but rose to 1.94 in 1973. To the extent that a feeling of civic obligation is a political resource, the youth sample gained in resources over time. Among parents, the ratio was 1.69 in 1965, dropping to 1.08 in 1973. In this respect the two generations drew much farther apart over the eight years. One could imagine a life-cycle explanation for these trends such that the young would shift back toward lesser participant emphasis later on or that the middle-aged would later re-emphasize the participant mode, but the generational argument is much more compelling.

The second resource to be examined—"internal" political efficacy— is a complicated measure to analyze because there are tremendous educational differences which affect comparisons between the parent and young adult generations. As high school seniors in 1965, the young

[15] We are not unmindful that similar configurations in other portions of our analysis could also be interpreted in this fashion from a strictly statistical standpoint, the lacunae between age 26 (youth in 1973) and around 40-45 (youngest parents in 1965) notwithstanding. This is why interpretations must not only be advanced with caution but must be heavily influenced by side information, past research, and theoretical guidelines.

people gave more efficacious responses than their parents by a fairly wide margin, but when we looked at parents with at least a high school education this difference evaporated almost completely. From this, as well as from cross-sectional election study data, we concluded that few life-cycle changes should be expected apart from perhaps a small decline among well-educated, older adults.

These considerations are important in enabling us to interpret the results for internal efficacy. Figure 5.7 shows the mean scores on the two-item index. These results represent a combination of period ef-

FIGURE 5.7: Internal Political Efficacy

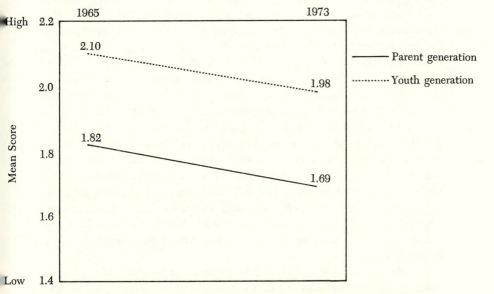

fects and generational differences caused by the greater education of the young adults. The same events over the past decade that led to a decline in political trust seem to have led both generations to lose a degree of political efficacy which they would probably not otherwise have lost. The decline in efficacy, however, is very slight, and bears little resemblance to the precipitous drop we will observe for political trust. Nonetheless, members of both generations felt a shade less able to understand and influence the government than they had previously. Importantly, this conclusion extends to the item stating that voting is the only way in which an individual can affect what goes on in government. One might have thought that the demonstrations in the 1960s, particularly with regard to civil rights and the Vietnam War, would have led Americans to enlarge their view of the possible ways

of influencing government. Instead, both generations were more willing to agree with the "voting only way" stimulus in 1973. Given the
decline common to both generations, the filial cohort remained the
more efficacious over time.

A somewhat different perspective is offered by the responses to two
other questions which were put to parents at both time points but to
young adults only in 1973. The questions asked whether people "like
me" have any say in the government and whether public officials
"don't care" about what people "like me" think. These two questions
are often cited as denoting external efficacy in that they center on aspects of the political structure. In each instance, the efficacy of the
parents declined about 10%, or slightly more than for internal efficacy.

The generational differences in 1973, however, are much smaller
than was true for internal efficacy, being 7% and 3%. Not only that, but
the generational advantage has altered so that the parents have higher
scores on external efficacy than do their offspring. Despite what we
took to be an advantage in internal efficacy among the young due to
their extended education, that same educational superiority does not
render them more externally efficacious. If one assumes, though, that
the young were more susceptible to cues and trends at work in the political environment—and if one concludes that these cues and trends
were in the direction of discouraging a sense of external efficacy—then
the disadvantage of the young becomes explicable. Whereas their
higher educational levels would help them retain a stronger sense of
self in coping with the political world, that same educational advantage (and what it entails) might well lead them to be more doubtful
about how responsive the political system would be to them during a
period of struggle.

Our third indicator of political resources is a measure of capturing
the respondents' political sophistication about the ideological nature
of the party system. A capacity for abstraction is generally viewed as
a desirable trait. Indeed, much of the recent discussion about the
place of ideology in American politics has revolved around the public's ability to use ideological yardsticks in general and to connect the
parties with policy positions in particular.

Unlike partisanship, knowledge of presumed party differences is not
widespread among children.[16] And while such knowledge grows rapidly during the high school years, high school graduates are still less
knowledgeable than their parents. We would expect youths' compre-

[16] Fred I. Greenstein, *Children and Politics* (New Haven: Yale University Press,
1965), Chapter 4; and Jack Dennis, *Political Learning in Childhood and Adolescence* (Madison: University of Wisconsin Research and Development Center for
Cognitive Learning, 1969), Chapter 2.

hension to expand somewhat in the early years of adulthood. In contrast, parental views would change very little on the basis of life-cycle developments. However, images of the parties have certainly changed over the past decade, and it is possible that some aggregate adult movement would also be observed in the 1965 to 1973 period.[17]

Based on replies to several questions about party differences, more change occurred among the young than among their elders. For example, the proportion of those believing that there are important differences in what the parties stand for rose from 37% to 47% among the young versus a stable figure of 38% among the middle-aged. By the same token, those professing that one party is more conservative or liberal than the other climbed from 60% to 73% among the young compared with 67% to 74% among their parents. Considering only those saying that one party was more conservative than the other, the percentage of the young citing the Republicans rose from 74% to 83% compared with 82% to 84% among their parents. On all counts, then, the net alteration was sharper among the young and moved them from a position of being less knowledgeable than the parental generation in 1965 to one of being, if anything, more knowledgeable by 1973.

As in Chapter 2 we combined answers to these and other questions to locate respondents along a five-point continuum calibrating their recognition and understanding of the liberal-conservative dimension. The distributions and mean scores for each generation at each point in time are presented in Figure 5.8. (Table 2.7 contains a short description for each category in the measure.)

Turning first to the filial generation, it is apparent that a substantial jump occurred in their levels of conceptualization. Decreases in the two lowest categories were almost perfectly matched by increases in the two highest. That the gain was as high in the fifth as in the fourth category is crucial because the former contains references of a more abstract and general nature, explanations that are sometimes referred to as being in the domain of broad philosophy. The increasing ability to distinguish between the parties in terms of such overarching concepts is a sign that the upcoming generation has a sizeable segment that can deal with the parties and their activities in at least a quasi-ideological fashion.

Aggregate shifts among the parents were but a dim reflection of those among the young. True, the mean score shifted upward, but on a much lower scale. Significantly, the gain in the highest category was only 2%, compared with 11% among the young adults. On balance, the

[17] Trend analysis dealing with related (but still distinct) measures of ideological sophistication shows an increase occurring by 1968. Nie, Verba, and Petrocik, *Changing American Voter*, Chapter 7.

FIGURE 5.8: Recognition and Understanding of Liberal-Conservative Dimension

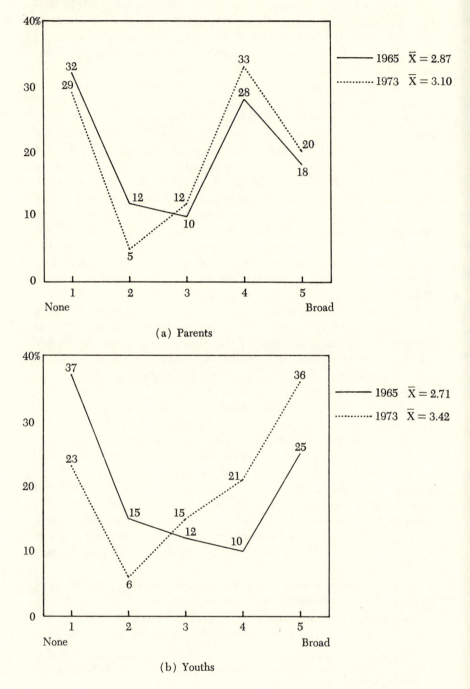

(a) Parents

(b) Youths

parents' view of the party world was scarcely more ideologically struc-
tured in 1973, after a series of bitter interparty fights, than it was in
1965.

As a result of the different trends at work among the two generations, their positions relative to each other underwent a reversal over
the years. The mean scores provide the easiest method of comparison.
In the earlier period the parents held an edge, modest to be sure.[18]
But the sharp increase among the young, coupled with the much
smaller one among the middle-aged, produced a fairly substantial advantage for the new generation by 1973. A close inspection of the two
graphs reveals that the basis for the 1973 advantage rests very much
in the juxtaposition of categories 4 and 5, i.e., narrow versus broader
definitions used in describing the liberal/conservative differences between the parties. Even in 1965 the young were more likely to employ
the broader term and the parents the narrower term. Nor was this
strictly a matter of a higher level of average education among the
young. As we shall see subsequently, however, the culture associated
with higher educational aspirations and achievements does promote
more usage of the ideologically sophisticated terminology.

More so than with other measures we have used, it is unclear to
what extent true generational effects account for the patterns observed.
The significance of our results seems to be the speed with which
young adults learned the classical view of political party differences.
However, it is difficult to say how much this was due to the particular
circumstances of the late 1960s and early 1970s. That the young not
only caught up with but also surpassed their elders suggests the operation of both life-cycle and generational processes. The complexities
of information acquisition deserve more attention, and we now turn
to another aspect of that topic.

While perhaps not as crucial as goals, values, and attitudes, an
awareness of current and past political history and a comprehension
of the machinery of government undoubtedly make for a difference in
individual political behavior. Although the six factual questions posed
to our panel respondents by no means exhaust all types of factual information, the workings of a variety of dynamic processes can be seen
in the differential response patterns.

In the aggregate parents are unlikely to have changed differentially
across the types of questions that we used. They should have about the
same retention levels for significant historical phenomena that occurred

[18] Distributions for the parents are quite similar to those for a representative
sample of adults in the late 1950s. Philip E. Converse, "The Nature of Belief
Systems in Mass Publics," in David Apter (ed.), Ideology and Discontent (New
York: Free Press, 1964), 219-27.

during their lifetimes as they do for facts and figures about governmental machinery gleaned either from textbooks or political experience. Surely the older generation would have increased its knowledge of individuals and events primarily of recent significance (such as Vietnam), but on the questions we asked very little net change ought to be observed.

In contrast, young people ought to show a definite decline in one area, namely, the technical operations of government. Eight years after high school graduation fewer of the young adults are likely to answer questions on this topic correctly, just as they have probably forgotten specific names, dates, and places from their history books. Less clear-cut is what is likely to take place in the younger generation's knowledge of major historical events of the recent past. Young people obviously cannot relive these events, so that we would rarely expect dramatic increases in their knowledge of them. They may, however, come to know more about such events as they enter the adult environment where much of the population assumes that one knows about such things, and where considerable political interaction presupposes knowledge of the forces shaping the contemporary world. Thus youthful awareness of recent historical events and personalities should rise, though not very steeply.

The data for the six questions are rich in their variety and rewarding in the extent to which they fit these theoretical expectations. As can be seen in Figure 5.9, parents were remarkably stable on every question. A saturation point seems to be reached by the middle years. Over this eight-year span the greatest change in parental response was a 3% gain in the number who were able to indicate correctly the number of Supreme Court justices. Given the amount of attention devoted to the Supreme Court during this period, this very meager climb strongly suggests that older adults' knowledge of many features of governmental structure and processes is firmly fixed.

In contrast to the stability of parental responses is the movement in both directions observed in the young adults' answers. As expected, the declines come in their knowledge of governmental structure. We would expect some further decline in the percentage able to answer these questions in the future. The percentage will probably remain higher than for the parents, however, because of the youths' higher education level.

Most interesting to us are the increases in young people's knowledge of historical events and current personalities. Two features are important—that there is an increase, and that the rise is no greater than it is. Nearly three in ten youths are still ignorant of the partisan era in which their parents matured. Despite the small gain registered, there

FIGURE 5.9: Knowledge of Political Facts

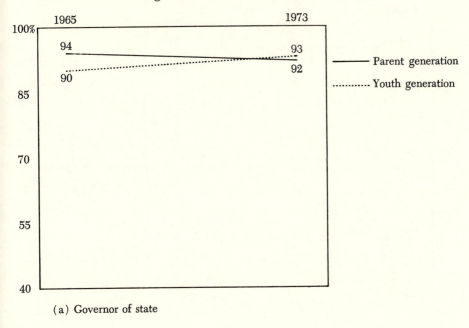

(a) Governor of state

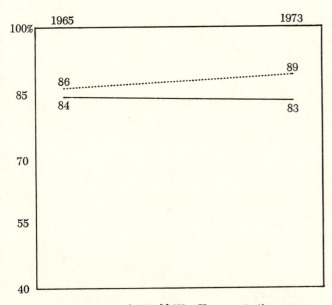

(b) Country with World War II concentration camps

FIGURE 5.9 (cont.)

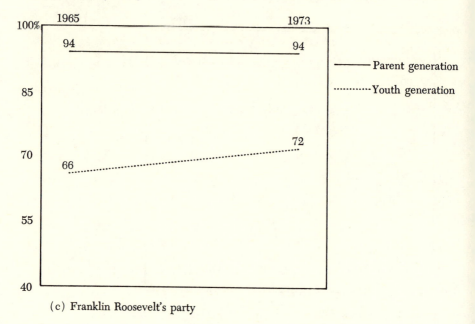

(c) Franklin Roosevelt's party

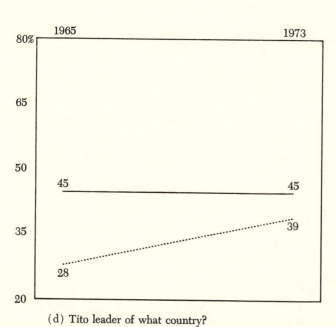

(d) Tito leader of what country?

FIGURE 5.9 (cont.)

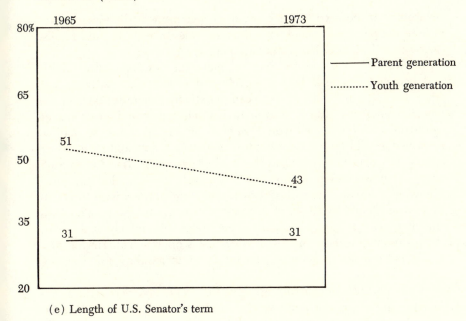

(e) Length of U.S. Senator's term

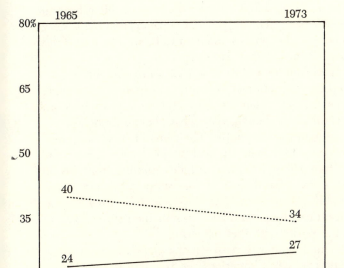

(f) Number of Supreme Court Justices

continued to be a true and substantial generational difference. Only where the personality is of contemporary relevance (Tito) did familiarity grow by more than five to six percent.

Returning to a theoretical point of view, the development of political knowledge reveals both life-cycle and generational patterns, but they are patterns from which we can tentatively generalize beyond the specific questions asked. Information about forms and processes of governmental operations would seem to be among the most shallow knowledge held by the new adult. Command of facts and figures may rise slowly over generations as the level of education rises; but in each generation we can probably witness a cycle of expanded technical knowledge toward the end of formal schooling coupled with the trailing off of the ability to recall this information as one leaves school. In the aggregate this drop probably occurs relatively quickly at first and then slowly as a more or less steady state is approached. Here a life-cycle pattern seems most significant in understanding the learning process.

A sharply different picture emerges for events and personalities occurring in the present and recent past. Because of their recent entry into the adult world of politics and increasing exposure to politically relevant media content, the rising generation improves on its awareness. On the other hand, the parental generation has reached a near-saturation point: those who will learn have learned, as the results at the individual level suggest. Set off against these life-cycle effects are generational effects, as exemplified by the difference in identification of Franklin Roosevelt's party. This type of discrepancy, and the variety of images, experiences, and emotions attached to it, are likely to stand as a permanent part of the political landscape.

The upshot of these different thrusts is that scores on the overall information index—i.e., the number of correct responses to the six questions—remained virtually identical across the eight years for both generations. It is significant, though, that what change there was resulted in a small net gain for the youths. Their loss in "book-learning" was compensated for by their gain in "real-world" learning, with the mean score rising from 3.61 to 3.69. On an index running from 0 to 6, this is a very small shift. Nevertheless, it does support the suggestion that information holding is responsive to life-cycle as well as generational forces. By contrast, the parental scores remained stable, 3.73 to 3.72, keeping them at parity with their offspring.

Additionally, the high similarity between the generations on information holding versus the clear superiority of the filial generation on conceptual sophistication underscores the differential basis of these two cognitive orientations to politics. The latter is more dependent on higher levels of education and exposure to the world of abstractions, whereas political information is more a matter of meeting a threshold of education and of paying attention to politics. There is, in all probability, an enduring generational gap on the sophistication measure and an equally enduring generational continuity on the information measure.

POLITICAL PARTICIPATION

As in the case of our individual-level analysis, it would be desirable at this point to move directly from resources to political participation. Inasmuch as the young were not eligible to vote at the time of the 1965 study and were otherwise discouraged from entering the full array of political activity, we did not ask them specific questions about participation in the larger political realm. Over-time comparisons for the parents are likewise limited because they were asked a series of questions that summed up their previous ten years' worth of political action—due to our interest in parents as agents of socialization. We can, however, pick up the threads of voting participation beginning in 1968 (1964 for parents) on the basis of retrospective questions. We can also present some preliminary evidence about participation throughout the eight-year period that will enable us to determine whether the tendency toward convergence in psychological involvement and political resources is also present for political participation.

Turning first to voting turnout, we find strong evidence for convergence based on life-cycle effects. The pattern of initial low turnout rates, which then grow rapidly and level off, has been observed so frequently that it would be surprising were it not found in our panels. As Figure 5.10 shows, parental turnout—the figures for which are inflated due to the middle-aged character of the sample—is high and relatively steady for all four elections. The reduced turnout in 1972 compared to 1968 is consistent with the lower national balloting in the later year.

In contrast, the younger generation began its voting history with a turnout markedly below that for the elder generation. This is so even though the youth sample includes the better educated three-fourths of the total cohort (i.e., high school graduates). Predictably, turnout decreased in the off-year election, but in an exaggerated fashion. Finally, in 1972, while the nation's overall turnout was dropping from its 1968 level, voting in the young cohort rose by 11%, reflecting a development of the voting habit. By 1972 the large 1968 difference between the two generations had been sharply reduced. In its voting record this young generation registers the same slow start and rapid growth that has been

FIGURE 5.10: Voting Turnout

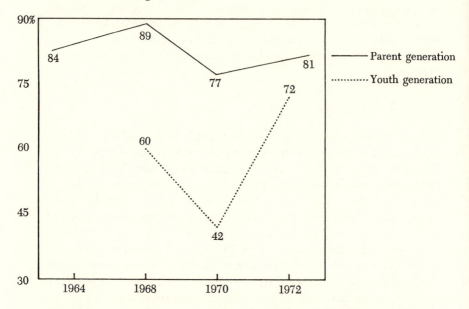

observed almost universally in the past. Life-cycle effects are clearly at work in this process, as they are in the much less volatile performance of the senior generation.

Is this tendency toward convergence as evident if we move to other, usually more demanding, political acts? In the sense that the levels of our young adults, qua high school seniors, could only rise in the interim there would have to be some convergence. But how much is more problematic. In Chapter 2 we described a thirteen-point political activity index constructed from responses to questions covering a wide range of behaviors over the seven to eight years preceding 1973. We use that index here to take a brief glance at the question of convergence between the generations.[19]

If voting is included in the activity index, the parents hold an edge over the young of 4.7 to 4.1 in mean scores. This is what one might very well expect based on the usual assumptions about participation increasing to a high around middle age. Based on this combined index, and assuming the young started from a base approaching 0 in 1965 (though the young do engage in such activities as wearing buttons), this would fit a model of life-cycle effects drawing the generations together.

[19] The following borrows from work done in collaboration with Paul Allen Beck. See Beck and Jennings, "Political Periods and Political Participation," *American Political Science Review,* 73 (September 1979), 737-50.

Removing the voting component reveals a rather different picture. As would be expected from the figures presented on turnout, the over-all voting mean for the four elections is higher for parents than for youths, 2.97 to 2.04. It almost necessarily follows, then, that the non-voting activity levels are actually *higher* among the young than among their parents. That is precisely the case, the means being 1.7 for par-ents versus 2.1 for young adults. Clearly, a big component of the youth score is life-cycle in nature. Opportunity and motivation rise once the age of majority is reached. But should the surge in activity actually surpass that of their seasoned elders?

The full answer to that question cannot be attempted here, but two or three observations are in order. First, the youth margin is not sim-ply a consequence of exceptionally high performance on unconven-tional activities outside the electoral domain. Figure 5.11 shows the proportions of each sample that had engaged in (at least once) the nine activities listed. Certainly the young had more often taken part in protest activities, as would be expected of this particular cohort. Yet they also had slight to moderate leads in trying to influence others

FIGURE 5.11: Performance of Specific Political Activities

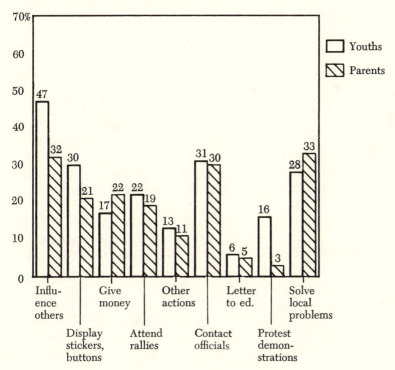

how to vote, attending rallies, wearing buttons and using campaign stickers, other campaign activities, and contacting public officials. Parents led only in donating money and community problem-solving. Thus the young were about as likely or more so to engage in so-called traditional political action. Far from being a generation that eschewed conventional means of exercising influence, the class of 1965 almost reveled in it, if the participation levels of their parents are taken as a criterion.

Second, although the performance of these various activities almost inevitably accompanies entry into young adulthood, the presence of generational effects seems likely in the rapidity with which this cohort reached levels equaling or going beyond those of the parental generation. It requires no elaborate rendering of the political history between 1965 and 1973 to assert that it was a period in which the opportunities for participation were highly conducive to youthful action. Many of the issues about which the political tempest raged directly involved the fate of the young—the Vietnam War, the draft associated with it, the later stages of the civil rights movement, student power on he campuses, and the new morality in public and private life. Various political and cultural leaders attracted and sometimes symbolized the attitudes and preferences of the dissident young, the most obvious figures being representatives of the "left," though the right was not without its heroes also. By all odds, the times were especially propitious for excessively quick and intense politicization of the emerging generation.

A third point to make is that here, as is sometimes true at other places in our analysis, the differential educational profiles of the two generations complicate any easy interpretation of a life-cycle or generational sort. On the one hand, it is true that education was moderately to strongly related to participation in each generation, and since the young have more of the better-educated, their overall level of participation was given a significant boost (see Chapter 8). So part of the presumed generational effect is, indeed, most likely compositional in nature.

But that is not quite the full story. As noted elsewhere, "Education probably functioned in two ways to enhance the participation of the young. First, it provided many of the young with 'tools' for participation—confidence, verbal abilities, etc.—that many of their parents did not possess. Second, it also provided the young with much greater opportunities for participation because a great deal of the political activity of the period was centered on college campuses. Since the college-educated among the youth sample were on campuses during this period, education here may merely be a surrogate for exposure to opportunities. It seems likely also that the distinctive participation style of the young owes substantially to their college environment—an environment which directly affected virtually no parents."[20] This exposure to opportunities and the milieu in which it was embedded constitutes a genuine generational effect because it embodies a community of shared experiences. Simply controlling for education attainment across two lineage generations will not make the environments and the experiential histories equivalent.

In this chapter we have surveyed a range of political traits lying primarily in the cognitive and behavioral domains. When laid against the sometimes hyperbolic portrayals of the generation gap provided by the media and some scholars, our findings seem to demonstrate considerable intergenerational convergence or relatively constant divergence. There were exceptions, to be sure, but the prevailing pattern did not support the picture of an ever-widening gulf between the generations. Much of the hoopla surrounding conflict between the generations, however, centers on attitudes, values, and goals, on questions of affect and evaluation. In the next chapter we examine our generations with respect to these dimensions, in the expectation that the configurations emerging will form an overall pattern different from that observed for involvement and resources.

[20] Paul Allen Beck and M. Kent Jennings, "Generations, Time, and Political Participation," unpublished paper, 1977, 31.

CHAPTER SIX

Continuity and Change at the Aggregate Level: Political Preferences and Attitudes

FOR a variety of reasons the 1965-1973 period witnessed a number of clashes between representatives of the younger and older cohorts. These years abounded in contrasting definitions of the political order, opinions on issues of the day, and perceptions about how and by whom policy should be made. Some of the differences involved new items on the public agenda, others had a longer history. Thus materials dealing with such topics as partisanship and voting, a variety of public issues, and evaluations of actors in the governmental process are available for over-time analysis, and will be dealt with in this chapter. Many of the events and personalities that engaged the American public occurred after our initial data gathering in 1965, so we cannot track preferences and attitudes associated with them. It will be possible, though, to take stock of the generational differences on key issues as of 1973 and, more significantly, to lay the real against the imagined generation gap. This chapter will also offer illustrations of continuity and change outside the political realm, so that comparisons can be made between political and nonpolitical configurations.

PARTISANSHIP AND ELECTORAL BEHAVIOR

Virtually all previous work on partisanship leads to one clear expectation about the eight-year period of the panel. Aggregate partisan distributions among the parents should change very little if at all. Even in unsettled times, such as realigning periods, it is the young who are peculiarly susceptible to the currents of partisan sentiment flowing in one direction or the other. Parents, having had many years in which to develop and nurture a partisan attachment, should be highly resistant to short-term ebbs and tides in party fortunes. That this is true is borne out nicely by the data in Figure 6.1a, which shows the entire partisan distribution for parents in both years. The fact that the proportion of strong partisans declined by 4% may slightly contradict the life-cycle processes that have been evident in earlier years. But the great similarity of the overall distributions in the two years wholeheartedly supports the view that partisanship among middle-aged adults is stable in the aggregate.

Figure 6.1: Party Identification[a]

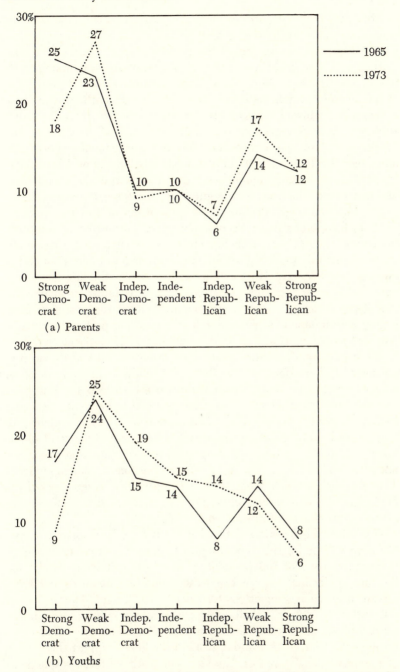

(a) Parents

(b) Youths

[a] These figures exclude the mailback respondents of 1973, thus accounting for slight discrepancies with the results reported in M. Kent Jennings and Richard G. Niemi, "Continuity and Change in Political Orientations," *American Political Science Review*, 69 (December 1975), at p. 1324.

More change in partisanship should be apparent among the younger generation, but exactly what changes should be expected are not altogether clear. On the one hand, the generation is maturing at a time marked by a significant rise in the proportion of adults claiming to be free of allegiance to either of the major parties. Thus the proportion of Independents might be expected to rise above what it was in 1965.

Working against this possibility are two factors. First, these young adults are several years into the adult life cycle. All have been able to vote in at least one congressional and one presidential election, and many have been able to vote in two presidential elections. Past studies indicate that partisan feelings begin to jell fairly quickly after the individual enters the active electorate.[1] If this force is operative, we would expect a slight decline in the proportion of Independents already to have taken place. Second, compared with other orientations, the transmission of party attachments across generations is carried out quite successfully except, possibly, in realignment periods. Though the question has been raised repeatedly as to whether the late 1960s and early 1970s constitute such a period, opinion is far from unanimous that it does. Hence it would not be surprising if the offspring, after flirting with independence while in high school and perhaps in college, returned to the partisanship of their parents in fairly large numbers.

These two countervailing tendencies should at least keep the proportion of Independents among the young adults from rising much, if indeed it rises at all. With these thoughts as a backdrop, the change in the partisan distribution of the filial generation between 1965 and 1973 is startling (Figure 6.1b). The proportion of Independents, already very high in 1965, rose another 11%, reaching almost half of the sample. At the same time, the proportion of strong identifiers was cut nearly in half. Such an increase in the proportion of Independents at a time in the life cycle when we would ordinarily have expected the beginning of a long-term decline, provides a compelling argument for a generation effects interpretation.

This raises the question as to what the future development of partisanship will be for this generation. Although there may be a decline in the proportion of Independents in the future, it seems likely that the rate of decline will not bring the proportion down to levels observed in previous generations for some years, if ever. The decline of political trust which we shall observe later, along with negative implications about parties and the party system generated by disclosures through the Watergate scandal, would very likely support this feeling of independence. Moreover, the fact that many of these respondents

[1] Philip E. Converse, "Of Time and Partisan Stability," *Comparative Political Studies*, 2 (July 1969), 139-71.

have felt a degree of independence from parties for several years is also likely to make them more resistant to future changes. On the other hand, sustained psychological attachment to the nonentity of "independence" seems intuitively more difficult than attachment to the entity of a political party.[2]

Generation effects also emerge when considering voting behavior. Of equal or greater importance, however, are the short-term period effects. Looking at the reported vote in the presidential elections of 1964, 1968, and 1972 and the congressional elections of 1970 and 1972 demonstrates these effects very nicely (Figure 6.2). While the younger

FIGURE 6.2: Republican Voting in Five Elections

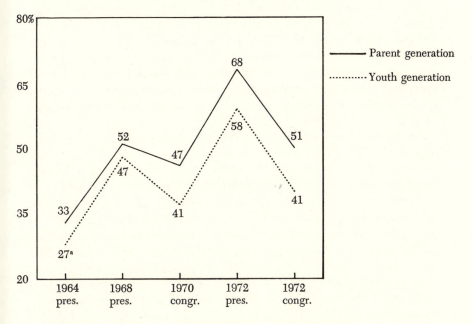

[a] Because youths were ineligible to vote in 1964, this percentage indicates those preferring the Republican candidate.

generation consistently voted more Democratic by a small margin, the movement from one year to another followed very much the same pattern in both generations. Thus both generations manifest signs of the Goldwater debacle in 1964, Nixon's hairline victory in 1968, the tradi-

[2] Implications for the party system of a sharply decreasing partisanship in the population are discussed in Paul Allen Beck, "A Socialization Theory of Partisan Realignment," in Richard G. Niemi and Herbert F. Weisberg (eds.), Controversies in American Voting Behavior (San Francisco: W. H. Freeman, 1976).

tional "decline" of the presidential party in the off-year election, the spectacular "surge" represented by Nixon's landslide of 1972, and the general GOP weakness shown by the accompanying congressional vote. These parallel movements occurred despite intense Democratic attempts to woo the young in 1972 and despite the much greater proportion of Independents among the young adults. Especially given the differential composition of the two generations, Figure 6.2 appears to be a good example of a hybrid generation-period effects model.

What is perhaps most surprising about these results is the proximity of the two generations. Images of a vast generational gulf in the electoral arena simply dissolve in the face of these figures. Nevertheless, the consistently lower affinity of the young for Republican candidates bodes no succor for the minority party, especially because there is evidence that the crack between the generations is widening. Beginning in 1968—the first year for which there is an actual vote report among the youths—the distance between the two generations begins to grow. It is an infinitesimal growth, to be sure, and is smaller than the difference that sampling error alone could produce. At the very least, however, the widening difference does nothing to undermine the argument of emergent generational effects.

An historical footnote of more than incidental interest lies in the appeal of the Wallace candidacy in 1968. Much to the surprise of those inclined to equate youth with liberalism, Wallace did disproportionately well among voters under 30 years of age. Recalled voting behavior and preferences elicited from our respondents are very much of a piece with the evidence from cross-sectional studies of the American electorate. Indeed, in some respects they are even more persuasive. In the youth sample the Wallace proportion of the three-party vote was 12%, as compared with 10% in the parental sample. Adding to these figures the expressed preferences of those not voting raises the youth figure to 14% while the parent figure remains at 10%. What is impressive about these figures is that the young respondents were all at least high school graduates in 1968, with a large proportion attending college at the time. Their mean level of education was already well above that of their parents. Clearly there was a sizeable pocket of young adults not yet inured to the call of appeals outside the two-party system and not yet "conditioned" to remain with one of the two parties. That the Wallace candidacy could have held more attraction for the younger than the middle-aged cohort testifies loudly to life-cycle effects.

OPINIONS ON PUBLIC POLICY ISSUES

Much of the work on age and generational conflict has centered on the question of diversity of views on issues of the day. It is not unusual to see age breaks in popular polls which reflect sizeable differences between young and old. Divisions of opinion on material, economic matters have traditionally been based much more on divisions of social class than of age. But claims to prestige and recognition, differences of views on life styles, competing moral structures, conflicts over means to achieve ends, as well as polarization over basic changes in the political order often have an age-based component.[3]

We draw on judgments made about four issues in comparing our two generations over time. The resulting patterns illustrate very nicely the diverse nature of issue continuity and change. Emerging as a classic example of generational cleavage is the subject of prayers in the public schools. Despite what seemed to be court rulings unfavorable to the use of prayers, this negative position is agreed to by only a minority within each generation at both points in time (Figure 6.3a). More interesting from our point of view, there has been scarcely any change in either generation, with the younger group maintaining its moderate edge over the older. Given this continuing difference, it seems best to interpret the result as generationally inspired. The older generation was socialized in a time when religious interests were clearly more prominent than they are now and before the courts had drawn yet sharper lines on the separation of church and state. Only a marked dip later on in life would bring the junior generation into accord with the older.

Another issue involving religion and the state yields a similar pattern of movement, although the opinions expressed are considerably different from those on the prayers in school question. Figure 6.3b demonstrates that support for allowing speeches against churches and religion has remained very high among both generations. And the visible gap between the two generations remains, suggesting again a more or less permanent schism. Beyond that, there is evidence of a growing division. The increasing secularization of society and perhaps the residues of the free speech movement have pushed the younger generation almost to a point of unanimity on this issue.

Although prayers in school is a continuing issue which occasionally blazes into life, the third issue at hand is one which has burned with a sustained flame over the eight-year period. To say that the federal government's role in integrating the schools has been a matter of dispute and one which has seen some shifting of sides is to state the obvious. During the mid-1960s, at what may well have been the height of the civil rights movement, opinion among our respondents was very much on the side of a positive federal role in integration. Consistent with the

[3] On the point see Anne Foner, "The Polity," in Matilda White Riley, Marilyn Johnson, and Anne Foner et al., *Aging and Society*, Vol. III (New York: Russell Sage Foundation, 1972).

FIGURE 6.3: Opinions on Public Policy Issues

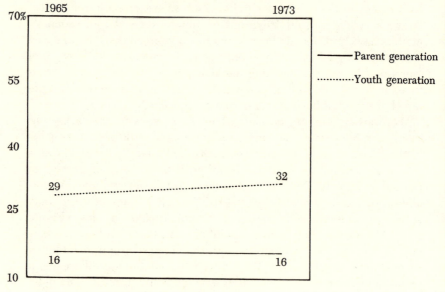

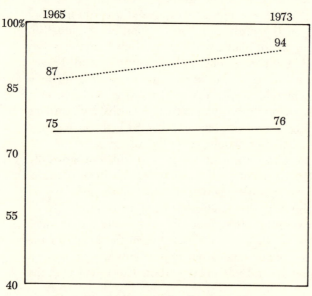

(a) Prayers should not be allowed in schools

(b) Speeches against religion should be allowed

FIGURE 6.3 (cont.)

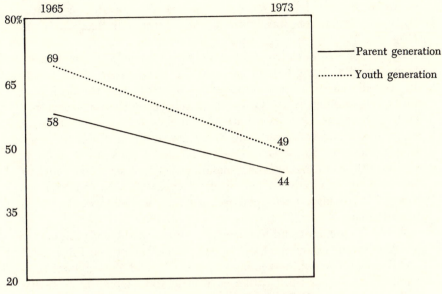

(c) Federal government should help integrate the schools

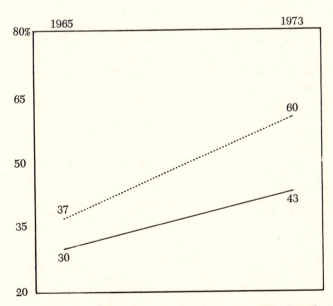

(d) Communist should be allowed to take office elected to

theme of being socialized during a more racially liberal *Zeitgeist*, the upcoming generation was more positively disposed than the older (Figure 6.3c).

By 1973 a downturn had set in. Slightly under half of each generation favored a strong federal role and the former edge of the young adults had come close to disappearing. So strong was the decline in youth support that by 1973 they were well below the point occupied by their elders in 1965. There are any number of reasons for the fall, the busing controversy certainly being among them. From the long-term perspective, however, the key point is the evidence of a strong secular pull operating on both generations. In contrast to the previous issue where essentially no period effect could be observed, this one shows it in abundance, with perhaps an extra kicker effect on the young in particular.[4]

While the secular trend has been away from the liberal position (*as of 1965*) on the school integration issue, it has been toward liberalism on an issue reflecting the waning years of the Cold War and anticommunism. About one-third within each generation agreed in 1965 that a Communist should be allowed to take an office rightfully won. By 1973 the figure had climbed appreciably for each generation, especially so for the younger one (Figure 6.3d). Since there is no plausible reason to suspect that Americans become less anticommunistic as a function of passing through middle age, period effects would seem to explain the increasing liberalism of each generation. As the plots reveal, however, the very modest excess liberalism of the young adults in 1965 has grown to a net difference of fifteen percent. It would be difficult to construct a life-course explanation for the enlarging gap. Rather, it would seem that the era in which the young have been socialized has led them to be more receptive to the secular trends.[5]

As is true of many of the other domains covered in this inquiry, no single model adequately describes the issue positioning of the two generations over time. That the youth cohort remains more liberal after

---

[4] This kicker effect conceivably resulted from the altered perspectives accompanying a change in status from dependent child in the nuclear family to that of independent adult and prospective parent of school-aged children.

[5] A cross-sequential design (basically a replicated cross-sectional survey) covering the 1956-1972 period reached very similar conclusions. Stephen J. Cutler and Robert L. Kaufman, "Cohort Changes in Political Attitudes: Tolerance of Ideological Non-Conformity," *Public Opinion Quarterly*, 39 (Spring 1975), 69-81. See also Clyde A. Nunn, Harry J. Crockett, and J. Allen Williams, *Tolerance for Nonconformity* (San Francisco: Jossey-Bass, 1978). An argument that an increase in tolerance is misperceived is presented in John L. Sullivan, James Piereson, and George E. Marcus, "An Alternative Conceptualization of Political Tolerance: Illusory Increases 1950s-1970s," *American Political Science Review*, 73 (September 1979), 781-94.

an eight-year interim suggests a standing generational contrast along a liberal-conservative dimension. And thus far it is difficult to see any life-cycle effects at work. On the other hand, there are two marked instances of secular shifts overlaid on the generational differences. One seems to be drawing the generations together, while the other separates them still farther.

SUBJECTIVE PERCEPTIONS AND THE GENERATION GAP

The trend analysis demonstrates that the much-fabled generation gap appears to have substance with respect to specific political issues. Our youth cohort began with a somewhat more liberal disposition and, if anything, increased the distance between itself and the parent cohort during the eight-year interim. Views on school integration proved the exception to the rule, an exception that is explicable in terms of massive period effects and possibly life-cycle effects operating on the young. However, the number of issues that we were able to introduce was exceedingly small. Nor did all of them necessarily have the salience and concreteness that are desirable in looking for consequential divisions of opinion in the populace. In the 1973 wave of the study we expanded the coverage of issues and introduced an additional format, as noted in Chapter 2. Examining these data will permit us to ascertain the extent and degree to which the generations diverge over a wider range of other issues. We will also be able to compare the "real" gap with the "perceived" generation gap.

Respondents located themselves on seven-point scales, running from the most conservative position to the most liberal position, for each of seven current issues as well as for a general purpose liberal-conservative scale of political views.[6] For purposes of comparing the generations as well as to obtain some appreciation of where they stand in absolute terms, we shall first treat self-placements in the 1-3 positions as representing a liberal (or at least less conservative) stand, and self-placements in the 5-7 positions as representing a conservative (or less liberal) stand. The middle location of "4" will be disregarded for the time being.

A number of operations can be performed using this approach. First, we can see for each generation the sheer degree of "liberal" sentiment on each issue. Only on the issues of equality for women and protecting the rights of the accused was there an absolute liberal majority among the youths. On no issue was there an absolute liberal majority among the parents. One conclusion to draw from this is that even

[6] These are the same issues referred to in Chapter 3, pp. 60-61. Abbreviated headings are listed in Table 6.1.

though the young have been accused of being too liberal across the
board, that charge would have to be severely qualified. At the same
time, however, it is true that the young are more liberal than their
parents on every issue examined. So taking only the proportion of liberal answers as a first approximation, the patterns found in our trend
data are repeated here. The generational model, by inference, is substantiated.

Considerably more information can be adduced from these self-
placements. By subtracting the percentage of conservative answers
(scores 5-7) from the liberal ones (1-3), we can obtain the net liberal
or conservative leanings of each generation. Especially because there
is a varying tendency for respondents to use the middle position on the
scale, this subtraction procedure adds a refinement that will put the
relative position of the two generations in sharper perspective. It turns
out that the filial generation has a net score in the liberal direction
five out of eight times, thereby lending support to the view that it is a
predominantly liberal generation. On the other hand, the parental generation shows a surplus of conservative stands on each issue, perhaps
confirming the view that middle-aged, middle America basically slants
toward the conservative side. Moreover, in every instance the net
score of the young is more liberal, or less conservative, than is that of
the middle-aged. By simple count, then, the young emerge as the more
liberal, and the generational model is upheld, *ceteris paribus*.

A more parsimonious way of presenting these issue-position results,
and one that will prove useful for subsequent comparisons, is to employ the mean scores for each generation. These are shown in the first
two columns of Table 6.1 and conform in general to the message conveyed by the percentage distributions just described. Although the
young are less conservative than the middle-aged on each issue, the

TABLE 6.1: Real and Perceived Generation Gaps on Political Issues, 1973

	Self-report			Parent perception			Youth perception		
	P	Y	Dif.	P	Y	Dif.	P	Y	Dif.
Gov't guarantee jobs	4.7[a]	4.4	.3	4.8	4.1	.7	5.1	4.1	1.0
Busing for integration	6.3	5.6	.7	6.1	4.9	1.2	6.0	4.9	1.1
Gov't help minorities	4.4	3.8	.6	4.8	3.7	1.1	5.1	3.7	1.4
Protect rights of accused	4.4	3.4	1.0	4.7	3.3	1.4	4.8	3.2	1.6
Change form of gov't	4.9	4.0	.9	4.9	3.3	1.6	4.9	3.3	1.6
Equality for women	4.0	3.0	1.0	4.6	2.8	1.8	5.1	2.9	2.2
Legalize marijuana	5.7	4.1	1.6	5.9	3.2	2.7	6.1	2.9	3.2
Liberal-conservative views	4.4	3.8	.6	4.8	3.0	1.8	5.2	3.2	2.0

[a] Entries in the "P" and "Y" columns are the mean scores on the 1-7 issue scales; the
higher the score the more conservative the responses.

difference is from quite modest to very substantial. The magnitude of the generation gap depends very much on the issue being discussed.

The issues and the corresponding intergenerational differences group themselves into three clusters that reveal much about the nature of the generation gap as it applies to political issues. The smallest differences are in the fairly traditional New Deal era issues of guaranteed jobs and help for minorities, and in the visceral, complex issue of busing to achieve integration. The next set of issues form part of the new politics so widely spoken of during the late 1960s and early 1970s and extending in milder form to later years as well. Protecting the rights of the accused, bringing about equality for women, and questioning whether some fundamental changes were not needed in the government were all part of the new political climate that seemed to take on age as well as class dimensions.

Finally, we come to a single issue which for many people has come to symbolize the separation between the generations in both a cultural and political fashion, viz., the use of marijuana. Here the youth liberal margin is huge, though it is interesting to observe the components upon which that margin is built. There was actually a bare *conservative* majority among the young adults on this issue, a finding which indicates a very divided cohort, as of 1973 at any rate. However, this bare majority is completely overwhelmed by the lopsided conservative leanings of the older generation, thereby producing a gap of massive proportions.

If these are a reasonable cross-section of issues facing the American public in 1973, the case can be sustained that these biologically linked generations have contrasting ideological postures. Assuming that the differences would have been adumbrated by 1965 results on identical or surrogate issues, we would be prepared to conclude that a generational model characterizes these findings. True, inequalities in education help explain the disparities, so that there are compositional generational effects as well as "experiential" generational effects—though, as we have argued before, the acquisition of higher education during different historical times constitutes in itself a different socializing experience. Indeed, this is precisely what one would expect. Battle lines form much more readily on new content, where the residues of prior socialization are weaker and where innovations are more easily mounted.

The foregoing demonstrates that there was indeed a conflict between the generations on issues, whether we want to label this a true or artificial generation gap. Yet to some eyes that gap might not seem as large as the gulf that was widely popularized during the period and which is still often reflected in general discourse. Only with respect to the

marijuana issue was there the spectacular difference that popular accounts might have led us to expect. Was the gap simply smaller than
had been imagined all along, or had it receded as early as 1973? The
answer to the puzzle may lie in the difference between perception and
reality, between how people constructed the gap based on their perceptions and the actual, self-revealed nature of the gap. So far we have
dealt only with self-reports from members of each generation. These
were then aggregated to form a profile for each generation. Although
the resulting profiles definitely showed a more liberal face for the
young, profiles based on how each generation was *perceived* vis-à-vis
the other are likely to yield a more dramatic picture.

In addition to placing themselves on the issue scales, the respondents also placed various other social groupings. Included among these
were, for the young, where they thought "most people about your
age" would be and where "most people your parents' age" would be.
For the parents the referents were also "most people about your age"
and "most people around the age of 25." The latter was used, of
course, because that was the approximate age of at least one of their
children. Each generation, then, was asked to generalize about its own
peers and about the opposite generation. These additional placements
make possible two more major pairs of comparisons: differences based
on parental perceptions and differences based on youth perceptions.
There are other combinations, but these serve best to illustrate the
varying images of the generation gap.

Turning to the figures based on parental perceptions (Table 6.1,
cols. 3 and 4), we observe a quite noticeable upward shift for every
difference score, ranging from a gain of .4 on the issue of guaranteed
jobs to a 1.1 on the legalization of marijuana. Now this increase comes
about as a result of two complementary shifts. First, compared with
how they rate themselves, parents are inclined to see other people their
age as more *conservative*, the only definite exception being enforced
busing. Second, compared with how youths rate themselves, parents
without exception see the youths as being more *liberal*. As a consequence of these twin "misperceptions" the gap appears to be larger
than it was based only on self-reports from members of each generation. The discrepancies between the self-reports and the perceptions
are clearly not a function of the former somehow being biased in a
direction that would favor or encourage discrepancies. Since our
young adult respondents are better educated than the cohort as a
whole, and since education is related to more liberal answers, the
youths' self-reports are, if anything, biased in a liberal direction already. To some extent the parental respondents are also better edu-

cated than the parental cohort as a whole, but the relationship with education is not nearly as pronounced.

Finally, we come to the scores generated by youthful perceptions (cols. 5 and 6). The most striking fact is that the distance between the generations now reaches its zenith on six of the measures, is tied with parental perceptions on a seventh, and barely trails the parent-perceived gap only on the issue of busing. From the perspective of the young adults there is nearly a cross-generational chasm on virtually every issue considered. As in the case of the parental perceptions, this widened gulf arises from two complementary movements. On the one hand, our young adult respondents saw their peers as being more *liberal* than they themselves were in the aggregate. That overestimate is especially noticeable in the cases of busing, marijuana, and liberal-conservative political views. Like the parents, then, the young exaggerated the proclivities of their own kind—where these are defined by the ideological juxtapositioning of the two generations. On the other hand, the young overestimated the conservatism of their parents' generation on all save the busing issue and the proposal for changing some governmental forms (where a tie ensues). Again, they resemble parents in the perceptions of their opposite numbers. Parents thought the young were even more liberal than the young actually were, whereas the young thought parents were more conservative than the parents actually were. Each invested its opposite with disproportionate quantities of the ingredients which, in fact, had some basis in reality.

Confronting the near steplike character of the generation gap as we move from self-reported differences to parent-perceived differences and then to youth-perceived differences, we can begin to understand the vehemence and certainty attached to proclamations about the generation gap. Just as important as the "real" gap between the generations was the gap between that reality and the perceived reality. For the young the size of that gulf was often over twice as large in their perceptual world as it was in the world anchored by the revealed sentiments of representatives from each generation.

Why the perceived distance was greater among the young than their elders is not an easily resolved question. As the group supposedly responsible for the gap as a consequence of rebelling from their elders or, alternatively, acting out the normative imperatives of their elders' teachings, it was perhaps not at all unnatural for them to visualize a breach of devastating proportions. And, of course, that vision was fed by the mass media and underlined by verbal and physical power confrontations that indeed pitted the young against the middle-aged.

A key question for the future is whether this pluralistic ignorance[7] on the part of both generations—but especially the young—will continue. Is an image of sharp divisions inherent in the process of entering adulthood regardless of the historical setting? Does the lessened cleavage perceived by the parental generation represent a diminution of such strong feelings as people move through the life cycle? These questions are offered as alternatives to the obvious explanation that the period under study was unique, that perceived *political* conflicts between the generations were running at high tide under the impetus of an exceptionally strong *Zeitgeist*. Certainly all the side information at our disposal would incline us toward a generation/period effects interpretation. It is difficult to recall another era when a phrase such as "you can't trust anyone over 30" could have epitomized the perceived political tensions between generations. Yet it may be that the young simply responded to that *Zeitgeist* more fervently than did their parents because of their being in the middle of their identity formation. Thus we leave hanging the question of whether the greater perceived generational conflict on the part of the young will endure, and thereby constitute a lasting generational marking, or whether it will recede with time, thus constituting more of a period/life-cycle effect. At the very least, however, we can conclude that whatever model may best describe the results, the gap lay as much or more in the eyes of the beholder—and thus had a crucial political reality of its own—as it did in the actual issue distance separating the views of the two generations.

Evaluations of the Political System and Governmental Actors

If *Zeitgeist* means anything it should mean that individuals within a political system are sensitive to and affected by the critical problems

---

[7] The term is from Floyd H. Allport, *Social Psychology* (Boston: Houghton Mifflin, 1924), and originally referred to the assumption by individuals in a group that their own attitudes were unshared by others in the group when in fact similar attitudes were held by other group members. Merton expanded the concept to include the situation where individuals believe their attitudes *are* shared by others but in fact they are not. See Robert K. Merton, *Social Theory and Social Structure*, enlarged ed. (New York: Free Press, 1968). Our usage refers in part to the misperception members of each generation have about their peers but also to the misperceptions existing across the generations. For related work see James M. Fields and Howard Schuman, "Public Beliefs about the Beliefs of the Public," and Hubert O'Gorman, "Pluralistic Ignorance—A Replication and Extension," *Public Opinion Quarterly*, 40 (Winter 1976-1977), 427-48, 449-58, respectively. A provocative political interpretation is Elisabeth Noelle-Neumann, "Turbulences in the Climate of Opinion: Methodological Applications of the Spiral of Silence Theory," *Public Opinion Quarterly*, 41 (Summer 1977), 143-58.

of the time. It would be absurd, for example, to think that the traumatic events of the Civil War, World Wars I and II, and the Vietnam War were not perceived by people experiencing them as tests of the nation's ability to survive either physically, morally, or both. Similarly, the various economic panics and depressions have not passed unnoticed among those experiencing them. Broad social-political ills and gains also help set off major and minor political periods. To the extent that they are recognized and experienced, these events and movements form the citizenry's image of the political periods through which they are passing. They constitute, in short, one barometer of the "spirit of the times."

We have tapped this spirit by asking our respondents what things they are least proud of as Americans. Answers to this free-response question were coded under a great number of specific categories, which in turn fall under a few general rubrics. By observing the marginal distributions of these rubrics for each generation we can catch the kinds of events and processes which struck them as constituting national negative images. These images may be taken as one indicator of a political era.

One clear result emerging from answers to this question is that both generations were caught up in the general disillusionment that swept the country during this time frame. In the first place, there was a decrease in the proportion rejecting the premise of the question. Whereas in 1965 some 14% of the parents avowed that there was *nothing* of which they were not proud, by 1973 that proportion had dwindled to 8%. Although only a handful of the youths had felt that way in 1965, even that fraction declined over the years (6% to 5%). Thus, the general acceptance that there was, indeed, something wrong with America had become virtually ubiquitous as the second Nixon administration got underway. Given the seeming plethora of topics that could have been mentioned, one can perhaps only wonder at those individuals in each generation who still went out of their way to contest the validity of the question.

An even more telling indicator of the period effects operating on both generations lies in simply comparing the mean number of codable responses that were evoked in each year (Figure 6.4). The percentage increases in the means were quite striking, rising by about a third in each case. Stated another way, those giving two or more national faults constituted 45% of the young in 1965, but 68% in 1973. Comparable figures for the parents are 35% and 58%. Nor was this leap a reflection of greater general verbosity during the 1973 interviews. We saw with respect to the "good citizen" inquiry, for example, that there was scarcely any change in the mean number of responses over time. Rath-

FIGURE 6.4: References to Qualities Least Proud of as an American

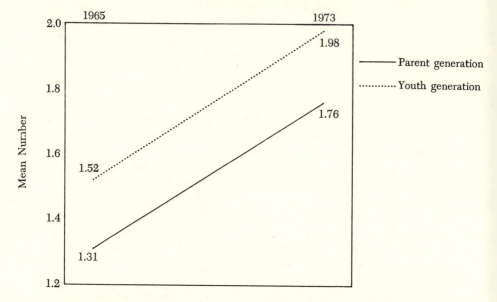

er, the same stimulus brought forth a much greater number of answers in 1973 because the cataloguing of national ills and alleged wrongdoing had proliferated greatly during the interim. Our respondents gave us a faithful reproduction of that changing canvas.

Both the decrease in the proportions rejecting the premise of the question and the remarkable increase in the number of negative features give witness to strong period effects. At the same time, however, it is apparent that the generations remained some distance apart over time. The young were more generous in owning up to disturbing elements in 1965 and they continued to be so in 1973. Indeed, Figure 6.4 would seem to be a very handsome illustration of what we have called a hybrid generation-period effects model. Especially in view of the circumstances surrounding the young generation's entry into the adult political world, it seems doubtful that this generational disparity would dissolve easily. Any tendency the young might have had to take a less damning view of the nation was severely hindered by the events of the 1965-1973 era.

Although these overall results are telling in their own right, there were some intriguing cross-currents of attitudinal change also at work. Political historians are already referring to the 1960s as the civil rights decade. Beginning with the sit-ins of the late 1950s and early 1960s, and culminating with riots, strong legislation, favorable court decisions, and administrative enforcement, the civil rights movement centered primarily on the struggle for black equality. The question at hand is whether this sense of the times is shared by our two generations, and whether it is shared to the same degree. If our data are a sure guide, the judgment of political historians is matched by the images of the mass public. We have taken as an indicator the total percentage of respondents referring to civil rights in answer to the "least proud" question. In 1965 both generations placed extraordinary emphasis on the civil rights area (Figure 6.5). Responses of this type were more than double those in other areas. And the great majority of these responses dealt specifically with white-black problems, with only a scant few being overtly hostile to the movement.

The relative and absolute focus on civil rights as of 1965 strongly suggests a period effect at full tide. But without another observation point, that developmental state would be difficult to document. By using exactly the same coding scheme on the 1973 replies, except for adding new categories, we are able to replicate the 1965 procedures. As Figure 6.5a shows, there was a staggering drop in the salience of civil rights on the part of both generations. The attrition was slightly sharper for the younger generation, virtually removing the modest edge it possessed in 1965. Aside from this small difference, the two generations moved almost in parallel, pointing toward a decisive *Zeitgeist* phenomenon.[8]

Exactly what the long-range consequences of the absorption with civil rights in the mid-1960s will be on the two generations is beyond the scope of this analysis. So also is the equally significant question of the consequences of its eclipse by early 1973. It is worthwhile, however, to offer one vivid piece of fall-out from the civil rights movement, one which shows in fairly concrete terms the behavioral consequences of the historical period.

In both 1965 and 1973 our respondents were asked if they had any close friends of the opposite race. Blacks of both generations responded much more in the affirmative, and exhibit little change over time. Not so among the whites. While noticeably less than half of each generation claimed close black friends at either point in time, the trend was definitely up for both cohorts over the eight-year span (36% to 45% for the younger generation and 28% to 38% for the older one). Other explanations are possible, but it is difficult to account for this in any way other than as period effects flowing directly out of the civil rights movement. This explanation is all the more convincing be-

---

[8] One might challenge data of this type on the grounds that people simply report "what's in the news" at the time. To a great extent that is precisely the point, but only when that "news" is continuously repeated and reinforced by other phenomena—as was clearly the case for civil rights.

FIGURE 6.5: Specific Objects Least Proud of as an American

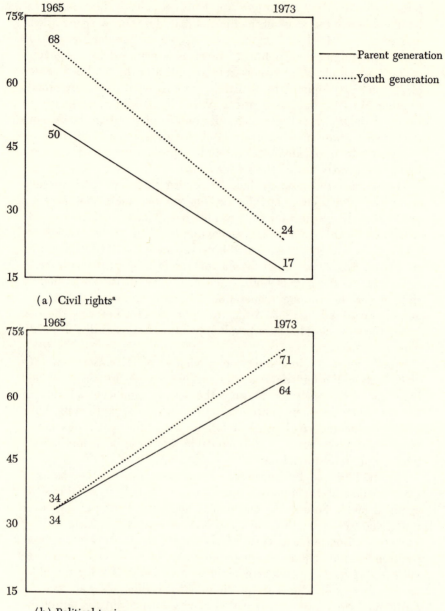

(a) Civil rights[a]

(b) Political topics

[a] These figures differ from those previously reported because they are based on the total number of respondents rather than responses. See M. Kent Jennings and Richard G. Niemi. "Continuity and Change in Political Orientations," *American Political Science Review*, 69 (December 1975), 1316-35.

cause movement among the parents parallels that for the youths. If it were due only to the "compositional" effects derivative of the younger generation being better educated, the shift should be less among the parents. That the filial generation still holds an edge over the older one does point toward a continuing generation gap in an absolute sense, however. Parents by 1973 had reached just about the same level occupied by the young as of 1965. Overall, the pattern suggests strong period effects leavened by generational ones. The edge for the young would seem to be very much a function of being socialized in an environment more sensitive to racial injustice and strife.

Given the monumental decline in the visibility of civil rights as an object of embarrassment if not outright shame, what sorts of objects were cited to such an extent that the overall level of negative references actually *increased* over time? Our respondents were remarkably adept at singling out a myriad of events, actions, processes, institutions, and actors. Some, such as the Nixon presidency, were not even present at the time of the first wave of interviews. Others were of a more generic quality and transcend the years. One way of summarizing this challenging array is to group together those that are clearly political in content.[9] When this is done, we find the sharp rise depicted in Figure 6.5b. Summing across all responses, the mean number rose from .42 to 1.02 among the young, and from .43 to .91 among the parents. The "vacuum" created by the fading salience of civil rgihts was filled in by other types of explicitly political topics. Alternatively, one might say that a variety of other topics helped drive down the saliency of civil rights. In any event, political objects as negative referents rose dramatically. This rise is underscored by showing the ratio of political objects to all objects cited at each time point. In 1973 they formed at least one-half of all mentions for each cohort; in 1965 they comprised about three in ten of all mentions.

Curiously enough, the villains and culprits cited with much greater frequency in 1973 were no more likely to be formal government actors and institutions than they were in 1965. All of the explicitly political references were divided into those naming agents, institutions, or actions of the government on the one hand, and all other objects on the other. Most of these other references were to Americans in general or to specific segments and characteristics of the population (e.g., too apathetic, no pride, draft evaders, welfare cheaters, demonstrations,

[9] We have separated civil rights from "pure" political citations not because civil rights is not a political problem but because it is so much more than that and because it has distinctive features. Moreover, the majority of civil rights mentions in the interviews stressed the societal and interpersonal nature of the civil rights phenomena rather than the strictly governmental aspects.

disrespect, etc.). In both years references of the first type—those to the political system—outran by a large margin the nonsystem references. But as these figures show, the ratio of system to nonsystem responses was about the same among the young; among the older generation the proportion of system references actually fell somewhat.

	Youths		Parents	
	1965	1973	1965	1973
System references	27%	58%	29%	46%
Nonsystem references	7%	13%	5%	18%
Proportion system to all political references	.79	.82	.85	.72

What is a bit surprising about these findings is the absolute increment in references to one's fellow Americans, an increase that kept pace with that for system blame among the young and exceeded that increase among the parents. The accelerated citations of system properties and actors were expected. In contrast, the rising castigation of nonofficial actors and events was less anticipated and suggests that members of both generations came to see fault in more than just the "system" and its executors. We have, then, further evidence of the widely cited declining faith in America and its peoples. If anything, the older generation is the more pessimistic when it comes to assessing the people.

Reinforcing this observation are the results for another dimension emerging from the "least proud" descriptions. A range of answers fell under what we have labeled "moral, ethical, and religious practices and values." These are distinctly outside the realm of political phenomena as well as that of civil rights. If our respondents were becoming less enchanted with their fellow citizens during the eight-year period, we should expect to see an increase in references to negative qualities of this sort. Parents lead the way in this respect with the proportions going from 20% to 30%. But their offspring are not far behind, with an increase of 18% to 24%. Americans were not only becoming less praiseworthy politically, but morally and spiritually as well.

As a final indicator of political system evaluations we turn to the most widely discussed of all recent changes in mass public attitudes— those regarding political trust. Cohort and cross-section analyses[10] have shown remarkable drops in the level of trust accorded the national

[10] See especially Arthur H. Miller, "Political Issues and Trust in Government: 1964-1970," *American Political Science Review*, 68 (September 1974), 951-72, and in the same issue a "Comment" by Jack Citrin and a "Rejoinder" by Miller, 973-1001. A recent update on trust levels is Arthur H. Miller, "The Majority Party

government. Our unique contribution will be to trace that pattern for two distinct generations over an extended time frame.

We have relatively well-developed theoretical expectations about the course of development of political trust. Two kinds of processes are expected to structure jointly the patterns of change for the older and younger generations. On the one hand, strong period effects are likely to be found. Trust in the government has been declining for a number of years, particularly since 1964. Thus the level of trust shown by the parent and the young adult samples should decline markedly; conversely, levels of cynicism should rise.

In addition to these period effects, a life-cycle change should also be observed. It has been shown repeatedly that young children are more idealistic about political authority than older persons. This is true even of the late 1960s and early 1970s when the extremely positive views of earlier years were no longer so evident.[11] By late adolescence, idealistic views decline, but in 1965 we still found the seniors to be much more positive about the government than were their parents. In the years since then we would expect their cynicism to have grown due to their encounters with the "real" world of politics, quite apart from any period effects.

Combining these two expectations, we should find growing cynicism among both generations, but a faster rate of change among the young adults. Strong confirmation of these expectations is observed in Figure 6.6, which shows the mean scores for the additive scale based on responses to the five items making up the standard political trust measure. Exceptionally strong *Zeitgeist* effects are seen in the diminution of trust among both generations. One seldom sees in longitudinal data the precipitous changes summarized here and presented in more detail in Appendix B.

But the young have changed more. Whereas in 1965 they were extraordinarily more positive than were their parents, by 1973 they had become equally negative, even though parents themselves were more cynical than they had been in 1965. In more normal times we would have expected the younger set to change by a relatively small amount, perhaps approaching the degree of cynicism held by parents in 1965.

Reunited?: A Summary Comparison of the 1972 and 1976 Elections," in Jeffrey Fishel (ed.), *Political Parties and Elections in an Anti-Party Age* (Bloomington, Ind.: Indiana University Press, 1977).

[11] Jack Dennis, "Dimensions of Support for the Presidency," paper presented at the annual meeting of the Midwest Political Science Association, Chicago, April 1975; and Fred I. Greenstein, "The Benevolent Leader Revisited: Children's Images of Political Leaders in Three Democracies," *American Political Science Review*, 69 (December 1975), 1371-98.

FIGURE 6.6: Trust in Political Authorities

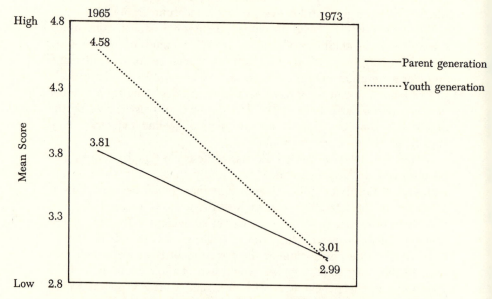

Under the impetus of events beginning in the middle 1960s, however, this generation was catapulted well beyond what probably characterized most preceding cohorts.

Despite the very rapid shifting among the young, on three of the five items comprising the scale they still remain more trusting than the older generation. This suggests that there is room for yet a further increment in the cynicism of the younger population due solely to life-cycle effects. That likelihood is also supported by data from adult cross-section samples showing change well into adulthood among individuals as well educated as our young adults.[12] Moreover, we would speculate that having reached this degree of cynicism, a rapid return of trusting attitudes is unlikely even when the political atmosphere becomes less charged. If this is borne out, the greater than usual cynicism among the young adults would keep the overall adult level of cynicism quite high even if the young are replaced over the next few decades by new, less cynical cohorts. We may be witnessing not only period and life-cycle effects, but also the makings of generational effects.

As political trust in the national government has declined dramatically in absolute terms, the relative place of the national government

[12] M. Kent Jennings and Richard G. Niemi, *The Political Character of Adolescence* (Princeton, N.J.: Princeton University Press, 1974), Chapter 10.

in the three-tiered U.S. system has also declined. In contrast to absolute trust, however, there are also marked age-related contrasts. These contrasts suggest the additional workings of life-cycle effects.

Our evidence comes from questions about the level of government —national, state, or local—in which the respondents have the most faith and confidence and the least faith and confidence. In 1965 a majority of each generation vested more confidence in the national government, but there was a chasm between the overriding majority point of view of the younger group and the more moderate margin among the older (Figure 6.7a). Based only on those figures, and making no allowance for period and life-cycle changes, one might well have predicted a continuing generational cleavage. What happened in the eight years approached landslide proportions among the young and was more glacial among the old. Both generations recorded a decline, thereby fitting our presumption of period effects. But the decline was momentous among the young, bringing them to virtual congruence with their elders.

Strictly speaking, it is difficult to distinguish between life-cycle and generation effects in accounting for the exaggerated movement of the filial generation. Evidence from other work suggests a similar dip at that age range among previous cohorts.[13] This would support a period-life course hybrid model. On the other hand, as noted earlier, period effects often fall unequally on the generations. Because of their still impressionable years it is conceivable that the secular trend is being felt especially strongly by the young. Nor should we rule out the possibility that while period effects account for virtually all of the shift among the parents, it is a combination of period, generational, and life-cycle processes that is operating on the young adults.

Although this is a good example of the complexities of trying to unravel the threads of change and continuity, of one thing we can be sure: the trust position of the federal government declined relatively as well as absolutely, and it seems safe to say that this occurred across the board. The main beneficiary of that decline was local government and to a much smaller extent state government. Figure 6.7b shows that local government gained slightly in the senior generation and very substantially in the younger. Again, there is presumptive evidence for a secular shift affecting both, along with a heavy impact on the young of either life-cycle and/or generational processes. Regardless of the processes, the two generations now stand in much closer proximity than they did eight years previously.

[13] Ibid.

FIGURE 6.7: Faith and Confidence in Levels of Government

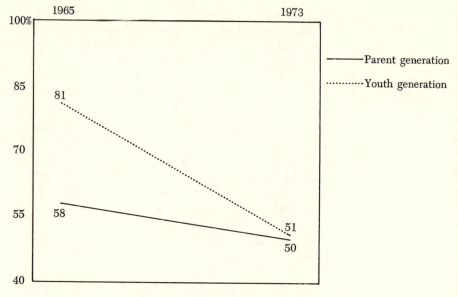

(a) Most faith and confidence in national level of government

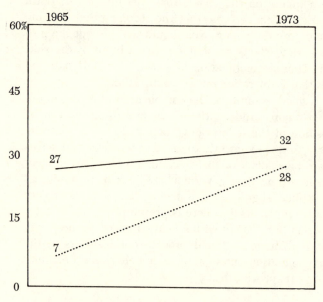

(b) Most faith and confidence in local level of government

Evaluations of Sociopolitical Groupings

In our discussion of individual-level stability we found at least a moderate degree of persistence with respect to how a number of broad sociopolitical groupings were rated. As usual, the parents proved more stable than did their offspring. Because these groups were all easily recognizable by name, at any rate, it is a bit surprising that even greater stability was not observed. It should be recalled, however, that the time period under study was one during which broad collectivities often came to be praised or stigmatized in the heat of political battles. Our effort in this section will be to ascertain the net effects of these tempestuous times on the assessments made of these groupings, and the degree to which the generations moved together or apart.

We begin by noting the mean ratings applied to each of the eight groups on the 0-100° thermometer scale. Figure 6.8 contains a separate chart for each generation. Although there are minor variations, the *relative* esteem in which the groups were held was approximately the same for each generation at both time points. Whites and Protestants anchored the high end of the evaluations and labor unions and big business the low end. The three religious-ethnic minority groupings of Catholics, Negroes, and Jews, plus the regional minority of Southerners, fell in between. Thus the most inclusive, majoritarian categories garnered the highest recordings, whereas the most specific, noninclusive, and special purpose groupings reaped the lowest ratings. In part, of course, this flows from the fact that the study sample is primarily white and Protestant and not, for the most part, identified with big business or labor unions as such.[14] The differential assessments also emanate from the fact that the more inclusive and less specialized the grouping, the less is the likelihood that any particular negative feature will submerge the generally positive affect felt toward other components. That both generations responded in about the same relative fashion over time suggests a general kind of continuity.

Beyond that, however, some significant contrasts occur. A visual inspection reveals that the mean group evaluations supplied by each generation were very closely allied in 1965. In fact, the largest difference, that for Southerners and Protestants, amounted to only four points. Moreover, the young rendered slightly higher ratings in two instances and the generations were tied in two other cases. By 1973 this coziness had evaporated. Each generation tended to lower its evaluations, a tendency that was realized seven out of eight times among the young and five out of eight among the middle-aged. These declines

[14] Not surprisingly, respondents who are members of any particular one of the eight groups tend to give higher ratings to that group than do nonmembers.

FIGURE 6.8: Mean Evaluation of Sociopolitical Groupings[a]

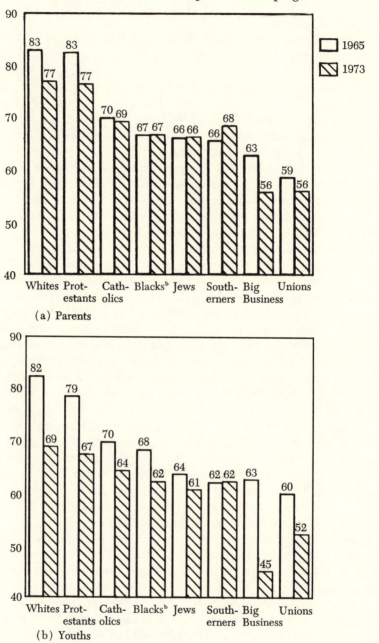

(a) Parents

(b) Youths

[a] Entries are mean scores on the 0-100° thermometer scale; the higher the score, the more favorable the rating.
[b] The term "Negroes" was used in 1965, and "Blacks" in 1973.

suggest a period effect. At a time when most institutions in society were being challenged if not maligned, the lowering of positive feelings for even broad social groupings is perhaps an inevitable byproduct. But these period effects fell much more heavily on the young adults. Without exception their favorableness declined more than did parental favorableness; the pitch shown in Figure 6.8 is especially sharp for whites, Protestants, and big business. Additionally, the absolute scores in 1973 were always higher among parents. Hence the general configuration suggests a mixture of period and generational effects.

While one might certainly have expected the younger generation to lower its assessments of such mainstream entities as white and Protestants, and especially its affect for big business and even labor unions, it is not at all expected that they would wind up being less keen than their parents about blacks, Jews, and Catholics. Nor was it expected that their absolute scores for these groupings would be lower in 1973 than in 1965 nor that Southerners would be the one grouping where the mean scores did not change at all. Does this mean that the young actually became less tolerant of minorities as well as becoming disillusioned with mainstream groupings? Considering that the offspring took more liberal stances on a number of policy issues and in their voting preferences, it is difficult to accept this proposition. There are two threads of evidence that explain, if not outright refute, the interpretation that the young became less tolerant in both an absolute sense and relative to their parents.

The first piece of evidence lies in the evaluations assigned to a number of groupings asked about only in 1973. If it were true that the young had become uniformly less enthusiastic than their parents about groups and collectivities in America, then their ratings even of patently liberal groups should be no higher than those of their parents and their ratings of patently conservative groups no lower than their parents'. That clearly does not hold. Illustratively, the mean scores applied to marijuana users was 42 among youths, 20 among parents; for the women's liberation movement the respective scores were 54 and 47; and for radical students, 32 and 22. Even though these ratings do not represent warm endorsements in either generation, the younger one had the more benign outlook. Evaluations of conservative actors provide a mirror image. Whereas parents gave policemen a mean rating of 77, youths gave them 66. Similarly, the military scored 72 among parents, 55 among youths. Both generations tended to place conservative groups higher than the liberal ones listed, but the intergenerational comparison leaves little doubt as to the young adults' more liberal position. The ratings applied to these criterion groups effectively refute the speculation that the young had somehow become more jaundiced about so-called liberal elements in the society.

What, then, is the explanation for the absolute and relative decline in the evaluations of Catholics, Negroes, and Jews? Here we introduce a second piece of evidence. One of the options available for respondents when using the "feeling thermometer" to rate various stimuli is the 50° mark, defined as not feeling particularly warm or cold toward the group. Respondents can use this location to express either ambivalent or ambiguous feelings. It is in the differential usage of this location that we find the explanation for the filial generation's slippage.

In 1965 there was little difference between the two generations in the usage of the thermometer midpoint, the range being from 0% to 7%, with only three exceeding 5%. Nor was one generation consistent in its greater usage of the 50° mark. By 1973 the pattern had altered. Now the range was from 3% to 21%, with all but one exceeding a 5% difference. The great bulk of this change arose from young adult shifting. Only one shift among the parents resulted in a change greater than 5%, whereas all but one shift among the young *exceeded* 5%. What is crucial is that in all cases except labor unions and big business (about which more in a moment), the young increased their use of the ambiguous or ambivalent temperature mark by anywhere from 11% to 24%. Significantly, the largest gain was registered for the two most heterogeneous social groupings, whites and Protestants. Since the mean evaluations in 1965 were all well above 50°, the almost inevitable result of the rise in the use of the 50° mark in 1973 was to lower the overall scores for each of these six large groupings.[15]

It remains to be explained just why the young adopted the neutral position so much more in 1973 than in 1965. A plausible explanation is that of increasing political sophistication and involvement. Although Catholics, blacks, and Jews are in one way or another more distinctive than whites and Protestants, they are still very inclusive groups. A hallmark of the politically sophisticated individual is to reject the notion of stereotyping broad classes of individuals, which are nevertheless highly subject to stereotyping. The easiest way to do that in the situation at hand was to opt for the 50° placement indicating neutrality or a reluctance to categorize. If our thinking is correct, there should be a relationship between an indicator of sophistication and involve-

[15] The scores could have been lowered in other ways, of course. A cross-tabulation of the ratings at the individual level reveals, however, that the bulk of the loss came from individuals lowering their 1965 scores to the 50° mark. It is instructive that the two biggest overall declines among the parents (whites and Protestants) also occurred where the use of the midpoint figure rose the most.

ment, such as political activity, and the use of 50°. That, indeed, proved to be the case.[16]

The immediately foregoing applies to the six more general population groupings, leaving out big business and labor unions. These two have unique properties compared with the other six. They are more clearly identified with particular interests of a political and economic sort. They are often thought of in terms of leaders and the "big shots" rather than in terms of people who work in big business or the rank and file labor union member. More importantly, though, they are less like a general demographic group, where one presumes to find all stripes of individuals. Our results in terms of how frequently the neutral point was employed in evaluating these two groups are consonant with this line of reasoning. In direct contrast to the more general collectivities, the use of the neutral point actually declined among the young (6% for labor unions and 5% for big business). Therefore, the young were not necessarily less willing to make judgments, per se, in 1973 versus 1965. Rather, they were more willing to do so when the object had sufficient, singular properties stamping it politically and economically.[17] As it turned out, a disproportionate number of those who had been at the midpoint in 1965, especially in the case of big business, lowered their scores in 1973, thus helping contribute to the overall decline in esteem for big business and labor unions.

NONPOLITICAL CHARACTERISTICS

In order to evaluate more fully the nature of change and continuity in the political world it is helpful to draw on a few comparisons from the nonpolitical realm. There are two reasons for doing so. In the first place, some ostensibly nonpolitical orientations have political significance. For example, one of the measures taken up is belief in the authenticity of the Bible. When used as a surrogate for a more comprehensive measure of religious fundamentalism, we have found that measure to be highly associated with a number of political attitudes and behaviors, even after controlling for characteristics associated with fundamentalism and the political variables at issue. Noticeable changes in the aggregate distributions of such nonpolitical variables

[16] The frequency of using the 50° placement tended to vary directly with scores on the political activity index described in Chapters 2 and 4. Although increases were observed at each level of activity, the magnitude was lowest among the low activists and highest (with one exception) among the high activists.

[17] Political activity level was not related to the decreasing use of 50° for labor unions, but it was for big business—the drop being 3%, 4%, and 9% for low, medium, and high activists, respectively.

could be politically consequential. A second reason for drawing on nonpolitical traits is that only by looking at nonpolitical phenomena can we determine if the process of political change and continuity is *sui generis*. To this end it will be especially important to employ non-political measures that have at least rough analogues in the political sphere.

Our prime materials come from the religious domain. A prominent portrayal of young people in the 1960s is that they fell away from or-ganized religion in droves, drifted toward agnosticism and atheism, to say nothing of being attracted toward more occult religions. Our first piece of evidence is in accord with that portrayal even though the abso-lute differences are not large. In 1965 there was virtually no difference between the generations in terms of their disavowing any religious preference, the figures being 1% for the youths and 2% for the parents. While this figure scarcely changed among the parents (4%), the gain put it up to 12% among the young. It is hard to distinguish between life-cycle and generational effects in interpreting this growing cleav-age. Young adulthood is clearly a time when traditional observances, such as church attendance, decline.[18] On the other hand, the outright rejection of any religious identification suggests more than temporary backsliding. Hence we may be witnessing a generational effect setting in, abetted in large part by the general discontent and criticism of es-tablished institutions so prevalent during the span covered by our two soundings. By the same token we would expect parents as a whole to be more impervious to such challenges, at least to the point of not in-creasing their open disavowal of religious identification.

Although giving up a religious identification is ordinarily a much more serious affair than renouncing a party preference, the compari-son is an apt one and is, in any event, the closest we can come to draw-ing a parallel. We observed a marked contrast between the generations with respect to party identification, a contrast we attributed primarily to generational effects. Especially important in the present context was the rising gap between the generations in terms of those claiming to be Independents. If we treat religious identification in the same vein, we find a similar development. Religious "independence" has grown among the young in the same fashion as has party "independence." In each instance what is involved is a greater rejection by the young of conventional ideologies and institutions.

A second indicator of religious belief provides strong support for this interpretation. The strongest positive alternative in the question involving the nature of the Bible states that "the Bible is God's word

---

[18] Data on church attendance from repeated cross-section samples are available in George Gallup, *The Gallup Poll* (New York: Random House, 1972).

and all it says is true." Figure 6.9a presents the proportion of each generation at each point in time subscribing to that belief. Already modestly differing in 1965, the generations came to disagree rather vividly by 1973. All of this widening gap stems from the exceptionally strong drop among the young because there was even a slight diminution among the middle-aged as well.

Without doubt there are generational effects at work here. Some portion of the dramatic decline among the young might be due to the traditional surge of religious skepticism said to occur in young adulthood, but the small drop among the parents argues against this as the sole or even major component. Rather, there would seem to be some element of period effects moving both generations. These effects clearly fall more heavily on the young, so much so that the intergenerational differences already present in 1965 were broadened considerably. Thus a hybrid generation-period effects model would seem to fit most adequately.

Perhaps the closest political analogies present in our study consist of the responses to the issue questions that have a religious element. We concluded that generational effects characterized the disparity between parents and youths on those issues, with the young increasing their already-greater liberalism and the middle-aged holding steady. Similarly, on the formerly delicate issue of whether "atheistic" Communists should be allowed to take office, the liberal margin of the young increased over time, even though both generations became more liberal. Consequently, the behavior of the generations in the pure religious belief realm provides a sequel to that in the political sphere.

The final measure dealing with religion is behavioral in nature, the frequency of church attendance. We observed in Chapter 3 that individual-level persistence in church-going was considerably higher for parents than for their children. A comparison of the proportions reporting weekly church attendance reveals the major consequence of that difference in stability. Figure 6.9b shows a landslide drop in attendance by the young, accompanied by a very modest decline among their parents. Next to the precipitous declines reported for political trust, the youth drop in church attendance is one of the sharpest to be encountered in our study. What is all the most remarkable is that the young started out as much *more* faithful than their elders in 1965, only to wind up being *less* faithful by about the same margin eight years later.

This is a very curious pattern, one of the few of its type uncovered in our analysis. It clearly represents a hybrid model, perhaps containing strong elements of life-cycle, generational, and period effects. The abnormally high proportion of the young reporting weekly attendance

FIGURE 6.9: Religious Beliefs and Practices

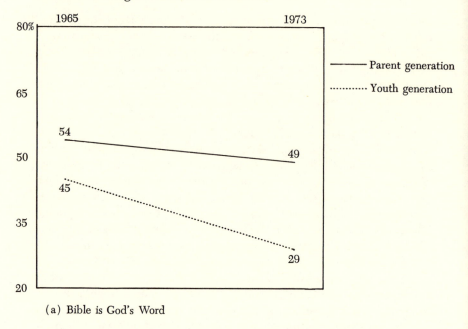

(a) Bible is God's Word

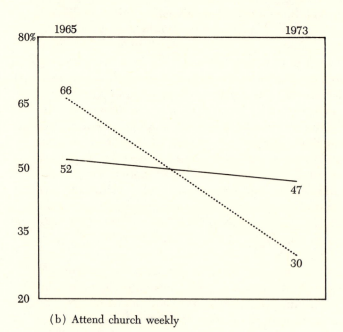

(b) Attend church weekly

in 1965 is probably both a function of life stage, church-going being a very social activity for teenagers, and a methodological artifact (to be discussed in the following chapter). And the drop-off in attendance would surely be expected as a result of leaving the familiar environs of home and home town. Still, the decline is so steep that one suspects generational effects as well, especially since there is, if anything, a fall among the parents also. Whatever processes best describe the movement, the end state again involves the young taking up a less traditional, less conservative position, just as they do on most of the political measures having a valence.

Finally, we may turn to the three sociopsychological variables for which we have over-time data: personal trust, opinion strength, and self-confidence. Since none of these, except possibly personal trust, involves societal institutions or reactions to historical developments, one would expect less net change than on comparable political measures. If there were differences between parents and youths in 1965 on personal trust, for example, we would expect those differences to continue.

For the most part our expectations are borne out. Personal trust provides a good illustration of what would appear to be a hybrid generation-period effects model. It has been widely claimed, especially before the calamitous drop in political trust, that there was a close connection between trust in people and trust in government, that the latter proceeded from the former during the childhood socialization process. Although there is probably some substance to this claim, it is patent that by the time people reach adulthood they make their assessments of the government versus their fellow humans on a rather independent basis. There was a modest decline of mean scores among both generations on the 1-7 personal trust scale used: from 5.1 to 4.6 for youths, and from 5.4 to 5.1 for parents. (The complete distributions are given in Appendix B.) This drop pales by comparison with that found for political trust. Clearly, the evaluative mechanisms are such that political institutions and actors are defined separately from the populace as a whole, a not very surprising finding in one sense, though the contrast is more dramatic than prior writing about the connection between the two would have suggested.

That both generations revised downward their personal trust in others suggests a period effect. However, they began from moderately different positions in 1965, thus producing a combined generational-period effects model. Curiously enough, the young were less trusting initially and remained so in 1973. What is especially odd about that is that the youth were more trusting of government initially than were their parents. The new generation has seemingly begun its trek through life with a less sanguine view of fellow Americans, whereas we might well have expected the middle-aged—who presumably have viewed with alarm some of the developments in American society—to have turned more doubtful. In any event, the essential points are that much greater continuity exists at the level of personal than political trust for each generation, and that the younger generation continues to be less trusting.

Our two indicators of personal efficacy illustrate continuity in an even stronger fashion. Both opinion strength and self-confidence exhibit virtually no net change in either generation over time. We saw in Chapter 3 that there was a good deal of instability at the individual level. However, the net effect of this instability was to leave each generation unchanged. To an even greater degree than in the case of personal trust, these levels of personal efficacy would seem to be much more induced by individual-level propensities and fortunes than by systematic, structural forces operating in a directional fashion. So the gains ostensibly experienced by some individuals are balanced by the losses experienced by others. Moreover, scarcely any difference exists between the generations at either time point for the self-confidence measure, thereby yielding an example of almost perfect continuity. Opinion strength, on the other hand, runs consistently at a modestly higher level among the young (see Appendix B). Barring life-cycle developments, this would appear to substantiate a pure generational effects model, though the gap is not large.

The closest political analogue to these measures of personal efficacy is the political efficacy measure. As we saw earlier, internal political efficacy declined modestly between 1965 and 1973 in each generation, with the young having a substantial edge in efficacy over their elders at both time points. Inasmuch as there was virtually no shifting on personal efficacy—in fact there were very slight increases in a couple of instances—the political analogue appears to be less stable at the aggregate level, as was the case in the comparison between personal and political trust. Not surprisingly, however, the disparity in the efficacy domain is much less marked than in the trust domain. This would seem to be a consequence of the place of "ego" in the political efficacy measure, as contrasted with the basic emphasis on other (i.e., political actors) in the political trust measure. Evaluations of institutions and actors are much more subject to unidirectional shifting than are evaluations of the self.

We close with an example that probably reflects both life-cycle and period effects. In 1965 parents and their offspring had remarkably similar views about whether teenagers were getting worse, better, or were about the same as always. Approximately three-fifths thought they were about the same, with the youths saying slightly more often than their parents that teenagers were better, while the parents took a dimmer view a bit more often. By 1973 the proportion picking the "same" category remained at about three-fifths, but both generations increased their disapproving votes and decreased their approving ones. Since the generations began with very similar views in 1965, this tandem movement suggests a rather pure period effects model. This view is supported by the ample public discussion, perhaps even greater than is usually the case, about the evils and afflictions of recent adolescent cohorts.

Yet there are reasons for suspecting life-cycle effects also. Having only recently moved out of the teenager classification, it would be surprising if the young adults more often took the position that the current crop of adolescents was better than their own. By the same token, at least half of the parents no longer had teenagers in their households; to say that a later cohort showed a net improvement would seem to be a critical commentary on their own children and on their roles as child-raisers. Whatever the process, the relevant point for us is that the generations did not draw apart on a contemporary youth-related issue, where the youth in question are members of a succeeding cohort about which both parents and young adults could feel somewhat removed.

CONCLUDING REMARKS

We began our discussion of aggregate comparisons between the generations and over time by noting the controversy and ambiguity surrounding the question of conflict between the generations. We offered a number of models to help guide us through the results showing the configuration of the two generations as they moved from 1965 to 1973. One conclusion can be drawn with certainty. Configurations compatible with each of the suggested models emerged in the findings and analyses. Not that these models accommodated or definitively accounted for all of the many patterns uncovered across the wide range of phenomena included in our inquiry. Yet there was evidence pointing very strongly toward continuity as well as change growing out of the pure and mixed impact of generational, life-cycle, and period effects.

Although the diverse findings defy easy generalization in terms of the generational conflict argument, some broad assessments can be ventured. In many respects the flow of the two generations over time had, if anything, brought them closer together than they had been initially. Only in certain issue areas, in partisanship, and in some elements of cognition could it be said that there was a noticeable pulling apart of the generations. To the extent that differences increased, they

took the form of the younger generation's having emerged with slightly to moderately more liberal political views, greater independence in
partisanship, marginally higher Democratic voting behavior, and greater ideological sophistication. Differences on contemporary issues,
while certainly present, were not nearly as severe as they were perceived to be by each generation. Of the other orientations covered,
the pattern tended to be either one of little change over time or of
visible convergence. Considering that three-fifths of our young generation attended college, that approximately one-half of the males served
in the military, that the country was in an uproar during much of the
eight-year period, and that open efforts were made to pit the young
against the middle-aged, one can only marvel that the gulf did not
widen rather than narrow.

Part of the explanation lies in the sorts of indicators we have used.
Rather than restrict ourselves to matters of affect and preference we
have also introduced measures of involvement, resources, and participation. To the extent that the generation gap hypothesis rests purely
on contrasting issue preferences, the examination of these other dimensions establishes the limitations in scope of any existing gap.

More fundamentally, however, the presence of other processes can
be seen either drawing the generations together or, less often, pulling
them apart. Clearly, life-cycle effects were present, working primarily
(but with significant exceptions!) to hold the parents on a plane while
drawing their offspring toward them. We saw this most vividly in the
domains of involvement, resources, and participation. Period effects
sometimes prompted parallel shifts in both generations, most notably
regarding evaluations of the political system and of governmental actors. And there were, indeed, some visible signs of lasting generational
effects as in information inventories and certain issues of our time.
There was also suggestive evidence of nascent generational effects
which may not fully crystallize for some time.

Despite these multiple processes at work and some instances of
growing divergence, what stands out as we watch these two generations over time are the strong vectors acting to bring them in line.
These come, in substantial part, from the life-space changes accompanying the aging process among the young. Those forces, while perhaps weaker now than in the past, are still massive shapers of behavior
and belief. Complementing this source of convergence are the forces
of contemporary history which touch the lives of young and middle-
aged alike. If the middle-aged were unresponsive to these effects, differences between the generations would persist or increase. While
malleability is higher among the young, there is graphic evidence in

our materials that change occurs in the middle years also. Society-wide forces exert their influence on each generation and thus help bind them. The frequent upshot of the two sets of forces is a smoothing out of intergenerational antagonism, a smoothing out accomplished even over eight turbulent years of political history.

CHAPTER SEVEN

The Identification of Generations:
Cohort versus Panel Change

I N the two previous chapters we utilized panel data from the two generations to explore questions of aggregate change and continuity.
Three major processes were observed: historical or period effects
which seem to be operating on both the older and younger generations, generation effects which appear to be distinguishing the two
generations, and life-cycle effects which presumably characterize
each generation as it ages. While such effects were sometimes relatively pure, as in the case of political trust, there were other instances
where hybrid models applied or where interpretation remained ambiguous.

Particularly vexing was the problem of trying to distinguish between
generational and nongenerational (i.e., life-cycle or period) effects.
This difficulty arises from both technical and theoretical considerations. On the technical side, a major problem is the absence of panel
data covering the entire life cycle or data for several distinct generations. For example, if youths are "lower" than parents on some measure—and even if they have increased slightly over the eight-year panel
—the difference could be due to the fact that youths are in a much
earlier stage of the life cycle than parents, or it could be because the
youths belong to a new political generation. Without elaborate
amounts of data over an extended time frame, it is virtually impossible
to conclude firmly that one explanation rather than the other is correct. The *amount* of change observed sometimes provides useful clues.
If young people have surpassed parent levels by age 25, it is likely that
there are generational effects, perhaps in combination with life-cycle
effects. Yet even in this case some ambiguity remains.

The usual way out of this dilemma is to rely on theoretical knowledge about life-cycle development and about the historical era in question. Theory will often suggest that one explanation is much more
plausible than another. Here, however, theory provides relatively little
assistance. As discussed extensively before, there are good reasons to
expect life-cycle changes, particularly in the younger generation. But we
also observed that there is both popular and academic work suggesting
that a new political generation had come into existence. And of course,

period effects of some sort were almost certain. All of this leaves us in a particular quandary with respect to generational effects.

In order to explore these concerns more fully, we take advantage of an additional set of data along with the youth and parent panels. Part of the original 1965 data gathering included the administration of paper-pencil questionnaires to all available members of the senior class in 79% of the 97 sample schools, for an unweighted N of 20,674. In 1973 we were able to administer a similar questionnaire to high school seniors in 88% of the original schools, for an N of 16,929. Although the 1965 and the 1973 questionnaires differed in some respects, they included questions on a number of political and personal variables that were identical in the two years and were as similar as possible to the interview questions. These questionnaire data, along with the companion youth and parent panel data, are the basis for the analysis in this chapter.

With appropriate weighting, the two mass questionnaire samples can be characterized as reasonably representative of the high school senior universe in the two years. The 1965 mass sample is not as representative as the original 1965 interviewees' sample due to the refusal of some schools to allow the administration of the questionnaire and to the fact that local conditions and absenteeism contributed to less than full response rates on the self-administered questionnaires. In addition, the 1973 sample is biased to the extent that the universe had changed its parameters since 1965, e.g., through school consolidation. Also, schools that were nonexistent in 1965 are unrepresented in the 1973 sampling. However, a number of cross checks and comparisons with contemporaneous data collected by the United States Bureau of the Census' Current Population Surveys and by the Bureau of Labor Statistics lead us to the conclusion that the amount of bias does not seriously affect the results to be reported here.

For convenience, we will refer to the questionnaire materials as *youth cohort data*, since each sample represents a cohort defined as those who were high school seniors in the respective years. These replicated cross-section data are to be distinguished from the *youth and parent panel data*, which consist of materials gathered from the same respondents in 1965 and 1973. While the word "cohort" correctly describes the two senior class samples, our analysis should not be confused with typical "cohort analyses," in which birth cohorts are studied by means of successive cross-section samples (each covering a wide age span) taken at different points in time.[1]

---

[1] The introduction of the 1973 cohort is especially helpful in reducing the threats to validity stemming from maturational (life-cycle) effects. For example,

MODELS OF COHORT AND PANEL CHANGE

The availability of the replicated surveys from the senior classes of 1965 and 1973 gives us a powerful tool for determining which models best describe aggregate continuity and change over the 1965-1973 period. This is best seen by considering ideal models like those shown in Chapter 5, but with the youth cohorts added. Of course, even setting up ideal models showing cohort and two-panel movements is a complicated task, and the following models are offered only as general guides. Nonetheless, they show how the addition of the youth cohort data clarifies some configurations.

The first ideal model (not shown) is virtually the same as Figure 5.1a. In it there is no change among either the panel members or the youth cohorts. In the terminology of the parental-filial comparisons this would be called absolute continuity. Because we observed relatively little complete continuity when comparing the two panel generations—in part because the filial generation usually registered some visible movement—this should be an infrequent pattern. If found, however, continuity in the youth cohort is an important factor since it shows that the absence of a generational cleavage carried over to 1973.

A second model is an ostensibly pure period effects model and is the same as Figure 5.1b (with a third parallel line added for the youth cohorts). Even this relatively pure model shows how data from the youth cohorts is useful for sorting out of life-cycle from period effects. In Chapters 5 and 6 we interpreted congruent shifts by parent and youth panels as evidence of period effects. Yet more or less congruent moves by parent and youth panels—especially if the changes among the youths were slightly greater—could be the result of life-cycle developments in which change does not stop in early adulthood. But if we now detect the same kind of movement between the cohorts as in

---

if both the youth panel and the youth cohorts change in a similar fashion over time, we are on much safer ground in inferring period or generational effects than if we have only the youth panel data in hand—despite the helpful presence of the parent panel. The topic of complex designs such as this is taken up in Leslie L. Roos, "Panels, Rotations, and Events," in Leslie L. Roos and James A. Caporaso (eds.), *Quasi-Experimental Approaches* (Evanston, Ill.: Northwestern University Press, 1973). See also Paul B. Baltes, "Longitudinal and Cross-Sectional Sequences in the Study of Age and Generation Effects," *Human Development*, 11 (No. 4, 1968), 145-71; and K. Warner Schaie, "A General Model for the Study of Developmental Problems," *Psychological Bulletin*, 64 (August 1965), 92-107. For an ingenious design in the field of political socialization that includes cross-sectional, panel, and cohort components see Kenneth D. Bailey, "The Development of Political Orientations in Children: A 'Telescoped' Longitudinal Approach," paper presented at the annual meeting of the American Association for Public Opinion Research, Buck Hill Falls, Pa., May 1977.

the two panels, it would be doubly difficult to reject the probability of period effects. Of course, even this expanded data base offers no fool-proof way of determining which of several alternative explanations is correct. In the case at hand it might be that period effects account for the movement between the cohorts and life-cycle effects for the move-ment of the panels. Yet this configuration—especially if supported by theoretical expectations—lends added credence to our interpretation of period effects.

As we have indicated, the addition of the youth cohort data is useful in assessing both the pure continuity and period effects models. But the particular virtue of this added data base is that it helps in detecting the presence or absence, as well as the duration, of generational ef-fects. Consider, for example, the model shown in Figure 7.1a. With only the youth and parent panel data, it is difficult to detect genera-tional influences. Although parental continuity and youthful conver-gence toward the parents are suggestive of life-cycle effects, they could equally well result from some combination of life-cycle and genera-tional effects. Adding the line for the youth cohorts, while not a perfect solvent, helps distinguish among these possibilities.

To see this, compare Figures 7.1a and b. In both cases, parent and youth panel data are identical, but the conclusions we would draw are different. Figure 7.1a makes the best case for pure life-cycle effects. The youth panel is converging toward the parents, while the new group of twelfth-graders is identical to the youth panel when they were high school seniors. There is no guarantee that the youths will con-verge to the exact position of the parents; some generational forces may prevent them from ever reaching that level. Yet one can quite confidently conclude that the youths of 1965 and of 1973 are part of the same generation, and that as they age they are moving in the di-rection of parental states. Figure 7.1b, by contrast, shows an example in which the 1973 cohort diverges from that of 1965. Presumably a generational shift has occurred. While the same life-cycle tendencies apparent in the youth panel may lead to a subsequent increase in the 1973 cohort, it begins farther removed from current parental attri-butes than did the preceding generation.

Purely generational models are also more interpretable with the ad-dition of the youth cohorts. Figure 7.2 makes this apparent. In 7.2a the parent and youth panels display absolute continuity. But something happened to the 1973 cohort which made it deviate from the 1965 cohort. The most obvious explanation for this is generational; since the youth and parental panels did not change, life-cycle and period effects would seem to be ruled out.[2]

[2] As usual, this is not foolproof evidence. For example, the panels might ordi-

FIGURE 7.1: Models of Aggregate Continuity and Change

1965   1973

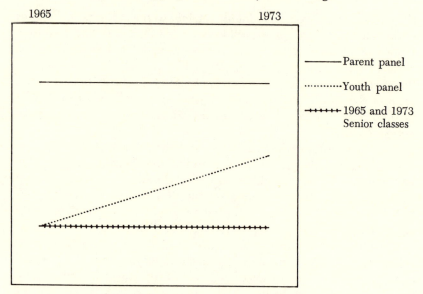

———— Parent panel

············ Youth panel

++++++ 1965 and 1973
Senior classes

(a) Life-cycle effects: youth panel converges with parent panel, youth cohorts remain the same

1965   1973

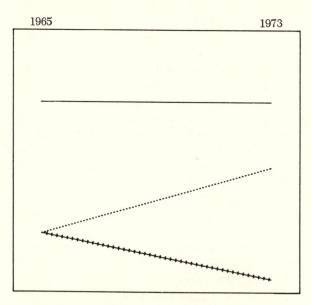

(b) Life-cycle-generational effects: youth panel converges with parent panel, youth cohorts diverge

FIGURE 7.2: Models of Generational Effects

1965   1973

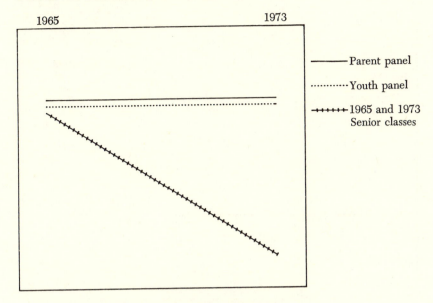

——— Parent panel

············ Youth panel

++++++ 1965 and 1973
        Senior classes

(a) 1973 cohort a new generation: youth and parent
panels remain the same, youth cohorts change

1965   1973

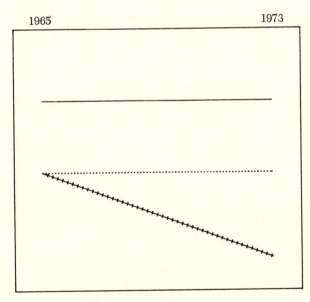

(b) 1965 and 1973 cohorts are new generations: gap
persists between youth and parent panels, youth cohorts
change

FIGURE 7.2 (cont.)

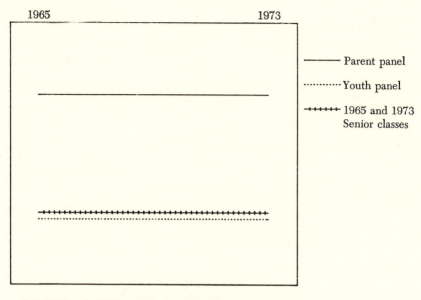

1965   1973

———— Parent panel

············ Youth panel

+++++ 1965 and 1973
      Senior classes

(c) 1965 and 1973 cohorts are part of same new generation: gap persists between youth panel and cohorts versus parent panel, youth panel and cohorts remain the same

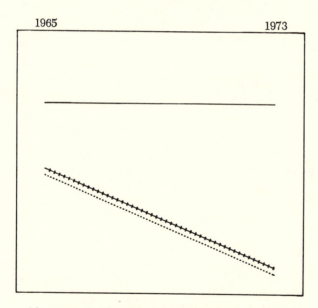

1965   1973

(d) 1965 and 1973 cohorts are part of same new generation: gap persists between youth panel and cohorts versus parent panel, youth panel and cohorts change

Note, however, that more than just the presence of generational effects is revealed. In 7.2a the youths who were high school seniors in 1965 appear to be part of the same generation as parents. The generational shift occurred sometime after 1965. For contrast, consider the rather similar configuration in Figure 7.2b. Parent and youth panels are stable and thus no life-cycle or period effects are inferred; and the change in the youth cohorts suggests a new generation in 1973. But the high school seniors of 1965 were already different from their parents. Thus there are at least two generational shifts—between parents and 1965 seniors and between '65 and '73 seniors. One can also imagine, of course, situations intermediate between these two in which one generational change is large and the other is small.

Still another configuration which we might encounter is depicted in Figure 7.2c. Neither the panels nor the youth cohorts change across the eight years, but a sizeable gap exists between the parental panel versus the youth panel and cohorts. This pattern, like the previous one, strongly suggests generational differences. But here 1965 and 1973 high school seniors are part of the same generation. Apparently the processes setting off the filial and parental generations were sufficiently long lasting to color the makeup of the cohort coming along eight years later.

The last figure, 7.2d, is rather similar to 7.2c. Here a sizeable gap exists between the parent panel and the youth panel and cohorts, but the latter two change between 1965 and 1973. Presumably the same forces that created the divergence between parents and youths in 1965 continued to operate, forcing both the youth panel respondents and the 1973 seniors even farther from parental levels.

These various models by no means exhaust the logical possibilities. For example, we could encounter a hybrid generation-period effects model similar to that shown for parent and youth panels in Figure 5.1e. In some degree ambiguity will still pervade our interpretations. Nevertheless, the ideal models shown here nicely reveal the added interpretive power made possible by the youth cohort data.

A Methodological Note. A methodological point with substantive implications should be made about the entries on the graphs to follow. Over half of the time (15 of 26 cases) the 1965 entries for the youth panel and cohort respondents are very similar, within 5% of each other. This matching is desirable for the kinds of comparisons we wish to make. The rest of the time, however, the difference between the two entries is more substantial, complicating cross-time comparisons.

---

narily have increased due to life-cycle factors, but strong period effects held them constant. Theoretical interpretations must still be relied upon to help distinguish among possible alternative explanations.

There are two possible explanations for the discrepancies. One involves sampling. Panel respondents were randomly drawn from class lists in the participating schools; the response rate was 99%. Cohort respondents came from about three-fourths of the schools, and there was a differential take across schools. Although the bias appears to be slight, it is conceivable that this difference sets off the cohort from the panel respondents on some variables.

A second possibility is that the differences might result from instrument effects. There is no question that the setting for a personal interview is quite different from that for a self-administered questionnaire. While a personal interview is preferable for open-ended questions, and while it discourages respondents from making random answers or playing games with answer patterns, it also is affected by role expectations. The presence of the interviewer is obtrusive and affects responses primarily in the direction of socially desirable answers.[3] In contrast, the self-administered instrument, while deficient on the qualities noted above, has the advantage of being essentially an asocial experience. The respondent is taking few personal cues and is not trying to please an interviewer.

Looking at the discrepancies that occurred lends support to this explanation. Panel respondents typically gave more socially acceptable answers than did cohort respondents. On the political trust items, for example, the panel members invariably gave the more trusting answer. The same was true of political efficacy and two of the three interpersonal trust items. The panel respondents also professed to be more interested in governmental affairs. More of them said that they went to church every Sunday. In the context of 1965 at any rate, these are all in the direction of more socially acceptable answers.[4]

As it turns out, these discrepancies do not constitute a severe problem, whatever their cause. Instrument effects operative in 1965 were undoubtedly also operative in 1973. Thus questionnaire response comparisons over time, or interview comparisons over time, should be equally valid. And on the positive side, one gain from having both types of data is that inferences can be made about instrument effects.

[3] For a comprehensive treatment of various effects see Seymour Sudman and Norman M. Bradburn, *Response Effects in Surveys: A Review and Synthesis* (Chicago: Aldine, 1974). See also Jean M. Converse and Howard Schuman, *Conversations at Random: Survey Research as Interviewers See It* (New York: Wiley, 1974), and Robert L. Kahn and Charles F. Cannell, *The Dynamics of Interviewing* (New York: Wiley, 1974).

[4] Since three-fifths of the 1965 interviewees also subsequently completed the self-administered questionnaire, it is possible to compare directly the responses of the same individuals under the two different circumstances. These comparisons revealed that the personal interviews did elicit, on the whole, more socially desirable responses. A brief treatment of these comparisons is presented in Appendix A.

Another gain is that where the cohort and panel responses are virtually identical we have a better estimate of the true population values since we are reasonably sure that instrument effects are absent. Where the two figures differ we are less certain about true values. But that does not hinder our ability to assess the *patterns* of change and continuity.

Another methodological point to make is that the socioeconomic background of the class of 1973 is higher than that of 1965. Illustratively, whereas 43% of the students' fathers in 1965 had not graduated from high school, the same was true of only 35% in 1973. Comparable figures for the students' mothers were 36% in 1965 and 29% in 1973. These changes represent significant gains, both statistically and substantively, over an eight-year period even though the absolute differences may seem small. Their importance lies in the fact that many of the variables to be analyzed in this chapter are related to socioeconomic status (SES). Other things being equal, rises in family SES should have produced corresponding changes in the student profiles. Therefore, if the class of '73 remains the same as the class of '65, or if it actually moves in a direction contrary to that expected on the basis of a higher SES background, we would be inclined to sort the two youth cohorts into two distinct generations, especially if the youth panel fails to show a parallel movement.

Our concern with the possibility of instrument effects leads us to alter the manner of data presentation in this chapter. We will present the results for single questions and items rather than for the composite measures extensively used in the preceding chapters.[5] In addition, a number of questions are used here which are not used elsewhere.

Psychological Involvement in Politics

The small rise in political interest on the part of the youth and parent panels was attributed primarily to life-stage developments. Political interest evidently increases with age well into the adult life span. If this interpretation is correct, we would expect the 1965 and 1973 senior class cohorts to show little or no change in the amount of attention paid to "what's going on in government." As it turns out, the cohort data show little movement, declining only slightly across the eight years (Figure 7.3a).

Although we would not want to overemphasize the small decrease between the two cohorts, it does suggest that, if anything, the secular

[5] This has the added virtue of enabling us to detect particular nuances at work on some of the composite measures such as political trust, political efficacy, and interpersonal trust.

FIGURE 7.3: Interest in Public Affairs

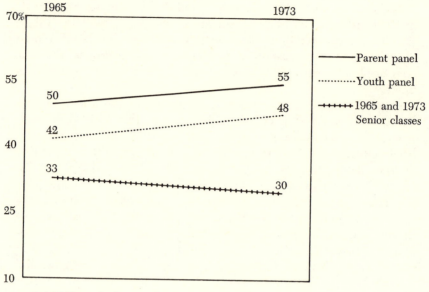

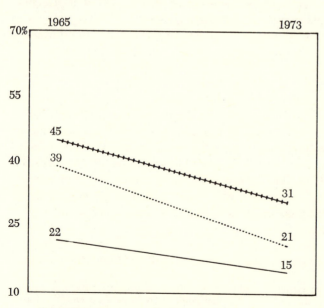

(a) Follow what's going on in government most of the time

(b) Follow international affairs most

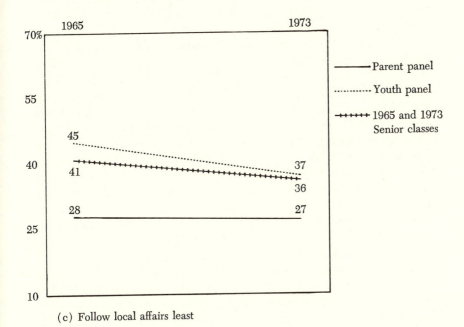

(c) Follow local affairs least

pressures among the young were in the direction of lesser concern with politics. Thus the small though expected gain among the panel respondents was actually working against the effects of Watergate or whatever else was at the base of declining cohort interest. Overall, then, our interpretation remains that the rise in political interest among the panelists was a function of life-stage developments—significantly, developments that do not stop in early adulthood.

Further evidence of cohort differences comes in the form of reports on reading magazines "pretty regularly about public affairs and politics." Because the question was not asked in the 1965 mass-administered survey, our comparison is tainted, but fully congruent with other results. The 1965 youth panelists reported a reading rate of 55%. Even assuming some inflation due to instrument effects, that figure contrasts sharply with the 39% registered by the 1973 cohort in the mass-administered survey. Thus the apparent cohort decline in involvement indexed by the question on general interest in politics does not appear to be specious.

Turning to the focus of political interest, a different and much more complicated sort of over-time change emerges. We contended in Chapter 5 that decreasing cosmopolitanism among the young was primarily a consequence of life-cycle factors as well as, in part, the tenor of the times. The data in Figures 7.3b and 7.3c do not contradict this contention, but they suggest that elements of all three types of change were present.

First, the addition of the cohort data indicates what must be a generational change between 1965 and 1973. The senior class of 1973 is substantially less cosmopolitan in outlook than the class of 1965. In fact, if we allow for the instrument effects or sample bias that raise the 1965 questionnaire responses above the more representative panel group, the 1973 senior class cohort may be only about as international-ist as middle-aged parents were in 1965.[6] We cannot tell whether seniors in 1965 were following the path laid down by the parental genera-tion. The difference in their responses may be life-cycle in origin (see below). But a marked generational shift did occur in the years after 1965.

A second set of forces probably affecting the focus of political inter-est are the life-cycle factors discussed in Chapter 5. Entry into the adult world has long been suspected of shifting young people's atten-tion away from the more remote features of the world scene to the more immediate concerns of one's own country and community. The precipitous drop in the youth panel is consistent with this change, es-pecially considering that the decline was much greater than among the parents.[7] The same conclusion can be drawn from the proportions fol-lowing local affairs least closely, where parents are virtually unmoved while a noticeable drop occurs in the younger generation. Significant-ly, the decline in following *international* affairs most is not completely taken up by greater attention to *local* matters. Thus, a further decline in the youth panel line of Figure 7.3c is likely, which would bring it close to the levels observed for parents.

Even the generational and life-cycle factors together probably do not account for all of the movement in the foci of political interest. Two features of the data suggest that period effects are also involved. For one thing, there is a decline in the proportion of parents following international affairs most, though the drop is not as great as among youths. Moreover, note that the youth panel respondents end up in

[6] The proportion following international affairs most among the 1965 question-naire respondents was 7% more than among the representative sample (45% vs. 38%). If the 1973 questionnaire sample also appears this much more internation-alist than a representative group of interview respondents would be, they are very nearly the same as parents in 1965 (about 25% vs. 22%).

[7] The possibility of floor effects has to be considered when proportions approach levels observed among the parents. In this case, however, there are no absolute floor effects preventing the parental value from declining as much as the youths'. Nor are there theoretical reasons to expect a realistic floor level substantially above zero. And finally, the proportions in the local affairs figure (7.3c) are not subject to this problem.

Figure 7.3b looking even less cosmopolitan than did their parents in 1965. If only life-cycle factors were present, youthful interest in international affairs would have declined, but would probably not have reached parents' 1965 levels for several years.

Overall, then, changes in the salience of varying levels of public affairs are among the most complex of those we have observed. It is impossible to rule out any of the mechanisms responsible for fluctuating adult values. On the contrary, there is evidence that generational, life-cycle, and period effects were all at work in the declining cosmopolitanism of the late 1960s and early 1970s.

POLITICAL RESOURCES: EFFICACY

The circumstances of the mass questionnaire were such that the only political resource items included were the two "internal" and one "external" political efficacy questions. Our previous treatment of efficacy revealed a modest decline in the internal variety among both filial and parental generations, with each generation being about equally affected. Although the cross-generational decline pointed toward period effects, the continuing higher efficacy of the young adults suggested a long-run generational difference—albeit a difference partly based on compositional disparities in the two generations.

With the introduction of the cohort data we have a better purchase on the nature of the dynamics at work during this period. Compared with the senior class of 1965, that of 1973 was visibly less efficacious (Figure 7.4). This applied to the two internal efficacy statements as well as the one external statement included in both surveys. These sharp declines point toward a pronounced generational cleavage, especially in light of the higher SES of the 1973 class. Even allowing for instrument effects, which appear to lead to higher self-declarations of efficacy among the interviewees, the 1973 cohort seems destined to enter young adulthood less confident than was the 1965 cohort about its ability to influence governmental policies. This new generation in fact represents a return to the efficacy levels found in the parental generation, judging by a comparison with the parents' 1965 responses. Thus the generation of the student protests, the Vietnam War, and the anti-heroes turns out to be singular for its greater efficacy.

But these generational tendencies are overlaid on the period effects referred to earlier. All generations, insofar as we can tell, were becoming less efficacious over the panel period. Hence, the generational surge in efficacy apparent in 1965 among the 1965 seniors was partly nullified by the overall decline in the subsequent years. The 1965 senior cohort was still relatively more efficacious than its lineage predeces-

FIGURE 7.4: Political Efficacy

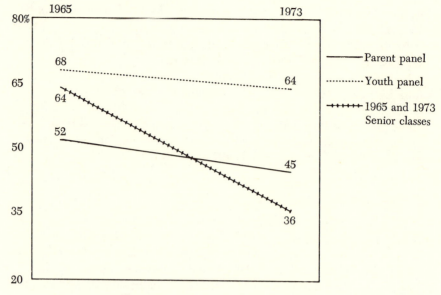

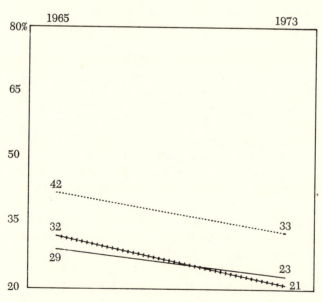

(a) Voting is not the only way to have a say in how the government runs things

(b) Politics is not too complicated to understand

FIGURE 7.4 (cont.)

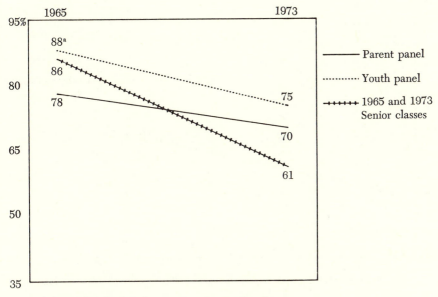

(c) My family does have a say about what the government does

ª Based on response from panel members (N = 1,012) who were part of mass-administered data set.

sor and a succeeding age cohort, but in absolute terms it had, by 1973, declined toward levels of self-confidence expressed in prior years by earlier generations.

PARTISANSHIP AND VOTING BEHAVIOR

One of the most noticeable features of the youth panel was the rise in independence across the eight years, a rise unmatched in the parental generation. From this comparison we were led to deduce a generational effect. Addition of the 1965-1973 cohort trend adds credence to this interpretation. The lines in Figure 7.5a for the youth panel and for the cohorts are virtually overlapping. Whatever forces of disillusionment with the parties or independence of thought were pushing the young adults toward increasing independence as they aged eight years were also affecting the upcoming cohort. In this instance the 1965 and 1973 cohorts are clearly part of the same generation. And it

FIGURE 7.5: Partisanship and Voting

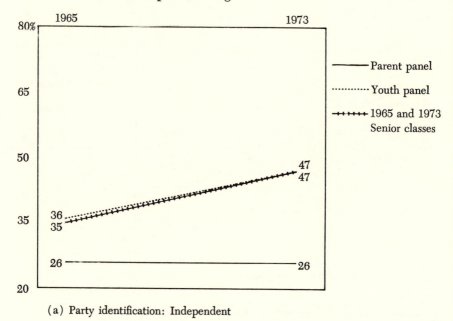

(a) Party identification: Independent

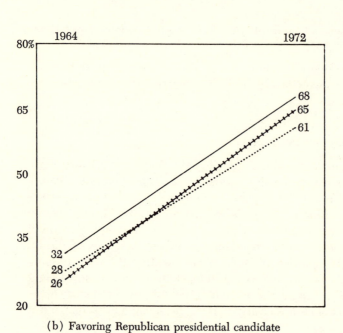

(b) Favoring Republican presidential candidate

seems likely that this trend is still continuing, with the end of the "independent generation" not yet in sight.[8]

Another indicator of partisanship is the reported presidential favorite in the years 1964 and 1972. Once more the results for the youth panel and for the cohorts are virtually identical, and in this instance both are similar to the parent panel (Figure 7.5b). The massive preference for Johnson in 1964 is almost equally matched by the lack of support for McGovern in 1972. Short-term period effects is the immediately suggested model, although additional data on the behavior of the panels in 1968 and 1970 suggest a small generational difference as well. It is unclear from the youth cohort results whether this difference —the greater Democratic preferences among offspring than among parents—also characterizes the 1973 cohort. In any event, the similar slopes and positions of all three lines make it clear that we are primarily viewing strong period effects.

Partly as a methodological note, we should point out that there is essentially no difference between the youth panel and cohort respondents of 1965 for either partisanship or voting. Except in severely homogeneous and politicized environments there would not be any pressure for the youthful interviewees to categorize themselves one way or another with respect to these measures. Hence we have no *prima facie* evidence, at any rate, of instrument effects. We are in a correspondingly better position to say that the sample estimates in Figures 7.5a and 7.5b are exceptionally close to the population values.[9]

OPINIONS ON PUBLIC POLICY ISSUES

Our present discussion of political issues will differ from that of the previous chapter. Neither in 1965 nor in 1973 did the mass questionnaire contain the two school-issue questions—the legitimacy of prayers

---

[8] As of 1973 the youngest cohort is also the least convinced about the efficacy of the American political party system. In response to the statement, "Neither the Democratic nor the Republican party is interested in the needs of people like me," some 42% of the class of 1973 offered agreement. In contrast, only 15% of the youth panel and 19% of the parent panel agreed with that sentiment. Similarly, when confronted with the bald statement that "America needs some new political parties," 57% of the youthful cohort agreed, as contrasted with 42% of the youth panel and only 31% of the parental panel. Although one might well expect the opinions of the 1973 high school seniors to become a little less harsh in the post-Watergate period and as they accumulate a sense of electoral history, their dispositions as of 1973 were scarcely a harbinger of good times for the parties.

[9] There is no contradiction between this conclusion and our indecision in the previous paragraph. Instrument effects in Figure 7.5b are small. But when a difference of a few percentage points is important, as in voting, the apparently minor instrument effects (and sampling bias) make it difficult to be precise about the relative preferences of the 1973 cohort.

in school and the federal government's role in integration. These were omitted primarily because of anticipated and voiced opposition to such questions on a mass basis. On the other hand, there is an additional issue question included in the youth panel interview schedule, the parent schedule in 1973, and in both administrations of the mass questionnaire. This question elicited the respondent's opinion about the superiority of the American form of government. All three issues used here, then, deal with what we have called a civic tolerance dimension.

Our earlier discussion concluded that the rising tolerance of the youth panel (for the two questions treated) was primarily a generational phenomena, though conditioned also by putative period effects, since the parental generation became more liberal on the Communist holding office issue. The panel data for the "American superiority" item, though complete only for the youths, support this interpretation (Figure 7.6c). The youth panel registered a sizeable gain in the proportion disagreeing with the jingoistic statement, and this proportion was greater than that among parents. The 1965 generation appears to be a strikingly tolerant one.

Examining the results for the youth cohorts does nothing to temper our interpretation (Figure 7.6). True, the 1973 class is more tolerant than the class of 1965 on the proposition that a Communist should be allowed to hold office, though the gain is by no means as pronounced

FIGURE 7.6: Opinions on Public Policy Issues

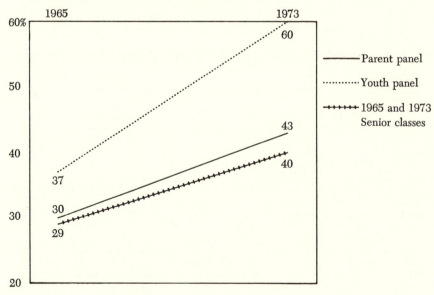

(a) Communist should be allowed to take office elected to

FIGURE 7.6 (cont.)

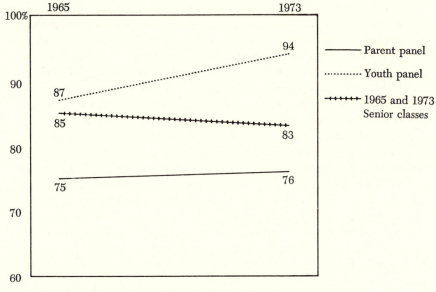

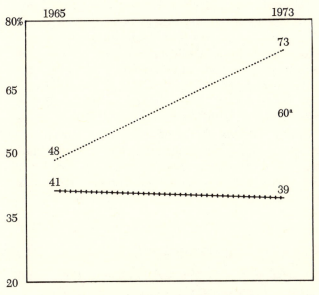

(b) Speeches against religion should be allowed

(c) American system of government is not the system all countries should have

[a]Not asked of parents in 1965.

as that for the youth panel. On the other two items there is actually a small *decrease* in the liberal response. Let us be generous and say that no intercohort differences emerged. This would still place the panel in the much more tolerant posture in 1973. If the trend was toward greater tolerance, as seemed to be the case, the 1973 cohort should have at least shown some increase. Yet it did not do so in two cases out of three. Why should the 1973 cohort not be characterized by the same generational effects which we argued applied to the panel?

One explanation is that the 1965 seniors are different, that the political climate experienced by them helped breed a much more liberal generation. Not having been nurtured by the traumatic events of the 1965-1973 period, the younger cohort may in fact be less sensitive to the issues of civil liberties and tolerance implied by these statements. These data are among the most impressive we have for supporting an argument that the Vietnam generation was not only distinctive from previous ones but distinctive from succeeding ones also.

As attractive as this line of reasoning may be, it is not without weaknesses. It does not square, for example, with other data showing that proximate cohorts of college age have become more tolerant on similar issues.[10] Nor does there seem to have been any massive reactionary trend at large which would make these youngsters less tolerant. An alternative, perhaps complementary, process may be at work. A breakdown of the panel by education shows remarkable gains in tolerance by those going on to college and decidedly smaller gains by those not going on. An appreciation for the kinds of values raised by these issues seems especially dependent on higher education and, to a lesser extent, on the sophistication that comes with more political experience. If that is the case, we would expect the 1973 cohort to have an upsurge in liberal sentiments as it went through the next few years. Of course, we have no way of demonstrating this, since we cannot introduce subsequent data on that cohort. Assuming that our portrayal is realistic, however, the discrepancy between the panel and cohort comparisons can be seen as life-cycle in nature. It would evaporate as the 1973 cohort acquires more education.

EVALUATIONS OF GOVERNMENT: POLITICAL TRUST

The extraordinary decline in trust accorded officials of the federal government in the parental generation was exceeded only by the even

[10] Fewer students in 1971 than in 1969 felt that "belonging to some organized religion is important in a person's life." Fewer in 1970 and in 1971 than in 1969 agreed that "the American way of Life is superior to that of any other country." See Daniel Yankelovich, Inc., *The Changing Values on Campus* (New York: Pocket Books, 1972), 41, 68.

more severe drop in the filial generation. Our interpretation of similar movements in both generations was that of exceptionally strong period contributions, with perhaps some small components of both generational and life-cycle impact in the case of the younger generation. Introducing the opinions of the 1965 and 1973 cohorts reinforces this view. Figures 7.7a-7.7e show the percentages accorded the most trusting, least cynical, alternative among the standard five items used to elicit feelings of political trust. Both the panels and cohorts register extraordinarily sharp movements, all in the direction of less trust. Coupled with the information from successive cross-sectional national surveys, these trend lines point unequivocally toward strong period effects.

A singular characteristic of the panel and cohort comparisons, however, is the lower reported trust in 1965 of youths who filled out the questionnaire as against those who were interviewed. Again, the very probable reason for the discrepancy is the anonymity provided by the nature of the paper-pencil administration. Thus, if one were trying to estimate the true levels of trust or cynicism among youth in 1965, the mass-administered results are probably more realistic. Especially as long ago as 1965, the more socially appropriate answer to a question about the rectitude, wisdom, and judgment of national officials was positive rather than negative.

Although the presence of period effects is dramatic, it is also possible that generational effects are present. Observe that the pitch of the cohort trend line is considerably steeper even than that for the youth panel on three of the five items. The same is true of a sixth item closely related to the five trust items (Figure 7.7f). As a result, even allowing for instrument effects, the 1973 cohort was less trusting than the young adults in that same year.

We should point out, however, that here is the one instance where the difference in timing of the personal interviews in 1973 versus the administration of the questionnaires in that same year assumes importance. Interviews began in January and were largely completed by the end of March, whereas the mass administrations did not begin until mid-April and were not completed until the end of May. Recalling the political history of those months reveals that the Watergate disclosures became increasingly dramatic and negative in their impact. It is undoubtedly no accident that the biggest differential between the cohort and panel soundings occurred on the statement about dishonest people running the government. We might, then, be observing an artifact of the timing in data-gathering.[11] On the other hand, the greater mallea-

---

[11] Preliminary analysis indicates that cynicism scores did, indeed, increase even over the course of the mass-administered phase of the study.

FIGURE 7.7: Political Trust

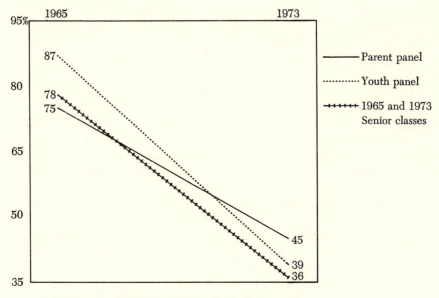

(a) Government is run for the benefit of all the people

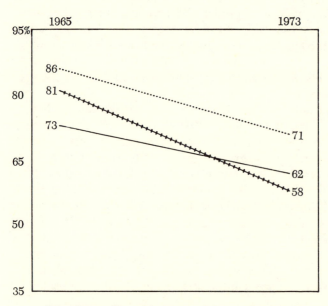

(b) Almost all people running the government know what they are doing

FIGURE 7.7 (cont.)

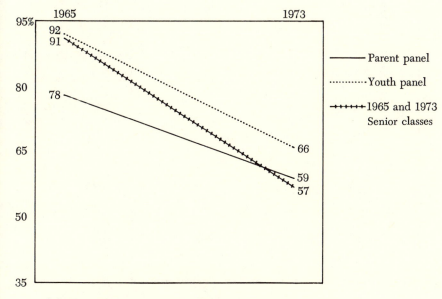

(c) Trust government in Washington about always or most of the time

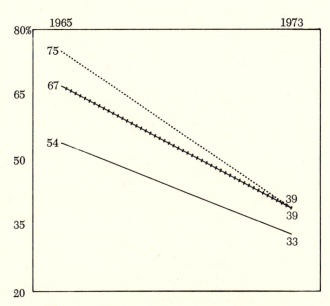

(d) Government wastes not much or some money

FIGURE 7.7 (cont.)

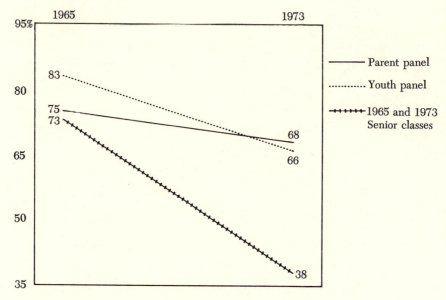

(e) Hardly any or not many people running the government are dishonest

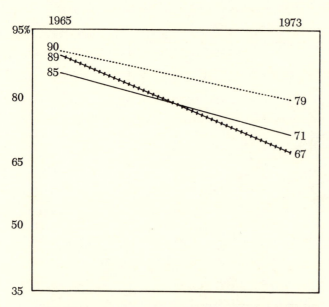

(f) Government pays a good deal or some attention to what people think

bility of the 1973 seniors meant that these revelations and the general ambience of the times had a greater impact on them.

Just as the absolute trust accorded the operations of the federal government underwent a drastic decline over the eight-year span, so too did the relative trust accorded the national government. There was a corresponding rise in the relative positioning of local and state governments, especially the former. We attributed part of this movement to period effects because there was some movement in both generations. But the modest nature of the parental shift led us to conclude that life-cycle and generational effects also influenced the filial generation.

Cross-cohort change is even more marked than that for the youth panel, but both testify to the diminished standing of the national government (Figure 7.8). Combined with the evidence for the parental generation, these results underscore the presence of period effects. But the much more dramatic results in the youth panel and cohorts point toward processes well beyond simple effects of the time period. In particular, a strong presumptive case for generational effects can be made, effects that apply to both the youth panel and the cohorts. The 47% decline registered by the 1973 cohort on high faith and confidence in the national government is steeper than any other observed in our data, while the 31% figure for the youth panel approaches the steepest. Again, it is possible that the 1973 cohort was reacting to the further Watergate disclosures, thereby adding to the downward plunge. In any event, the much greater change in both the youth panel and cohorts than among the parents suggests a strong generational component. Of course, life-cycle effects were also most likely at work in the panel, much as they were for previous cohorts. But the thrust of the movements is so strong that both the 1965 and 1973 cohorts had attained a level of relative distrust of the national government apparently reached by earlier cohorts only at a much later stage in the life cycle.

NONPOLITICAL ORIENTATIONS

The heightened secularization of the youth panel, especially when compared with the parent panel, was noted in the previous chapter. Strong generational and moderate life-cycle effects were posited. The cross-cohort data substantiate this interpretation. In the first place, the incidence of nonaffiliation with formal religious groups rose from 6% in 1965 to 12% in 1973, a rise similar to that of the youth panel (2% to 13%), but noticeably greater than that of the parent panel (2% to 4%). This is strong support for the inference of a generational change.

FIGURE 7.8: Faith and Confidence in Levels of Government

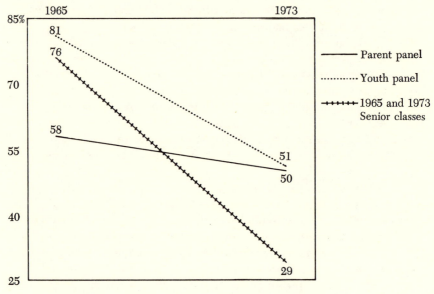

(a) Most faith and confidence in national level of government

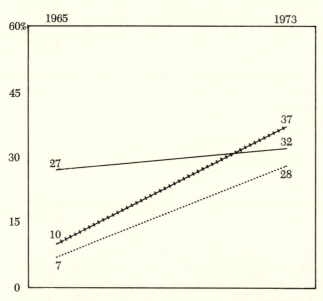

(b) Most faith and confidence in local level of government

Reported weekly church attendance also declined substantially between the 1965 and 1973 cohorts. In fact, it declined to the point that
the 1973 seniors were regularly attending church less than the parents
had in 1965 (Figure 7.9). Again this supports the view that some gen-

FIGURE 7.9: Weekly Church Attendance

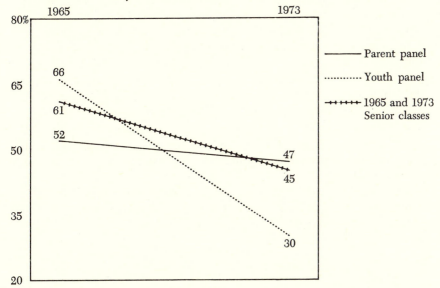

erational change was occurring. Still, the drop in cohort attendance,
while sizeable, was much less than the sharp drop-off in the youth
panel data. While it is possible that the youth panel respondents represent a unique segment of the under-thirty generation, a more reasonable expectation is that the 1973 cohort will show similar erosion
of religious devotion as it ages eight years. Thus a combination of generational and life-cycle effects would seem to be at work. Both youth
cohorts as of 1973 were considerably less religious in the conventional
sense than the parental generation, thereby demonstrating a generational effect.[12] But the gap between the two youthful cohorts suggests

[12] Church attendance normally drops off in early adulthood and then rises later
on. But the decline was probably not so great in past generations. For example,
Gallup polls in the late 1950s and early 1960s showed a difference in weekly
church attendance between people in their twenties and those fifty and older
which averaged about 4%. In the late 1960s and early 1970s, this difference averaged about 12%. Moreover, the increase in nonaffiliation suggests a less religious
generation. Data on church attendance are found in George Gallup, *The Gallup
Poll* (New York: Random House, 1972).

that the younger will undergo yet further declines, something that we would ascribe to life stage.

In the area of social-psychological attributes, we have over-time cohort and panel data for two characteristics. A rather uniform set of results emerges with respect to the measure of interpersonal trust. It will be recalled that both generations registered a moderate decrease in the trust attached to other people. We surmised that a period effect was at work. Although the declines in interpersonal trust are but pale shadows of those for political trust, they are symptomatic of the more general malaise which appeared to be gripping the nation. In most respects the intercohort comparison is even more convincing on this point. Declines in trust are more substantial for the cohorts than for the panel on all of the items comprising the interpersonal trust index (Figure 7.10). These downward movements approach 20% for each question. In general these results weaken the alternative interpretation of declining trust over the life cycle. Mild period effects seem to be at work plus a possible added generational distinction marking off the youngest cohort.

The other measure for which we have data is the degree of self-confidence. We observed earlier that both generations changed very slightly in the direction of higher self-confidence. In the cohort data

FIGURE 7.10: Interpersonal Trust

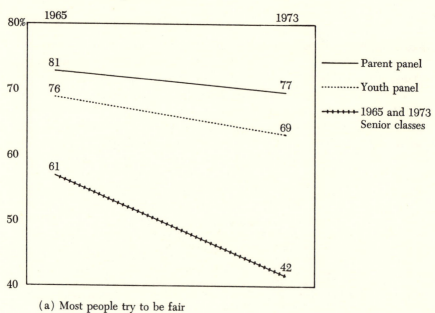

(a) Most people try to be fair

FIGURE 7.10 (cont.)

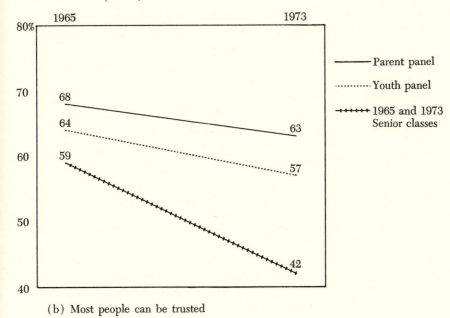

(b) Most people can be trusted

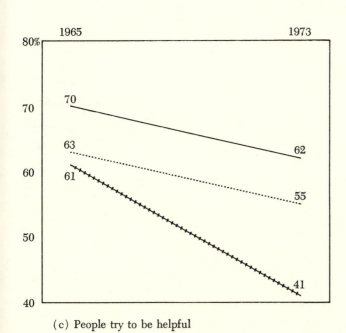

(c) People try to be helpful

there is a slight hint that the 1973 senior class is blessed with somewhat less self-confidence than its predecessor of eight years previously
(Figure 7.11). There is a modest drop from 1965 to 1973 on two of
the three items making up the index and essentially no change on the
third. This contrasts with virtually no change for the youth panel on
two of the items (but not a drop) and a small 4% rise on the third;
for the parents there were small increases on two of the measures and
a somewhat larger surge on the third item. We may, then, be seeing
the makings of a generational effect which would set off the 1973 cohort from both the parental generation and the cohort of 1965.

FURTHER COMPARISONS OF THE 1965 AND 1973 COHORTS

The self-administered questionnaires used in the canvassing of the
entire senior classes contained several questions that were not asked in
the personal interviews. Responses to these questions can be used to
shed further light on the strong suggestion already offered that generational differences were emerging between the class of 1965 and the
class of 1973. If the response patterns of the two classes to the same
stimuli differ appreciably, then we will have additional evidence for
inferring a generational gap between these two cohorts separated by

FIGURE 7.11: Personal Efficacy: Self-Confidence

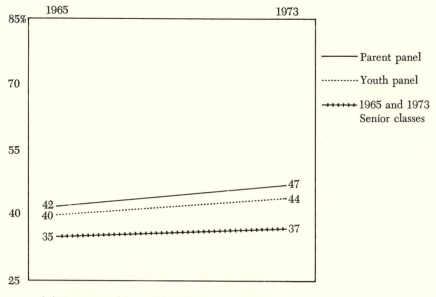

(a) Pretty sure life would work out the way I want it to

Figure 7.11 (cont.)

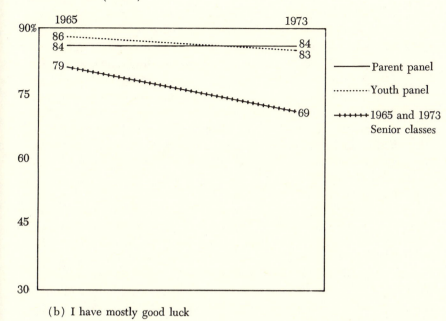

(b) I have mostly good luck

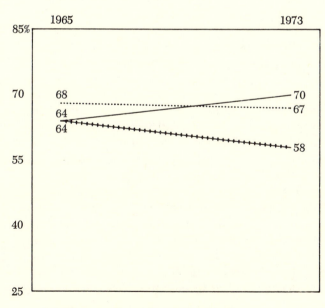

(c) Plans usually work out as expected

only eight years. Our basis for inference will not, of course, be as strong in the absence of data showing how the class of 1965 would have responded to these stimuli in 1973. At the very least, however, we can say that as they stood on the verge of adulthood the two cohorts had different characteristics. The presumption is that if two cohorts begin the race with different traits, then the race will be run in a different fashion and with possibly different outcomes. When coupled with the results from the more complete analysis based on panel and cohort respondents, the data from the responses unique to the questionnaire will give us strong grounds for claiming true generational differences.

At the outset it is worth noting that the two classes differed widely on several properties that, while not explicitly political in nature, nevertheless have political overtones. For example, the proportions reporting that they drink beer at least occasionally rose from 39% to 61%; a comparable rise occurred with respect to hard liquor—35% to 60%. These are extraordinarily sharp increases, signaling a much earlier entry into forms of social behavior more typically reserved for adults. Although reported usage of marijuana was much lower, at 28%, this figure was already nearly as high as the 35% figure reported by the youth panel respondents in 1973. (The question was not asked in 1965.) On the very likely assumption that marijuana usage increased in young adulthood, the 1973 class again stands out for showing early signs of "adult" behavior. In the measure that the use of alcohol and marijuana reflects in varying degrees an alteration in social norms, if not indeed in legal norms, the 1973 cohort may be said to be more indulgent and adultlike than was its 1965 predecessor at the same stage. This pattern is congruent with the findings concerning religious behavior.

The greater distrust of others evidenced by the class of 1973 seems to be part of a general syndrome of more cynicism and dissatisfaction with others, especially with authorities. Manifestations of that syndrome are readily apparent in how the students viewed authority relations in their schools at the two different points in time. For example, agreement that "teachers treat everyone fairly" in their schools dropped from 43% in 1965 to 24% in 1973. By the same token, agreement that teachers had never treated them personally in an unfair manner dropped from 47% to 36%, and that administrators had never treated them unfairly from 82% to 65%. On all counts, then, the class of 1973 was less sanguine about the place of students in the authoritative and decision-making processes within the school—in short, about the school as a political system. It seems unlikely that the "objective" conditions sparking these declines had really changed that much between

1965 and 1973, especially in view of developments in the area of student rights, affirmative action, and citizen oversight. Rather, the students' sensitivity was raised. Perhaps they were simply more realistic by 1973; clearly they were more suspicious and imbued with a sense of unfairness.

Attitudes and behaviors in the realm of student autonomy and influence also underwent alteration over the eight-year period. Although students are always inclined to think they are unduly circumscribed in the confines of the school, the percentage claiming that to be the case increased from an already high figure of 83% in 1965 to an even higher mark of 91% in 1973. In a somewhat broader vein, support for the statement that students participate a good deal in running school affairs (as opposed to teachers and administrators deciding everything) declined from 47% in 1965 to 31% in 1973. Overt forms of "political" participation also declined. Whereas in 1965 some 56% of the students claimed to have run for office either in or out of school, that figure had declined to 42% in 1973. By the same token, even the proportion of students having held two or more offices or committee heads dropped slightly from 39% to 31%. Significantly, the decreases in competing for office and in holding positions occurred despite the fact that the average size of the schools surveyed in 1973 was smaller than was the case in 1965, an important datum because size of class is inversely related to amount of extracurricular participation. On balance, then, the 1973 cohort felt more ineffectual in school and was less participative in student body governance.

Although we have argued that the school is but a poor microscopic reflection of the real world of politics, and that attitudes and behaviors observed at the high school level do not necessarily have their political parallels later on, there is evidence of at least modest connections—as we saw in looking at the relationship between political trust and perceived school fairness with the 1965 data,[13] and in looking at the association between school participation levels and adult political participation levels in Chapter 5. Assuming that these admittedly modest relationships hold as the level of high school dissatisfaction and participation varies, it follows that increases in the perceptions of unfairness and inequity and of decreases in participative orientations can have a net impact on the magnitudes of certain subsequent political manifestations. Perhaps more significantly, and less directly, the general syndrome of greater distrust and dissatisfaction combined with lesser engagement could spill over into the world of *realpolitik* in a

---

[13] M. Kent Jennings and Richard G. Niemi, *The Political Character of Adolescence* (Princeton: Princeton University Press, 1974), 223-25.

number of unanticipated ways. In this respect, the class of 1973 began its adult political history with a quite different set of prepolitical experiences than did the class of 1965.

Shifting to the explicitly political domain, we find further evidence of the contrast between the two high school cohorts. We observed earlier (Figure 7.3a) that the 1973 cohort registered fractionally lower general interest in politics. This decrease is more strongly reflected in the frequency of political conversations reported by the two classes. Table 7.1 shows the degree of political discourse with family members and with friends. The class of 1973 clearly falls behind its predecessor. These are by no means precipitous drops, but they are greater than that for interest in general. These are also reports of behaviors rather than attitudes. As we have seen, the aggregate profiles in behaviors tend to be less susceptible to severe changes over time than do profiles in attitudes and evaluation. It should also be reiterated that the 1973 cohort comes from homes where the average educational level is higher than that for the 1965 cohort. Despite this, the class of 1973 began its political history with less psychological involvement in politics.

TABLE 7.1: Political Conversations with Family and Friends

	Class of 1965	Class of 1973
With family		
Several times per week	37%	30%
Few times per month	45	41
Once or twice per year	13	17
Never	6	12
With friends		
Several times per week	29%	24%
Few times per month	48	40
Once or twice per year	15	17
Never	7	15

This somewhat less active orientation to the political world is also demonstrated in the traits most frequently selected by the class of 1973 as attributes of the good citizen. As Table 7.2 reveals, both classes put a premium on obeying laws. Beyond that, however, there were some distinct differences between the two cohorts. In particular, the more recent class played down the two explicit political characteristics of being proud of one's country and, an especially telling point, of voting

TABLE 7.2: Attributes of the Good Citizen[a]

	Class of 1965	Class of 1973
Obey the laws	72%	74%
Proud of their country	73	67
Vote in elections	70	56
Tolerant of other races, nationalities, religions	64	72
Go to church	12	9
Mind their own business	5	16

[a] Respondents were asked to select three out of the list of six. Totals do not add to 300% due to rounding and to the failure of some respondents to make three selections.

in elections. On the other hand, being tolerant of others was emphasized more, as was minding one's own business.[14]

Combining these results with those already presented, we can categorize the 1973 cohort as distinctly less imbued with the traditional virtues associated with civic training. Politics was less central in their lives and the participant culture was less valued. Indeed, one sees signs of a withdrawal, of a turning inward. In the normal course of events a goodly proportion of the high school class of 1973 became the college senior class of 1977. Both academic and other observers have noted the striking contrast between the latter-day college cohorts and their predecessors of the late 1960s and early 1970s.[15] What is rather remarkable from our perspective is that we can see the adumbrations of the quiescent mood as early as 1973, before the cohort even entered the changing college milieu.

Part and parcel of the new mood apparently sweeping the young cohorts of the mid-1970s was a greater skepticism and cynicism about people and societal institutions. We had convincing glimpses of that in the comparisons based on political and personal trust, with the 1973 cohort emerging as less trusting than the class of 1965 and, significantly, also less trusting than the class of 1965 as assessed some eight years later. Adding materially to this appraisal of the newer cohort are the results from a question dealing with the negative aspects of the United States (Table 7.3). As with its predecessor, the class of 1973 ranked

[14] Fully of a piece with these trends is the fact that when asked how active they expect to be in public affairs and politics when "on their own," 12% of the class of 1965 vs. 6% of the class of 1973 expected to be "very active."

[15] In addition to the everyday evidence, the annual surveys of entering students by the American Council on Education reveal a retrenchment in some respects and a general centrist tendency in political matters.

TABLE 7.3: Qualities Least Proud of as an American[a]

	Class of 1965	Class of 1973
Slums and poverty	70%	75%
Prejudice and discrimination against minorities	62	63
Dirty politics in government	54	63
Lack of interest and participation in public affairs	41	24
People only out for themselves	38	50
Way other countries take advantage of us	29	23

[a] Respondents were asked to select three out of the list of six. Totals do not add to 300% due to rounding and to the failure of some respondents to make three selections.

slums and poverty and prejudice and discrimination at the top of a list of six characteristics presented to the respondents.[16] The classes also resembled each other in not placing much emphasis on the advantage being taken of the United States by other countries, though it is significant that the later cohort thought that less crucial than did the earlier one.

There are three strong differences, however, and they reflect a decided change in societal outlook. Not surprisingly, dirty politics was more salient in 1973. Watergate was taking its toll. What is perhaps more unexpected was the decline in the proportion lamenting the lack of interest and participation in public affairs. Two likely sources for this decline can be cited. On the one hand, the later cohort might simply be saying that there is a plenitude of participation, that the country has nothing to be ashamed of on that score. On the other hand, they may be saying that, compared with other evils, the lack of political activity is not serious, that there are other shortcomings far more crucial. One can see in this playing down of the active political role an echo of the de-emphasis on activism in descriptions applied to the good citizen. If the seniors of 1973 were not as concerned about political participation, they were more concerned about the selfishness and callousness of their fellow human beings. Assertions that people are only out for themselves rose by 12% across the eight years.

Again it should be stressed that the forces that were causing the

[16] It is ironic to note the widespread acknowledgment of slums and poverty as deplorable qualities when respondents were presented a list of predefined problems compared with the scarcity of such replies when they were responding to the open-ended version of this same question. Slums and poverty are seen, therefore, as being important but not terribly salient.

later cohort to differ from the earlier one might also be affecting that earlier one as it aged. We saw some signs of that in comparing panel and cohort data in the previous sections of this chapter. But we also saw that in some respects the two cohorts were distinctive. The material presented in this section, based only on comparisons of the two youth cohorts is, without exception, sympathetic to the proposition that the two cohorts showed definite signs of becoming unique political generations. Even if one assumes that the class of 1965 also underwent subsequent changes, as it surely did in several respects, and even if one assumes that the class of 1973 will undergo modification, as it surely will, it nevertheless remains true that the starting points for the two cohorts were quite different. It is difficult to conceive of their reacting to and engaging in the world of politics in the same fashion, given this contrast.

Conclusion

In one respect the results from adding the youth cohort data are gratifying for what little new they have told us. In only one instance did the added material significantly revise our interpretation of the panel-only data. With respect to civic tolerance, our initial explanation was that the 1965 cohort was considerably more tolerant than the parent generation. The lack of further movement in this direction by the 1973 cohort, along with the connection between tolerance and education, altered our view in the direction of a life-cycle interpretation. But typically the youth cohort trends simply added welcome support to our previous explanations.

From a different perspective, however, the results in this chapter are most gratifying for their positive contribution. We remarked at the outset that the introduction of the youth cohort data would be most useful for distinguishing generational change. That it has done well, chiefly by making clear the extent to which the 1973 cohort stands apart from its 1965 counterpart. Rather surprisingly, it is only in the movement toward independence on the party identification spectrum that the two younger cohorts seemed clearly to be part of the same generation and distinguishable from the parents. Religious differences possibly set off the younger cohorts, though a generational shift in church attendance appeared between 1965 and 1973.

As we noted more fully in Chapters 5 and 6, the thrust of our results suggests, first of all, that even the 1965 seniors were not so widely separated from the attitudes and behavior of their parents as the more extreme proponents of the generation gap thesis insisted. Along with life-cycle forces that have brought them still closer together in some domains, the notion of an unbridgeable or irreversible gap between this generation of parents and their offspring seems weak indeed. What we are able to add now is that the case appears to be as strong or stronger for the emergence of a generational shift between the 1965 and 1973 senior class cohorts. To the extent that the 1965 seniors were defiant of their parents, they did not win the support of high school seniors coming along less than a decade later. Supportive evidence came from the results restricted to the self-administered replications as well as from the fuller, more dynamic results employing both panel and cohort data.

What should not be overlooked in observing this generational change is that the direction of the move was sometimes away from and sometimes in the direction of the orientations of the older, parental generation. The declining interpersonal trust and self-confidence made the 1973 seniors less like the parents than were the seniors of 1965, and also distinguished them from the 1965 cohort. But on the more political items the tendency was for the 1973 cohort to change in the direction of the parents' responses. In some cases the 1973 cohort was actually more like the parents than were the parents' own offspring. For example, with regard to political efficacy, the parents were less efficacious than their children. Consequently, the shift toward lower efficacy levels among the 1973 seniors made them rather similar to the parents—in fact, more similar to the parents than to the high school senior cohort of eight years earlier. On some of the political trust items the younger cohort actually "overshot" the parents, with their declining trust leaving them below the levels of the parents.

This last observation is a fitting conclusion to this chapter. The existence of generational shifts in the eight years following the mid-1960s did not open up wide rifts between the newest cohort and the generation(s) represented by the parents. In fact, the 1965 senior class and the immediately surrounding cohorts are in many respects the deviant case and the 1973 cohort represents a return to more typical pre-adult models. What characterized the generation of the mid- to late-1960s, of course, was its atypical politicization. As we have seen, this manifested itself in heightened political interest and involvement as well as in a host of opinions and feelings about the manner, efficacy, and targets of political participation. Perhaps this is not surprising in light of the momentous events that had taken place even by the middle of the decade. What is enlightening is how quickly this change took hold even of precollege-age young people,[17] and how it receded just as

[17] This applies even to pre-high schoolers. See Roberta S. Sigel and Marilyn Brookes, "Becoming Critical about Politics," in Richard G. Niemi and Associates, *The Politics of Future Citizens* (San Francisco: Jossey-Bass, 1974).

quickly in the 1970s. This recession took the form of the two movements observed in this chapter. The 1965 generation often swung in the direction expected of young adults, thus bringing them closer in attitudes and behavior to their parents' generation. At the same time, the new generation of high school seniors was also changing—in comparison with that of 1965—so that as these students entered adulthood there was a smaller gulf between them and the generation of the parents.

Finally, we reiterate a point made earlier that our conclusions are in part a function of what indicators are used. In this chapter especially, our analysis has dealt little with contemporary issues. On these matters, as on partisanship, a different picture of generational change and cleavage might exist. But for the concerns that we have studied here, the tendency has been for parent and offspring generations to be drawn together, and on most political attributes for the 1973 seniors to shift in such a way as to reduce whatever parent-offspring differences had existed in the mid-1960s. Despite eight exciting, tempestuous years, and despite a good deal of individual and aggregate change, a remarkable degree of intergenerational continuity, or of only short-lived discontinuity, was present.

CHAPTER EIGHT

The Prominence
of Educational Stratification

Of all the demographic characteristics used to account for and specify the distribution of political attitudes and behaviors, none is so pervasive as education. Virtually every major study of American public opinion, electoral behavior, and political participation has devoted at least some energy to pointing out the relationship between level of formal schooling and various attributes. The broad contours of these relationships are well known. In general, the more durable and widespread correlates of education lie in the field of political participation and its preconditions. Psychological involvement in politics, political resources, and a great deal of political activity vary with educational attainments.[1] Standing in contrast to these almost universal regularities are the more uneven correlations in the areas of political preferences, attitudes, and evaluations. However, there is persuasive evidence that education is positively related to a cluster of values and attitudes that are generally called elements of the liberal democratic creed.[2]

While the topography may be reasonably familiar, the forces generating that topography are less well charted. Typically, explanations for education's seeming impact have been ambiguous and ad hoc in nature. But the cursory as well as the more systematic explanations can be grouped under one of two theories.[3]

---

[1] The literature approaches the voluminous. See, inter alia, Angus Campbell, Philip E. Converse, Warren E. Miller, and Donald E. Stokes, *The American Voter* (New York: Wiley, 1960); Gabriel Almond and Sidney Verba, *The Civic Culture* (Princeton, N.J.: Princeton University Press, 1963); Sidney Verba and Norman H. Nie, *Participation in America* (New York: Harper, 1972); Lester Milbrath and M. L. Goel, *Political Participation*, 2nd ed. (Chicago: Rand McNally, 1977); and Herbert H. Hyman, Charles R. Wright, and John Shelton Reed, *The Enduring Effects of Education* (Chicago: University of Chicago Press, 1975).

[2] The seminal study is Samuel A. Stouffer, *Communism, Conformity, and Civil Liberties* (New York: Doubleday, 1955). See also Herbert McClosky, "Consensus and Ideology in American Politics," *American Political Science Review*, 58 (June 1964), 361-82. For an update of the Stouffer study see Clyde Z. Nunn, Harry J. Crockett, Jr., and J. Allen Williams, Jr., *Tolerance for Nonconformity* (San Francisco: Jossey-Bass, 1978). A comprehensive secondary analysis of thirty-eight national surveys is found in Herbert H. Hyman and Charles R. Wright, *Education's Lasting Influence on Values* (Chicago: University of Chicago Press, 1979).

[3] The following paragraphs rely heavily on the lucid presentation by John W.

The older, more prominent model takes the socialization perspective. Schools are viewed as processing institutions. Students are assumed to be imbued with different sets of skills, motivations, and values depending (usually) upon the quantity or (less commonly) the quality of their schooling. These differential effects then guide and influence the individuals' lives for years to come, long after they leave the original site of inculcation. Exactly what it is about the schooling experience that results in different socialization outcomes is often vaguely defined, but most observers conclude that a variety of factors are at work rather than any single factor. The socialization model has often been employed to "explain" how rising educational levels change a political culture.

A second approach has been stated informally for some time but has recently received a more formal exposition in reaction to and as a result of frustration with the socialization model. Most frequently called allocation theory, this approach views educational systems as sorters and selectors of the individuals passing and *not* passing through their portals. The emphasis is more on outcomes than processes. Schools confer success on some and failure on others over and above any socialization outcomes. Schools are viewed as certification institutions with social charters that give them the right to invest their graduates with distinctive properties and qualifications. These qualities are recognized by their possessors and by others in society as qualifying them for given statuses and roles—irrespective, say, of ability level. Credentials provide the basis for allocation, and this allocation in turn leads to differential behaviors, values, and attitudes.

Despite the considerable heat generated by extreme proponents of these two views, there would appear to be, as is customary, points of reconciliation. Thus, Meyer proposes that "students tend to adopt personal and social qualities appropriate to the positions to which their schools are chartered to assign them."[4] Adoption is a mode of socialization. That is, these appropriate qualities do not just magically appear once an individual has been sorted out. By the same token, even some years after one's education is completed, "adults tend to adopt qualities appropriate to the roles and expectations to which their educational statuses have assigned them,"[5] thus building and enlarging upon earlier socialization experiences.

Of course, the higher the level of education the more generous and expansive are the roles and expectations. Life prospects vary according

Meyer, "The Effects of Education as an Institution," *American Journal of Sociology*, 83 (July 1977), 55-77.
[4] Ibid., 60.   [5] Ibid.

to educational attainments (and perhaps in advance of them) and go on doing so throughout life by a system of subsequent allocations that continue to set off the better from the less well educated. Consequently, long after any direct socialization effects of schooling have faded, reinforcement occurs through repeated application of the expectations associated with differential allocation. As Meyer notes:

> . . . schooling is a fixed capital asset in the career of the individual.
> . . . Is it surprising that the attitudes of and orientations of [better] educated individuals continue to reflect such enhanced life prospects over long periods of time? They perceive these prospects and are surrounded by others who see them too.[6]

There will be examples from the following materials that could be seized upon by adherents of either model as well as by those leaning toward a mixed view. Regardless of the superiority of either the socialization or allocation model, however, an important property shared by both constructs is an educational stratification system that has strong links to political behavior and attitudes. Our aim is to consider the *dynamics* of education as a stratifying mechanism in American politics. We wish to determine how quickly our young adults become distinguished politically according to their eventual educational achievements, the expansion or contraction of the differentiation over the eight-year period marked by rapid individual and societal change, and a comparison of these patterns with those displayed by representatives of a more stable, mid-life group, the young adults' parents.

Contained within these larger aims is a particular one which, for many observers, is of transcendent importance: the immediate and longer range impact of college education. Whether one is talking about the association between college education and political traits among adult populations, or comparing college versus noncollege youth, substantial differences are often noted. Yet it is unclear to what extent these differences rest on college training per se. This lack of clarity stems from several chronic problems that have characterized research in the area.[7] First, the great majority of studies do not have precollege readings on the traits being assessed, thereby precluding before-and-after comparisons. This shortcoming obviously makes it impossible to determine the rate and direction of change. A second, accompanying shortcoming is the lack of control or comparison groups of same-aged,

---

[6] Ibid., 61-62.

[7] Similar discussions will be found in Kenneth A. Feldman and Theodore M. Newcomb, *The Impact of College on Students* (San Francisco: Jossey-Bass, 1969), Chapter 2; and Alexander W. Astin, *Four Critical Years* (San Francisco: Jossey-Bass, 1977), Chapter 1.

noncollege youths. In the absence of such groups it is difficult to assess the consequences of self-selection; college-bound students may
already differ from those not matriculating. The absence of control
groups also renders problematic the ascription of change to college experience versus maturational, life-course, and period effects that may
be affecting both college and noncollege youths alike. A final defect
of much of the work is that dynamic statements about the effects of
college have often been made based on static, cross-section observations. Samples of college students are often divided up according to year
in school. Inferences about the impact of college are then made based
on the year-to-year comparisons. An obvious peril here lies in the differential mortality of student populations. Drop-out rates are not only
sizeable but also variable according to several characteristics, such as
social class, that have a bearing on political orientations.

Our youth panel is ideally suited to overcome many of the customary shortcomings. Initial observations occurred several months before
any of the college-bound students had been exposed to their collegiate
environments. Later observations took place after the great majority of
them had terminated their higher training but not so long past that
certain kinds of effects would have eroded completely. And, of course,
many finished their schooling with high school graduation. Thus our
requirements of pre- and post-observations and of same-age comparison
groups are fully met.[8]

Assessing Educational Achievement

By any absolute standards the class of '65 achieved a remarkably
high level of schooling over the eight-year study period. Approximately one-third held a four-year degree and about one in twenty-five already
had a degree beyond the bachelor's level. As this cohort makes its way
through the life cycle the educational attainments will rise even higher,
as advanced degrees are obtained by some and as the bachelor's degree
is obtained by still others. Indeed, 8% of the respondents were enrolled
in college as of the 1973 interviewing.

[8] Two of the few other national studies meeting these criteria are Jerald G. Bach-
man, Patrick M. O'Malley, and Jerome Johnston, *Adolescence to Adulthood:
Change and Stability in the Lives of Young Men* (Ann Arbor: Institute for Social
Research, University of Michigan, 1978), and Bruce K. Eckland and J. P. Bailey,
Jr., *National Longitudinal Study of the High School Class of 1972: A Capsule
Description of the Second Follow-up Survey—October 1974* (Washington, D.C.:
U.S. Government Printing Office, 1977). The first is a five-wave panel beginning
with sophomore boys in high school in 1966 and ending in 1974, and the second
is a three-wave panel starting with high school seniors in 1972. Political orienta-
tions were a minor concern of each project.

It is apparent that this educational range is restricted in two senses. First, it excludes the estimated 25% of the birth cohort that did not graduate from high school in 1965, largely as a result of having dropped out of school. To the extent that education is related to the topics under investigation, this truncation means that the statistical relationships will be muted compared with what they would be for the cohort as a whole.

A second consequence is that the range and variability are also relatively narrow when compared with the parental generation. Most noticeably, there are large numbers of parents without high school diplomas. Specifically, 9% of the parents had less than an eighth-grade education, 12% eighth grade only, 19% some high school, 36% a high school diploma, 13% some college, and 10% a bachelor's degree or higher. Thus, two-fifths of the parental generation fell below the *lowest* level achieved by the filial generation. And only one-tenth was in the highest category (college level) occupied by one-third of the young adults.[9] The greater variance in parental education would be expected, *ceteris paribus*, to result in stronger statistical relationships than in the case of their offspring.

If our major intent was to focus on the consequences of the absolute amounts of education, the inequalities between the two generations would present serious obstacles. For example, there would be no matching youth group for the two in five parents without a high school diploma, to say nothing of the great inequalities existing at the upper ranges. However, a concept of equivalency can be employed that directly confronts the problem of absolute inequalities. We noted earlier that whether one subscribes to the socialization or to the allocation theory about the political effects of schooling, both are sympathetic with the emergence and perpetuation of an educational stratification system. Although this system is one of achievement rather than ascription, it tends to be rather rigid—from the individual's point of view— once young adulthood has passed by. As attested to by a voluminous literature, this stratification system has, in turn, substantial connections to a variety of political and politically relevant subjects.

From the stratification point of view, the lack of absolute compara-

---

[9] It is undoubtedly true that the parental cohort is itself better educated than the entire parental cohort for the 1965 youth cohort, since parental education is a solid predictor of offspring education. In our own data, for example, the rank order correlation between parent and offspring education is $\tau_b = .36$, $\gamma = .52$. Correlations between the parents' education and that of their own parents are .42 (γ) for their mothers and .39 for their fathers. These cross-generation continuities mitigate the consequences of the secular trends that make the 1965 youth so much better educated than their lineage predecessors.

bility or even of functional equivalence across generations becomes less of a handicap. For what is of interest now is the relationship of the stratification classes to political qualities across generations and over time. By analogy, income strata probably continue to be associated with differential consuming and saving patterns even though the absolute levels change and even though the income distribution flattens and swells over time. More germane for present purposes, education continues to be related to occupational achievements even though the average level of education has climbed sharply and the occupational structure has altered.[10] One way of framing the question, then, is to ask what are the developmental properties and patterns of stability between the education stratification system and political attitudes and behavior.

From this perspective we are free to categorize each generation according to relative or rank-order amounts of education, because this will guarantee a stratification system for each generation. Yet we also wish to retain elements in that ordering that reflect both the socialization and certification processes. Fortunately, the empirical distributions lend themselves to satisfying both these requirements. The youth cohort can be stratified into three nearly equal groupings of high school graduates (36%), some college (32%), and college graduates (32%). These provide discrete boundaries from both the socialization and allocation points of view. Having a high school diploma implies a certain level of socialization as well as qualification or certification for given statuses and roles in society. But having a college degree signifies quite a different set of expectations and achievements. The "some college" category becomes a less well-defined stratum though one that is clearly intermediate between the two.

On the parental side the resulting categories are less than high school (40%), high school graduates (36%), and some college or more (24%). Again, these divisions comport well with both allocation and socialization assumptions about schooling effects. For the older generation, not finishing high school carried a stamp in much the same fashion as does "only" finishing high school for the younger generation. By contrast a high school diploma marked the crossing of a distant visible threshold in terms of the socialization and certification processes. Finally, to have matriculated at college was a clearly recognizable differentiation in an earlier era.

It is well established that colleges vary dramatically in terms of aca-

10 Peter M. Blau and Otis Dudley Duncan, *The American Occupational Structure* (New York: Wiley, 1967); and Robert M. Hauser and David L. Featherman, *The Process of Stratification* (New York: Academic Press, 1977).

demic quality. Since we have the specific educational histories for all of our respondents, it would be possible to categorize them according to the qualitative features of their alma maters. There are two major reasons why we will not pursue that strategy. First, and foremost, the bulk of the evidence in the literature suggests the overwhelming importance of quantity rather than quality within quantity as the key differentiator.[11] This is not to deny the unique importance of certain qualitative features, but rather to emphasize the overall strength of socialization and certification effects as represented by level of attainment. A second reason is simply one of economy. With two generations, two time points, and a variety of orientations to cover, the matter of qualitative gradation would require more space and time than we have available—the intuitive appeal of the subject notwithstanding.

Because the young adults all had the same educational attainment in 1965, it is impossible to compare the same educational strata over time, as we can for the parents. As anticipated in our earlier remarks, however, we can do something that is in many respects more interesting and certainly more singular. Since we know the educational destinations of the young, we can stratify them in 1965 by their *eventual* attainments yet *before* these attainments had actually come to pass. By so doing we can specify more sharply the questions that will occupy our attention: (1) Do rates of individual-level stability differ for those who were in the process of obtaining higher education during the study period compared to those who completed their formal schooling at the beginning of the panel? (2) To what extent is the connection between educational stratification and political characteristics already in place by the end of twelfth grade? (3) To what degree is that connection maintained in the wake of post-high school experiences, where one set of experiences consists of formal education itself? With the introduction of the parental results we can go on to ask: (4) How stable are the educational-political relationships for this younger cohort, caught at a time of life-space and educational transition, compared with those of the older cohort observed during a period of virtual educational stasis? (5) Do the absolute magnitudes of the relationships across time and generations appear to be weakening or strengthening? It is to these questions that the remainder of this chapter is devoted.

[11] The evidence against the lack of specific school effects has been particularly formidable at the secondary school level, as in James S. Coleman et al., *Equality of Educational Opportunity* (Washington, D.C.: U.S. Government Printing Office, 1966). At the college level the evidence is often constrained by the fact that many studies deal only with the variance among college student populations, rather than college plus noncollege. Still, the argument is decidedly toward amount rather than type. See Feldman and Newcomb, *Impact of College on Students*; Bachman, O'Malley, and Johnston, *Adolescence to Adulthood*; and Astin, *Four Critical Years*.

Individual-Level Dynamics

Our initial concern is with individual change or its obverse, individual stability. We know from other studies that college students do undergo change.[12] We also know from Chapters 2 and 3 that this young sample—nearly two-thirds of whom had some college exposure —was subject to considerable instability even though stability typically outweighed change. Consequently, our emphasis is on a comparison of change rates among those with and those without a college education. Our hypothesis is that those who did not go beyond high school changed least and those who completed college changed most, with the "some college" group intermediate.

It should be made clear at the outset that this initial analysis is by no means a complete test for the effects of education. If our hypothesis is unsupported, it does not necessarily mean that college has no impact on students. It might be, for example, that half of each group changed their degree of political interest but the changers who went to college uniformly increased their interest while those changers not matriculating all lost interest, with those in the intermediate group showing some gains and some losses. Moreover, nonstudents are also experiencing many new situations in the young adult years, often including important factors such as finding and working at a job, marrying and starting a family, and spending time in the military. Therefore, even if gross and net change in each group were the same, it would prove only that college had no distinct impact on young adult rates of change.

Despite all of these qualifications, if college has an impact on students, it seems plausible that it will show up in greater rates of change among those who go through the experience. If college makes people more interested in politics, more knowledgeable, more liberal, less religious, and so on, it has to change them in order to have this effect. Because nonstudents are not having *these* experiences, we make the tentative assumption that they are changing less.[13]

[12] A summary through 1968 of such studies is Feldman and Newcomb, *Impact of College*, esp. Chapter 2. For more recent evidence see Astin, *Four Critical Years*, esp. Chapter 2, Appendix, Tables A-C. Of course the classic example of college effects remains the Bennington study. See Theodore M. Newcomb, *Personality and Social Change: Attitude Formation in a Student Community* (New York: Holt, Rinehart, & Winston, 1943); and Theodore M. Newcomb, Kathryn E. Koenig, Richard Flacks, and Donald Warwick, *Persistence and Change: Bennington College and Its Students After 25 Years* (New York: Wiley, 1967).

[13] Few studies have ever looked at this question. One which did found that 48% of a sample of college graduates and 53% of a sample of employed youths were "average" changers (the rest being greater than average) on a finely graded scale of social maturity. See James W. Trent and Leland L. Medsker, *Beyond High School* (San Francisco: Jossey-Bass, 1968), 188.

To test our hypothesis, we generated 1965 × 1973 turnover tables exactly as in Chapters 2 and 3 except that there were now three such tables for each measure, one for each educational group. As in the earlier chapters, we employed both correlations and gross stability (percentage not changing). It is important to examine both kinds of measures. The correlation still has the advantage of being sensitive to the degree of change. But in this context the gross stability percentage has two things in its favor. First, it provides a very direct answer to the question of whether, proportionately, *more* college-educated than non-college-educated changed over the panel years. Second, the correlations are sensitive to the initial distributions, and are sometimes misleading inasmuch as these distributions vary considerably by education. Fortunately, our conclusion does not depend on which measure is examined.

That conclusion is that higher education is little, if at all, related to the rate of change of political attributes during the young adult years. The correlational results seem particularly indicative of no strong, consistent relationship between education and change (Table 8.1). It is true that there are some instances in which a monotonic relationship exists, especially in the resources and participation areas and in group evaluations. But the direction of the relationship is inconsistent with our hypothesis in two cases, including one (knowledge) which exhibits one of the largest absolute differences in the correlations for the extreme groups. Most revealingly, however, the magnitude of the differences between educational groups was small in most cases. Even ignoring the absence of monotonicity, consider the difference in the τ_b's between those who completed college and those who had no college experience. In only four instances (recognition and understanding, turnout, least proud of political features, and ratings of Jews) was the difference larger than .10, and many of the differences were on the order of .05 or less. The correlational evidence, therefore, suggests a very mild and uneven relationship between education and stability, with perhaps a slight edge in changeability of college graduates.

The percentage figures add support to the conclusion of a minimal relationship by suggesting, almost as strongly, that the edge in instability belongs to the high school graduates. As with the correlations there are a number of instances of a monotonic relationship between education and gross stability. But most of the cases (interest in public affairs, cosmopolitanism, magazine reading, candidate preferences, speeches against churches, and both personal efficacy scores) indicate higher stability among the college graduates, with partisanship, two of the policy issues, and lack of pride in political features showing the reverse. Overall, the extreme differences are generally less than 10%, and more often than not, college graduates are the most stable. Even on the subject of voter turnout, for which the correlations showed the largest decline from high school to college graduates, the percentage stable is highest among the latter. What happened in this instance was that relatively few of the college-graduates-to-be failed to vote in 1968; subsequently, most of them voted in 1972, yielding low stability in a correlational sense but having little effect on the percentage stable.

The important point is probably not the divergence between the two stability measures, although that should make us think carefully about what we mean when we say that college changes people. The major result is the lack of support for the hypothesis that college graduates undergo more change than those with less education. To be sure, all three groups moved about considerably. But none seems more prone to change than the others. There are a few tantalizing possibilities. College graduates were universally among the most stable on all but one of the social-psychological measures. Partisanship showed a moderate decline in stability (on both measures) as education rises. Nonetheless, without independent confirmation of these possible exceptions, the conclusion stands that among young adults rates of change on political and nonpolitical attributes are at best minimally related to educational achievement.

Results in nonpolitical domains are of a piece with those in the political. Religious beliefs and practices are a case in point. College is widely believed to have a liberalizing and secularizing impact. While that may be true, and will be put to the test subsequently in this chapter, such aggregate shifts are not matched by disproportionate individual-level change according to education. Thus our conclusions about relatively equal rates of stability in political traits are bolstered by similar findings outside the political realm.

Although there are several reasons why stability does not vary appreciably by education, the major immediate interest for us lies in the meaning of these results for our subsequent analysis. In the first place, we can be reasonably certain that any differences in aggregate-level figures over time do not derive from differential rates of change at the individual level. Second, and related to the first point, we will also know that any shifting in the fit between education and political attributes over time is not a consequence of variable individual-level stability across the three educational strata. Our analytic tasks are thereby eased.

Involvement, Resources, and Participation

Having surveyed the topic of individual-level stability, we are now in position to examine the aggregate picture. Several pieces of information will be conveyed in our typical mode of presentation. The most

TABLE 8.1: Stability and Change among Youths, by Education

	τ_b			γ			Gross Stability		
	H.S. Grad.[a]	Some Coll.	Coll. Grad.	H.S. Grad.	Some Coll.	Coll. Grad.	H.S. Grad.	Some Coll.	Coll. Grad.
Good citizen—political qualities	.16	.15	.09	.22	.20	.13	29%	32%	29%
Interest in public affairs	.27	.33	.26	.41	.52	.45	46	50	56
Cosmopolitanism	.22	.11	.19	.26	.15	.27	20	21	24
Read newspapers	.25	.21	.22	.35	.31	.34	42	39	48
Read magazines	.19	.24	.21	.33	.40	.39	51	55	58
Watch television	.16	.16	.16	.24	.23	.23	35	36	36
Listen to radio	.11	.06	.15	.16	.09	.22	37	34	40
Good citizen—active qualities	.13	.18	.13	.18	.24	.18	33	34	29
Internal political efficacy	.19	.26	.18	.31	.42	.31	45	48	46
Recog. & underst. lib-cons.	.27	.23	.16	.36	.31	.24	39	28	36
Knowledge of political facts	.43	.49	.53	.54	.61	.66	35	30	43
Voting turnout, 1968 × 1972	.34	.15	.09	.62	.34	.27	66	63	70
Partisanship	.45	.42	.38	.53	.49	.45	63	58	55
Candidate preference, 1964 × 1972	.26	.23	.23	.73	.50	.46	50	56	60
School integration	.19	.18	.09	.37	.32	.16	48	50	49
School prayers	.37	.40	.35	.71	.68	.62	77	70	62
Communist holding office	.25	.32	.29	.53	.63	.66	65	62	62
Anti-church speeches	.12	.06	.12	.41	.40	.62	78	87	90

TABLE 8.1 (cont.)

	τ_b			γ			Gross Stability		
	H.S. Grad.[a]	Some Coll.	Coll. Grad.	H.S. Grad.	Some Coll.	Coll. Grad.	H.S. Grad.	Some Coll.	Coll. Grad.
Least proud—political qualities	.15	.00	−.01	.28	.01	−.01	37	34	29
Political trust	.20	.16	.17	.26	.22	.23	20	15	16
Labor unions	.15	.19	.17	.18	.23	.21	54	50	47
Southerners	.29	.38	.31	.35	.45	.36	53	59	54
Catholics	.30	.25	.29	.37	.32	.37	60	53	54
Big business	.19	.06	.18	.23	.08	.22	51	43	35
Jews	.20	.30	.20	.28	.39	.26	62	64	55
Whites	.25	.24	.22	.34	.32	.31	60	52	49
Protestants	.22	.19	.16	.28	.26	.21	58	51	47
Blacks	.22	.26	.27	.27	.31	.33	54	53	56
Religious preference	.50[b]	.54	.59		.69	.69	61	61	60
Belief in Bible	.41	.40	.42	.68	.69	.58	64	60	62
Church attendance	.33	.28	.35	.51	.46	.35	36	35	37
Personal trust	.20	.33	.27	.27	.43	.27	34	43	44
Opinion strength	.26	.16	.16	.34	.21	.20	30	30	21
Self-confidence	.18	.19	.21	.24	.26	.32	31	33	42

[a] N's before missing data are deleted: high school 492; some college 426; college graduate 430.
[b] Because religious preference is a nominal variable, the symmetric lambda statistic is used here. The gross stability figure is computed on the basis of specific denominational preference.

basic information is the absolute value of the variables in both years, at each of the three levels of education achieved by the youth. In the majority of cases the entries represent mean scores. Although we recognize the loss of information incurred and the interval-level assumptions involved, a summarizing device was mandatory in view of the large amount of material to be covered. Mean scores and standard deviations for the samples as a whole are presented in Appendix B. To demonstrate the relationship between education and the dependent variables, an ordinal measure of association, gamma, will be given as well as a simple "difference score" between the absolute values of the lowest stratum (high school graduates) and the highest stratum (college graduates or higher). In order to compare the absolute change among the three strata over time we will also usually present the "difference score" between the 1965 entry and the 1973 entry.[14] Finally, exactly the same procedures will be followed in analyzing the parental sample, so that cross-generational comparisons can be easily made.

Although education is positively related to every indicator of psychological engagement among young adults, the range and over-time development of that relationship vary considerably. Not surprisingly, the weakest absolute magnitudes occur in the use of the ubiquitous electronic media for following public affairs. Even in the case of radio and television usage, however, there is a small increase in the strength of the relationship, a first indication that differentiation increased over the eight years.

All of the other indicators of involvement reflect more fully the stamp of educational differences (Table 8.2). More interest in politics, greater use of newspapers and magazines, more frequent political conversations in the family, and more cosmopolitan forms of interest characterized the better educated even *before* they left high school. With the exception of general interest, these differences expanded across the years.[15] Sometimes this enlargement came about as a result of absolute gains by the college graduates and absolute losses by the other two strata, as in the case of newspaper reading. One of the largest shifts (magazine reading) occurred, however, where the absolute scores of all strata dropped—but progressively less as education rose.

What is intriguing about the case of magazine reading is that the impact of education comes at the expense of predictions that college

---

[14] As is apparent from these remarks, and as was discussed in Chapter 1, our goal is not to specify the contribution of education to the Time$_2$ scores. That would, of course, require a different mode of analysis, most likely one involving multiple regression. As a general rule, the Time$_1$ score was by far the best predictor of Time$_2$ scores when such analyses were carried out.

[15] A similar finding is reported for interest in politics by Bachman, O'Malley, and Johnston, *Adolescence to Adulthood*, 134.

raises the absolute levels of the more demanding acts of political involvement. Interpretations of education-related differences in print media consumption among adult samples implicitly assume that going to college *elevated* the consumption rate. Indeed, if we had only the 1973 data in hand, that would be our initial interpretation. But our longitudinal results indicate that higher education simply *retarded* a more general decline in magazine usage. On the other hand, the parental figures suggest that period effects were at work because the same pattern holds there also. Thus we cannot dismiss the presumption of absolute positive effects during some historical eras.

Whether one wants to emphasize the early emergence of differences or their tendency to increase is a subjective matter. Given the overwhelming emphasis in the literature on college effects, however, the pre-exposure results are perhaps the more significant. Another way of highlighting the importance of the $Time_1$ relationships is to enter both education and the $Time_1$ scores in a regression equation where the $Time_2$ score is the dependent variable. Without exception, the $Time_1$ score is a better predictor than is educational achievement.

Regardless of the emphasis put on the findings for the young adults, parallel comparisons with the parental generation are instructive. In the first place, the magnitudes of the relationships tend to run higher. At first we attributed this to the presence of more variance in education among parents. As we shall see in a moment though, there are other relationships that run stronger among youths than parents. Thus it is conceivable that increasing age might bring further differentiation in the youth generation. While that must remain a speculative point, a second difference between the two generations rests on firmer ground. Differences between the educational strata did not widen as often in the parental generation, and when they did, the shift was much less marked. Indeed, the associations may be regarded as virtually stable. The contrast between the two generations would seem to rest in the relative openness of the young to new influences and in the fact that they were in the process of achieving their education in contrast to the static character of parental education.

Comparing the generations by educational strata typically reveals a noticeable shift in the "advantage" held by the stratum in one generation over the matching stratum in the other. Consider newspaper reading. In both 1965 and 1973 the lowest youth stratum has an absolute edge over the lowest parental stratum. At the middle level, that advantage shifts in favor of the parental stratum, and in the highest level the advantage increases still further for the parents. Although the precise values differ for the other measures, the pattern holds with few exceptions: as one moves from the lower educational strata to the

TABLE 8.2: Psychological Involvement in Politics, by Generation, Education, and Year[a]

	Youths			Parents			Correlation (γ)	
	12 yrs.	13-15 yrs.	≥16 yrs.	<12 yrs.	12 yrs.	≥13 yrs.	Y	P
Interest in public affairs								
1 (Low) - 4 (High)								
1965	3.04	3.30	3.45	2.90	3.31	3.62	.31[b]	.41
1973	3.08	3.33	3.50	3.08	3.39	3.70	.31	.38
	+.04	+.03	+.05	+.18	+.06	+.08		
Cosmopolitanism								
1 (Least) - 7 (Most)								
1965	4.83	5.34	5.62	3.95	4.18	4.98	.25	.25
1973	4.37	5.03	5.31	3.74	4.09	4.61	.28	.22
	-.46	-.31	-.31	-.21	-.08	-.37		
Read newspapers								
1 (Don't read) - 5 (Almost daily)								
1965	3.78	4.04	3.96	3.55	4.37	4.68	.14	.47
1973	3.62	3.93	4.19	3.39	4.20	4.62	.23	.47
	-.16	-.11	+.23	-.16	-.17	-.08		

TABLE 8.2 (cont.)

	Youths				Parents				Correlation (γ)	
	12 yrs.	13-15 yrs.	≥16 yrs.		<12 yrs.	12 yrs.	≥13 yrs.		Y	P
Read magazines										
1 (Don't read) - 3 (Regularly)										
1965	1.97	2.32	2.46	+.49	1.81	2.19	2.59	+.78	.33	.48
1973	1.66	2.13	2.40	+.74	1.56	1.96	2.47	+.91	.45	.53
	-.31	-.19	-.06		-.25	-.23	-.12			
Talk politics in family[c]										
1 (Don't talk) - 5 (Very often)										
1965	2.86	3.13	3.17	+.31	2.25	2.68	3.01	+.76	.17	.36
1973	2.12	2.69	2.86	+.74	2.22	2.62	3.01	+.79	.34	.41
	—	—	—		-.03	-.06	0			

[a] N's before missing data are deleted: youths, see Table 8.1; parents, <12 yrs., 475; 12 yrs. 420; ≥13 yrs., 282.

[b] Entries are the correlation between education and the various measures for each generation in each year. Y = youths, P = parents.

[c] For parents the referent in each year is the respondent's spouse; for youths the referent is family members in 1965 and spouse in 1973. Because the referent is different for youths, the 1965 minus 1973 values are not reported.

higher ones the relative youth advantage decreases or, conversely, the relative parental advantage increases. Separating out those parents with a college degree simply sharpens the contrast between the best educated in each generation.[16]

This pattern, which is not nearly so evident in the other domains covered by our inquiry, appears to result from two processes that reflect both the importance of absolute levels of education and movement over the life cycle. The greater youth advantage at the lower educational levels seems to flow directly from the fact that all of these individuals have a high school diploma. Whether through allocative or socialization processes, these young adults are brought to a threshold of psychological involvement that puts them ahead of the counterpart elders, none of whom completed high school and half of whom did not go beyond the eighth grade.

Despite a general rise in the salience of politics among the poorly educated parents between 1965 and 1973—a rise actually higher than that for the better educated—the disadvantage under which they have labored since leaving school still leaves them only on a par with the lowest youth strata. As one moves up the educational hierarchy, however, the encumbrances become less of a strain on the parents, and the product of more opportunities and inducements to become psychologically involved emerges.

On balance, then, the generally acknowledged preconditions of political action and informed position-taking are well marked by educational strata in both generations. Significantly, the demarcation has become firmly rooted by late adolescence—prior to post-high school educational pathways—though it often becomes sharper by young adulthood. At mid-life, at least as represented by the parental generation, the association is somewhat stronger and more stable.

In many respects the results in the domain of resources are a carbon copy, writ large, of those for psychological involvement. Among the young, differences in resources were already well in place even before the eventual education destinations were reached. And these disparities tended to widen over time. Similarly, among parents all the relationships were moderate to strong in 1965 and were altered very little as of 1973. Eventual education is thus an early, strong, and persistent concomitant of resources. Yet there are variations in emphasis within this configuration that merit attention and that distinguish resources from involvement.

[16] General interest paid to public affairs provides an illustration. Whereas 60% of the young college graduates said they paid attention most of the time, the same was true of 75% of all parents who had at least some college but of 85% of those with a college degree.

A measure derived from answers to the open-ended query concerning the qualities of the good citizen provides a first glimpse into the workings of the educational stratification system as it affects political resources. In Chapter 2 we noted that in addition to characterizing the model citizen descriptions as nonpolitical or political, the latter could be categorized into allegiant versus active modes. Because it sets out a prescriptive norm of duty to participate, the active mode was considered to be a political resource.

Education was moderately related to the mean number of active mode responses at both points in time, but it was also related at about the same level to the mean number of total responses to the question. A fruitful way of introducing some standardization is to compute the ratio of active to allegiant responses. These ratios are presented in Figure 8.1.

FIGURE 8.1: Ratio of Active to Allegiant Descriptions of Good Citizen, by Years of Schooling

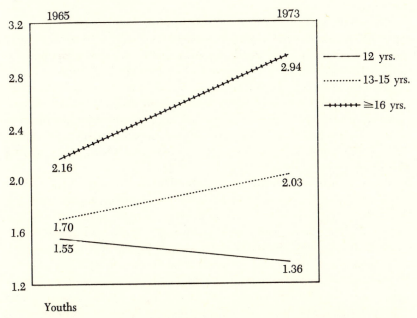

It is readily apparent that by the end of the twelfth grade the young adults already had different emphases according to eventual education. The moral imperative of participation versus passivity and rule-following was more deeply ingrained among those destined to obtain college degrees. By 1973, the young adults had sorted themselves out even more vividly. While the ratio had dropped among the high school graduates, it had risen modestly among the some-college group and rather strongly among the college graduates. The upshot was the enlargement of gaps by education. By contrast the parents changed in a uniform direction and kept closer to each other (not shown).

These results are similar to others in the resources area that lead to the conclusion that education in some instances is as powerful (or more so) a discriminator among youth as among parents. By 1973 education marked off the young a shade more powerfully with respect to ideological sophistication and political knowledge (Table 8.3). It is no accident that education exerts such a strong influence in these two dimensions. Both have an extremely strong cognitive component, in the one instance relying on the ability to handle abstractions and in the other on the possession of concrete pieces of information. Whether they actually acquire such an awareness in school or are allocated to social locations offering more subsequent exposure early in adulthood, the better educated retain these elements and concepts to a much higher degree.

This result leads in turn to a second point. The largest gain in the correlations among the young was on ideological sophistication; and even though of a more modest nature, there was also an increase among the parents. It will be recalled that the measure employed here reflects the respondent's ability to apply and describe correctly the abstract concepts of liberalism and conservatism with respect to the two political parties. Now if more, especially higher, education means anything in a political sense it means the developed capability of recognizing and understanding abstract concepts and fitting them to real world examples.

Even though all educational strata shared in the general rise in sophistication, the lowest stratum in each generation lagged well behind the other two. Given the perceived changing world of the political parties along ideological dimensions, one would expect those least well-versed in the nature of abstract, logical thought to absorb less quickly and deeply the currents at work. By contrast the political knowledge measure, reflecting as it does the correct identification of much more stable entities and not relying upon the ability to handle abstract concepts, shows virtually no change in either absolute value or in its strong association with education.

A rather different set of findings and interpretations applies to another commonly recognized resource, internal political efficacy. As the table entries show, only minor alterations occurred within each generation in the absolute scores across time and in the overall relationship between education and efficacy. A greater sense of being able to affect

TABLE 8.3: Political Resources, by Generation, Education, and Year

	Youths				Parents				Correlation (γ)	
	12 yrs.	13-15 yrs.	≥16 yrs.		<12 yrs.	12 yrs.	≥13 yrs.		Y	P
Internal political efficacy 1 (Low) - 3 (High)										
1965	1.84	2.17	2.33	+.49	1.50	1.89	2.24	+.74	.39	.52
1973	1.68	2.03	2.25	+.57	1.42	1.71	2.08	+.66	.45	.49
	−.16	−.14	−.08		−.08	−.18	−.16			
External political efficacy 1 (Low) - 3 (High)										
1965	—a	—	—		2.24	2.58	2.74	+.50	—	.43
1973	2.15	2.42	2.47	+.32	1.99	2.38	2.63	+.64	.25	.45
					−.25	−.20	−.11			
Recognition and understanding of liberal-conservative dimension 1 (None) - 5 (Broad)										
1965	2.23	2.66	3.32	+1.09	2.36	2.89	3.68	+1.32	.33	.40
1973	2.64	3.62	4.22	+1.58	2.53	3.18	4.08	+1.55	.51	.47
	+.41	+.96	+.90		+.17	+.29	+.40			
Knowledge of political facts 0-6 (Number correct)										
1965	3.79	4.66	5.48	+1.69	4.04	4.91	5.65	+1.61	.52	.54
1973	3.87	4.83	5.62	+1.75	4.04	4.91	5.70	+1.66	.54	.53
	+.08	+.17	+.14		0	0	+.05			

a Not available for 1965.

political outcomes is often ascribed to higher education. Yet the results for the youthful generation are unequivocal not only in demonstrating that education-related disparities were already in place by the twelfth grade but also—and this is more surprising—that higher education did not produce a gain in efficacy. In fact, the only beneficial effect of higher education was to retard slightly the small downward drift characterizing all educational strata. Had only the 1973 data been available, we might well have concluded that it was higher education per se that generated the strong differences among the young. Thus even though education has a healthy association with all political resources, we see that this linkage comes about in diverse ways.

Turning to political participation, we find the same general patterns. Consider voting turnout, the most commonly employed barometer of political participation (Figure 8.2). Although absolute turnout rates by educational strata vary across years and generations, the nature of the relationships varies little. Patterns take hold and maintain themselves early on in young adulthood. The edge of the better educated youth is all the more impressive because they have been more geographically mobile than have other youths. Overall, 24% of the youth sample had not moved from their home communities during the study period, but the figure varies from 38% of the high school graduates to 18% for the some-college and 15% for the college grads.

More intensive, less common forms of political participation engaged in during the 1965-1973 period are also characterized by vivid differences according to educational strata. On each of the five electoral and four nonelectoral activities we inquired about, there was a moderate to strong relationship with education in both generations. The additive index combining all of the items has virtually an identical association for both: $\gamma = .44$ for young adults, .45 for parents. Overall, young adults were already marked by lines of cleavage as distinct as those in their parents' generation. The consequences of stratification emerge quickly and with strength. A breakdown of activity rates by year bolsters this contention. For each activity named we ascertained the timing and circumstance of the involvement. It is clear that the better educated began to outdistance their former high school classmates quite early in the 1965-1973 period.

A more graphic way of demonstrating the links with education, and one which reveals several variations within the larger pattern, is to array the distributions for each type of activity. Figure 8.3 arranges eight acts (excluding "other" electoral behaviors) according to the overall frequency within each generation. As we saw in Chapter 4, the rank orders of most-performed actions do vary a bit across the two groups. Notwithstanding the rank-order differences, there is enormous similar-

FIGURE 8.2: Voting Turnout by Years of Schooling

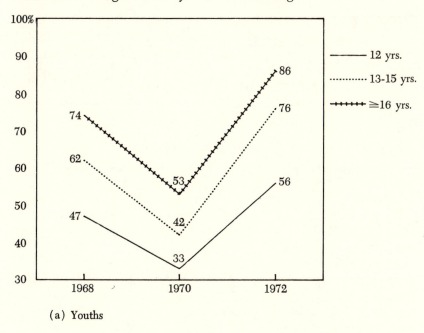

(a) Youths

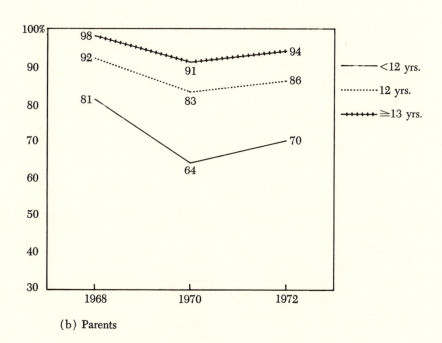

(b) Parents

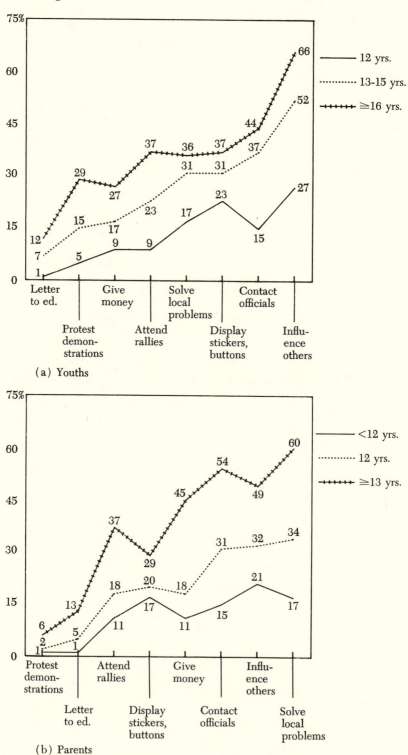

FIGURE 8.3: Performance of Specific Political Activities, by Years of Schooling

(a) Youths

(b) Parents

ity in one respect. Despite the fact that the participation net was cast widely, it is uniformly true that the higher the education the greater the participation, with the margins usually being very substantial.

Among the young the distances are especially noticeable for demonstrating, attending political rallies, contacting officials in writing or in person (and giving them one's opinion), and trying to persuade others to vote in a certain way. Some or all of these differences resulted from the better educated having been in environments during a time when both conventional and unconventional participation was running at high tide.[17] Campuses were repeatedly the locus, and sometimes the focus, of demonstrations, rallies, and confrontations with officials and fellow citizens. As the detailed descriptions offered by the respondents revealed, these proceedings dealt with several major issues, such as the Vietnam War, and with particular candidacies. The latter were often linked to issues of hot interest on the campuses.

Thus higher education served in a very direct fashion as a precipitator of political action. Campuses and their student bodies provided an immediate opportunity structure for intense and dramatic political activity that was "denied" those on the outside. Colleges have become less politically fevered since that era. It is doubtful that succeeding cohorts participated at such high rates, especially with respect to physical demonstrations, marches, and sit-ins. In this sense there may well have been a generational effect at work.

Although the campuses provided a ready channel of participation, it is apparent that differences by education would have emerged among the young in any event. The better educated also engaged in more actions outside of what might have been inspired by the campus. Participation was higher in contemporaneous electoral contests with no obvious connections to campus-related events or issues; long after they had left the campuses the better educated continued to outperform others in regard to new issues and candidacies; and the rate of "working with others to solve some community problems"—clearly outside the pale of the glamour issues of the times—was twice as high among those having gone to college as among the high school graduates. Those matriculating may have been given an extra boost by the nature of the times, but there is little reason to believe they would not have sorted themselves out, or been sorted out, anyway.

Additional support for this argument, if needed, comes from the results for the parental generation. During the same historical era parental participation was also easily distinguished by educational attain-

[17] Similar contrasts between college and noncollege youth are reported in Daniel Yankelovich, Inc., *Generations Apart* (New York: Columbia Broadcasting Company, 1969), 29.

ments. Interestingly, though, the widest gaps occur in somewhat different areas. What most sets off the parents having gone to college from those without a high school diploma are higher rates of donating money, contacting officials, and solving local problems. These contrasts are most likely both life-cycle and generational in nature. In middle age the income gap broadens and political donations become less burdensome for the better educated. Similarly, the role of community activist or civic leader is more likely to be taken on by the better educated as they acquire standing in the community.

It is significant that the wide gap on contacting officials transcends the generations. This is the most personal, direct means of trying to exert influence. What public officials see and hear is obviously being skewed toward whatever the better educated are presenting. Even though substantial disparities in absolute years of schooling characterize the two generations, the patterns are similar. The replication of differential patterns of access and voice shows no signs of abating. On the other hand, the large gap on demonstrations among the youths versus the tiny difference among the parents is a function of the college-educated young having been on campuses during a turbulent era as well as the lower opportunity costs associated with being young and a student.

Given the strong static associations in each generation between education and participation, we would expect reasonably strong longitudinal ones as well. Direct comparisons can be made for the parental generation. The activity index based on electoral participation in the decade preceding 1965 was positively related to education, $\gamma = .37$. This compares with the .50 correlation for the electoral index built up for the 1965-1973 period. If anything, the tie became stronger across time. The earlier pre- or parapolitical analogue for the youth generation is the high school participation index. Predictably, the association is not as robust as for the index reflecting participation in the "real world" of politics ($\gamma = .30$ vs. .49). Yet even this level of association suggests some continuity in the stratification-participation link.

PREFERENCES, ATTITUDES, AND EVALUATIONS

Up to this point we have seen that the stratification system represented by educational achievement has a moderate to strong bearing on psychological involvement, resources, and activity in the political world—both in the older and younger generations and in the earlier and later time periods. Very significantly, we found that the youth could be readily distinguished by educational strata well in advance of

their actual educational destinies. Such consistent educational differentiation is not, however, invariant across the political landscape.

Party identification and candidate preference provide illustrations
of two patterns absent in the foregoing domains. Among the youths,
education was barely related to the likelihood of identifying with the
Republican party in 1965, $\gamma = .10$. By 1973 even that thin link had
completely disappeared ($\gamma = .0$). Nor does the incidence of Independents vary by education. Rising education was at least visibly and
consistently related to party identification among parents, however:
$\gamma = .25$ in 1965 and .26 in 1973. Thus the theme of greater stability in
relationships among parents appears again even though the magnitudes are not high. But the presence of a relationship in one generation and not in the other suggests that generational effects are medi-
ating the older linkage between education and party identification.
The absence of this linkage in the youth generation also means that
the results dealing with voting behavior (below) are not due to a
common tie of education to both party identification and voting preference.

Voting behavior provides an illustration of another pattern and also
supplies a perspective on the evaluation of candidate preference
among the young. Although party identification was, as usual, the personal trait most closely associated with the direction of the vote, it is
also true that education was directly or indirectly linked to the vote
in a very curious fashion among the young (Figure 8.4). The presidential preferences of the young reveal a pattern of countershifting
positions by educational category. With one minor deviation, each
stratum joined in the rising Republican vote across the three elections.
But there was an inverse relationship between education and the GOP
increase, resulting in a gradual reversal of the positive association between education and Republican voting.

Here is an example, a rare one, of how education continues to sort
out the cohort but where the directional flow of that sorting out
changed. In passing it might be noted that this finding offers presumptive evidence for the effects of higher education, not simply of self-
selection. It is no secret that recent and contemporary denizens of the
campus were less enamored of Nixon than were their noncollege peers,
especially in 1972. What our data add to that picture is the greater
resistance of the better educated to the national short-term electoral
forces favoring Nixon—despite their having begun as more favorably
disposed to the conservative candidacy of Goldwater in 1964.

A comparison with the senior generation simply heightens the contrast. Although the differences narrowed in 1972, those with high

FIGURE 8.4: Proportion of Young Adults Favoring Republican Presidential Candidates, by Years of Schooling

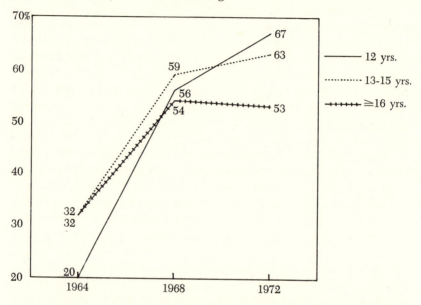

school degrees or better consistently gave more support to the GOP candidates than did the poorly educated. The same was true for the 1970 and 1972 Congressional elections, whereas among the young the differences were trivial. A revealing comparison is the gap between the best-educated strata of each generation in 1972. The difference of 17% in support for Nixon is the largest contrast across any of the same-rank strata for the three elections.

There is another historic piece of evidence indicating that the nexus between education and the vote was more fluid among the young. In Chapter 6 we showed that the 1968 Wallace candidacy actually enjoyed more support in the junior than the senior generation. Not surprisingly, Wallace's drawing power was grossly maldistributed by education. Even though each educational category represented about one-third of the youth sample, the Wallace backing was distributed 53%, 33%, and 14% across the three strata, running from low to high. Alternatively, the proportion voting for Wallace from each of the respective strata was 21%, 15%, and 6%. Matching figures among parents were much more compressed and, with one exception, considerably lower in magnitude—14%, 8%, and 8% from the least to best educated. The greater susceptibility of younger, have-less cohorts to the radically inclined voices of the right has been a frequent subject of speculation and occasional confirmation.[18] Our evidence is remarkably acute on that score.

Distinct from partisan preferences are attitudes about public policy issues. Because our questions tap a liberal-conservative dimension outside the arena of bread-and-butter issues, we would expect education to be positively related to taking the liberal stance. It is widely believed that college education has a liberalizing effect with respect to such issues. Studies of adult and college-age populations routinely report such findings, though the mechanisms at work are not at all well understood.[19]

Results from the youth panel lend support to the hypothesized effects. By 1973 there were moderate to strong relationships for each of the five issues. That was universally true in the later year, whereas the picture had not been clearcut earlier. As Table 8.4 shows, there was an irregular and slight association on the integration and prayer issues, whereas the greater liberalism of the higher strata was already in place with respect to the civic tolerance measures. What seems to explain this difference is the nature of the issues. Both the integration and prayer issues are school-related and have a very concrete, specific context. By contrast the other three are more hypothetical and deal with more abstract matters. In the absence of explicit empirical referents, we would expect the more liberal and tolerant proclivities of those with higher education to materialize as they "fill in" the lacking information and interpret the hypothetical questions in terms of their understanding of liberal democratic thought. In a sense, there was an excess of information on the prayer and integration issues.

Eight years later the effects of stratification were apparent across the board, having been strengthened in the civic tolerance area and moved to substantial levels on the two school-related issues. What accounted for the emergence of the latter was the smaller decline of pro-integration sentiments among the better educated and a rise in their anti-prayer-in-school sentiments. Again we see that the distance between strata can increase over time even though exposure to higher education does not generate absolute gains in the conventionally as-

[18] E.g., Philip E. Converse, Warren E. Miller, Jerrold G. Rusk, and Arthur C. Wolfe, "Continuity and Change in American Politics: Parties and Issues in the 1968 Election," *American Political Science Review*, 63 (December 1969), 1083-1105, and James Lamare, "Inter- or Intragenerational Cleavage? The Political Orientations of American Youth in 1968," *American Journal of Political Science*, 19 (February 1975), 81-90.

[19] Regarding college-age group see Yankelovich, Inc., *Generations Apart*; Daniel Yankelovich, *The New Morality: A Profile of American Youth in the 70's* (New York: McGraw-Hill, 1974); and Bachman, O'Malley, and Johnston, *Adolescence to Adulthood*, Chapter 7.

TABLE 8.4: Opinions on Policy Issues, by Generation, Education, and Year

	Youths				Parents				Correlation (γ)	
	12 yrs.	13-15 yrs.	≥16 yrs.		<12 yrs.	12 yrs.	≥13 yrs.		Y	P
School integration										
% pro										
1965	73	67	67	-6	55	62	56	—[a]	.07	—[a]
1973	42	46	58	+16	46	37	49	—[a]	.23	—[a]
	-31	-21	-09		-09	-25	-07			
School prayers										
% anti										
1965	26	33	29	—[a]	13	16	23	+10	—[a]	.22
1973	20	33	47	+27	13	13	25	+12	.41	.23
	-06	0	+18		0	-03	+02			
Anti-church										
speeches										
% pro										
1965	81	88	93	+12	62	79	89	+24	.34[b]	.48
1973	89	97	96	+7	63	81	90	+27	.41[b]	.50
	+08	+09	+03		+01	+02	+01			

TABLE 8.4 (cont.)

	Youths				Parents				Correlation (γ)	
	12 yrs.	13-15 yrs.	≥16 yrs.		<12 yrs.	12 yrs.	≥13 yrs.		Y	P
Communist holding office										
% pro										
1965	23	39	50	+27	21	28	47	+26	.38	.36
1973	40	63	79	+39	27	43	69	+42	.53	.51
	+17	+24	+29		+06	+15	+22			
All gov'ts. be like U.S.										
% anti										
1965	30	52	66	+36	—c	—c	—c	—c	.47	—c
1973	52	76	93	+41	44	64	80	+36	.65	.49
	+22	+24	+27							

a Difference scores and correlations not given because relationships are not monotonic.
b Gamma coefficients assume high values with highly skewed distributions.
c Not available for 1965.

sumed direction. Rather, exposure to college can have the effect of slowing down an apparent conservative secular trend.

With the exception of the free-speech issue, where ceiling effects are at work, the differential rates of change on issue positions are among the sharpest we encountered in comparing the educational strata. This would seem to be presumptive evidence favoring the view that post-high school education, either through socialization or allocation processes, makes a difference. A broader inventory of similar issues would probably have shown a similar pattern, whereas bread-and-butter issues might well have shown differences in direction of change and perhaps magnitudes as well. It is also obvious of course, that all educational strata were in flux. Without our threefold categorization we would not have been aware of the broader secular trends at work. Nevertheless, there seems to be a clear net educational effect, apart from the larger trends.

A comparison with the parental cohort is instructive in that it highlights the greater lability of the younger one during this period. This is visible primarily on the integration and prayer issues. Education shows no orderly relationship to integration in either year and a modestly positive one to the prayer issue in both years. That is, education did not function in quite the same way for the two generations, a departure from our more typical findings. For the more abstract issues, however, the strength of the relationships is roughly the same in each generation.

Although each generation is, with the exceptions noted, distinguished by a positive relationship between education and liberal stances, the comparison of same-rank strata across generations illustrates the probable importance of absolute levels of education. Except for the reversed positions of the lowest strata on the integration issue in 1973, the youth are in every instance more liberal than their same-rank parental counterparts. Since the absolute level of education is, at each rank, higher for the young adults, these differences could simply be reflecting those disparities rather than any generational effects in the direction of greater liberalism.

However, it can be easily demonstrated that youthful members are not necessarily more liberal than parents with the same absolute amount of education. Comparisons between the filial and parental high school graduates in 1973 (categories 1 and 2, respectively) show that the young adults are more liberal on three of the five issues, less liberal on two. Thus, the absolute amount of education appears to be quite crucial and, judged only on the basis of the high school educated, exerts roughly the same effect on each generation. Additional support for this contention rests on the comparison between college degree holders in each cohort. Although the youthful graduates occupy the more liberal position on all five issues, the gap between the two generations is less than 5% on all but one of the issues. From a larger perspective, these twin pieces of evidence suggest that many of the dissimilarities in the attitudinal profiles of the two generations are compositional in nature, i.e., they stem from divergent demographic or social make-up rather than from intrinsically different sociopolitical histories that, in turn, yielded generational effects.

Based solely on the issues for which we have over-time readings it appears, if anything, that education is more closely linked to issue position in the junior than in the senior generation. This, despite the presence of much greater variance on the independent variable, education, in the parental generation. A brief examination of issue questions asked only in 1973 underscores that point. Within each generation, education was related to taking a more liberal stance on the six-policy issues presented to the respondents in the form of the 1-7 self-placement scales. On four of these the association was clearly stronger in the youth generation, while on the remaining two there were no intergenerational differences. In addition, self-placement on the liberalism-conservatism scale, while by no means strongly related to education among young adults ($\gamma = .20$), was not a factor at all among parents ($\gamma = .03$).

Despite being more homogeneous in its educational achievements, the younger generation is more politically divided along educational lines than the older. With time these divisions may flatten out a bit, though the panel returns for the parents are not suggestive of such a trend. These results, as well as those already advanced, strongly support the idea that educational stratification, however finely divided in absolute terms, will continue to be a strong political demarcator in the rising generation and, by extension, in those to come. There seems to be a self-governing mechanism whereby differential amounts of education act to divide the populace politically.[20]

Moving from political attitudes to political evaluations, we find that education had very little impact either across time or generations. Trust in government is a case in point. In 1965 education had virtually no relationship to political trust in either generation. All educational strata shared in the momentous drop of trust accorded the government. Due largely to the moderately smaller drop among the young high

[20] A similar conclusion is reached in Hyman, Wright, and Reed, *The Enduring Effects of Education* and in Hyman and Wright, *Education's Lasting Effects on Values.*

school graduates, the relationship by 1973 was negative, but only on the order of −.15.[21] In the parental generation it was the least educated who underwent the greatest loss in trust, resulting in a very weak positive relationship between education and trust.

Much the same was true of the companion measure assessing in which level of government one had the most faith and confidence. In 1965 the better educated in both generations more often picked the national government; but they led the way in the general downward plunge, so that the weak positive relationships of 1965 had turned into weak negative ones.

Nor were the outcomes very different when looking at the evaluation of eight sociopolitical groups instead of governmental actors. Mean thermometer scores did not vary appreciably by educational strata. Illustratively, of the thirty-two possible relationships (2 generations × 8 groups × 2 observations) the highest was $\gamma = .22$. To be sure, there were some consistencies in the results. Education was uniformly negatively related to ratings of labor unions, Southerners, and whites, and positively related to ratings of Jews. And the signs tended to remain the same across time within a generation. Altogether, though, group evaluations are rather poorly understood by looking at educational strata.

Aside from demonstrating continuity in weak relationships, the only intriguing aspect of these findings is the longitudinal behavior of the college-educated youth. Without exception, those who matriculated registered a greater drop in ratings than those who stopped at the twelfth grade. And in a majority of cases it was the college graduates who dropped the most. For example, the decline in mean evaluation of Protestants ran 7.2, 12.6, and 14.6 across the high school graduate, some-college, and college graduate categories. Comparable drops for ratings of whites were 11.8, 13.7, and 16.0; for big business, 14.1, 18.9, and 20.8; for Jews, .9, 3.4, 6.0, and for labor unions, 4.2, 10.2, and 10.1.

There are two processes involved in these differential net declines. One is the greater caution and unwillingness among the college graduates to generalize about broad social groupings such as whites and Protestants. This state of mind is represented by somewhat greater usage of the 50° indifference mark on the 0° = 100° thermometer used to generate group affect. Such growing wariness toward stereotyping and generalizing about heterogeneous groupings is an oft-cited consequence of the collegiate experience. It truly seems to be absorbed from the prevailing liberal ethos dominating the majority of campuses. A second process is involved in the ratings of the two more specific

[21] A similar pattern is reported in Bachman, O'Malley, and Johnston, *Adolescence to Adulthood*, 135.

groups, labor unions and big business. Although all three educational
strata employed the midpoint location *less* in 1973 than in 1965 when
evaluating these two groups, this was particularly the case with the
college educated. Thus the greater drop recorded by them with respect to unions and big business reflects more of a true loss in positive
affect, rather than a rise in cautiousness.

Nonpolitical Comparisons

As in earlier chapters, it is useful to introduce concepts and measures outside the political realm in order to determine whether the political is in some sense special. Our questions here are quite simple:
(1) Do the political consequences of educational stratification have
their nonpolitical parallels? and (2) Does cross-time and cross-generational stability obtain? Taking up the latter point first, the answer is
a resounding yes. Without exception, the signs of the relationship are
the same in each generation and the relationships tend to be remarkably stable within a generation over time. Having said that, it is nevertheless true that distinctions and nuances are to be found, especially
when set alongside equivalent political characteristics. It will be con-
venient to treat the six measures in groups of two.

We have often used religious orientations in direct comparison with
political, especially partisan, orientations. Religious identification is a
case in point. A common fear among devout parents is that their children will lose their religious identity when placed in an environment
that offers alternative religious approaches, including nonreligion.
These fears are reasonably well founded in one sense, taking our results and others as a guide.[22] As high school seniors all but 1% or 2%
in each educational stratum professed to some religious identification.
By 1973 the ranks of the nonidentifiers had grown to 7%, 14%, and 18%,
ascending with educational attainment. Although secularism had set
in across the board, the college-goers were hit the hardest.[23] Significantly, the analogue of independence in party identification was not
characterized by differential attrition.

Religious beliefs, as expressed in attitudes about the divinity of the
Bible, are mightily affected by education, with the impact being a bit
higher among parents (Table 8.5). However, these varying evaluations
of the Bible appear with nearly equal magnitudes at both points in
time; the degree to which the college-educated young were more skep-

[22] E.g., Astin, *Four Critical Years*, 55-59.
[23] Interestingly enough, defection to nonbelief was most frequent among students who had been Catholic in 1965, a finding applicable across all three educational strata.

TABLE 8.5: Nonpolitical Orientations, by Generation, Education, and Year

	Youths				Parents				Correlation (γ)	
	12 yrs.	13-15 yrs.	≥16 yrs.		<12 yrs.	12 yrs.	≥13 yrs.		Y	P
Church attendance										
1 (Never) - 4 (Almost every week)										
1965	3.42	3.50	3.49	—[a]	3.06	3.20	3.17	—[a]	—[a]	—[a]
1973	2.61	2.60	2.55	-.06	3.00	2.98	2.94	-.06	.03	—[a]
	-.81	-.90	-.94		-.06	-.22	-.23			
Belief about the Bible										
1 (Irrelevant) - 4 (God's Word)										
1965	3.56	3.38	3.22	-.34	3.67	3.45	3.21	-.46	-.36	-.47
1973	3.34	3.14	2.90	-.44	3.60	3.35	3.09	-.51	-.43	-.47
	-.22	-.24	-.32		-.07	-.10	-.12			
Opinion strength										
1 (Low) - 7 (High)										
1965	4.36	4.69	4.68	—[a]	3.99	4.19	4.30	+.31	—[a]	.07
1973	4.27	4.92	4.59	—[a]	3.82	4.10	4.26	+.44	—[a]	.12
	-.09	+.23	-.09		-.07	-.09	-.04			

TABLE 8.5 (cont.)

	Youths				Parents				Correlation (γ)	
	12 yrs.	13-15 yrs.	≥16 yrs.		<12 yrs.	12 yrs.	≥13 yrs.		Y	P
Self-confidence										
1 (Low) - 7 (High)										
1965	4.51	4.77	5.40	+.89	4.41	4.93	5.18	+.77	.26	.19
1973	4.42	4.98	5.59	+1.17	4.71	5.11	5.38	+.67	.33	.19
	−.09	+.21	+.19		+.30	+.18	+.20			
Personal trust										
1 (Low) - 7 (High)										
1965	4.84	4.97	5.39	+.55	4.81	5.60	6.13	+1.32	.13	.36
1973	4.30	4.64	4.92	+.62	4.31	5.45	5.97	+1.66	.14	.39
	−.54	−.33	−.47		−.50	−.15	−.16			
Today's teenagers										
1 (Worse) - 3 (Better)										
1965	2.07	2.14	2.18	+.11	1.97	2.09	2.12	+.11	.11	.18
1973	1.18	2.00	2.03	+.24	1.77	1.92	2.04	+.27	.18	.30
	−.26	−.14	−.15		−.20	−.17	−.08			

[a] Difference scores and correlations not given because relationships are not monotonic.

266 Educational Stratification

tical than others in the cohort increased only slightly. Religious fundamentalism appears not to be differentially affected by going to college as such.

Since beliefs about the divine nature of the Bible are one (crude) way of defining a liberal-conservative religious dimension, we can compare these results with those reflecting a liberal-conservative dimension in politics, more specifically the issues listed in Table 8.4. The statistical associations for Biblical beliefs compare very favorably with those for political issues, both in magnitude and stability, as well as in the onset of the differentiation. Consequently, the patterns for political issues are not unique.

Participation in religious affairs offers a stunning contrast. If religious participation is to be gauged by church attendance, then education accounts for virtually no difference. Whereas political participation was strongly associated with education, there was essentially no connection with church attendance at either point in time. All strata shared in the downturn in church attendance.

Despite the fact that educational attainment is strongly related to religious beliefs but not to religious behavior (as measured here), there is a strong sense in which the relationships make a joint, dramatic statement. The decline observed in religious orthodoxy and observance among college students is typically inferred to be a consequence of attending college. But our figures leave no doubt that the some-college and high school graduates were registering approximately the same absolute declines, albeit the direction of the findings supports the hypothesis of greater change among college graduates. Nevertheless, the prime message is that apparently common forces were acting on all educational categories. As with many of our political variables, it is erroneous to conclude that college attendance necessarily inspired the observed changes.

The two measures reflecting what we call ego strength may be roughly compared with political resources, especially internal political efficacy. Given what is known about the self-image-enhancing aspects of more education, it is not surprising to note the positive signs in Table 8.5. What is perhaps unexpected is that with the exception of youths' self-confidence, they are not stronger. The result for self-confidence bears interest, however, because this measure provides the better reflection of how successfully individuals see themselves as coping with the world in general; opinion strength basically taps self-assuredness—some would say stubbornness or opinionatedness. Accounting for the widening gap between the youth strata was the absolute decline in the self-confidence of the high school graduates versus the modest increase among those attending college. Here is another instance where the presumptive evidence when coupled with what is known about the greater opportunity structure opened up by higher education, would lead to the inference that college, per se, made a difference. Even among young adults, however, the relationship of education to political self-confidence is higher than it is to personal self-confidence.

Finally, we came to two measures assessing one's confidence in nonpolitical objects. In contrast to political trust, education is positively related to trust in nonpolitical objects, especially among parents. Thus, whether the objects being appraised were people in general or the relative quality of contemporary versus previous teenage cohorts, better-educated parents were far more likely to weigh in with higher positive feelings. Although the results are in the same direction among the young, the magnitudes are weak. In terms of absolute scores, it is significant that college students shared in the general declines of trust in nonpolitical objects. This is another case where larger trends were superimposed on any differentiating effects that higher education might have had.

CONCLUSION

With one major exception (political evaluations) our findings corroborate the hypothesis that educational stratification provides a fundamental, early-emerging, and persistent link between individuals and their political worlds and, in a broader sense, to the fabric of American politics. The unique contribution of our investigation lies in the ability to pinpoint the early, strong appearance of the link in late adolescence, its tendency to widen in young adulthood, and its relative vibrancy when compared with the reasonably strong links forged by middle age. Of special importance is the demonstration that many characteristics commonly attributed to college education are already established before high school is completed. Although higher education typically exaggerates the pre-existing differences, that does not come about because of any greater shifting about at the individual level by those attending college.

If anything, our results probably understate the role of educational stratification because the data base excludes that education stratum which is typically the least politicized and which holds some of the most conservative views on noneconomic public policy issues. Despite that, the relationships observed were often stronger in the younger than in the older generation, where educational attainment was much more heterodox. Whether the younger generation will continue to be more differentiated than its lineage predecessor is problematic. Future observations would be necessary to establish that point.

Another longitudinal question is more amenable to an immediate answer. Based on the over-time cross-generational analysis, we would have every reason to expect the continuing appearance of education as a sorting device. Drawing on the questionnaires administered to the 1973 high school seniors, we can demonstrate that a much more recent cohort shows all the signs of perpetuating the relationship. The seniors were divided between those saying they expected to go to a four-year college versus all others. Based on similar data from the youth panel, we know that this intention is strongly related to post-high school education. There is little reason to expect much difference in the class of 1973. Moreover, in the measure that self-designation and anticipation are the vital processes involved, the differences should be readily apparent when students are classified in this way.

Our comparison, then, is between the mass-administered data for the class of '65 and that of '73. This comparison tells us whether there has been a generational effect at work such that the class of '73 is marked by different forms of relationships than was the class of '65. If the links between educational plans and political orientations are noticeably stronger in 1973, then it could be argued that educational stratification is in fact increasing in its impact. Conversely, weaker connections would suggest a deterioration.

Although there were occasional variations, the configurations look much the same in the two years. Correlations in the modest to sizeable range were observed for both years in the areas of psychological involvement in politics, cosmopolitanism, internal political efficacy, tolerance of nonconformity, and in the nonpolitical domains of self-confidence, personal trust, and church attendance. Similarly, the same low to nonexistent associations were found for each year in the areas of political trust and partisanship. Whatever social and political currents may have rocked the youth culture between 1965 and 1973, they were not of sufficient force to disturb the basic ties between educational stratification and political traits. Barring unforeseen developments, it seems highly likely that these associations will persist and that they will continue to manifest themselves before all educational destinations are reached.

At the outset of this chapter we noted that two major theories have been advanced to account for the striking differences often observed across educational classes. Briefly put, socialization theory posits that differential values, skills, and motivations are instilled directly or indirectly by educational systems and that these carry on into adult life. Allocation theory contends that different levels and types of training certify or legitimate the recipients to occupy different statuses and play different roles, and that sociopolitical disparities grow out of these differential allocations. Since our own position was that both processes were most likely at work, we did not develop a case for one or the other in presenting our findings. Nevertheless, we should at the very least consider whether our evidence informs or challenges either theory. Evidence from the youth generation is the more appropriate in this regard inasmuch as the parental generation is anywhere from two to four decades beyond formal schooling and has long since found its status and role niches.

The crucial piece of evidence is the visible differentiation among high school seniors according to their ultimate educational destinations. At first glance, this major finding seems to support neither theory. On the socialization side, how could individuals with exactly the same amount of absolute education differ so much if in fact the schools are trying to infuse them all with the same values, skills, and motivation? From the allocation perspective, how can such differences exist even before the students have received their varied certifications and before they have begun to occupy their "assigned" positions in the polity?

The answer, of course, is that students at the same given level of schooling within the same school are actually being processed and allocated in quite different ways, both formally and informally. The tracking system, culminating in the college preparatory versus nonpreparatory curriculum, is perhaps the key distinction. Thus the formal and informal socialization experiences, with their attendant political consequences, vary by *likely* educational attainments. Different values, skills, and perspectives are being learned by those who anticipate further schooling and those who do not. If we also think of curriculum distinctions as a form of chartering,[24] however, then the bridge between socialization and allocation perspectives is accomplished. Students are sorting themselves out and are being sorted out by peers and school authorities. A consequence of this selection process is the development of different aspirations and expectations about the political lives of people destined to occupy different positions in society as a result of their formal schooling. So even before distinctions and designations in the "adult" world have been made students have been differentially allocated according to the educational context of curriculum type.

Of course, far more is at work in determining a person's political profile than schooling, regardless of whether an allocation, socialization, or hybrid perspective is adopted.[25] Primary and secondary groups,

[24] Meyer, "Effects of Education as an Institution," 61.

[25] Multiple regressions were performed with the replicated 1973 measures as the dependent variables, and education, sex, race, and the 1965 measures as the independent variables. Although education usually trailed the 1965 measure, its

the larger community, the mass media, and exposure all have direct and indirect effects in molding, reinforcing, modifying, and sometimes in recasting an individual's political profile over time. Yet educational institutions are uniquely situated to, and expected to, influence the lifelong political orientations of those passing through their portals. While schools are in one sense supposed to perform a leveling function, they are also expected to make distinctions, and to encourage and facilitate varying interests, skills, and predispositions. Our results speak very much to the latter expectation. Educational institutions may indeed accomplish a leveling, but it is abundantly clear that before students leave secondary school they have become politically stratified in many respects and that this stratification by no means diminishes over time. Both socialization and allocation processes would seem to be at work in producing these outcomes.

---

effects were significant at the .001 level about three-fourths of the time and it was customarily the second strongest predictor.

CHAPTER NINE

Sex, Gender Roles, and the Challenge to Tradition

ALONG with religion and politics, sex serves as a major topic of conversation and controversy in everyday lives as well as a major demarcator of status. In the United States the three topics have often been linked to each other, perhaps never more so than in the period marked by the contemporary women's liberation movement. Traditional prescriptions about the roles of women (and men) in society, anchored in part by religious and quasi-religious values and by political and legal practices, have been severely challenged. The long list of feminist grievances and the attempts to redress them have inevitably become part of the political agenda. When added to the customary concerns about the intersection between sex and politics—such as differential political socialization and variable political behavior—the onset of the women's movement makes the study materials available to us all the more intriguing.

Partly in response to the movement's exhortations, the nomenclature surrounding the topics of sex and gender has been changing, so much so that multiple usages and not a little confusion abound. Since these are not simply trivial differences in semantics, we should state at the outset our own general rules of usage. For the most part when we refer to gross comparisons between men and women we will speak of these as sex differences, recognizing full well that these differences do not (in the absence of scientific evidence to the contrary) spring inherently from biological status. Technically, we could refer to such comparisons as gender differences, but we wish to reserve gender and gender roles for more specific meanings. Unlike strictly biological sex roles, gender roles are culturally defined. "Gender role consists of all optional and prescribed attributes, attitudes, and behaviors defined appropriate for and expected of females and males within the culture."[1]

Illustratively, being employed has been virtually a mandatory gender role for men whereas for women it has moved from a deviant role to a widely recognized and accepted optional role and, for some seg-

[1] Reesa M. Vaughter, "Review Essay: Psychology," *Signs*, 2 (Autumn 1976), 120-46, at note 14.

ments of the populace, a modal role. In a different vein, even though both men and women become parents, being a mother continues to be freighted with different role specifications than being a father. The heart of the controversy over the so-called women's issue lies precisely in the area of the culturally imposed role expectations and perform-ances attached to people as a result of their sexual traits. In this chap-ter comparisons based on gender roles will follow upon a consideration of basic male-female (sex) differences.

Unlike education-related differences, which are often thought to crystallize in the late teens and early twenties, sex and gender role differences are often regarded as fixed and invariant over the life cycle. It has been argued that observed adult variations in political interest, resources, and involvement all have their roots in pre-adult-hood.[2] More recently, suspected causes of many sex differences have been traced back to early childhood, as in analyses of active males and passive females in stories and illustrations in children's literature. Gen-erational and cohort analyses treat changing sex differences over time, but they seldom consider alterations in sex-related attitudes or behav-ior within a single generation.

The work on sex and political attributes, therefore, reveals little about the life-cycle dynamics of sex and gender role differences. Yet there are strong reasons for suspecting variations. Indeed, one line of thought stresses the small likelihood of strong pre-adult differences be-tween the sexes simply because there is little opportunity or reason for them to be expressed; rather, gender-related norms become more visible later on because the opportunities emerge and adults feel re-sponsible for enacting gender norms acquired (but latent) during childhood.[3] One might hypothesize, then, that male-female differences will be greater during some stages of the life cycle and smaller during others. In particular, the transition period from adolescence to adult-hood would seem to be one of those points at which sex differences are likely to undergo considerable alteration.

Awareness of sex-appropriate roles and values, as they have been traditionally defined, undoubtedly begins at an early age, but the school works in a number of ways to qualify this awareness. Girls and boys both must undergo recurring formal and informal lessons in civic

[2] Herbert Hyman, *Political Socialization* (Glencoe: Free Press, 1959), Chapter 2; Fred I. Greenstein, *Children and Politics* (New Haven: Yale University Press, 1965), Chapter 6; Robert D. Hess and Judith V. Torney, *The Development of Po-litical Attitudes in Children* (Chicago: Aldine, 1967). The latter authors point out changes in boy-girl differences as well.

[3] Virginia Sapiro, "Socialization to Political Gender Roles Among Women," pa-per presented at the annual meeting of the Midwest Political Science Association, Chicago, April 1977.

training. The rights and obligations of citizenship, which form a major part of this training, are not defined by sex or gender role. Both sexes are encouraged to participate in school activities such as student government. Evidence from our 1965 wave indicates that, if anything, girls were more involved in school politics than were boys.[4] And factors that may be important later, such as being a homemaker, are not relevant at the high school stage.

By age 25 or 26 all this has changed. Males are almost all working away from the home while many women are not. And even though strides have been taken in the direction of job equality in recent years, females who work are still more often in jobs that are of lower status and that involve less decision-making power. Children have arrived in many families, and the primary responsibility for the day-to-day care is still viewed as more of a female than a male role. As a consequence of these changes, sex-related political contrasts might be expected to increase. Sex-appropriate norms, which were perhaps apparent to adolescents but subdued by the formal and informal school curriculum, are now reinforced by marital, occupational, and parental roles. At least for a portion of the women, conventional political interest and activity are discouraged or at least not encouraged. For our sample, these life-cycle considerations mean that sex and gender role differences should tend to be greater in 1973 than they were in 1965.

While these life-cycle forces may seem uncontestable, the picture is complicated by strong period effects setting in at the time the 1965 high school seniors began their move from late adolescence into adulthood. In fact, just the opposite prediction about sex-related differences flows from a consideration of historical forces during the period of our study. Equality of the sexes has by no means been achieved, but steps have been taken in that direction in a number of realms. One would anticipate that emerging equality would be reflected in declining political differences where they existed in 1965 and that no increase in differences would develop where they were already very small.

Convergence should be especially true for the kinds of orientations we are studying. If our concern were primarily overt political participation, marital and occupational roles might override any potential influence of the changing societal perspectives on gender roles. But all of our panel measures related to involvement were designed with high school seniors in mind, and consequently were not dependent on manifest participation. Attitudinal and judgmental characteristics were al-

---

[4] For example, 62% of the girls and 51% of the boys had run for a school office. Thirty-two percent of the girls had been an officer several times compared to 21% of the boys.

so not so likely to be influenced by motherhood and other factors that are thought to account for lower female politicization. Thus, if the feminist movement has had an effect on this generation of youths, it should be readily apparent in weakened or continued low 1973 relationships between sex, gender role, and political attributes.

What of the parental generation and of intergenerational differences? Since parents consistently exhibited less aggregate and individual change than did youths, it seems likely that the differences between subsets of parents would be less subject to alteration than among comparable subsets of youths. It also seems likely that gender roles would be more firmly established among the parents, so that shifts associated with the women's movement would have less impact on the older generation. Thus sex and gender role differences among the parents should remain relatively unchanged. What characterizes intergenerational comparisons should then depend on whether life-cycle or historical forces are more influential among the young. Analysis of the 1965 wave showed a marked decline in sex differences among the younger generation in those cases where mothers and fathers differed. If life-cycle factors predominate, this decline will be reversed and male-female differences will tend to be equalized in the two generations. If historical forces predominate among the offspring, differences should still be apparent among the parents, but will be virtually nonexistent among the youths.

All of the foregoing propositions can be analyzed using the format developed in Chapter 8. In the first part of the chapter, after briefly contrasting individual-level change among men and women, we will concentrate on overall male-female comparisons. Since sex is a dichotomous variable, a single two-by-two table for each generation shows aggregate turnover for each sex and mean or percentage differences between males and females in each year. Comparison of the two tables yields the intergenerational perspective. After this analysis for the entire sample, we will observe variations in the younger generation of women according to their marital, maternal, and employment statuses, and in the older generation according to the age of their child(ren) and their eight-year employment record. These analyses shed additional light on the life-cycle dynamics of sex and gender role differences. Because the results depend heavily on the interplay of historical forces and life-cycle developments, the findings also yield critical insight into the pathways likely to be taken by future cohorts.

RATES OF CHANGE

Most work and indeed most of our introductory remarks about sex differences concern aggregate comparisons. However, it is worth considering briefly the matter of individual rates of change. Previous work, rarely based on longitudinal data, offers little in the way of guidance here, and theoretical considerations are of scarcely more help. Life-cycle development, for example, is an ambiguous factor. Women who become homemakers may lower their interest and involvement while males and employed women are unchanging, or they may fail to increase their awareness and activity while males and employed females are surging ahead. Either process would result in the sex and gender role differences traditionally observed. Historical forces, we suppose, did promote greater individual change among women during this period. We might especially look for greater lability in the realm of attitudes where, as we noted, factors such as motherhood need not be an inhibiting force. On the other hand, the women's movement has by no means been directed solely at females, so one wonders how great the differences would be in the relative frequency of change.

As it turns out, the soundest conclusion is that there is little difference in rates of change by sex. In fully half of the cases for each generation, the 1965 $\times$ 1973 correlations for men and women were within .03 of each other. When relatively large differences (over .10) did occur, it was women who were more stable among the young. In the parental generation, only one difference was this large. Thus there is particularly little support for the expectation of greater female changeability.

Nor were differences in stability rates concentrated in any one area; for the most part, rough equality characterized each set of correlations. It is true that in the critical domain of public policy issues, two of the largest differences were found between male and female youths. But contrary to expectations, it was women who were more stable: $\tau_b = .20$ and .10 for women and men, respectively, on the question of school integration, and .17 versus .04 on the matter of speeches against churches. Moreover, differences on the other two issues were small (.04 and .01). And among the parents, the over-time correlations for policy issues were all within .01 of each other.

In short, as individuals, neither men nor women were more prone to change, either in the early or middle adult years. As we shall see, however, aggregate changes are much more differentiated. We take up each set of attributes in turn.

PSYCHOLOGICAL INVOLVEMENT

The area of political interest and media usage offers a useful opening into the question of evolving sex-related patterns at the aggregate level. Political interest itself is one of the few topics about which prior research has been decisive. Males almost without exception have proclaimed more interest in politics than have females.[5] However, the differences have often been quite small,[6] and the results from our 1965 wave showed a much reduced male advantage in the filial compared to the parental generation. This reduction between generations, added to the historical force of increasing feminine concern with politics, suggests that by 1973 the younger generation might show virtually no sex differences in political interest. This is especially so inasmuch as expressing interest requires no overt activity.

Viewed from this perspective the results in Table 9.1 are striking. It was among the parents that male-female differences declined. Among the youths the small sex gap in 1965 actually grew larger. This surprising turn of events was brought about by contrasting changes in the two generations. Young males increased their interest, as would be predicted for new adults, while young women as a whole were no more interested than they had been as high school seniors. At the parental level, it was the women who changed. In fact, they changed more than any of the other groups. The thesis of eroding sex differences in the new generation with little change in the older one is severely contradicted in this instance.

A second aspect of involvement—cosmopolitanism, or geopolitical focus—is particularly subject to the crosscutting influences of the women's movement and of traditional life-cycle development. Women have been found to be more interested than men in local matters, especially school affairs, but less involved in other domains of political activities.[7] Based on these participation modes, we would expect young adult women to reorient their attention away from larger domains and toward more local concerns. At the same time, the push for greater involvement of women in formerly masculine pursuits suggests a possible revision of previous patterns of development.

The results support the more traditional, life-cycle argument (Table

[5] At the pre-adult level see, for example, Greenstein, *Children and Politics*, 115-18; Hess and Torney, *Development of Political Attitudes in Children*, 188; Herbert Hyman, *Political Socialization*, 29-39. Among adults, greater interest among males is typically inferred from their more frequent participation. See, for example, Lester W. Milbrath and M. L. Goel, *Political Participation*, 2nd ed. (Chicago: Rand McNally, 1977), 116-18.

[6] In addition to the references in footnote 5, see Roberta S. Sigel, "The Adolescent in Politics: The Case of American Girls," paper presented at the annual meeting of the American Political Science Association, San Francisco, 1975; Sidney Verba and Norman H. Nie, *Participation in America* (New York: Harper and Row, 1972), 100-101, 180-81.

[7] M. Kent Jennings, "Another Look at the Life Cycle and Political Participation," *American Journal of Political Science*, 23 (November 1979), 755-71; M. Kent Jennings and Richard G. Niemi, "The Division of Political Labor Between Mothers and Fathers," *American Political Science Review*, 65 (March 1971), 69-82.

TABLE 9.1: Psychological Involvement in Politics, by
Generation, Sex, and Year

	Youths[a]			Parents			Correlation (γ)	
	Female	Male		Female	Male		Y	P
Interest in public affairs								
1 (Low) - 4 (High)								
1965	3.20	3.30	+.10[b]	3.03	3.49	+.46	.13	.42
1973	3.20	3.39	+.19	3.22	3.50	+.28	.23	.30
	.00	+.09		+.19	+.01			
Cosmopolitanism								
1 (Least) - 7 (Most)								
1965	5.18	5.31	+.13	4.09	4.57	+.48	.08	.19
1973	4.76	5.05	+.29	3.97	4.24	+.27	.12	.11
	−.42	−.26		−.12	−.33			
Read newspapers								
1 (Don't read) - 5 (Almost daily)								
1965	3.89	4.00	+.11	3.99	4.30	+.31	.10	.20
1973	3.76	4.04	+.28	3.84	4.16	+.32	.17	.23
	−.13	+.04		−.15	−.14			
Read magazines								
1 (Don't read) - 3 (Regularly)								
1965	2.22	2.26	+.04	2.14	2.12	−.02	.04	−.02
1973	1.96	2.13	+.17	1.89	1.97	+.08	.15	.08
	−.26	−.13		−.25	−.15			
Watch television								
1 (Don't watch) - 5 (Almost daily)								
1965	3.86	3.76	−.10	4.28	4.21	−.07	−.01	−.06
1973	4.23	4.10	−.13	4.39	4.30	−.09	−.12	−.07
	+.37	+.34		+.11	+.09			
Listen to radio								
1 (Don't listen) - 5 (Almost daily)								
1965	3.39	3.22	−.17	3.42	3.41	−.01	−.08	−.01
1973	2.91	3.11	+.20	2.81	2.98	+.17	.08	.09
	−.48	−.11		−.61	−.43			

[a] N's before missing data are deleted: male youths 672, female youths 676, male parents 491, female parents 688.

[b] Plus sign signifies a male advantage, negative sign a female advantage.

9.1). Though cosmopolitan outlooks in the offspring declined among both sexes, the decline was greater among women. This increased the sex difference, which already had women a bit less oriented to national and international affairs as high school seniors. Particularly significant was the increase in primary attention to local matters, which rose from 10 to 16% among women but only from 11 to 13% among men. The contrasting results for parents are again intriguing. Scores for both sexes declined somewhat, due to lowered interest in international events, but the older generation of women changed the least of any group. In 1973 male-female differences were actually a bit lower among parents than among youths.

Once we are armed with these results for general political interest and focus of interest, the data on media usage are less unanticipated. In three of the four cases, a sharp increase is apparent in male-female differences among the youths. In each of these instances the change brings the contrast more in line with traditional stereotypes. Males read more in both years, but the gap was wider in 1973. Radio listening, which showed a decided female advantage in 1965, reversed itself into a numerically larger male advantage eight years later. The exception to this pattern was television, where sex differences were perhaps minimized by its becoming the dominant form of news gathering.

The results for the parental cohort are more mixed, with virtually no change in a couple of instances and a large increase in sex differences for radio usage. Again with the exception of television, where we shall find that homemakers keep viewing rates high, the changes increase at least minimally the male advantage. If the women's liberation movement has had an impact on attention to politics via media usage, it is not apparent in these data.

The way in which these changing sex differences came about also supports the view that media usage patterns are not responding strongly to suggestions for more female involvement in politics. For each medium except television, usage rates actually declined among women, and always declined more than among men. It would seem that if both sexes were responding to period effects away from the other media and toward television, and with respect to these other media, that women were acting in such a way as actually to increase the gap between the sexes.

Changes in the frequencies underlying the mean scores yield still further insight into what was happening. For political interest, slightly fewer young males were in the lowest categories in 1973 (follow public affairs only now and then or not at all) than had been the case in 1965. Young females, on the other hand, more frequently gave these responses. Infrequent newspaper reading (three or four times a month or less) was stable among males but rose significantly among females. For radio usage and magazine reading, sporadic attention increased among both sexes, but much more so for women. Increasingly, therefore, there was a cadre of women well insulated from the political process, except possibly that of television news coverage.

Psychological involvement, then, presents us with something of a surprise. On every measure except television viewing, men outdistanced women in 1973. Of greater significance, however, was the fact that the sex differential, far from declining among young adults, consistently increased; it was the older generation that revealed some slackening of sex differences. Two tentative conclusions follow from these findings. First, it appears that the adolescent years may indeed suppress male-female contrasts in political involvement, with traditional differences becoming more apparent early in adulthood. This happened in our cohort despite the movement toward sex equality in legal and other domains. Second, the parent findings further support the idea, stressed in Chapters 2 and 3, that adults continue to respond to their changing environment well into middle age. Exactly what lies behind the changes is unclear, since increasing political interest among the middle-aged females was not matched by greater use of the media. Yet it is clear that sex differences continue to show alterations beyond the high school-young adult shift observed in the younger generation.

POLITICAL RESOURCES

As with psychological involvement, so too with resources: most studies report that males hold a slight to moderate edge among both adult and pre-adult populations. Women tend to be less able to cite ways in which they could influence government, to have less factual information at their command, and to be armed with a less sophisticated and systematic conceptual apparatus for evaluating politics.[8] As in the case of involvement it should be stressed that differences between the sexes are ordinarily not large[9] and that there are certain socioeconomic

[8] See, for example, Angus Campbell, Philip E. Converse, Warren E. Miller, and Donald E. Stokes, The American Voter (New York: Wiley, 1960), 49-93; Gabriel Almond and Sidney Verba, The Civic Culture (Princeton: Princeton University Press, 1963), 209-13; and, at a pre-adult level, Greenstein, Children and Politics; Hess and Torney, Development of Political Attitudes in Children; Anthony Orum, Roberta S. Cohen, Sherri Grassmuck, and Amy W. Orum, "Sex, Socialization, and Politics," American Sociological Review, 39 (April 1974), 197-209. From a comparative perspective differences between the sexes tend to be smaller in the United States than in other Western countries. See M. Kent Jennings and Barbara G. Farah, "Ideology, Gender and Political Action," British Journal of Political Science, 10 (April 1980), 219-40.

[9] See, especially, the mixed results on feelings of political efficacy among pre-

strata wherein women outperform men. Following the logic used in the previous section, we can entertain contrasting expectations about change in the filial generation. If there are more encumbrances standing in the way of young women than of young men, then whatever gaps existed in 1965 should have been heightened by 1973. On the other hand, if the feminist movement and other social trends have exerted their anticipated sway, then those differences should have diminished and perhaps even been completely overcome.

Political efficacy offers an example in support of the life-stage hypothesis. Since efficacy was declining during this period for the whole sample, increasing sex differences would probably stem from a sharp decline in women's feelings of competence rather than from an increase in men's. Table 9.2 confirms this expectation. Male youths dropped only slightly from the earlier levels, whereas females dropped a good deal more, thus increasing the male advantage. What occurred, more specifically, was a considerable increase in the proportion of females with very low efficacy, suggesting that some fraction of them underwent a serious loss in perceived ability to cope with the political world after high school graduation, just as some withdrew psychologically from the world of politics. By contrast, what little change was transpiring in the parental generation worked in favor of reducing the male advantage.

Turning to the cognitive components of political resources, we find a somewhat confusing picture of change. For retention of political facts the results are about what one would expect. Among parents there was virtually no change of any kind. Men retained a very substantial advantage. Both male and female youths increased their storehouse of information, but only slightly, so there was no major change in the sex differential. Still, the male advantage in 1973 is fractionally above its already healthy size eight years earlier.

On the other hand, the measure of the understanding of political party differences shows a declining male advantage among the youths alongside an increase of similar magnitude among the parents. The decline in the youth generation is due to an unusually low level of

---

adults. Easton and Dennis found no consistent differences between boys and girls in the second through eighth grade. Merelman found high school senior girls slightly more efficacious than boys, while our results from 1965 show just the opposite. David Easton and Jack Dennis, "A Child's Acquisition of Regime Norms: Political Efficacy," *American Political Science Review*, 61 (March 1967), 25-38; Richard M. Merelman, *Political Socialization and Educational Climates* (New York: Holt, Rinehart and Winston, 1971), 125. Differences tend to be greatest and most consistent in the area of information and understanding. See especially Orum et al., "Sex, Socialization, and Politics," and Merelman, *Political Socialization and Educational Climates*.

TABLE 9.2: Political Resources, by Generation, Sex, and Year

	Youths			Parents			Correlation (γ)	
	Female	Male		Female	Male		Y	P
Internal political efficacy 1 (Low) - 3 (High)								
1965	2.06	2.15	+.09	1.74	1.92	+.18	.11	.19
1973	1.84	2.11	+.27	1.63	1.76	+.13	.31	.15
	−.22	−.04		−.11	−.16			
Recognition and understanding of liberal-conservative dimension 1 (None) - 5 (Broad)								
1965	2.57	2.86	+.29	2.68	3.12	+.44	.13	.20
1973	3.34	3.50	+.16	2.87	3.43	+.56	.07	.25
	+.77	+.64		+.19	+.31			
Knowledge of political facts 0-6 (Number correct)								
1965	3.32	3.89	+.57	3.41	4.16	+.75	.26	.38
1973	3.39	4.02	+.63	3.40	4.17	+.77	.28	.38
	+.07	+.13		−.01	+.01			

recognition and understanding among partisan (Republican and Democratic) males in 1973. In 1965 this group was reasonably well informed relative to other youths. Over the next eight years, however, their improvement was rather slight. It is not apparent just why they showed so little change.

In any event, it is clear that the male advantage in regard to political resources at the time of high school graduation by no means disappears immediately thereafter and can, in fact, widen. However, the evidence in this section offers less support for a strict life-cycle interpretation of changing sex differences, inasmuch as there was little change in male-female differences in regard to knowledge of political facts and a declining difference among the youths on the recognition variable. Still, there is no strong support for the idea of vanishing sex differences in the rising generation. Extrapolating into the future, it appears that sex differences will not disappear altogether for some time.

POLITICAL PARTICIPATION

Men continue to dominate the elite positions of politics, although substantial inroads are being made by women in state and local politics. At the mass public level men have usually been found to be more participative also, but the cross-sex differences have been moderate at best and have been declining over time. Women have come close to holding their own despite the generally discouraging effects of socialization practices, unfavorable structural conditions, and inhibiting situational factors.[10] Most investigators, however, have not been able to focus on particularly crucial points in the life course. Nor have they been able to compile participation histories. Our young cohort offers an especially apt target for observing whether the traditional, though diminishing, participation gap is still extant and how this cohort compares with a generation which has a sex-linked discrepancy in participation. As in our earlier discussion, it should be noted that our materials are necessarily limited because of the youthfulness of the junior cohort in 1965.

We turn first to voting in national elections. Based on their self-reports about their very first opportunities, women turned out just a bit more often in both 1968 and 1970, thus violating the expectation of higher initial engagement by men. However, the 1968 and 1970 figures are distorted by the fact that upwards of one-half of the males were in the military service at some point during the eight years. As shown elsewhere, men in the service voted less frequently than did other men, thereby accounting for the lower male turnout in these first two years of eligibility.[11] By 1972, even with some vestiges of the military impact still in evidence, the "expected" male advantage emerges:

Percent Voting

	Youths			Parents		
	Female	Male		Female	Male	
1964	—	—		81	88	+ 7
1968	62	59	−3	86	93	+ 7
1970	43	41	−2	71	84	+13
1972	70	74	+4	76	88	+12

The disparity is obviously small, but the fact that it emerges at all is noteworthy. Among parents the stereotypical male advantage holds

[10] Kristi Andersen, "Working Women and Political Participation, 1952-1972," *American Journal of Political Science*, 19 (August 1975), 439-53; Marjorie Lansing, "The American Woman: Voter and Activist," in Jane S. Jaquette (ed.), *Women in Politics* (New York: Wiley, 1974); Nancy E. McGlen, "The Impact of Children on Political Participation," unpublished paper, State University of New York at Buffalo, 1976; Susan Welch, "Women as Political Animals? A Test of Some Explanations for Male-Female Differences," *American Journal of Political Science*, 21 (November 1977), 711-30.

[11] M. Kent Jennings and Gregory B. Markus, "Political Participation and Vietnam Veterans: A Longitudinal Study," in Nancy L. Goldman and David R. Segal (eds.), *The Social Psychology of Military Service* (Beverly Hills, Calif.: Sage, 1976).

across all four elections. Indeed, it is larger for the last pair than for the earlier pair. Assuming that the difference among the young does not increase, the comparison across the two cohorts suggests a generational effect of diminishing sex inequalities.

A fuller picture of participation rates is obtained by drawing upon the political activity index summarizing the levels of participation over the 1966-1972 period. For convenience we have collapsed the thirteen-point index into a trichotomy of low, medium, and high. As shown in Table 9.3, young men held but a small advantage over women. Al-

TABLE 9.3: Political Activity Index in 1973, by Generation and Sex

| | Youths | | Parents | |
	Female	Male	Female	Male
Low	31%	27%	28%	13%
Medium	41	39	42	44
High	28	34	30	43
	$\gamma = .11$		$\gamma = .32$	

though the direction of the results is in keeping with traditional expectations, the magnitude of the relationship scarcely suggests the perpetuation of serious sex-linked inequalities. Nonetheless, examining reported behavior for each of the specific activities making up the index shows just how uniform the small male advantage is. Apart from the nebulous "other" work for a party, candidate, or issue (on which there is a tie) young men were more participative on each measure, by margins ranging from 1% (wearing buttons) to 9% (influencing others). Females in the younger generation are catching up to males in their participation rates, but still lack full parity.

The parental generation exhibits about the same type of difference associated with males and females in the past—not overwhelming but clearly of a magnitude to warrant the conclusion that sex, in some fashion, helps segregate the more from the less active. Though an exactly comparable index cannot be computed for 1965, thus barring strict longitudinal comparisons, there was a substantial male advantage in the earlier period as well ($\gamma = .24$). When we examine specific activities reported in 1973, there is a male advantage in every one, and in most cases the difference is greater than in the offspring generation. Clearly, then, what we have here is a generational effect in which sex differences have declined to only a small margin. Still, in keeping with the results for psychological involvement and political resources, sex differences have not yet disappeared.

PARTISANSHIP AND ELECTORAL BEHAVIOR

In our treatment of psychological involvement, resources, and participation, our expectations and interpretations were fairly well anchored in bodies of knowledge and thought associated with passage through the life cycle and with the impact associated wih social movements such as the rise of contemporary feminism. As we turn to political preferences and attitudes, however, our perspectives have to shift and the directionality of the hypotheses is not so easily determined. Neither life-cycle nor social movement theories provide strong guidance.

Voting and partisanship are cases in point. First, we encounter an evaluative component not present in involvement, resources, and participation. The presumed processes lying behind the differences observed previously may not carry over into opinions about political groups and individual actors. Second, there is less evidence about preadults on which to base expectations or to make inferences about changes over the life cycle. Part of the reason for this is the third new factor. Sex differences in evaluations of contemporary candidates, issues, and parties probably fluctuate widely depending on the exact stimuli under consideration. Therefore in this and succeeding sections we will have to be cautious in generalizing beyond our specific results.

Figures on the direction of the vote are presented in Table 9.4. What we find surprising about them is the greater difference between male

TABLE 9.4: Partisanship and Voting, by Generation, Sex, and Year

	Youths			Parents		
	Female	Male		Female	Male	
Candidate preference						
% preferring Republican						
1964	24	32	+ 8	30	34	+4
1968						
(Dem)	39	35	− 4	39	39	0
(Rep)	49	45	− 4	52	48	−4
1970	40	34	− 6	49	44	−5
1972	63	59	− 4	68	68	0
Party identification						
% Independent						
1965	33	40	+ 7	25	28	+3
1973	40	54	+14	25	28	+3
	—	—		—	—	
	+7	+14		0	0	

and female youths than parents. We do not attach a great deal of significance to the direction of the difference, although it is perhaps significant that in each presidential election young women reported more frequently that they had voted for the winner. This happened despite the fact that fewer women are Independents and, consequently, more likely to be swayed by short-term electoral forces. In neither generation is the contrast sharp enough that candidates could ignore one group while courting the other. Yet throughout the 1964-1972 period there remained a small difference in young men's and women's candidate preferences.

The results regarding candidate preferences must be regarded lightly because the numerical differences and even the direction vary from one election to another. Preferences are especially likely to vary unpredictably depending on the short-term factors influencing a particular contest. More meaningful, then, are comparisons of male-female partisanship. To our surprise, there is a contrast among the young that must be regarded as rather sizeable, and which doubled in magnitude between 1965 and 1973. Both sexes have a substantial proportion of Independents, but it is especially high among males. Moreover, the discrepancy is greatest among "pure" Independents. In 1965, only three percent more males than females were nonleaning Independents. By 1973 this amounted to a nine percent difference.

A possible explanation for the greater number of male Independents lies in each sex's response to contextual pressures. The difference in the more recent sounding can be attributed to male responsiveness to historical forces favoring nonpartisanship. But males were also noticeably more often Independent in the spring of 1965, just before the proportion of Independents started its dramatic rise in the national electorate. It may be that as high school seniors the males were responding to typical classroom rhetoric in favor of independence from parties. In each year, then, males were more attuned to external currents, which happened to be in the same direction each year.

Whether or not this explanation is correct, the fact that more young men than women are Independent was unanticipated. Sex differences in partisanship have typically been nonexistent or very small,[12] such as the three percent difference between mothers and fathers observed here in each year. Moreover, if differences existed, we might have expected greater partisanship among males because of their perceived greater willingness to tolerate and engage in conflict.[13] Moreover, our

[12] Campbell et al., *The American Voter*, 49.
[13] Sigel, for example, cites this argument though she finds it unconvincing. Nonetheless, among the nonpoliticized portion (over 80%) of her sample, boys

own data below show that males do not uniformly respond more strongly to period effects. Thus, at least for 1973, it must be regarded as something of an anomaly—owing to historical circumstances and differential reactions to them—that young adult males were considerably more often Independent than were females.

The effect of this divergence cannot be judged adequately without data on later time periods. We have already seen that the difference in candidate preferences in 1973 was less than the difference in partisanship, and could not readily be explained by the partisan difference anyway. Nor was there any sex difference in the relative proportions of Democrats and Republicans among those who did identify with the party. And in absolute terms the male-female difference is not large, even though it is contrary to our expectations. Thus the practical consequences of this contrast may be negligible unless it persists and grows in subsequent years. Yet it is significant in the present context as another example of the failure of sex differences to disappear in the new generation of adults. Though the gap may decline later as more youths marry and husbands and wives exert mutual influence, sex differences in partisanship, as in involvement and political resources, had reached surprising levels by 1973.

Opinions on Public Policy Issues

Men and women have ordinarily tended toward convergence with respect to specific questions of public policy. The major exceptions have been over issues in which the moral dilemmas are especially acute, e.g., war and capital punishment.[14] While pre-adult opinions have been infrequently studied, the same conclusions apparently apply. Our results follow precisely this pattern. For three of the four policy items there was little variation by sex in either generation and no meaningful change over time. There was a slightly greater shift among women away from support for school integration, but it left men's and women's opinions virtually identical in 1973.

On the remaining issue, however, there was a large gap between men's and women's opinions in both generations in 1965, and that gap had widened by 1973:

---

more often score high on acceptance of the need for partisan conflict; Sigel, "The Adolescent in Politics." See also Hess and Torney, Development of Political Attitudes in Children, 192-93.

[14] See, for example, Alan D. Monroe, Public Opinion in America (New York: Dodd, Mead, 1975), 96, 206; Milton J. Rosenberg, Sidney Verba, and Philip E. Converse, Vietnam and the Silent Majority (New York: Harper and Row, 1970), 75-76; The 1972 Virginia Slims American Women's Opinion Poll, Louis Harris and Associates, Inc., 1972.

Communist holding office, % pro

	Youths			Parents			Correlation (γ)	
	Female	Male		Female	Male		Y	P
1965	31	43	+12	23	39	+16	.25	.35
1973	49	70	+21	34	54	+20	.43	.39
	—	—		—	—			
	+18	+27		+11	+15			

At the extremes, more than two-thirds of the male youths in 1973 were in favor of allowing an elected Communist to take office, while two-thirds of the older women opposed this position. That a difference exists on this particular issue is significant inasmuch as Stouffer found women less tolerant of Communists and suspected Communists twenty years prior to our second wave.[15] He argued that women are not more intolerant than men in general, which is consistent with the failure to find sex differences on all civil liberties questions.[16] But on questions involving Communists, he found a small difference that was maintained at differing ages, education levels, regions, etc. As our results and a national replication show,[17] that difference seems to have persisted into the 1970s, despite the period effects also observed in our data.

Equally important with respect to this question is that the division between males and females increased most among the young. From the 1965 evidence alone we might infer a gradual decline in sex differences because the younger generation showed a slightly smaller difference than the older one. In eight years' time, however, the young adults had managed to increase the gap to a notch above that in the parents' generation. It is difficult to account theoretically for this large gap because of the lack of consistency across all issues and because the "Communist" question does not have an obvious connection to factors which are affected by movement through the life cycle. Nonetheless, it is clear that we cannot yet predict the disappearance of some male-female differences of opinion.

Although the four issues already treated are the only policy questions for which we have longitudinal data, questions introduced in the 1973 survey provide an additional source of information on male-female attitudes. In general, differences are not large in either genera-

[15] Samuel A. Stouffer, *Communism, Conformity, and Civil Liberties* (New York: Doubleday, 1959), Chapter 6.
[16] For example, in H. H. Remmers and D. H. Radler, *The American Teenager* (Indianapolis: Charter Books, 1962), 210-20.
[17] Clyde Z. Nunn, Harry J. Crockett, Jr., and J. Allen Williams, Jr., *Tolerance for Nonconformity* (San Francisco: Jossey-Bass, 1978), Chapter 7.

tion. This conclusion applies even to feminist issues. One of the larger discrepancies, for example, occurs in the younger generation on the question of whether women have "too much," "too little," or "just about the right amount" of influence in American life and politics. Yet the difference is only 8%; 48% of the females compared to 40% of the males responded "too little." On a seven-point scale where the extremes were "women and men should have an equal role" (scored 1) and "women's place is in the home" (scored 7), men in both generations were actually more favorable toward sex equality than were women. But again the difference was not large, especially in the younger generation where men averaged 2.96 and women 3.05. Similarly, on thermometer scores accorded three prominent women and "the women's liberation movement," male and female ratings differed, on average, by only 2.4 points, and not always with the same directionality at that.

Still, sex differences have not disappeared altogether. In both generations, for example, men were slightly more favorable toward a government guarantee of "a job and a good standard of living" (differences of .15 and .36 on a seven-point scale). Among the younger adults, men's and women's feelings about marijuana were surprisingly variant: men scored 3.71 and women 4.43, where 1 represented "make use of marijuana legal," and 7 was "set penalties higher than they are now." The frequency and location of these variations are not easily predicted, and on the whole they may be decreasing. But we are confident that issues will continue to arise here and there, the feminist movement notwithstanding, which divide the population along sex lines.

EVALUATIONS OF GOVERNMENTS AND GROUPS

As with opinions on policy items, sex differences in evaluations accorded political institutions, actors, and groups can be expected to vary somewhat from one object to another. In addition, as we noted in Chapter 3, group assessments are highly susceptible to changes in the objects themselves as well as in the observers. This means that the magnitude and direction of sex differences might reasonably vary across time just as across objects. Finally, group attachments have not generally been thought to vary much by sex.

Our first piece of evidence suggests that young males and females have grown apart over the eight-year period. In Chapter 5 we saw that responses to an open-ended question about what features the respondents were least proud of as Americans could be grouped into a few main categories. One large category is simply whether the feature referred to fell within the political domain, and under that heading whether the referent was the political system per se. Although both men and women joined in the rising chorus finding fault with the political system, the gap between the two widened. Whereas in 1965 the γ correlation between sex and system references was .12 (indicating more political system responses by males), by 1973 it had climbed to .24. This growing cleavage occurred despite the fact that women, who gave more overall responses in each year, had a slightly higher lead in mean rate of responses to the question in 1973 compared to 1965. Whatever impact the feminist movement may have had in terms of raising the salience of an imperfect political system among young women in particular was more than offset by other forces acting on young men. A final point to make is that the greater male emphasis on system deficiencies contrasts in each year with the greater female emphasis on race relations and on moral turpitude.

Generalized criticism of the political system provided a first glimpse into the possibility that young males more quickly manifest the emerging skepticism or cynicism that develops in young adulthood or, from another point of view, the skepticism that began to mark the historical era. Another indicator is found in the declining levels of political trust:

Political trust, 1 (Low) - 6 (High)

| | Youths | | | Parents | | | Correlation (γ) | |
	Female	Male		Female	Male		Y	P
1965	4.64	4.51	−.13	3.77	3.86	+.09	−.08	.05
1973	3.12	2.89	−.23	2.98	3.01	+.03	−.12	.01
	−1.52	−1.62		−.79	−.85			

Both sexes lowered sharply the trust they accorded government officials, but the drop was larger among males. Consequently, the male-female gap widened a little between the two soundings. As with the "least proud" references, the parental generation showed little in the way of sex differentiation on political trust.

That this characterization of sex differences has some generalizability comes from the data on group evaluations. Once again, young males were already less positive toward societal groups in 1965; for seven of the eight groups they awarded lower thermometer ratings than did females. Even though starting with lower ratings, male youths typically (six times out of eight) dropped their ratings more than did their female counterparts, so that by 1973 the difference between their responses was most often a bit above the earlier gap. Among the parents the results were rather mixed, as on the generalized criticism and trust items. Overall, the average difference in the scores between male and female parents was only half that among the offspring.

Intergenerational contrasts provide another interesting perspective on male-female divisions. Consider political trust. In 1975 both male and female youths were much more trusting than their same-sex parents—differences of .65 and .87 for men and women, respectively. Levels of trust declined much more among the youths than among parents, but in 1973 female offspring were still slightly more trusting (+.14) than their mothers. Male youths, in contrast, were now less trusting than fathers (−.12). Young men evidently develop the more cynical views of adulthood rather quickly after entering the electorate, while young women take somewhat longer.

Thermometer ratings of groups yield a comparable pattern. In 1965 parent and youth ratings were not widely separated. Young females, on average, rated groups more highly than did their mothers, with a mixture of higher and lower scores, while male youths uniformly handed out slightly lower scores than their fathers. By 1973 young women were consistently less positive than their mothers, but young males had become less positive than their fathers to an even greater extent. As with political trust, this pattern suggests that men develop more quickly than do women the more negative views characteristic of adulthood.

These results lend added support to a life-cycle model in which male-female differences vary systematically over the life span. Young adult men and women differed in 1965, but they had become increasingly different by 1973. In most instances this came about because males led the way in becoming less positive in their feelings about political actors and institutions. It is as if the greater interest, knowledge, and participation on the part of young men helped them shed more quickly any remaining youthful idealism. As in other areas, sex differences in this domain appear to wear away or even reverse themselves among older adults. Thus, while in their twenties, males' and females' attitudes appear to coincide less frequently than either before or after.[18]

[18] In addition to the life-cycle interpretation, the evidence is also consistent with the view that young males are more reactive to external stimuli, which during this era were in a generally negative or cynical direction. This possibility was noted earlier in connection with changes in the proportion of Independents. While we favor a life-cycle interpretation here, faster reaction to the political system by young males also suggests variable sex differences across the life cycle, though the differences would not necessarily be as strong nor the direction as consistent from one era to another.

Nonpolitical Orientations

The recurring theme in our discussion of political variables was the surprising frequency of persisting or increasing sex differences in the younger generation over the eight-year period. Table 9.5 shows that the same strong tendency characterizes several nonpolitical orientations as well. The variety of the attributes covered—a religious belief, a religious behavior, and personality traits—suggests the breadth of this conclusion. Alterations were quite small in the religious domain, but it should be noted that the sex differences on church attendance

TABLE 9.5: Nonpolitical Orientations, by Generation, Sex, and Year

	Youths			Parents			Correlation (γ)	
	Female	Male		Female	Male		Y	P
Belief about the Bible								
1 (Irrelevant) - 4 (God's Word)								
1965	3.47	3.32	−.15	3.53	3.39	−.14	−.23	−.22
1973	3.23	3.05	−.19	3.48	3.25	−.23	−.24	−.29
	−.24	−.28		−.05	−.14			
Church attendance								
1 (Never) - 4 (Almost every week)								
1965	3.59	3.34	−.25	3.19	3.06	−.13	−.28	−.10
1973	2.72	2.44	−.28	3.05	2.88	−.17	−.19	−.10
	−.87	−.90		−.14	−.18			
Personal trust								
1 (Low) - 7 (High)								
1965	5.24	4.86	−.38	5.38	5.43	+.05	−.13	.02
1973	4.68	4.51	−.17	5.08	5.04	−.04	−.06	−.02
	−.56	−.35		−.30	−.39			
Opinion strength								
1 (Low) - 7 (High)								
1965	4.53	4.55	+.02	3.93	4.42	+.49	.01	.17
1973	4.30	4.86	+.56	3.83	4.31	+.48	.20	.17
	−.23	+.31		−.10	−.11			
Self-confidence								
1 (Low) - 7 (High)								
1965	4.89	4.86	−.03	4.63	4.98	+.35	−.01	.14
1973	4.90	5.02	+.12	4.82	5.24	+.42	.06	.16
	+.01	+.16		+.19	+.26			

remained sharper among the young than the middle-aged.[19] Where change was greatest (on opinion strength) there was virtually no difference in 1965, but a substantial male advantage in 1973. Only with respect to personal trust did the young men and women draw demonstrably closer together.

As usual, sex differences among the parents changed less consistently, making it difficult to predict a course for such divisions over the life cycle. What is clear, however, is that sex patterns are tending to reproduce themselves across the generations. Perhaps the most startling example of this is the match that developed over time with respect to opinion strength.

The alterations occurring on the personality variables are most meaningful when compared to their closest political counterparts. In the case of political trust we noted that young men were less trusting than young women, sufficiently so that as young adults the males were less trusting than their fathers while young women remained more trusting than their mothers. In the case of personal trust, the younger generation of both sexes was less trusting by the time of high school graduation. Yet in both 1965 and 1973 it was the young men who were least trusting. The rates at which cynical outlooks overtake the more trusting attitudes of childhood may therefore differ between political and personal spheres, but in both cases it is young males who are the first to shed the openly trusting images of childhood.

Feelings of efficacy likewise revealed differing rates of development among young males and females. Political efficacy declined for both sexes as they encountered the adult political world, but for males the drop was a minor one. Subjective assessments of their personal efficacy actually showed an increase among the men. Women's personal efficacy, in contrast, showed no change on one measure and a fairly sharp decline on the other. These results again suggest a possible contrast between personal and political arenas. But the important point here is that, barring subsequent life-stage developments, the differing rates and even directions of change between males and females augur for a continuation of mild sex differences in personal and political outlook.

YOUNG ADULT WOMEN: MARRIAGE, EMPLOYMENT, AND CHILDREN

Our results so far have shown surprisingly rare declines and relatively frequent increases in male-female differences between the end of high school and young adulthood. Many of these differences are

---

[19] The drop in the γ for church attendance is due to changing marginals. Relatively few females in 1965 were in the lowest two categories, and these small cells tended to inflate the γ.

consistent with the movement of a significant fraction of the women into traditional roles of housewife and (nonworking) mother and subsequent diminution in political involvement and awareness. We know, however, that many women are currently stepping into more varied roles, a phenomenon that almost certainly has consequences for political attitudes and behavior. Thus we are led to ask how women who have entered more versus less traditional female roles differ politically. Are the sex differences observed so far primarily attributable to women who have opted for the more traditional roles?

Initially our approach to this question is simply to ascertain whether women who occupy different statuses have, at a descriptive level, differing political perspectives. As we shall see, however, level of education in particular is sufficiently correlated with gender role that apparent effects of one factor could actually be due to another. Therefore, we shall try to assess whether gender role has an impact on political attributes independent of other factors. In this section we will concentrate on the offspring and afterward turn to women in the parental generation.

Several factors have a potential impact on political attitudes and behavior. Of these, marriage, employment outside the home, and the presence of children are the most prominent. Marriage has supposed effects on women for at least two reasons. The frequent and close presence of another person may serve to alter attitudes in the direction of that other person's feelings. Typically it has been assumed, though with indirect supporting evidence, that it is the wife who most frequently changes political preferences. Marriage also affects the variety and frequency of contacts outside the home, and this may alter political attributes. Yet it is not clear just what impact, if any, marriage alone has on political orientations.[20] For example, it is not at all certain that married women who have no children and who are employed have less opportunity or inclination than single women to be involved in political activities. Nor is it clear that attitudinal changes, if they occur, will be sufficiently unidirectional to be observable on an aggregate basis. Nonetheless, since the attitudes of married women have sometimes been found to differ from those of "comparable" single women,[21] we shall retain marriage as one of the key variables in our categorization of the young.

[20] David O. Sears, *Attitudes Through the Life Cycle* (San Francisco: Freeman, forthcoming), Chapter 8.

[21] Sapiro, for example, found that married workers were less supportive of the women's liberation movement than single workers, even after controlling for education. Virginia Sapiro, "Socialization to and from Politics: Political Gender Role Norms Among Women," unpublished Ph.D. thesis, University of Michigan, 1976, Chapter 3.

Employment and children seem much more likely to alter the attitudes and behavior of women, and indeed, empirical support for such an impact is greater than in the case of marriage alone. Andersen, for example, has shown that employed women now participate in political campaigns with the same frequency as men, while housewives continue to lag behind.[22] Welch demonstrates that employment is particularly helpful for less educated women.[23] McGlen found that the presence of young children tended to reduce a variety of kinds of participation, especially among the college educated; if women with young children were employed outside the home, however, they participated at rates close to or even exceeding those of males.[24] Studies by Lee, Kirkpatrick, Lynn and Flora, and Jennings have also detected significant, selective impacts of motherhood on participation at mass and elite levels.[25] Employment patterns and the presence of children have seldom been related to political attitudes rather than participation. It has been found, however, that employed women rate substantially higher on their feelings of political efficacy than do housewives.[26]

Having judged marriage, employment outside the home, and the presence of children to be the most likely factors affecting political preferences and behavior, we still need to specify how these variables, alone and in combination, are related to political orientations. The number of possible relationships is large. It might be, for example, that *type* of employment is an important factor. Or employment may be significant only for poorly educated women or for those with young children. The presence of very young children may be what is important and not the presence of children per se.

As an initial step in making our analysis manageable while preserving most of the relevant information, we created four categories out of the questions on marital status, occupation, and children. The first group ($N = 283$) consists of women with children. Given the nature of our sample, the children are all quite young, and we make no distinctions by specific age. Over 85% of these mothers are currently married, with most of the others widowed or divorced. A majority (60%)

---

[22] Andersen, "Working Women and Political Participation."

[23] Welch, "Women as Political Animals?"

[24] McGlen, "Impact of Children on Political Participation."

[25] Marcia Manning Lee, "Why Few Women Hold Political Office: Democracy and Sexual Roles," *Political Science Quarterly*, 91 (Summer 1976), 297-314; Jeanne Kirkpatrick, *Political Women* (New York: Basic Books, 1974); Naomi B. Lynn and Cornelia B. Flora, "Motherhood and Political Participation: The Changing Sense of Self," *Journal of Political and Military Sociology*, 1 (Spring 1973), 91-103; Flora and Lynn, "Women and Political Socialization: Considerations of the Impact of Motherhood," in Jane S. Jacquette (ed.), *Women and Politics*; Jennings, "Another Look at the Life Cycle."

[26] Andersen, "Working Women and Political Participation," 434.

of them are not employed outside the home, and of those who are, many work only part time (a third work fewer than 35 hours per week) and their jobs are predominately clerical. Therefore no distinction has been made between employed and homemaker mothers. The other three categories are easily defined: married, not employed ($N = 64$); married, employed ($N = 172$); not married ($N = 156$).[27] Almost all of the "not married" category are employed.

As suggested earlier, this classification is quite highly correlated with education. Of those with children, for example, 61% reported no college education, while 44% of those married but not employed, 30% of those married and employed, and 22% of the unmarried reported no college training. Conversely, only 9% of the women with children reported holding a college degree, while 26%, 46%, and 43%, respectively, of the remaining three categories held at least one college degree. This means, of course, that differences among the groups may be due to their relative education and not simply to life stage. Nonetheless, as a prelude to further analysis it will be important to see whether these categories of women are politically distinct from one another.

The results yield two firm conclusions. First, marriage alone (i.e., without children) and employment outside the home are not consistently related to political outcomes. There are occasional results suggestive of anticipated gender role differences. Unmarried women shifted from the most politically trusting in 1965 to the least trusting in 1973, and their feelings of political efficacy were highest in both years. Their personal trust was also the lowest among the three groups in 1973. This is consistent with a view of unmarried women as more realistic, self-reliant, and confident than others. Yet in terms of other political resources (knowledge of facts and understanding the liberal-conservative dimension) they were not generally more endowed than married women; they were no more interested or involved in politics than those who were married; and estimates of their personal efficacy hardly suggest strong egos. Similarly, married women who were employed sometimes differed from those who were not employed (e.g., political interest and newspaper usage), but the differences are not consistent (cf. the other media).

In contrast to the lack of differentiation by marriage and employment factors, the presence of children makes a frequent and often substantial difference. In a majority of cases, the young mothers are at one of the extremes in 1973—the least interested in politics, the least frequent readers of newspapers and magazines, the lowest in per-

[27] "Married" means currently married only; it does not include people simply living together. "Employed" means currently employed or temporarily laid off.

ceived efficacy, the most in favor of school prayers, the least self confident, etc.

The emergence of this distinctiveness and the lack of consistent or sizeable variations in the other three categories suggested that the young women could be divided into two classes, those with and those without children. Results based on this dichotomization were striking. Almost without exception the mothers in 1973 are less interested, attentive, and knowledgeable about politics, vote and otherwise participate less frequently, feel less efficacious and confident in both political and personal domains, are more conservative in their public policy as well as religious beliefs, and generally reveal a working-class outlook in their group ratings. The only exceptions to this pattern are roughly equal rates of viewing television, a slightly higher rating of blacks by the mothers, and lower personal trust.

Contrasting the 1965 and 1973 figures adds to our understanding of the dynamics of this divergence between mothers and nonmothers. In most instances, those who had become mothers by 1973 already differed from the rest of their cohort as high school seniors. But differences rather uniformly increased, opening wedges where none had existed before (radio usage, political trust, school integration, church attendance, and opinion strength) and widening the gap where it had already formed. These findings indicate that the 1973 differences are not entirely a matter of "selection effects" in the sense that those who became mothers always differed initially from those who remained childless into their mid-twenties. Sometimes they did differ initially, as noted. But whatever the case in 1965, those who had children became more divergent over the next eight years.

The growing divergence between mothers and nonmothers seems to have come about mostly through lack of continued development by the mothers, though there are a few understandable instances in which the mothers changed the most. As an example of the main tendency, consider voting turnout. In 1968 the difference between the "future" mothers (by three years after high school, some were already mothers) and nonmothers was only 3%. In the next presidential election turnout among nonmothers increased 11%, while for mothers the increase was merely 2%, so that the gap between the two groups was then quite large. Political trust is another example; the tendency toward declining trust was much weaker among the mothers. The other pattern is illustrated by political efficacy and by attitudes toward school integration; in these instances mothers underwent the most change. The sharper plunge in political efficacy is part of the general syndrome of more remoteness from the active mode of political life. Perceived threats affecting the welfare of their children, who are on the verge of entering school, almost certainly lie behind the mothers' greater disenchantment with school integration.

At a purely descriptive level we have established that young mothers are indeed different from nonmothers and that the distance between the two tended to grow over time. Given the directional components of this drift we have at least partially answered the question of why, contrary to what might have been expected on the basis of the feminist movement, the gap between men and women actually tended to increase in young adulthood. The increase almost without exception conformed to traditional patterns of male-female differences and did not reflect either feminist ideology or, more generally, growing equality and parity between the sexes. Basically, nonmothers had a closer political resemblance to men than did mothers.

The gender role of mother thus appears to be, in young adulthood at any rate, an important political and social-psychological demarcator. Yet we saw that mothers and nonmothers differ in two crucial respects —education and employment status. Since the former is related to a majority of the variables taken up here and since the latter is related at least to some and is in any event important theoretically, it would seem imperative that we control for the effects of these two properties. Because the three elements are intertwined with each other it is by no means certain that independent effects can be shown. Moreover, even within control categories the qualitative content may differ between mothers and nonmothers. For example, the particular type of college training may vary even if the number of years is the same. Nevertheless, it is necessary to ascertain at least at a global level whether it is motherhood per se, or other factors linked to motherhood, that seem to be the critical ingredients.

To see whether motherhood had any independent effects on political attributes, two linear regressions were run for each political characteristic on which the initial results showed a substantial difference between mothers and nonmothers. In each case three independent variables were included in the equation: education (high school, some college, completed college), employment (currently employed or not) and motherhood (mother or nonmother). One equation used as a dependent variable the 1973 measure of a given attribute. From this equation, of course, we could tell whether mothers and nonmothers differed significantly in that year. By using a second equation—identical to the first except that the dependent variable was the comparable 1965 measure—we could see whether future mothers already differed in 1965. These are the same questions asked previously, but now we have controlled for education and employment.

The results lend substantial support to the conclusion that the gender role of mother has an important impact on political attributes, especially involvement and resources. Even after we impose controls for education and employment, the 1973 results show that mothers were less oriented toward national and international affairs (less cosmopolitan), paid less attention to politics and news via radio and magazines, felt less politically efficacious, were less knowledgeable about political facts, more often favored school prayers and opposed seating an elected Communist, and were more trusting politically than were nonmothers. Only on three measures—political interest, understanding of the liberal-conservative dimension, and voting turnout—did an initial difference between mothers and nonmothers disappear when controls were imposed. Also as indicated by the uncontrolled comparisons, differences in 1965 were usually of the same sign, but often failed to be statistically significant (.05 level). Therefore, it seems that selection factors play a minor role in explaining the post-high-school contrasts, and that motherhood itself has a great deal to do with the differences observed.

The effects of motherhood do not so clearly extend to nonpolitical factors. Only on the question of interpreting the Bible was there a significant difference in 1973, with mothers hewing to a more fundamentalist viewpoint. In their personal trust and in their feelings of personal efficacy, mothers and nonmothers differed initially, but this gap disappeared after controls were imposed. Of course, the small number of nonpolitical variables we measured suggests caution in interpreting these results.

These findings from our brief excursion into adult gender roles support the notion that sex differences are not about to disappear in the onrush of the women's movement. If women continue to occupy what are labeled feminine gender roles with much greater frequency than men, the consequences are likely to be a continued overall difference between males and females. Women who do not choose to occupy these roles will resemble men more closely in their political characteristics, but the female average will differ due to the presence of more traditionally oriented women. Since changes in traditional family roles are typically brought about rather slowly, we foresee declining but still existing sex differences for at least the next generation.

MIDDLE-AGED MOTHERS: AGE OF CHILDREN AND EMPLOYMENT

In the younger generation motherhood sharply differentiates the political orientations of women while employment does not. It does not follow, however, that similar conclusions apply to later adulthood. The impact of motherhood in particular may vary if it is the presence of very young children that accounts for the observed results. In order to gain some insight into these matters for the present generation of middle-aged women, we can utilize the parent sample. Our analysis will be confined to the topics of involvement, resources, and participation since there are no apparent reasons for preferences and attitudes to vary as a result of changes in family composition at this stage of life.

By definition all of the women in our parent sample are mothers, but the number and ages of their children varied widely. For some the high school senior respondent was the oldest child and preteenage children were still in the home in 1965. For others the high school senior was an only child or the youngest one, and no children lived at home after our first wave of interviewing. To take account of these differences we grouped women into three categories. The first group are those who in 1965 had a child 10 years or younger. Typically these mothers had a child at home throughout the eight years spanned by our panel.[28] The second group consists of those whose youngest child in 1965 was 11-13 years of age. These mothers had a child at home for more than half of the panel period but had no pre-adult in the home for at least a year prior to the second interview. In the third group are those whose youngest child in 1965 was 14 or older. These mothers had a child at home for no more than half of the panel period and had no pre-adult in the household for at least four years. Unlike the categorization used for young women above, these groups averaged close to the same level of education. Age of course is correlated with this threefold classification ($\tau_b = .41$ when age is grouped into five-year spans). Consequently, both life-cycle and generational effects might confound our analysis, as we will note below.

In the areas of involvement, resources, and participation, mothers with the youngest children are most often on the low end; those with the oldest children are most frequently on the high end.[29] Even a casual inspection of the results, however, reveals some inconsistencies, with the middle group sometimes at the extremes. In part this may be due to the lower number cases in this group and the consequently greater sampling fluctuations. But it surely derives also from the fact that the group differences are typically small.

To facilitate comparisons with women in the filial generation, women in the parental generation were divided into those having a child in the home during the entire panel period and those not having one

[28] Our categories are based solely on the ages of children in 1965. We did not inquire whether children actually lived with their parents throughout high school.

[29] We checked to be certain that we were not overlooking significant effects on other political orientations. As expected, differences were minimal and/or inconsistent in direction.

at home for all or part of the period. Comparisons with the mother/
nonmother differences among the younger generation show that those
differences are always larger, in several cases by a considerable margin.
On political resources in particular, young mothers are severely disadvantaged when compared with nonmothers, whereas among the parents, mothers with children still at home trail behind other mothers by
scant margins.

Two factors are probably at work here. Motherhood seems to be
most crippling when children are in their preschool and early elementary school years. Nurturing and custodial demands are at their height
during that time. As children age, the immediate constraints lessen and
the political world becomes more salient. As this happens, the disadvantages in involvement, resources, and participation begin eroding
well in advance of the leave-taking. Hence the lack of difference among
women in the parental sample.

We have, then, a rather coherent picture of changes that are associated with initial parenthood among women and with what happens as
children and mothers get older. Young mothers differ from nonmothers
on a wide array of political and nonpolitical orientations, including attitudes. At middle adulthood mothers with children still at home lag
slightly behind other mothers in involvement, resources, and participation, but on evaluative dimensions there is no evidence of differences
associated with stages of the life cycle. Nonpolitical characteristics—
particularly, personal trust and efficacy—seem to respond to aging in
a fashion similar to that for political attitudes. By middle adulthood
there are no differences clearly associated with life stages, even without accounting for educational and other confounding factors.

One additional point should be made about the changes associated
with motherhood. There are no strong, unidirectional changes that accompany movement through the years when children are preteens,
teenagers, and then adults. If one looks at media behavior, for example, frequency of usage did not climb sharply between 1965 and 1973
for those who saw their youngest child leave home in 1965 or a few
years thereafter. In fact, any incipient increases were submerged by
secular trends in media usage, and usage rates for three of the media
actually declined among these mothers just as for others. It is true that
increased use of television was greatest for mothers of children who
departed home soon after our first contact; they also reported the
smallest decline in newspaper and magazine reading. Yet our results
do not show that mothers freed of their children suddenly and dramatically increase their attention to politics. This means that life-cycle
effects are very difficult to detect because they will often be submerged
by changes brought about by generational and period effects. Nonethe-

less, there do seem to be reasonably regular effects on political orientations associated with motherhood.

To complete our look at the impact of marriage, motherhood, and employment let us consider the matter of employment in the parental generation. As we noted earlier, the traditional wisdom is that employment outside the home will tend to increase women's involvement in politics, and presumably their political resources as well. To test this proposition, we divided the women into four natural groupings: those unemployed both in 1965 and 1973 ($N = 253$), those employed in both years ($N = 222$), and those who moved into ($N = 112$) or out of ($N = 92$) the work force between these two years. Though the last two categories have relatively few cases, there are enough of them so that they can be kept separate.

If we contrasted only the extreme categories—those unemployed both years compared to those employed both times—there would be no surprises. Although the differences are quite modest, in both years the employed are more involved, have greater political resources, participate more, are less trusting politically, have more personal confidence, and, as befits their somewhat greater youth and higher education, reveal a generally more liberal position on issues along with higher evaluations of minority groups. On most of the measures the 1973 difference is greater than that in 1965, suggesting that the two groups are diverging over time. Not that the groups always moved in opposite directions; typically they changed in the same way. But the alterations left the employed *relatively* more politicized and liberal than before. Nonetheless, even for these extreme groups the results are not very supportive of the presumed effects of employment. Although there is only a small correlation between parental education and employment, educational differences account for most of the contrasts between the continuously employed and the not employed. Employment may have a small effect since the signs of the differences are uniformly in the expected direction, but individual comparisons typically fail to be statistically significant in either year (based on regressing political attributes on education and employment for those continuously employed or continuously not employed).

Moreover, when we turn to those who changed their employment status, the results are ambiguous in one case and absolutely contradictory in the other. The ambiguous case consists of those employed in 1965 who subsequently quit working. Even from a theoretical perspective it is unclear what should happen to these women. If employment had in fact stimulated their politicization, should they revert to an unpoliticized state if they stop work? Simply because of decreased opportunity, they might discuss politics less frequently, but in other respects we see little reason to expect sudden depoliticization. In actuality, the changes in this group are as mixed as these expectations. Their political efficacy, for example, dropped more than that of any other group (by a tiny margin), and their recognition of the liberal-conservative dimension rose only a little, even compared with those not employed the entire time. Yet their expressed political interest increased more than that of any other group, their newspaper reading declined at about the same rate as the continuously not employed, and their voting turnout dropped by only a single percentage point between 1964 and 1972 compared to 7½% for the nonemployed. Overall, a change from employed to unemployed, at least at this stage of the life cycle, seems to have no consistent effect on the behavior or attitudes of mothers.

The final group—those who became employed between waves of the panel—did show a quite consistent change in their politicization. However, the change was opposite the one expected. Their expressed interest in politics increased like that of all other groups, but the increase was by far the smallest. Their use of newspapers and radio declined, like everyone else's, but the declines were substantially greater than those of other groups. Only the unemployed-employed showed no increase in television viewing, and their magazine reading declined considerably, though not as much as among two other groups. Here the explanation would seem to be the sheer decline in disposable time. But the picture is the same in political resources. Their drop in political efficacy was the second largest, their political knowledge fell more than any other group's, and they were the only ones to show less recognition of the liberal-conservative dimension in 1973 than they had in 1965. Their voting turnout dropped more than that of two of the other groups. In all of these areas, then, employment is associated with *less* rather than more involvement in politics.

Undertaking employment did not systematically alter the mothers' views on public policy issues. However, there was a noticeable decline in their political and personal trust and in their evaluations of political and social groups. On both trust measures, scores of the newly employed mothers fell more than any other group; on personal trust they went from the most to the least trusting between 1965 and 1973. On the thermometer ratings their assessments declined in all but one case, and in five of the eight cases the decline was the largest of any of the four groups. Not only did employment fail to engage these women in politics, it seems to have increased their political as well as personal distrust. Finally, the personal efficacy of these women was affected very differently from its political counterpart. Their self-confidence increased much more strongly than for any others, and their opinion strength declined less than for two of the other groups. In this respect the anticipated salutary effects of gainful employment were met.

If this is an accurate portrayal of what happened to these women over the course of eight years, why did employment not have the anticipated consequences? One key to the situation may lie in a point made by Andersen.[30] She observed that increases in campaign participation between 1968 and 1972 were sharpest among young women (born after 1939) and least among an older cohort (born 1907-1923). Young women, she reasoned, were strongly affected by the women's movement, whereas older women were much less affected by it. Since most of the mothers in the unemployed-employed group in our study were born between 1916 and 1925, the same reasoning would lead us to expect employment to have relatively little impact on this group. In addition, when we consider that a large proportion of these newly employed women were in clerical and sales occupations, the fact that it did not increase their political participation becomes more understandable. Finally, it may be that even though political characteristics retain some flexibility throughout the life cycle, becoming employed at this stage of life simply does not have much political relevance.

CONCLUSION

From the perspectives of understanding contemporary distributions of opinion and predicting future trends, the initial, unelaborated results of this chapter are perhaps the most significant. On average, young adult women continued to differ from young men in ways consistent with traditional stereotypes. Sex differences were most consistent in the areas of psychological involvement, resources, and participation, but they were also apparent in a variety of evaluative areas as well as in nonpolitical attitudes and behavior.

Two further observations support a prediction of continued sex differences. One we have seen throughout the chapter. Male-female differences among young adults (i.e., in 1973) were not uniformly reduced between generations as had appeared to be the case in 1965. There is evidence of a narrowing gap between males and females in some areas, notably participation. But overall, the parent-youth comparisons do not suggest a withering away of this longstanding division within the population.

The other supportive observation comes from the questionnaires administered to high school seniors in 1973. Simply in terms of their direction the evidence is overwhelming that traditional sex differences continued unabated. On every measure of psychological involvement,

[30] Andersen, "Working Women and Political Participation."

females were disadvantaged compared to males. Women's feelings of internal political efficacy were lower than those of men. (External efficacy was the one exception; females scored higher.) Men continued to be more favorable toward seating an elected Communist, were slightly more oriented toward national and international affairs, rated the national government somewhat more highly, and were more cynical. Women continued to lead men in their frequency of church attendance and in their personal trust. Judging the relative magnitude of the differences is somewhat riskier, since the number of comparisons is not large and there are some fluctuations. (E.g., on the question of magazine reading the correlation for high school seniors in 1973—.15—is greater than that for seniors in 1965 and closer to the figure for the panel youths in 1973; on the Communist question the correlation is nearly identical to that for high school seniors in 1965.) Overall, however, the correlations are high enough to indicate that there was no meaningful decline in sex differences on these political characteristics between 1965 and 1973.

From a more theoretical than descriptive perspective, two other results are perhaps most noteworthy. One is the observation made repeatedly throughout the chapter that sex differences among the youths increased between the end of high school and the mid-twenties. Since the differences came about in part because of the effects of motherhood on both political involvement and attitudes, it is likely that this is a regular response to the situation in which new adults find themselves.

Having emphasized this regularity, it is important also to observe the limits of life-cycle and gender role effects. Marriage by itself did not have any systematic impact on the political attributes of young adults. Nor did employment seem to have any consistent effect. Among the older mothers the ages of their children had small effects and none at all in the evaluative domain. Surprisingly, differences in employment status—even moving into the labor force—either failed to have independent effects or had unanticipated consequences.

Still, it is noteworthy that life-cycle and gender role effects were limited because members of both sexes in the same generation, and most often in both generations, moved in the same direction over time. The most obvious case was that of political trust. Males declined more between 1965 and 1973 in both generations. Among the offspring this led to a greater difference between males and females, a result which was consistent with the notion of males becoming alert to and involved in politics more rapidly than females. Dominating these results is the substantial decline in political trust scores among both sexes in both generations. From other evidence we know that this was the result of a massive period effect taking hold of the population in the late 1960s and early 1970s. While other instances are less dramatic, the same can be said of other changes. Observe, for example, the changes in cosmopolitanism, in attention paid to radio and television, in magazine reading, in attitudes toward elected Communists, and in church attendance and beliefs about the Bible. In all of these instances and others, gender role and life-cycle effects are superimposed on changes that come about because of alterations in the political system or in the social system underlying it. Gender role effects themselves may be superimposed on life-cycle effects which alter both sexes.

This observation brings us back to the theme we have emphasized frequently—that adults in general seem to be more subject to influence and change than has previously been recognized. Younger and older adults may differ in their responses to political phenomena, and young mothers may react differently from nonmothers and young fathers. Even older mothers may react slightly differently depending on their family situations. But the reactions of these groups are never totally at odds. Rather, the reactions vary mostly by their intensity and very little by their direction.

None of this is meant to deny the importance of gender role effects or to belittle the search for them. In light of their superimposition on other effects, the fact that we have been able to isolate one prominent gender role effect makes our efforts worthwhile. Nonetheless, perhaps a fitting, though surprising, conclusion to this chapter is to note how little can be attributed to life-cycle and gender role effects and how much of what we have observed must be attributed to broad social and political movements acting with nearly equal force on men and women in general.

CHAPTER TEN

Race Comparisons in
an Era of Change

I F the multiplicity of forces at work complicated our sex and gender role comparisons, the same is true to an even greater extent in the case of racial comparisons. Momentous historic events, frequent generational cleavages, as well as the ever-present individual aging process all came together in the 1960s and early 1970s to affect racially related phenomena in a fashion seldom paralleled in American history. These circumstances resulted in an enormous investment in race-related studies, including many devoted to the politics of race. While some things became clear—the tremendous increase in blacks' political cynicism, for example—much remains unaddressed or unclarified.

Even the simplest theoretical expectations are confounded by the complexity of the situation. On the one hand, the civil rights movement had made considerable strides by the time of our first interviews in 1965, and there was further progress toward racial equality in the ensuing years. Among the aims of the movement were increasing the political awareness, involvement, and power of blacks, along with raising their levels of self-consciousness and personal pride. On all of these characteristics blacks were disadvantaged in comparison with whites, and it was felt that equality in many nonpolitical areas would occur only when blacks became a potent political force. Since blacks had gained considerable political clout by the early 1970s, with obvious leaps forward in the electoral arena, we might well expect severely curtailed racial differences in 1973 on all matters relating to political resources, involvement, and participation.

On the other hand, a number of countervailing forces were at work. For one thing, the 1965-1973 period was not one of peaceful, steady progress toward racial equality. Especially in the early part of that period, riots and angry confrontations were frequently the order of the day. It was during this time that the most prominent black, Martin Luther King, Jr., was murdered. Progress in voting rights was not always matched in other arenas. Educational and job equality were surely not attained. The difficulty with which progress came, and the unevenness of that progress, no doubt lay behind the growing cynicism of blacks. It is also demonstrably the case that the attitudes of blacks and whites did not always converge; many whites continued to hold unfavorable stereotypes of blacks and many blacks remained suspicious of the motives and sincerity of whites.[1]

Overlaid on these conflicting forces was a generational contrast that was often remarkable. Younger blacks were easily the more militant, cynical, and involved in regard to political matters, and this difference often carried over into nonpolitical concerns.[2] Our own data from 1965 reflected this pattern. On media utilization, feelings of efficacy, and recognition of party differences—all in the general domain of resources and involvement—black youths had surpassed their parents and pulled more nearly even with whites. Young blacks also reversed the parental pattern on political trust, showing themselves to be more rather than less cynical than young whites. Likewise, on personal trust and opinion strength the younger generation differed less than did the parental set. What this means for the analysis presented in this chapter is that we might well expect differing patterns among the parental and offspring generations in each year, and perhaps as well a pattern of change that lacks commonality across generations.

Finally, life-cycle factors, especially the larger and more frequent changes among the young people, may affect racial comparisons in the two years. Just as in the previous chapter we argued that sex differences may be suppressed while youths are in school, racial differences may also be hidden, only to appear as the young move into the adult world. Though racial prejudice and discrimination are certainly not absent from high schools, racial differences may be depressed by the rhetoric of civics classes and by conscious attempts on the part of school administrators to keep overt discrimination limited. This might have been especially true beginning in the early 1960s with the advent of the civil rights movement. More "typical" racial differences may begin to emerge as young people graduate from high school and as blacks

---

[1] For example, see the evidence from the early 1970s cited by Charles S. Bullock, III, and Harrell R. Rodgers, Jr., *Racial Equality in America* (Pacific Palisades, Calif.: Goodyear, 1975), 152, 154-55. Over-time data through 1970 are presented in Angus Campbell, *White Attitudes toward Black People* (Ann Arbor: Institute for Social Research, 1971), Chapter 7.

[2] Schuman and Hatchett, for example, comment that ". . . age has appeared to be the strongest 'background' correlate of black racial attitudes in most, if not all, recent studies. . . ." Howard Schuman and Shirley Hachett, *Black Racial Attitudes: Trends and Complexities* (Ann Arbor: Institute for Social Research, 1974), 56. On personal cynicism see David O. Sears, "Black Attitudes toward the Political System in the Aftermath of the Watts Insurrection," *Midwest Journal of Political Science*, 13 (November 1969), 515-44. Evidence of compositional differences lying behind some of these variations is presented in Joel D. Aberbach and Jack L. Walker, *Race in the City* (Boston: Little, Brown, 1973), 119-24.

are directly confronted by discrimination and prejudice in the tasks of locating a job and finding a home as well as in political life.[3]

There are additional life-cycle factors which, upon closer inspection, probably do not seriously affect this set of blacks and whites. Among young blacks, especially those who are less educated, unemployment might be a significant factor. In our sample, however, nearly equal numbers of blacks and whites were currently employed. A greater percentage of whites had married, but more blacks who were married had children, so that very close to the same proportion of young people in each race were parents. The fact that on these dimensions black and white youths are quite comparable could provide a small push toward uniformity, assuming that blacks and whites respond similarly to newly achieved adult status.

The preceding discussion has been couched in terms of blacks versus whites, and the (black) civil rights movement. However, many of the same considerations apply to other nonwhites, especially the Spanish-speaking population. Since there were too few "other" nonwhites to analyze separately, they have been included along with blacks to make up the nonwhite sample used throughout the rest of the chapter. Separate analyses show that on some measures this has the effect of making nonwhites more similar to whites than blacks alone, but that in other instances it pushes whites and nonwhites farther apart. Generally the effect is small since blacks make up 85% and 88% of the non-white sample for youths and parents, respectively.

RATES OF CHANGE

Given the turbulent race-related events marking the first part of our study period, and considering the efforts devoted to changing the political role of blacks in American life, we would hypothesize more fluidity among nonwhites than whites. In order to test this hypothesis we will employ the same procedure as in previous chapters. Individual turnover tables were generated for whites and nonwhites separately. Given the vast preponderance of whites in the population, roughly 90%, the turnover figures for whites differ little from the overall results given in Chapters 2 and 3. The question, then, is whether nonwhites

[3] Though schools may seek to minimize racial differences, there is evidence that blacks develop some "adult" orientations earlier than whites, especially political cynicism and an awareness of party differences. See, for example, Paul R. Abramson, *The Political Socialization of Black Americans* (New York: Free Press, 1977), Chapter 1; Anthony M. Orum and Robert S. Cohen, "The Development of Political Orientations among Black and White Children," *American Sociological Review*, 38 (February 1973), 62-74.

have stability rates that diverge from those for the majority population in some systematic way.

Complicating this question is the fact that whites and nonwhites occasionally differ sharply in their aggregate responses. This means that gross stability figures—the percentage stable—and correlational measures of stability may give us very different answers. On party identification, for example, nonwhite youths are substantially less stable as measured by the over-time correlation (a .2-.3 difference). Yet because nonwhites are so overwhelmingly Democratic, a slightly larger percentage of them remained unchanged between 1965 and 1973. A similar discrepancy exists for reports of candidate preferences in 1964 and 1972.

Fortunately, the discrepancy between the two stability measures is seldom this dramatic. Among the youths, both measures suggest that whites are more stable in their responses over time, but by only a small margin. Considering the correlations, for example, whites are more stable than nonwhites a bit over half of the time. About a third of the time, however, the margin is reversed (with the remainder virtually equal). Most of the differences are under .10, and in a couple of the cases in which there is a greater difference it is nonwhites who are more stable. Gross stability rates suggest, if anything, an even smaller margin of difference between the races. Judging by these figures, nonwhites were more stable than whites almost as frequently as whites were more stable. Understandably, the two really large differences—of over 20%—occurred on the question about school integration and on vote choice. In these instances nonwhites less often changed their minds than did whites. Otherwise, differences in stability rates were not clustered significantly by type of political or nonpolitical attribute. Among the young, in short, racial contrasts in sheer rates of change are not very great.

Among parents the picture is more one-sided, at least when the correlational measure of stability is used. A large majority of the time the correlation for whites is greater than that for nonwhites, and in about half of all cases the difference is greater than .10. More so than among the youths, however, this difference is explained on the basis of more skewed responses from nonwhites. As with the younger generation, party identification and the vote in 1964 and 1972 are the prime cases in point. Republican identifiers and voters were highly unstable, so that the correlation is much lower for nonwhites; but the rarity of these individuals makes the gross stability figure higher for nonwhites. The same kind of result is true of reported frequency of church attendance. A slight variation occurs on two of the policy issues—school integration and school prayers; the correlations for whites and nonwhites are identical, but the latter are considerably more stable as measured by gross stability figures. To a degree, some of the other items are also affected by distributional differences, so that gross stability figures show more similarity between the races than do the correlational comparisons.

Overall, a useful contrast seems to be between race-related topics and others. On questions that are closely related to racial concerns, and therefore show rather skewed marginal distributions, nonwhites appear to be less likely to change on a percentage basis, although there is considerable instability among those few who articulate the unpopular or unusual response. Indeed, among these latter individuals the responses are so unstable as to suggest that they are largely random in nature. On items that are not related to race itself, whites seem to have a fairly widespread, though small, margin of greater stability. These differences are somewhat accentuated among the parents.

The slightly reduced stability levels among nonwhite parents become more significant when we view the differences intergenerationally. In many instances (about a third of the total) nonwhite youths are actually more stable by the correlational statistics than are their parents. Among whites this did not occur even once. Gross stability figures also confirm that white youths are rarely as stable in their responses as their parents, while nonwhite youths are often equally or slightly more stable. This seems to be one of the first instances of a generational difference that goes beyond simple variations in marginal distributions. It suggests that nonwhite youths have developed opinions and behaviors which have roughly the same amount of stability characteristic of majority youths of the same age range. In achieving this, they not only express opinions that are often different from those of their parents, as we shall see, but their opinions are more firmly fixed. Though less obvious to the casual observer, this result may well be the most important change in racial contrasts that we will see. The lack of dramatic change in racial differences that will be observed in the next sections should not obscure this shift in longitudinal consistency.

PSYCHOLOGICAL INVOLVEMENT

In terms of their psychological involvement in politics, this group of minority youths was not noticeably disadvantaged in 1965. In fact, in some ways they were remarkably engaged in political matters (Table 10.1). Their use of the print media was only slightly below that of whites, their overall professed interest was virtually identical to that of whites, and they paid considerably more attention to news and political

TABLE 10.1: Psychological Involvement in Politics, by Generation, Race, and Year

	Youths[a]			Parents			Correlation (γ)	
	Nonwhite	White		Nonwhite	White		Y	P
Good citizen—political qualities								
Ratio of responses to total responses								
1965	.69	.75	+.06[b]	.43	.58	+.15	—[c]	
1973	.66	.71	+.05	.36	.61	+.25		
	−.03	−.04		−.07	+.03			
Interest in public affairs								
1 (Low) - 4 (High)								
1965	3.26	3.25	−.01	2.92	3.26	+.34	−.06	.22
1973	3.22	3.30	+.08	3.14	3.36	+.22	.04	.17
	−.04	+.05		+.22	+.10			
Cosmopolitanism								
1 (Least) - 7 (Most)								
1965	4.88	5.28	+.40	4.00	4.33	+.33	.22	.14
1973	4.41	4.92	+.51	3.83	4.11	+.28	.27	.13
	−.47	−.36		−.17	−.22			
Read newspapers								
1 (Don't read) - 5 (Almost daily)								
1965	3.87	3.96	+.09	3.54	4.19	+.65	.00	.40
1973	3.80	3.91	+.11	3.32	4.06	+.74	.04	.38
	−.07	−.05		−.22	−.13			
Read magazines								
1 (Don't read) - 3 (Regularly)								
1965	2.13	2.25	+.12	1.88	2.16	+.28	.12	.26
1973	2.26	2.02	−.24	1.67	1.95	+.28	−.22	.27
	+.13	−.23		−.21	−.21			
Watch television								
1 (Don't watch) - 5 (Almost daily)								
1965	4.20	3.76	−.44	4.20	4.26	+.06	−.34	.01
1973	4.05	4.18	+.13	4.17	4.38	+.21	.13	.10
	−.15	+.42		−.03	+.12			
Listen to radio								
1 (Don't listen) - 5 (Almost daily)								
1965	3.61	3.28	−.33	3.75	3.37	−.38	−.19	−.17
1973	2.87	3.03	+.16	3.04	2.86	−.18	.05	−.03
	−.74	−.25		−.71	−.51			

[a] N's before missing data are deleted: white youths 1,228, nonwhite youths 120, white parents 1,046, nonwhite parents 133.

[b] Plus sign signifies a white advantage, negative sign a nonwhite advantage.

[c] Correlation not given because ratios not determined for each respondent separately.

events via the electronic media. Nonwhites were quite distinctive in their relative emphasis on national (and to a lesser degree state and local) politics rather than international affairs, but this was almost certainly owing to the attention paid to racial politics in this country during the panel years. In any case, this is a measure of the focus of interest and not of the degree of interest per se. Consequently it is difficult to conclude that a group is disadvantaged in some way by a lower score.

Comparison of white-nonwhite differences between generations reinforces the view that nonwhite youths were not underinvolved in 1965. In their overall interest and their reading about politics, the racial gap was sharply reduced in the offspring generation. On television viewing the numerical gap was reversed. Moreover, as we emphasized in our earlier analysis, nonwhite youths were often even with or ahead of parents in their level of involvement, whereas whites lagged behind parental levels or were ahead by smaller margins.[4]

This perspective on racial differences as of 1965, together with the emphasis placed on black involvement by the very existence of the civil rights movement, would lead us to anticipate still further diminutions of white-nonwhite differences or even the development of a nonwhite advantage among well-educated nonwhites. This expectation was not realized. On several of the measures there was little or no movement in the relative advantage of whites compared to nonwhites. Shifting was most noticeable in the media field: nonwhites went from an advantage to a disadvantage in radio listening and television watching, whereas they achieved an advantage and an absolute gain in magazine reading. Recalling the traditional arguments that the print media represent a more difficult and active pursuit of the news, we would conclude that nonwhites did score an expected gain in this area. Taken as a *whole*, however, the 1973 picture is not appreciably different from that of 1965.

Changes in the parental generation do not show a clear directional tendency. In both years there is a consistent white advantage, contravened only with respect to use of radio for political news. Intergenerationally, radio usage (along with cosmopolitanism, which is an ambiguous measure here) is also the sole exception to an otherwise consistent result. Differences in the younger generation, even where they increased between 1965 and 1973, show a smaller white advantage than in the parents' generation. Viewed from the long-term perspective of generational replacement, we can confidently conclude that racial

[4] M. Kent Jennings and Richard G. Niemi, *The Political Character of Adolescence* (Princeton: Princeton University Press, 1974), 289-98.

differences in psychological engagement in politics are indeed declining. The fluctuations among the youths, however, remind us that this is not necessarily a smooth process or one incapable of some reversal. Racial differences in this domain may eventually disappear, but only after society traverses a lengthy, winding road.

POLITICAL RESOURCES

Racial variations in political resources differ from the area of involvement primarily in that young minority members had not come as close to bridging the gap in 1965. As high school seniors nonwhites less often defined the good citizen in terms of active rather than allegiant roles, and were lower than whites on each of the other measures, with a particularly large spread in factual knowledge (Table 10.2). Nonetheless, there was customarily a very substantial reduction in the difference at the offspring level compared with the parents. If we presume that knowledge and understanding will follow upon psychological involvement, though perhaps with a lag, then the degree of political interest and media usage shown by nonwhites in 1965 might prompt a later increase in resource availability relative to that of whites.

For the most part the results confound this expectation. Though the alterations were small, the white advantage increased on three of the five measures. Nonwhites did make a large inroad on the expression of the civic duty norm as indexed by the ratio of active to allegiant portrayals of the model citizen. On the other hand, the gap on external efficacy—for which we have only the 1973 sounding—is sizeable and to the whites' advantage. Parenthetically, we should note that the external efficacy measure has a heavy flavor of system responsiveness to it, thereby making the nonwhites' lower score more explicable. As with involvement, the racial difference is less in the younger than in the parental generation (save on external efficacy). But in the short run the evidence suggests no decrease, and perhaps even a small increase, in the differential resources of whites and nonwhites.[5]

Looking over the results for both resources and involvement, it is useful to note that a white advantage in the offspring generation did not necessarily come about because of depoliticization on the part of nonwhites. Racial groups tended to move in parallel; only on political

[5] In a study of Detroit it was found that younger blacks (and whites) were more dissatisfied with the amount of power they possessed and that power dissatisfaction was related to participation and political discontent. See Joel Aberbach, "Power Consciousness: A Comparative Analysis," *American Political Science Review*, 71 (December 1977), 1544-60.

TABLE 10.2: Political Resources, by Generation, Race, and Year

	Youths			Parents			Correlation (γ)	
	Nonwhite	White		Nonwhite	White		Y	P
Good citizen—ratio of active to allegiant responses								
1965	1.18	1.83	+.65	1.38	1.74	+.36	—ᵃ	
1973	1.72	1.92	+.20	.87	1.10	+.23		
	+.54	+.09		−.51	−.64			
Internal political efficacy 1 (Low) - 3 (High)								
1965	1.86	2.12	+.26	1.31	1.88	+.57	.34	.64
1973	1.67	2.00	+.33	1.35	1.73	+.38	.40	.49
	−.19	−.12		+.04	−.15			
External political efficacy 1 (Low) - 3 (High)								
1965	—	—		2.12	2.53	+.41	—	.42
1973	1.96	2.37	+.41	1.92	2.32	+.40	.48	.42
				−.20	−.21			
Recognition and understanding of liberal-conservative dimension 1 (None) - 5 (Broad)								
1965	2.58	2.71	+.13	2.32	2.93	+.61	.02	.24
1973	3.26	3.45	+.19	2.66	3.16	+.50	.11	.23
	+.68	+.74		+.34	+.23			
Knowledge of political facts 0-6 (Number correct)								
1965	2.67	3.70	+1.03	2.37	3.91	+1.54	.49	.75
1973	2.70	3.79	+1.09	2.54	3.88	+1.34	.50	.64
	+.03	+.09		+.17	−.03			

ᵃ See footnote c, Table 10.1.

interest and television viewing did nonwhites decrease while whites increased. Nevertheless, whether the process involved a greater decline (e.g., newspapers, efficacy) or a smaller increase (knowledge), nonwhites from the class of 1965 ended up in their mid-twenties with a more consistent deficit in spectator aspects of political involvement and in relevant resources. The differences were not always large, and there were exceptions. The point is that racial differences failed to vanish.

Nor were the continuing differences between white and minority youths a product of inequalities in educational levels. For one thing, there was only a modest relationship between education and race for this group of young people. (Thirty-three percent of the whites completed college compared to 23% of the nonwhites; 36% of the whites and 42% of the nonwhites had no college.) Still, controlling for education might "explain" racial differences of the magnitude found here. Alternatively, since the number of nonwhites is small to begin with, controlling for education might make it impossible to discern any pattern in the results.

Instead, the results with education controlled were extremely consistent with what we observed for the racial groups as a whole. In every comparison in 1973 for involvement and resources, at least two and usually all three of the education groups exhibited the same pattern of white or nonwhite advantage as for the whole sample. Moreover, in most cases the change between 1965 and 1973 was in the same direction for each category of education. Therefore, neither the frequent white advantage in psychological involvement and resources nor the changes over the early adult years could reasonably be accounted for by varying levels of higher education.

One further point should be made about what we have observed so far, viz., that the generation gap among nonwhites was as visible in 1973 as it had been in 1965. Simply in terms of magnitude, nonwhite youths and parents differed more than did whites in almost every instance in both years. Equally significant, the nature of the differences was not the same across racial groups. Among whites the younger generation was typically less politicized, thus providing no strong threat to older, established leaders. In contrast, when nonwhite parents and youths differed, it was usually the young who were more involved and endowed with greater resources, thereby challenging the continued leadership of the older generation.[6] Inasmuch as this gap showed no signs of abating in 1973, it has all the earmarks of a generational cleavage that will be erased only by the slow process of population replacement.

POLITICAL PARTICIPATION

Judging only by turnout in presidential elections, we might conclude that whites still held a slight advantage in active political par-

---

[6] A long-term white advantage in political "effectiveness" among pre-adults is documented and assessed by Abramson, *The Political Socialization of Black Americans.*

ticipation into the early 1970s. The level of turnout among white youths was 6% and 4% higher than that for nonwhites in 1968 and 1972, respectively. This difference is small, but it nonetheless exceeds the white advantage in the parent population (2% in 1968 and 3% in 1972, down from 5% in 1964). Two results, however, thwart such a conclusion. First, there is the puzzling outcome for turnout in the 1970 off-year election. Among the parents, the races went to the polls at equal rates, but among the youths minority members voted at a rate 13% above that of whites. This might be dismissed as a fluke were it not for the higher rates of nonwhite participation in other kinds of political activity.

More nonwhite than white youths participated—occasionally by substantial margins—in seven of the nine activities about which we inquired (Figure 10.1). No matter how one looks at these results the conclusion seems inescapable that nonwhites were more vigorous participants in the 1965-1973 period.[7] Higher activity levels were found in all sorts of actions—electoral and nonelectoral, traditional and nonconventional, those requiring monetary resources as well as those requiring writing skills, more glamorous actions associated with the civil rights and Vietnam protest movements, and the more pedestrian modes. Also important is the fact that nonwhites much more frequently reported working with others to try to solve community problems. These actions tended to occur more recently, suggesting that minority members were not moved simply to participate during the height of the civil rights movement, only to withdraw later. On balance, nonwhites surely overcame whatever deficiencies they may have had in resources and psychological involvement.

All of this is in sharp contrast to the behavior of the parents. Aside from the electoral arena, where there was one tie, nonwhite parents were invariably less participative than whites (Figure 10.1). Often the differences were not very large—in fact, less than one-half percent on protest activities—but the uniformity of the results is impressive. From Figure 10.1 we can also determine that the same kind of intergenerational cleavage exists for participation as for psychological involvement and political resources. White young adults had a more than trivial advantage in five of eight instances and an average margin

[7] Since our sample design is effectively a control on education, this conforms to the finding by Verba and Nie that black participation is greater than white participation once socioeconomic factors are controlled. Sidney Verba and Norman H. Nie, *Participation in America* (New York: Harper & Row, 1972), Chapter 10. An extended treatment of the participation phenomena among both of the black generations included in our study is found in Elaine Ader Friedrich, "Black Perspectives on Politics: The Emergence of an Alienated Subculture" (unpublished Ph.D. thesis, University of Michigan, 1977), Chapter 8.

of only 6%. Nonwhite youths, however, clearly outpaced their parents on every activity, for an average advantage of 13%. Not surprisingly, the widest gulf was in protest activity, where few parents of either race were involved. But the difference was also quite large on helping to solve community problems and on contacting public officials. Considering the infrequency of writing letters to editors, the difference on that item is significant as well.

Not surprisingly, education was related to participation levels in both races. Significantly, however, the combined effects of education and race sometimes acted to push the minority youths toward astronomically high rates of participation. This was most startling with respect to protest demonstrations. Among nonwhites who had attended college, some 42% (45% among blacks only) had taken part in demonstrations—surely among the highest participation figures ever obtained in a cross-section probability sample of a large nonelite population. The comparable figure for whites, while still high by ordinary stand-

FIGURE 10.1: Performance of Specific Political Activities, by Race

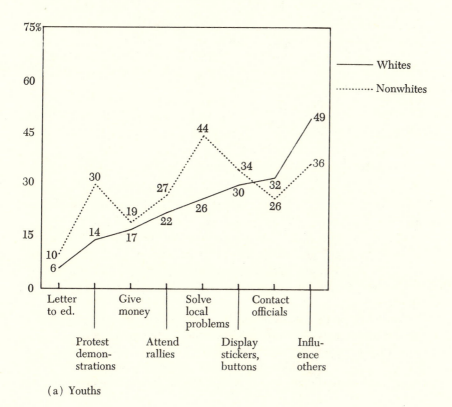

(a) Youths

FIGURE 10.1 (cont.)

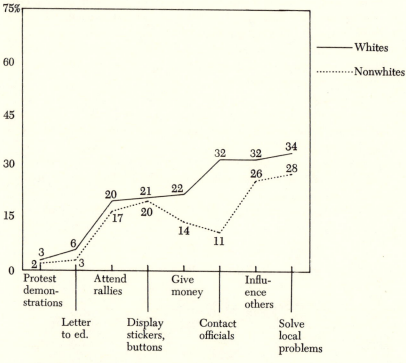

(b) Parents

ards, was 20%. Clearly, the much talked-about black activist college generation was a real phenomenon.

PARTISANSHIP AND ELECTORAL BEHAVIOR

As we move into attitudinal domains, it is no longer a matter of one group having an advantage that other groups seek to erase. Rather, the question is whether different groups see their interests and feelings as conflicting or coinciding. Racial differences are now likely to fluctuate, depending on the specific policies, institutions, or individuals being evaluated. While some differences can be expected, we should not anticipate the degree of consistency observed in the first part of this chapter.

Candidate preferences and partisanship are a case in point. While there is an obvious similarity between them—the extreme Democratic advantage among nonwhites—they cannot simply be lumped together. First, consider candidate preferences. Here the dominance of the Democrats tells virtually the entire story. While the Democratic vote or preference among nonwhites dropped as low as 74% (for both generations) in the 1972 election, each year was characterized by a white-nonwhite difference of at least 26% (youths in 1964). There was no indication that the Democratic edge was declining over the panel years or between generations. The generational cleavage observed so consistently above among nonwhites was nonexistent here. If anything, there was a small generation gap among whites, with parents preferring the Republican candidate by a margin of 4-9% in the four elections for which we have data.

In their partisan identifications the Democratic leanings of nonwhites are also obvious, with about 90% of the partisans professing to be Democrats in both years among both generations. But there are other important differences when we examine the percentage of Independents (Table 10.3). More whites claimed to be Independent in both generations, with little change in the margins between 1965 and 1973. The important results, however, are the generational comparisons. Among whites, the gap is quite large, especially in 1973. But it is even bigger among nonwhites. This in turn results in a smaller white-

TABLE 10.3: Partisanship, by Generation, Race, and Year, and by Race and Education

| | Youths | | | Parents | | |
	Nonwhite	White		Nonwhite	White	
Party identification						
% Independent						
1965	29	37	+8	15	27	+12
1973	41	47	+6	16	27	+11
	—	—		—	—	
	+12	+10		+ 1	0	

| | No College[a] | | | Some College | | | College Graduates | | |
	Nonwhite	White		Nonwhite	White		Nonwhite	White	
% Independent									
1965	16	36	+20	32	43	+11	48	33	−15
1973	26	47	+21	45	47	+ 2	67	49	−18
	—	—		—	—		—	—	
	+10	+11		+13	+ 4		+19	+16	

| | None | | | Some | | | Grad | |
[a] N's:	N	W		N	W		N	W
1965	50	434		41	380		27	402
1973	50	438		40	382		27	398

nonwhite difference among youths. The point, then, is that in their voting behavior nonwhite parents and youths behaved very much the same, whereas in their feelings about the parties, nonwhite youths were much more willing to desert the Democrats for an independent stance. Relative to their parents, they were even more willing to take an independent stance than were young whites.

Partisanship also differs from voting behavior, and indeed from every other attribute examined, in that education has an enormous impact on the racial difference. As shown in the bottom panel of Table 10.3, education had a relatively small effect on the proportion of self-proclaimed Independents among white youths. In contrast, nonwhites going on to higher education were considerably more willing than others to take an independent position in 1965, and the spread among educational groups grew even larger by 1973. Incredibly, nonwhite college graduates were substantially more often Independent than were whites. If this result continues to characterize nonwhite cohorts, while increasing proportions of these cohorts obtain a college education, the implications for the party system can hardly be overestimated.

OPINIONS ON PUBLIC POLICY ISSUES

Opinions on matters of public policy also show varying racial contrasts. Not surprisingly, whites and nonwhites differed sharply in 1965 on the topic of school integration (Table 10.4). As support for school integration efforts dropped in the 1970s with the intrusion of the busing issue, the racial difference grew still larger. Even though the younger generation differed less than the older one, the absolute difference was large in both groups.

A substantial racial contrast also characterizes two issues introduced in 1973 which directly involve race.[8] On the seven-point scale running from "bus to achieve integration" (1) to "keep children in their neighborhood schools" (7), whites took a relatively one-sided, antibusing stance (means of 5.78 and 6.47 for youths and parents, respectively), while nonwhites were quite sharply divided, evidently between those strongly favoring integration even at the expense of busing and those committed to neighborhood schools even if they are segregated (means of 4.07 and 4.26). On the seven-point scale inquiring whether "the government should help minority groups" (1) or "minority groups should help themselves" (7), whites were spread across the continuum with a moderately pro self-help mean (3.92 and 4.56); nonwhites

[8] Multiple regression analyses reveal that race continues to make a statistically significant contribution in accounting for the variance on those and other race-

TABLE 10.4: Opinions on Policy Issues, by Generation, Race, and Year

	Youths			Parents			Correlation (γ)	
	Nonwhite	White		Nonwhite	White		Y	P
School integration								
% pro								
1965	89	67	−22	78	55	−23	−.66	−.52
1973	76	46	−30	78	40	−38	−.60	−.67
	−13	−21		0	−15			
School prayers								
% anti								
1965	27	29	+2	7	18	+11	.12	.68
1973	32	33	+1	8	17	+9	.01	.49
	+5	+4		+1	−1			
Anti-church speeches								
% pro								
1965	85	87	+2	71	75	+4	.16[a]	.15
1973	97	94	−3	68	77	+9	−24.[a]	.26
	+12	+7		−3	+2			
Communist holding office								
% pro								
1965	37	37	0	32	30	−2	−.04	−.10
1973	62	59	+3	34	44	+10	−.07	.10
	+25	+22		+2	+14			

[a] Gamma coefficients can assume disproportionately high values when skewed distributions are present.

were much more in favor of the government helping minorities (2.62 and 2.93).

These three race-related issues are also distinguished by an interesting reversal of the usual intergenerational pattern. We have typically found more agreement between the two white generations than the nonwhite, where there was a moderate to large gap. Here, nonwhite youths and parents were remarkably agreed in their central tendencies, even though individual differences of opinion existed. Among whites, however, the young were more in favor of school integration, much more favorable when the subject of busing was introduced, and a full

related measures even when several relevant 1965 and contemporaneous variables are included in the equations. These findings underscore our contention about the persistence (and perhaps extension) of interracial differences on issues having a visible racial component. A similar conclusion, based on a different approach, is advanced by Friedrich, "Black Perspectives in Politics," Chapter 9.

step over on the "minority help" scale in the direction of favoring government assistance. On issues directly involving race, then, whites and nonwhites differed substantially,[9] with the white population more divided along generational lines.

A contrasting picture emerges on other policy matters, with smaller and less consistent differences between whites and nonwhites. Of course, racial contrasts do not disappear completely. Nonwhite parents, for example, were even more united than whites in the belief that schools should be allowed to start each day with a prayer (Table 10.4). We shall see later that this difference is not an isolated result, but reflects the greater religiosity of nonwhites. Another relatively large difference existed among parents on the question of whether the government should see to it that every person has a job and a good standard of living. Nevertheless, the most noteworthy characteristic of the nonracial issues is that whites and nonwhites differ by rather small, even trivial margins in the younger set.

Intergenerationally, differences on nonracial issues revert back to familiar forms. In virtually all cases youths of both races took a more liberal position than parents. But in every instance in Table 10.4 except on the "elected Communist" issue in 1965, and in every case of the seven-point scales from 1973, the nonwhite generations disagreed more than did the white. In these respects nonracial policy questions are much like party identification. Parent and youths differed in both races, but the gap is larger among nonwhites. Hence we continue to build a picture of a nonwhite population in which generational differences are consistently large except where racial concerns are rather direct and explicit. White youths sometimes disagree with their parents and sometimes share the same opinion. Nonwhite youths almost always disagree.

Evaluations of Governmental and Sociopolitical Groups

Having seen that whites and nonwhites differed sharply on racial questions, and knowing that racial concerns were related to more general feelings about the government during the 1960s and 1970s, it should not be surprising that racial contrasts exist on political system evaluations. In interpreting the results, however, it must be remembered that there was a considerable period effect in the late 1960s

[9] Persisting interracial differences on racial issues is noted in Sandra Kenyon Schwartz and David G. Schwartz, "Convergence and Divergence in Political Orientations between Blacks and Whites: 1960-1973," *Journal of Social Issues*, 32 (No. 2, 1976), 153-68.

which is acutely reflected in the cynicism of minority group members.[10] The 1965 results for both generations reflect the pre-change attitudes (Table 10.5). Nonwhites were more often "least proud" of the civil rights record of the United States (not shown), but whites of both generations were extraordinarily more willing to voice criticism in general. White and nonwhite youths differed only by a whisper on the political trust index, and nonwhite parents were actually more trusting than whites. Judgments about relative confidence in levels of government were similar, with the senior generation of nonwhites somewhat more confident in the national government.

TABLE 10.5: Evaluations of Government, by Generation, Race, and Year

	Youths			Parents			Correlation (γ)	
	Nonwhite	White		Nonwhite	White		Y	P
Qualities least proud of as American (Mean number of mentions)								
1965	1.26	1.55	+.29	.93	1.35	+.42	.35	.43
1973	1.99	1.97	−.02	1.56	1.78	+.22	−.01	.19
	+.73	+.42		+.63	+.43			
Political trust 1 (Low) - 6 (High)								
1965	4.56	4.58	+.02	4.02	3.78	−.24	.08	−.16
1973	2.45	3.06	+.61	2.75	3.02	+.27	.43	.16
	−2.11	−1.52		−1.27	−.76			
High faith and confidence in governmental levels 1 (Non-national) - 2 (National)								
1965	1.81	1.81	.00	1.60	1.57	−.03	.02	−.05
1973	1.39	1.52	+.13	1.43	1.51	+.08	.26	.17
	−.42	−.29		−.17	−.06			

By 1973 much had changed. The depth of negative feelings among nonwhites of both generations was apparent in their litany of complaints about the nation in general. Nonwhite youths equaled whites in their ability to cite features they were least proud of as Americans (Table 10.5). This is all the more persuasive because nonwhites tended

[10] On adults, see Arthur H. Miller, "Political Issues and Trust in Government," *American Political Science Review*, 67 (Spring 1974), 951-74, esp. 954-55. On pre-adults, see Abramson, *Political Socialization of Black Americans*, Chapter 1. For a thorough discussion of the causes, consequences, and corollaries of the decline in political trust among the black respondents in our own sample, see Friedrich, "Black Perspectives in Politics."

in general to be less forthcoming than whites in reponding to open-ended questions. Much of this "gain" came in the area of perceived weaknesses in the political system. In 1973 both whites and nonwhites placed relatively less emphasis on civil rights per se (though non-whites still led the way) and more on general system defects. But non-whites became especially more voluble. Indeed, nonwhite youths were now at least as willing as white (in absolute as well as relative terms) to criticize the political system per se.

Equally striking was the by now familiar shift in political trust. In both generations a massive change brought the nonwhite population into a more cynical position. The white-nonwhite difference changed by similar numerical amounts among parents and offspring, but with differing results due to their initial positions. Among parents the direc-tion of the relationship switched whereas among youths what was es-sentially no difference turned into a wide gulf.

Though on a reduced scale, the same pattern occurred in judgments of faith and confidence in the components of the federal system. In light of the initial role of the federal government in promoting racial equality, nonwhites' greater faith in lower governmental levels may be a bit surprising. But an analysis of the correlates of cynicism suggests that blacks, along with white integrationists, may have been less than satisfied with the pace of improvements in the late 1960s.[11] This led to a greater withdrawal of support for the national government along with the general rise of political cynicism.

Another indicator of the gap that had sprung up between the races was the response to the seven-point scale question inquiring whether "a change in our form of government" (1) was needed to solve prob-lems facing the country or whether "no change was necessary" (7). As of 1973, with the Vietnam situation still unsettled and the Water-gate scandal unfolding, most whites were nevertheless unwilling to en-dorse an extreme restructuring of the government. Mean scores (4.07 among youths and 5.01 among parents) reflected the feeling that change was needed, but that it should be less than total. Nonwhites, on the other hand—especially the young adults—often responded with the most extreme position, and means of 2.93 and 3.97 showed them much more willing than whites to endorse sharp breaks with the past.

While the white-nonwhite differences were the most salient features of system evaluations, shifts in the direction and degree of racial dif-ferences raise potential problems not only between the races. The gen-eration gap among nonwhites was as evident here as in most other areas we have surveyed. In 1965 both white and nonwhite youths were more trusting than parents of government in general (and of the na-

11 Miller, "Political Issues and Trust in Government," 957-58.

tional government in particular), a result we attributed to their life-cycle position. Eight years later white youths had pulled almost even with their parents (Table 10.5). In contrast, nonwhite youths had surpassed their parents on both measures and widened their emphasis on system-level defects. Similarly, on the seven-point scale regarding change in the form of government, white youths and parents differed but a tenth of a step while nonwhite youths were more than a point away from their parents. The generation gap remained as small as or smaller than that between the races, but it was large enough that if black unity were desired, it would be difficult and costly to achieve.

Evaluations of sociopolitical groups yield a mixed pattern of white-nonwhite differences reminiscent of results for policy issues. One kind of result is found in ratings of racial groups themselves. When whites and blacks are the subject matter, we would expect a large discrepancy in the ratings made by racial groups, an expectation that proved correct in both generations and both years (Table 10.6). Interestingly, the

TABLE 10.6: Evaluations of Sociopolitical Groups, by Generation, Race, and Year

	Youths			Parents			Correlation (γ)	
	Nonwhite	White		Nonwhite	White		Y	P
Whites 0 (Low) - 100 (High)								
1965	73.9	83.3	+9.4	74.6	84.1	+9.5	.41	.38
1973	61.2	69.7	+8.5	69.8	77.9	+8.1	.30	.28
	−12.7	−13.6		−4.8	−6.2			
Blacks 0 (Low) - 100 (High)								
1965	87.5	66.4	−21.1	85.2	64.5	−20.7	−.75	−.72
1973	81.6	60.1	−21.5	79.5	65.1	−14.4	−.77	−.57
	−5.9	−6.3		−5.7	+0.6			
Southerners 0 (Low) - 100 (High)								
1965	54.1	62.9	+8.8	57.5	66.7	+9.2	.25	.24
1973	56.7	62.9	+6.2	63.1	69.2	+6.1	.18	.20
	+2.6	0		+5.6	+2.5			
Jews 0 (Low) - 100 (High)								
1965	63.4	63.8	+0.4	66.8	66.1	−0.7	.02	−.02
1973	57.2	61.1	+3.9	61.3	67.0	+5.7	.16	.20
	−6.2	−2.7		−5.5	+0.9			

alteration that is perhaps most significant is numerically the smallest. White parents' ratings of blacks moved up a notch, while all other ratings were dropping. Intergenerationally, this meant that in 1973 white parents actually rated blacks higher than did their offspring by a full five points. In its own way this result, like so many others, belies the image of an older population resistant to change. If older adults were fixed in their racial views, based on years of dealing with blacks as social inferiors, one might well have expected their ratings of blacks to deteriorate during the civil rights struggle. Instead, the parents' appraisals rose slightly over this period, even as other appraisals involving race declined.

Changes in the ratings of racial groups were regionally concentrated, being much greater in the South. Among the youths change was in opposite directions inside and outside the South. In 1965, as one would expect, racial differences were considerably greater in the South in both generations. Among the young, however, racial differences in non-Southern areas actually increased slightly over the 1965-1973 period, while there was a sharp drop in the South. This meant that in the latter year the two regions were hardly distinguishable. Among parents the change was also greatest in the South, although there was some narrowing of the ratings gap in both regions.

Just as changes in the ratings of racial groups varied by region, ratings of Southerners varied by race (Table 10.6). This was quite obviously so in the early 1960s but less so a decade later. The negative image of Southern race relations at the time of the first interview, only a year and a half after Johnson assumed the presidency, resulted in relatively low overall ratings among whites. The intervening years saw marked improvement in the relative standing of the Southern population. While scores of other groups almost universally declined, those of Southerners stayed the same or rose. Though nonwhites still rated Southerners somewhat lower than did whites, the difference declined by approximately a third in both generations. We suspect that subsequent developments—migration, the rise to prominence of sunbelt cities, and the election of Jimmy Carter—have resulted in a further, slow upgrading in the relative standing of Southerners and a further decline in racial differences.

Changes in the appraisals of Southerners were regionally as well as racially concentrated. While evaluations of most groups were dropping, nonwhites in the South raised their ratings of Southerners by over nine points among the young and over ten points among the parents. As a result, racial differences in Southerners' ratings of their own population, which were very large in 1965, were significantly smaller in 1973. Among the parents, the 1973 ratings of white and nonwhite

Southerners were actually more in agreement than were the ratings of non-Southerners.

Ratings of the remaining groups represent more of a mixed bag of increases and decreases in racial differences. Changes in the evaluations of Jews are perhaps the most meaningful (Table 10.6). Jews were rated equally by whites and nonwhites in 1965, but a small difference had emerged by 1973. Though Jews have long been supportive of liberal causes, including antidiscrimination laws, blacks may have come to see themselves as having less in common with what they judged to be a high status group whose interests are basically antithetical to or nonsupportive of the upgrading of blacks.[12]

Intergenerationally, the most interesting result is that in almost every instance the absolute difference between parents and offspring increased from 1965 to 1973. Taking all groups together, the average parent-youth difference among whites jumped from 2.2 to 6.7 while it went from 3.5 to 6.5 among nonwhites. For certain groups the generational differences were actually larger than those between the races (notably big business and Protestants). This helps us to keep the racial comparison in perspective. With the exception of whites and blacks themselves, racial differences on group ratings are not large. To judge from these evaluations of sociopolitical groups, there is currently as great a prospect of generational as of racial cleavages.

NONPOLITICAL COMPARISONS

In their degree of independence from the political parties as well as on some policy issues, we found that racial differences were smaller among youths than among parents, and that the biggest gap was that between generations. Similar results characterize religious beliefs and practices. Nonwhite parents were substantially more fundamentalist and church-going than were white parents; the differences among youths were much narrower (Table 10.7). With the exception of the "Bible question" in 1965 the parent-offspring gap was wider than that between the races. In a further parallel with partisanship and policy positions, the generational difference was greater among nonwhites in three of the four comparisons. The basic similarity between the political and nonpolitical realms that has dominated our results all along continues to do so here.

---

[12] This argument is also made by Milton Himmelfarb, "The Case of Jewish Liberalism," in Seymour Martin Lipset (ed.), *Emerging Coalitions in American Politics* (San Francisco: Institute for Contemporary Studies, 1978), 304-305. See also the collection of essays by Nat Hentoff and others, *Black Anti-Semitism and Jewish Racism* (New York: Schocken Books, 1972).

TABLE 10.7: Nonpolitical Orientations, by Generation, Race, and Year

| | Youths | | | Parents | | | Correlation (γ) | |
	Nonwhite	White		Nonwhite	White		Y	P
Belief about the Bible								
1 (Irrelevant) - 4 (God's Word)								
1965	3.46	3.39	−.07	3.65	3.46	−.19	−.17	−.37
1973	3.29	3.12	−.17	3.64	3.36	−.28	−.22	−.46
	−.17	−.27		−.01	−.10			
Church attendance								
1 (Never) - 4 (Almost every week)								
1965	3.66	3.45	−.21	3.35	3.11	−.24	−.20	−.17
1973	2.71	2.57	−.14	3.40	2.92	−.48	−.05	−.28
	−.95	−.88		+.05	−.19			
Personal trust								
1 (Low) - 7 (High)								
1965	4.31	5.13	+.82	3.64	5.63	+1.98	.35	.60
1973	3.21	4.74	+1.53	3.04	5.31	+2.27	.54	.67
	−1.10	−.39		−.60	−.32			
Opinion strength								
1 (Low) - 7 (High)								
1965	4.59	4.53	−.06	3.99	4.16	+.17	−.04	.05
1973	4.59	4.57	−.02	3.95	4.04	+.09	−.04	.01
	0	+.04		−.04	−.12			
Self-confidence								
1 (Low) - 7 (High)								
1965	4.15	4.95	+.80	4.22	4.85	+.63	.37	.25
1973	4.08	5.04	+.96	4.26	5.09	+.83	.39	.32
	−.07	+.09		+.04	+.24			

Two of the three measures of psychological characteristics also yield racial differences that correspond to the closest political analogues (Table 10.7). In their personal as in their political trust, nonwhites declined more sharply between 1965 and 1973, so that by the end of this time whites in both generations were considerably more trusting. Especially dramatic is the increasing gap among the young. After eight years of dealing with the adult world black young adults suffered a severe drop in their regard for their fellow citizens. Whites also rated themselves considerably higher than nonwhites with respect to self-confidence, just as whites felt more able to deal effectively with the political system. The last measure—opinion strength—differs from the accompanying measure of ego strength as well as from political efficacy. Precisely why it varies is unclear.

That the personality measures are not exact duplicates of their political counterparts is clear from the generational contrasts. On personal trust there was a sharp reversal among nonwhites between 1965 and 1973, and in the latter year it was white youths and parents who differed most. In their self-confidence scores, nonwhites differed most in 1973, but by a small margin, and with parents being the more confident. Lastly, opinion strength by then showed the more usual pattern, with nonwhite parents and youths differing by a greater margin.

Despite these twists in intergenerational comparisons, the behavior of nonpolitical measures assures us that our results regarding white-nonwhite differences extend beyond the specifically political sphere, and that at least in the religious domain, generational differences among whites and among nonwhites parallel results for political behavior and attitudes.

Conclusion

If we were to take only a long-term perspective by concentrating exclusively on white-nonwhite differences in the young generation compared with those in the parental generation, we would surely conclude that racial differences were disappearing in most areas, especially those pertaining to involvement, political resources, and overt participation. A major exception comes from the index of political trust, and there are some exceptions in other evaluative areas. Nonetheless, the long-term picture clearly points to a general diminution of racial differences in the younger compared with the older generation.

While not contradicting this long-range perspective, comparison of the 1965 results with those from 1973 indicates that the complete eradication of racial differences is not yet at hand. Even in this youthful sample of high school graduates, wherein nonwhites are only minimally disadvantaged in overall educational attainment, whites surpassed nonwhites in psychological engagement and in their political resources; whites and nonwhites continued to exhibit differences in their policy positions and in their candidate and party preferences, with extremely large gaps when racial interests were directly involved, and nonwhites continued their greater religiosity and lower degrees of personal trust and self-confidence.

Further evidence that racial differences will not disappear immediately comes from the questionnaires administered to high school seniors in 1973. Racial differences of about the same magnitude as those in 1965 recurred in the 1973 sounding. The pattern of correlations was also similar to that in the earlier year. Of the comparable measures, the greatest differences among the 1973 seniors appeared in the areas of psychological involvement, resources, and nonpolitical orientations, just as in the 1965 and 1973 panels. As in 1965, there was little difference between the races on questions about prayers in schools and seating an elected Communist. Differences on political trust were larger than in 1965, but this is not surprising in light of the changes in the panel by 1973. Moreover, they were in the direction of heightening rather than decreasing racial contrasts.

Along with continued, if somewhat reduced, differences between whites and nonwhites, our results substantiated the presence of a considerable generation gap among nonwhites. With the exception of race issues and related phenomena such as candidate preferences that were directly and clearly related to minority groups' interests, the gap between nonwhite parents and offspring was widespread over the areas examined. Moreover, the magnitude was often as large as or even larger than the gap between whites and nonwhites. Perhaps even more important, however, is that the generation gap between younger and older nonwhites was not limited to specific attitudes and behaviors. This became evident very early when we looked at rates of individual change between 1965 and 1973. Middle-aged nonwhites appeared less stable than their white counterparts, while young nonwhites were much more nearly even with whites on this score. Thus, not only do young nonwhites frequently hold attitudes somewhat at variance from those of their elders, but the consistency with which they hold their attitudes is also more robust. The considerably greater opinion strength of young nonwhites would also seem to be suggestive of greater attitudinal clarity and consistency.

Finally, we come full circle by re-emphasizing that youthful nonwhites differed from the older generation by being more similar to the majority population. It is perhaps fitting, therefore, to conclude this chapter on the upbeat note of declining rather than continuing or expanding racial differences. Contrary to the gloomy prognosis of the Kerner Commission's 1968 report,[13] the younger generation does not appear to be increasingly driven toward irreconcilable political divisions and inequalities between the races. Especially persuasive in this regard are the commanding, higher than average participation rates among young nonwhites. Some racial differences will undoubtedly continue, particularly in the population as a whole. And they very probably will never disappear fully on matters of direct racial relevance. Yet the generational comparisons here offer an optimistic picture for those who would like to see the relevance of race diminished.

[13] The Kerner Commission, *Report of the National Advisory Committee on Civil Disorders* (Washington, D.C.: U.S. Government Printing Office, 1968).

CHAPTER ELEVEN

Protest Behavior and Its Legacy

Even a cursory recollection of the late 1960s and early 1970s brings to mind sharp images of student protests. Marches, rallies, sit-ins, boycotts, picket lines, pitched confrontations with authorities, and physical violence wracked the nation. Although the civil rights and "free speech" movements were critical immediate predecessors, and even though other objects of protest emerged, the issue that triggered so much of the student protest behavior was the Vietnam War. Protest often took the form of individual acts, such as various forms of draft evasion. More dramatic were the forms of collective, public protest. Collective behavior of an unconventional sort was not new to American politics, but the frequency, passion, and social locus of the student protest movement shook the nation to its core.

That protest behavior changes the quality and process attending the formulation and implementation of public policy can hardly be denied. An area of greater uncertainty is that of the political antecedents and consequences of protest activity at the individual level. Are protestors politically different to begin with or do protest phenomena represent a galvanizing, transforming experience? More importantly, what are the longer term impacts and corollaries of protest activity on political values, attitudes, and actions? Does having been caught up in the protest movement make a difference later on? These are the very general and not so tractable questions that we address in this chapter.

To guide our inquiry it will be useful to employ Mannheim's distinction about the meanings of the term "generation."[1] In its most general sense a generation refers to an age group sharing the same time and space. These age groups have an identity in terms of their historical-social location and thus have the *potential* of participating in a common destiny. But this is simply a potentiality brought about by the accident of biological and geographical commonality. An obvious derivative, therefore, is Mannheim's second concept, that of generation as actuality. Such generations form in periods of "dynamic destabilization," when same-aged individuals ". . . participate in the characteris-

---

[1] Karl Mannheim, "The Problem of Generations," English translation reprinted in Philip G. Altbach and Robert S. Laufer (eds.), *The New Pilgrims* (New York: David McKay, 1972), 101-38. Another historical and more normatively oriented approach to interpreting youth movements is Lewis Feuer, *The Conflict of Generations* (New York: Basic Books, 1969).

tic social and intellectual currents of their society and period, and insofar as they have an active or passive experience of the interactions of forces which made up the new situation."[2] Thus youth who are not exposed to these currents share the same generation location but do not share in the processes creating an actual generation.

A third conceptualization of generation arises from the fact that divergences may occur within actual generations, both in terms of behavior and in the directionality of goals and values. These divergences, born out of intense forms of shared responses to the unfolding history, lead to what are called generation units. The distinction between actual generations and generation units is summed up in Mannheim's famous dictum: "*Youth experiencing the same concrete historical problems may be said to be part of the same actual generation; while those groups within the same actual generation which work up the material of their common experiences in different specific ways, constitute separate generation-units.*"[3]

The contrast between the concept of generation as shared location in time and space versus the concept of actual generation is of doubtful utility in a society marked by high-speed mass communication and transportation and in an era during which certain political phenomena touched virtually every nook and cranny of the nation. Certainly these conditions characterized the momentous period of the late 1960s and early 1970s. The potentiality "of being sucked into the vortex of social change" was extraordinarily ripe. Thus we may think of the majority of our youthful respondents as comprising an actual generation as well as a potential one. Their "fresh contact" with the political culture occurred, by all accounts, during a period of incredible dynamic destabilization.

There are also strong a priori grounds for believing that distinctive generation-units emerged during this period. For example, sharp attitudinal differences were observed between college and noncollege youth of the same age, and even within the college ranks homogeneity did not prevail. But most observations in addition to suffering from the typical shortcomings in research design noted earlier, also suffer from a lack of focus on the critical events and shared experiences that presumably gave rise to and shaped the generation-units. To speak of generation-units we need to move beyond standard socioeconomic and environmental differences that characterize the typical analyses. What is needed instead are indicators that show more concretely how and

[2] Mannheim, 119.

[3] Ibid., 119-20, italics in the original. Mannheim stresses the concrete bonds formed in generation-units by virtue of the intense interaction (120-23) and (inferentially) the integrative "personally acquired memories" uniting the individuals within the unit (111).

with what consequences, certain groups worked up their historical experiences in unique ways. For as Mannheim observed, generation units ". . . are characterized by the fact that they do not merely involve a loose participation by a number of individuals in a pattern of events shared by all alike . . . but an identity of responses, a certain affinity in the way in which all move with and are formed by the common experiences."[4]

One ultimate objective of this chapter, then, is to determine the extent to which the protestors meet the standards of a generation-unit. From another perspective we will be exploring the proposition that post-adolescent *political* experiences can have an impact on a wide range of political orientations. Finally, the materials to be presented here will bring descriptive, substantive detail to topics (protest antecedents and consequences) about which considerable controversy exists.

A PROFILE OF PROTEST AND PROTESTORS

For those who lived through the protest period it may have seemed that nearly every young person was a protestor, in either incipient or manifest form. Of course manipulation by and of the mass media helped evoke that image. And it was not long before social scientists and more cautious observers began to amass hard evidence which showed that the proportion of actual demonstrators, as against sympathizers and fellow travelers, constituted a minority of the young—even at the universities in the forefront of the movement. Nevertheless, there was no gainsaying the sheer numbers of young people who were resorting to unconventional political action and the countless others who were participating vicariously.

Our efforts to place our young adult respondents within the protest environment included direct questions about their political participation histories since 1965. Specifically, the lead question ran: "Have you ever taken part in a demonstration, protest march, or sit-in?" For those responding positively, follow-up questions elicited the years and the particular circumstances involved. A total of 16% said that they had engaged in such behavior, a figure compatible with various other estimates resting on roughly similar bases.[5] In an absolute sense this is a small proportion, but several considerations enhance its significance. First, an extrapolation to the entire universe means tens of thousands of young adults took part in unusual, often dramatic political acts. Sec-

---

[4] Ibid., 122.

[5] E.g., the Yankelovich-CBS News surveys, as reported in Robert Chandler, *Public Opinion* (New York: R. R. Bowker Company, 1972), 74-75.

ond, approximately one-half of the participants were repeaters, having taken part in two or more events. A few were habitual demonstrators. Third, as will be shown shortly, this overall proportion was heavily concentrated in visible segments that were likely to be weighty political strata in the future. Finally, the one in six demonstrators among the young drastically outweighed the one in forty-five among their parents.

Although an eight-year period was referenced in asking about the incidence of protest activities, it comes as no surprise to find a sharp rise and fall across that time span. Figure 11.1 plots the proportion of all protest acts (rather than actors) over the eight years. The peak years of 1969 and 1970 alone account for over two-fifths of the acts. If we recall the chronology of the protest era, the pattern makes sense because the Vietnam War protests in particular were at their height during these two years. And the abrupt tailing off after 1970 echoes the popular impression of flagging political energy among the young.

FIGURE 11.1: Timing of Protest Activities[a]

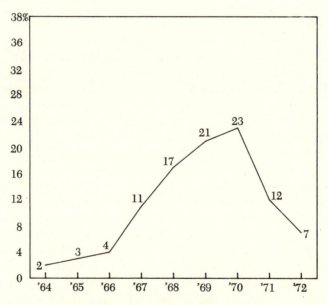

[a] N = 255, the total number of protest activities.

Yet there is a confounding factor at work. To a degree, the incidence of protest undoubtedly reflects the timing of college matriculation for this cohort. The majority of students started college within a year or so of high school graduation and were juniors and seniors near the end of the decade. To the extent that the campus provided the opportunity structure for protest activity, and that older students were more likely to take advantage of the opportunity, the curvilinear pattern of Figure 11.1 simply reflects the cohort's reaction to a conducive environment. Nonetheless, an historical interpretation is persuasive as well, inasmuch as the highest incidence of activity does not come in the years during which college-going for the entire cohort was at its height. Nor does the sharp drop after 1970 faithfully reflect the departures from college. Thus, while the timing of college attendance plays some role, the temporal distribution of protest activities also reflects the larger ebb and flow of the student protest movement across time.

Depending upon the phase of the student movement monitored, the focus of the protest activity would vary. A study capturing an earlier moment in time would undoubtedly have picked up a large number of demonstrators involved in the civil rights movement. For the time period embraced by our inquiry we expect the Vietnam War to occupy center stage as the object of protest behavior. Only the extent to which that is the case is problematic. Of all issues mentioned, those relating to the war constituted some 62%. Trailing far behind were student issues (13%), race-related issues (9%), labor-management conflicts (4%), and a hodge-podge of miscellany (11%). Even though strikes and take-overs involving issues of university governance and specific policies occurred on some campuses, the great bulk of demonstrators from the class of 1965 recall the war as the protest target.

If unconventional tactics were directed toward one primary and several secondary targets, the ideological component of the actions was overwhelmingly anti-official policy, anti-status quo, and—as it was often put—anti-establishment. In coding the descriptions of protest behavior we attempted to categorize the issue persuasion of the protestors. We uncovered some "pro" demonstrators, but these constituted less than 5% of the total. Thus we are dealing with a relatively homogeneous group in terms of their orientations at the time of their unconventional action.

Two main demographic characteristics served to divide the protestors and nonprotestors. Among whites the reported rate was 14% compared with 30% among nonwhites. By educational strata the figures rose from 4% among those with a high school degree, to 15% among those with some college, on to 29% among those with at least a college degree. These characteristics combine in an additive fashion. Among nonwhite college graduates the protest rate was 52%, compared with a 27% figure for similarly educated whites. In passing it should be confirmed that the object of protest behavior among nonwhites was predominantly in the race relations or student activities area. Because nonwhites comprise such a small proportion of the sample, however, the whites' concern with the Vietnam War dominates the overall figures reported above.

The strong "necessary but not sufficient" relationship between education and protest behavior ($\gamma = .58$) indicates the need to impose a control for the effects of education. We proceeded in the following way. Given the presence of only 29 protestors among the high school graduates, that educational stratum was discarded. This left the some college and college graduate groups, among whom the demonstrator N's are 63 and 129, respectively. Although we carried out much of the analysis in a twofold fashion, first combining these two groups and then looking only at the college graduates, we ultimately decided to concentrate only on the college graduates.

By confining the presentation to the relatively pure category of college graduates we substantially reduce the likelihood of bias and spurious effects associated with dropping out of college. For the major portion of what follows, then, we will be working with the subset of college graduates only. We will return occasionally to the entire sample for a multivariate analysis so that the impact of protest behavior may be gauged simultaneously with that of other factors.

Before launching into comparisons of protestors and nonprotestors along political lines it will be helpful to present some relevant academic characteristics of the two groups. A helpful standard to keep in mind is the 29% figure for protesting among college graduates as a whole. Students with higher grade averages were a bit more likely to have demonstrated—42% of the A students, 30% of the B students, and 22% of the C and below students. But it should be noted that A students made up only one in six of all protestors. Students attending private, nondenominational schools had a rate of 52% and such students comprised over one-fourth of all protestors. Size of school was an important ingredient also. Of students going to schools of $\geq 10,000$ some 43% had demonstrated, and these students formed almost one-half of all protestors. The widely held view that the social sciences contributed disproportionately is borne out: 46% of the social science majors had protested, versus 27% of the humanities majors, 23% of the natural science majors, and smaller proportions of other majors. And social science majors contributed 43% of all protestors. Subjective differences about college life also crop up. Retrospectively, 39% of the protestors versus 51% of the nonprotestors reported being very satisfied with their collegiate experiences. At the same time, protestors were more likely to report having had some of their important beliefs and values challenged while in school (69% vs. 53%).

These results fall pretty much within the boundaries of earlier studies working with smaller samples and with a narrower focus. The patterns associated with college major and type and size of school are especially important because of the magnitudes involved. Differences that we subsequently associate with or attribute to protest phenomena might stem instead from compositional differences among protestors and nonprotestors. We will treat that possibility more systematically in a section to follow. Suffice it for now to state that controlling for major, type, and size of school does not appreciably alter the differences in political traits between the two groups.

THE WIDENING GAP BETWEEN PROTESTORS AND NONPROTESTORS

As noted at the start of this chapter, it would be difficult to demonstrate conclusively that taking part in a more or less voluntary activity such as protest action leads to or causes changes in one's behavior or attitudes. The elements of self-selection are so pervasive and the lag in our measurements so long that we cannot assert that a widening gap between the protestors and nonprotestors over an eight-year period can be laid at the doorstep of the protest act itself. Nor would we necessarily expect that to be the case in a theoretical sense. While some participants may have experienced a breach with their past as a direct result of protesting, it seems much more likely that the act itself was part of a larger constellation, though surely one of its most vivid manifestations. We are on safer ground if we treat unconventional behavior minimally as an indicator of dissatisfaction, a desire to effectuate change, a reinforcement of previously held dispositions, and perhaps as a crystallizing event that helped change the actor's orientations.

Of course, even this more flexible view does not allow us to handle with complete satisfaction the probability that some of the same forces prompting unconventional behavior were also prompting other sorts of changes of the type for which we have both before and after measures. Here the intersection between the timing of the study and the frequency distribution of protest behavior provides some relief. Our observation point in 1973 comes two or three years past the great bulk of protest activity. Thus in a descriptive sense we will be able to see whether having been a demonstrator continues to be associated with a state of being that might have helped precipitate the act of demonstration, but well after the performance of the act itself and whatever mutual influences might have been operating at the time. This will allow us to determine if protesting is associated with some more or less lasting cleavages within this elite group of young adults such that we may speak of a generation-unit.

We may first address briefly the question of individual-level stability over time. Offhand, we might expect the protestors to show less stable orientations. They were the ones, after all, who broke the political norms by engaging in what were widely regarded as unconventional acts and not infrequently as illegal acts. A logical corollary of breaking with tradition would be greater alterations in political traits. By the same token, the absence of protest behavior suggests greater conservation of preexisting political characteristics. On the other hand, we already know that stability among college graduates as a whole was not visibly different from that of other members of the cohort.

To some extent our expectations about more instability among protestors are borne out. Across the various measures the demonstrators tended to have lower over-time stability in terms of correlation coefficients. This was especially noticeable whenever partisanship was involved in the measure. In most other respects the differences in the over-time correlations are modest ($<.10$) and occasionally are in the opposite direction. Significantly, on most nonpolitical orientations the protestors were more stable. Overall, then, the slightly greater degree of individual-level political "change" among the protestors will be sympathetic with a higher rate of aggregate shifts among them. We now turn to the questions of net changes and shifting differences between protestors and nonprotestors.

Involvement, Resources, and Participation

Given the behavioral display accompanying protest action, we have every reason to expect that protestors—as of 1973—will be more psychologically involved in politics, possessed of more political skills, and more participative in other respects than nonprotestors, even within this highly select group of young adults. An intriguing question, though, is whether there have been shifts in the distance between the two groups over time. Did the eventual demonstrators enter the protest era already better armed, or did the syndrome associated with protesting serve to elevate them above their fellow members? A converse hypothesis can also be posed. As will be shown subsequently, and as common observation would suggest, the demonstrators are more dissatisfied and disillusioned with the governing process. If they feel that protesting and other forms of political action have not generated favorable outcomes, they may be retreating and withdrawing from the political sphere. They might be prime candidates for the "privatization" behavioral mode. Therefore, the distance between the protestors and nonprotestors could actually have narrowed with respect to involvement and resources.

The results indicate unequivocally that the eventual protestors emerged from high school more politically oriented, more resourceful, and more cosmopolitan in their interests (Table 11.1, 1965 figures). These differences are sometimes relatively modest, but they all point in the same direction, and several are significant in a statistical sense.[6] The argument that the demonstrating students were self-selected in terms of political acumen has some merit. By the same token the counterargument that the demonstrators were fashioned overnight from the ranks of the politically unaware and unsophisticated is refuted.

Adding ammunition to this argument are some additional pieces of information gleaned from the 1965 interviews. At that time the incipient protestors also reported having more political discussions with family and friends. Among the protestors some 49% said they talked politics with family members several times a week and some 37% said the same about their friends. Comparable rates among the nonprotestors were 38% and 29%, respectively. Of even greater interest are the high school seniors' estimates about how politically active they would be as adults. Although we had little confidence in this question as a valid indicator of actual future behavior, it was useful in our earlier report as an index of contemporary involvement. As it turns out, however, this hypothetical query is a rather good predictor of eventual participation of the unconventional kind. Some 32% of the demonstrators versus only 13% of the nondemonstrators saw themselves as being "very active" in the future ($\gamma = .41$). On balance the protestors were disproportionately recruited from the ranks of the prepoliticized, the subjectively competent, and the politically knowledgeable. Observers have speculated that this was the case, but the data presented here are based on one of the very rare instances in which the cohort was assessed before leaving home, before the socializing effects of university life had set in, and before the major campus outbursts.

Having established that some self-selection processes were at work, we are now in a position to determine if being an unconventional participant is associated with a continuing gap within the ranks of college graduates. This can most readily be accomplished by comparing the 1965 and 1973 scores (Table 11.1). Demonstrators continued to distinguish themselves by their greater attentiveness, sophistication, and resource availability. Whatever disenchantment and frustrations may have prompted or emerged from their involvement in the protest movement were not sufficient to move them behind their less demon-

[6] Because of the small numbers of cases involved in much of the analyses in this chapter, we have paid more than the customary attention to levels of statistical significance in evaluating the results.

TABLE 11.1: Psychological Involvement and Political Resources among Protestors and Nonprotestors (College Graduates)

	Nonprotestors	Protestors		Correlation (γ)
Interest in public affairs				
1 (Low) - 4 (High)				
1965	3.38	3.62	+.24	.37
1973	3.42	3.67	+.25	.36
	+.04	+.05		
Cosmopolitanism				
1 (Least) - 7 (Most)				
1965	5.52	5.83	+.31	.14
1973	5.20	5.58	+.38	.22
	−.32	−.25		
Watch television				
1 (Don't watch) - 5 (Almost daily)				
1965	3.77	3.75	−.02	−.01
1973	4.26	4.03	−.23	−.16
	+.49	+.28		
Read newspapers				
1 (Don't read) - 5 (Almost daily)				
1965	4.05	4.07	+.02	.06
1973	4.10	4.40	+.30	.21
	+.05	+.33		
Read magazines				
1 (Don't read) - 3 (Regularly)				
1965	2.43	2.55	+.12	.16
1973	2.30	2.62	+.32	.40
	−.13	+.07		
Internal efficacy				
1 (Low) - 3 (High)				
1965	2.25	2.52	+.27	.35
1973	2.19	2.42	+.23	.33
	−.06	−.10		
Recognition and understanding				
1 (None) - 5 (Broad)				
1965	3.17	3.68	+.51	.24
1973	4.15	4.40	+.25	.12
	+.98	+.72		

Table 11.1 (cont.)

	Nonprotestors	Protestors	Correlation (γ)	
Knowledge of political facts				
0-6 (Number correct)				
1965	4.39	4.73	+.35	.19
1973	4.47	4.99	+.52	.30
	+.08	+.26		

strative peers.[7] The strengthened negative relationship with the use of television is simply the exception that proves the rule in that TV watching is a more passive, less demanding activity than is using the print media. Moreover, in absolute terms most of the indicators showed little change or a modest rise over time, thereby implying that the protest experience did not generate net negative effects.

With the notable exception of ideological sophistication, the gap between the two groups either remained stable or expanded in favor of the demonstrators. An additional sign is available showing that, if anything, the protestors increased their lead over the nonprotestors. Recall that the youths' descriptions of the good citizen were divided into political versus nonpolitical dimensions, and within the former between active versus allegiant portrayals. We argued that the greater the emphasis on the active mode the greater were the individual's resources, that a stress on the active dimension represented a positive approach to citizen duty. Loyalty and compliance with the laws, though necessary for system maintenance, are not the stuff of which the civic culture is formed. Based on their manifest behavior in the interim, we might well expect the protestors to have increased their subscription to the active versus the allegiant citizen.

Comparing the two groups reveals the degree to which this expectation is spectacularly met (Figure 11.2). In 1965 there was no difference between the two, with both emphasizing the active over the passive voice. Scarcely any change is apparent among the nonprotestors by 1973, but a whopping gain is recorded among the protestors. This change comes about primarily because of a sharp drop in the

[7] These and subsequent findings are sympathetic with a one-shot, post-hoc study of Southern civil rights student activists and two control groups from the early 1960s. See James M. Fendrich, "Activists Ten Years Later: A Test of Generational Unit Continuity," *Journal of Social Issues*, 30 (No. 3, 1974), 95-118. Another less direct effort to apply Mannheim's thesis to youth politics is Richard G. Braungart, "College and Noncollege Youth Politics in 1972: An Application of Mannheim's Generation Unit Model," *Journal of Youth and Adolescence*, 5 (No. 4, 1976), 325-47.

FIGURE 11.2: Ratio of Active to Allegiant Descriptions of Good Citizen among Protestors and Nonprotestors (College Graduates)

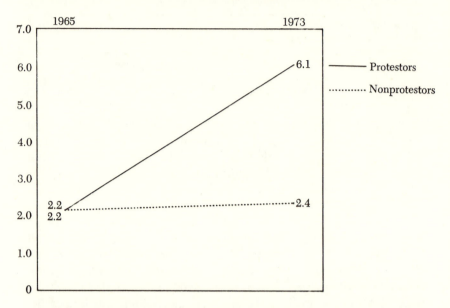

number of allegiant-type descriptions rather than because of an increase in the active ones.

An examination of the verbatim replies further substantiates a shift between 1965 and 1973. Among the protestors in particular there was an increase in outright calls for direct citizen action if things are not going well, declarations that one cannot simply sit back, that the good citizen goes out and organizes and even protests and demonstrates to achieve desired ends. The ethos of vigorous activism was alive and well among the veterans of the movement.

One popular image of the protest movement was that its practitioners were adopting these tactics because they had become disenchanted or felt thwarted by conventional outlets. A companion charge was that many protestors were literally bystanders who were caught up in the vortex of a particular riot or demonstration and that such people had neither the inclination nor the skills to practice conventional politics.[8] Both charges would minimize the rates of conventional activity by protestors. Contradicting this view was the apparent involvement of student protestors and protest sympathizers in electoral politics, especially the events revolving around the selection of the 1968 Democratic

[8] This is the student protest version of the "riff-raff" model applied to the urban riots of the late 1960s.

presidential nominee. We have also just presented evidence with respect to attentiveness and resources showing the greater politicization
of the protestors.

Fortunately, we have materials at hand to resolve the competing
views. Since we asked the respondents about their specific activities
over the eight-year span, we can address the issue by looking at the
frequency with which protestors and nonprotestors performed a variety
of political acts. Some of them may have been done in conjunction with
protestlike affairs, but they all fall within what are typically labeled as
conventional, normatively approved behaviors in American society. In
evaluating the results we should bear in mind that we are dealing with
an elite body of people who came of political age during an activist
era. We saw in our analysis by education (Chapter 8) that college
graduates in general have high rates of political participation in both
absolute and relative terms.

With this background in mind, the results are startling (Figure
11.3). It is not so much that the protestors also do more of everything
else; what is remarkable is the magnitude of that margin. Raw per-

FIGURE 11.3: Frequency of Other Political Activities among Protestors
and Nonprotestors (College Graduates)

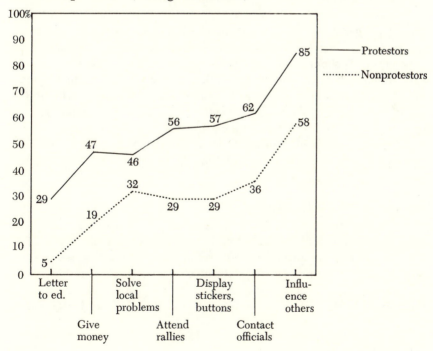

centage differences range from a low of 14% in the area of working with other people to solve local problems to highs of from 24% to 28% for *all* of the other activities. Or, in terms of the gamma correlation that we have been using, the range is from .29 to .79, with six of the seven correlations above .45. Although the activity levels of the nonprotestors are by no means meager, it is apparent that the protestors have by far the more extensive participation histories.

Nor was it necessarily the case that the protestors resorted to that mode after having tried the conventional route, nor that they gave up on the conventional mode after having tasted the excitement of demonstrations and sit-ins. Rather, a detailed examination of the respondents' participation calendars shows that the protestors were simultaneously employing diverse forms of behavior. Their political action repertories were more extensive and were being employed with greater frequency than was the case with nonprotestors. Significantly, there is no indication of a greater attrition in conventional activity among protestors in the most recent years (1971 through early 1973). The concept of an expanded action repertory in western polities has recently received extended empirical treatment,[9] but usually with insufficient numbers of actual unconventional participants to make the case emphatically. Here we have a superb illustration of an expanded repertory within a major element of the population.

A final touch emphasizes the eclecticism of the protestors. Voting is typically regarded as the "easiest" political act because it can be done rather quickly and because it incurs few obligations or expectations from others. It should come as no surprise, then, that voting turnout is very similar across our two groups. What difference there is, however, favors the demonstrators in the two most recent elections, with the biggest difference (58% vs. 51%) occurring in the low-stimulus, congressional election of 1970. Parenthetically, the fact that protestors vote as often as others is additional proof that the demonstrators of yesteryear have not rejected, any more than have others, the traditional arena of electoral politics.

Partisanship and Issue Preferences

We begin our comparisons of preferences and evaluations on the part of protestors and nonprotestors in the firm expectation that as of 1973, at any rate, the protestors more often occupied the "liberal" position on issues and candidates of the day. Of course there is no inherent reason why protest behavior should be coupled only with the left. Opposition to the civil rights movement and especially to integrated

[9] Samuel H. Barnes, Max Kaase et al., *Political Action* (Beverly Hills, Calif.: Sage, 1979).

schools has often manifested itself in a viciously unconventional form. So-called vigilante activity has typically been linked with right-wing activities. During the student protest era, however, it was predominantly leftist ideology that was being espoused—divisions within the left notwithstanding.

In any event, determining the directional differences is simply the beginning. First, the differences may be modest. After all, we have already established that the college graduates in general are considerably more liberal than their fellow members. And we know that many students identified with the demonstrators without necessarily being demonstrators themselves. Consequently, the demonstrators may be only marginally different in terms of political attitudes.

A further question is even more problematic and intriguing. A considerable controversy has sprung up regarding the "before" attitudes of protestors. Were they already more liberal than their fellow students or did they become transformed somewhere along the way? Approaches to this question include such divergent perspectives as the "red diaper" theory, which identified the latter-day protestors as the lineage descendants of liberal, left-leaning activist parents; the permissive society view, which depicted protestors as the spoiled, delinquent, unpatriotic products of affluence; and the moral superiority school, which saw the protestors as rejecting their materialistic, self-gratifying backgrounds and subscribing to a higher set of ethics.[10] When coupled with the 1973 bearings, our 1965 observations will help establish whether the protestors were initially distinctive and whether protestors drew even further away from their less vociferous classmates. A growing difference would support a crystallization or resocialization interpretation, one that would help stamp the protestors as constituting a generation-unit within the larger, actual generation.

Judging from the results in the area of partisanship, a strong presumptive case can be made for crystallization. Consider first the matter of party identification. In 1965 there was only a scant overall difference between protestors and nonprotestors (Figure 11.4). Although Democratic proclivities were more pronounced among the protestors, there were actually more strong Democrats among the nonprotestors, and there were—surprisingly enough—equal proportions of strong Republicans among the two groups. Declarations about the bias in

[10] The appropriateness of the various explanations depends in part upon what stage of the movement was being tapped, for the recruitment process changed as the movement aged. See, e.g., Milton Mankoff and Richard Flacks, "The Changing Social Base of the American Student Movement," in Altbach and Laufer (eds.), *The New Pilgrims*, 46-62; Patricia L. Kasschau, H. Edward Ransford, and Vern L. Bengtson, "Generational Consciousness and Youth Movement Participation: Contrasts in Blue Collar and White Collar Youth," *Journal of Social Issues*, 30 (No. 3, 1974), 69-94.

FIGURE 11.4: Party Identification among Protestors and Nonprotestors (College Graduates)

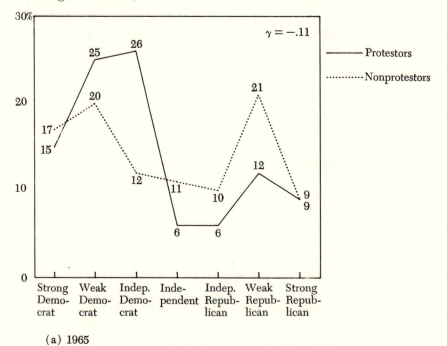

(a) 1965

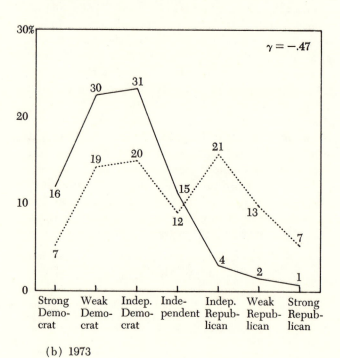

(b) 1973

partisan background of the protestors missed the mark. Those who eventually became protestors were certainly more Democratic than Republican, but the same was true of nonprotestors to only a slightly lesser degree.

At some point this partisan resemblance broke down. By 1973 a wide breach existed, with the "Democraticness" of the protestors becoming overwhelming. Even including Independent Republicans yields only a grand total of 7% for the GOP. Moreover, the proportion of strong Democrats failed to drop, in contrast to an absolute decline of 10% among the nonprotestors. While it is likely that the same forces pushing certain individuals in the direction of demonstrating were also pushing them toward the Democratic party, it seems more probable that becoming involved in the protest movement helped the swing to the Democrats rather than vice versa. For the peak years of protest occurred during the Nixon presidency, and the electoral hopes of protestors centered on supporting sympathetic candidates within the Democratic party (Lyndon Johnson not being one of the perceived sympathizers).

If party attachments showed a dramatic change over the eight-year period, the expression of party preference in terms of electoral choice was scarcely less dynamic. As with party identification, the protestors as high school seniors gave less support to the Republican side (Figure 11.5). But that difference pales when laid against the widening

FIGURE 11.5: Preference for Republican Presidential Nominees among Protestors and Nonprotestors (College Graduates)

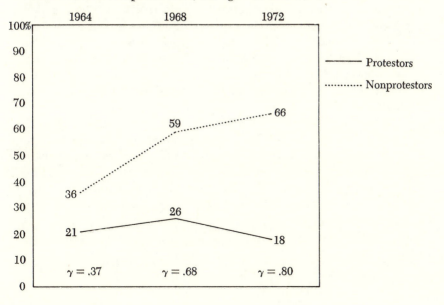

gap recorded in 1968 and 1972. Relatively few groups in the polity resisted the post-1964 swing toward the Republican nominee, Richard Nixon. Even our protestors, as they recalled their 1968 preferences, registered a small gain for Nixon compared with Barry Goldwater. Yet most impressive is the absolute decline for Nixon in the midst of his massive landslide victory of 1972. It is difficult to imagine any other identifiable subgroup in which support for Nixon in 1972 was, if any-thing, lower than that for Goldwater in 1964.[11] The differing track rec-ords of protestors and nonprotestors thus offer another piece of evi-dence for the thesis that the demonstrators were indeed "working over the historical materials" in a unique fashion.

Moving from partisanship to issue preferences, we find a similar pattern. As high school seniors, protestors voiced more support for a strong federal role in integrating the schools and more opposition to prayers in public schools (Figure 11.6). Although the differences are not large, they do support the view that self-selection was an impor-tant element in the metamorphosis of the protest movement. Never-theless, the percentage gap between the two approximately doubled over time. Especially striking in this respect is that support for school integration remained virtually unchanged among the protestors. As we have had occasion to note, the secular trend on this issue was down-ward among virtually all groups that we have examined. A high de-gree of resiliency against this secular trend sets off the protestors.

Parallel findings of an expanding gap emerge with respect to the more hypothetical, less immediately salient issues. To the two issues of whether an elected Communist should be allowed to take office and the right of citizens to make speeches against religion we have added the issue of whether "the American system of government is one that all nations should have." Responses to these three statements were added together to form a numerical civic tolerance index.[12] The under-lying dimension here is assumed to be a tolerance for nonconformity, a willingness to entertain unorthodoxy even when it runs against the normal grain.

Although protestors started out as the more tolerant, as expected, the edge is modest (Figure 11.7). In percentage terms the proportion of protestors in the highest category of the index (i.e., those giving the tolerant response to all three statements) is 40% compared with 34% among the nonprotestors. This is hardly the sort of difference that would enable one to predict with much success the likelihood of later

[11] We should reiterate that these are expressed preferences (not votes) in each instance and that the 1964 preferences were registered in 1965 when the respond-ents were still in high school.
[12] This index has not been used previously because the third item was omitted from the 1965 parent interview schedule.

FIGURE 11.6: Opinions on Two Public Policy Issues among Protestors and Nonprotestors (College Graduates)

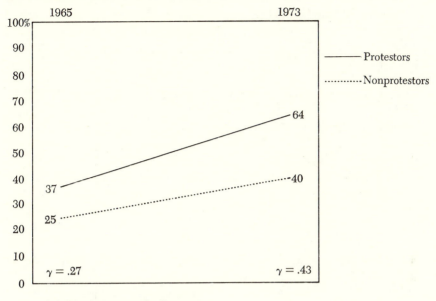

(a) Opposition to school prayers

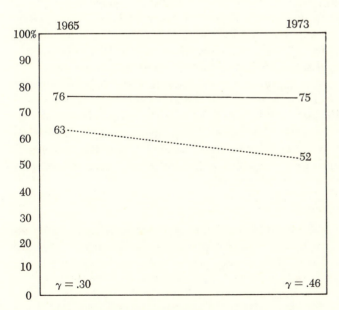

(b) Support for school integration

FIGURE 11.7: Levels of Civic Tolerance among Protestors and Nonprotestors (College Graduates)

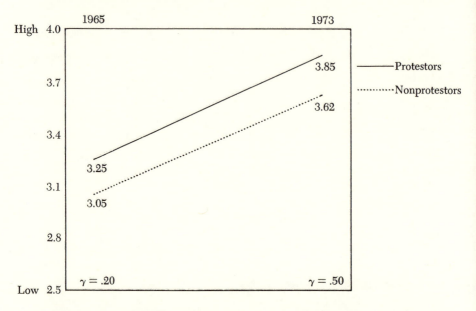

unconventional behavior. Both groups shared in a precipitous rise in
tolerance over the time span, a rise in tune with the secular trend as
well as one reflecting especially the enlightening effects of college
training (Chapter 8).[13] Nevertheless, the distance between the two
groups increased substantially, so that in percentage terms there is a
19% difference in the proportion choosing all three tolerant alternatives. Of course it would seem to be almost a denial of their own rhetoric if the protestors were to reject the civil libertarian element of any
of these assertions. Yet in one sense that is precisely the point. Within
an elite group with remarkably high tolerance levels, the demonstrators still managed to distinguish themselves for some years in the wake
of their own nonconformist behavior.

Trust in Government

Declining confidence in the government, its incumbents, and its policies was inextricably intertwined with the protest movement. We have
already chronicled the plummeting scores on the widely used trust in

[13] A recent study challenges the widely held view that tolerance has increased
over the past two decades by arguing that the objects of intolerance have simply
changed. See John L. Sullivan, James Piereson, and George E. Marcus, "An Alternative Conceptualization of Political Tolerance: Illusory Increases 1950s-1970s,"
American Political Science Review, 73 (September 1979), 781-94.

government measure, a decline fully shared in by the college graduate portion of the youth sample. Since analysis of our own and other youth data point decidedly toward the Vietnam War as the prime factor in the growing distrust among the young,[14] the demonstrators should have exceeded their fellow graduates in the pace of the developing distrust of government. What is not so clear is how substantial that difference would be as late as 1973, at a time when feelings of cynicism had permeated virtually every stratum of the polity. Even more problematic is the question of differing trust levels as of 1965. Were those who became demonstrators already more suspicious and cynical? Or were they the products of basically trusting environments, individuals who had been as "successfully" socialized as their friends, but who, when confronted with a perceived discrepancy between what they had internalized and what they observed in the everyday world, reacted even more strongly than did others?

Our results point decidedly toward the latter alternative. Consider first the results for the political trust index. Beginning in 1965 there was essentially no difference between protestors and nonprotestors in the high regard accorded the federal government (Figure 11.8). What meager difference there was, in fact, saw the protestors as a fraction *more* trusting. So the answer to part of our question is clear enough: as they prepared to enter the larger world of schooling and other endeavors the eventual protestors were imbued with a high degree of trust in the government, both absolutely and relative to their peers.

But if the two groups began the period on an equal footing, they did not end up that way. While nonprotestors dropped a full one and one-half points on the seven-point index, the protestors registered an even more severe drop of about two and one-half points. Many factors could have contributed to this steeper decline by the demonstrators. And in a causal sense, the sharper fall-off in trust might have preceded or coincided with the protest behavior. But when all is said and done, we still have the ultimate outcome that the protestors have separated themselves from others, that their experiences have rendered them the very least trusting.

Further evidence is at hand. According to popular democratic theory, a critical component of trust in governmental institutions is the belief that the authorities are responsive to public opinion. A major complaint of the protestors was that the government was not listening to (certain) people, that it was pursuing its own ends regardless. Vio-

[14] Gregory B. Markus, "The Political Environment and the Dynamics of Public Attitudes: A Panel Study," *American Journal of Political Science*, 23 (May 1979), 338-59; and Jerald G. Bachman and M. Kent Jennings, "The Impact of Vietnam on Trust in Government," *Journal of Social Issues*, 31 (No. 4, 1975), 141-55.

FIGURE 11.8: Political Trust among Protestors and Nonprotestors (College Graduates)

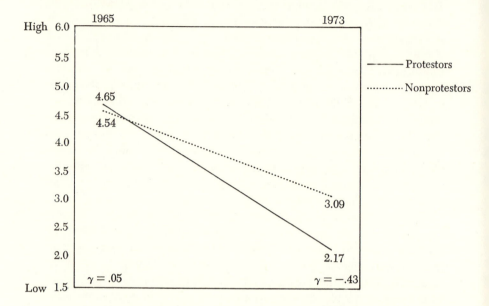

lent behavior often became a way of making the government pay attention. A single question used in both years' surveys asked about this aspect of trust in a direct fashion: "Over the years, how much attention do you feel the government pays to what the people think when it decides what to do, a good deal, some, or not much?"

As with the items making up the trust index, a huge decline in supportive responses occurred here. What is fascinating when comparing the protestors and nonprotestors is that the former originally saw the government as paying more attention ($\gamma = .20$); but in the interim the relationship reversed itself ($\gamma = -.28$). So the demonstrators began with a civics book presumption of a more attentive, responsive government in Washington. For them the disillusionment became more severe, perhaps because they started from a more positive base.

Further confirmation comes from the questions asking about the relative faith and confidence invested in the three levels of government. In 1965 the nascent protestors cast even more votes for the national government than did the nonprotestors ($\gamma = .12$). Again the difference is not large, but that it is there at all belies the contention that the student radicals entered the era disproportionately distrustful of the national government. Indeed, considering their greater liberal sentiments and the general linkage seen at that time between the national government and liberal causes, a finding of this order is not surprising.

Eight years later the relationship had been dramatically reversed. While the nonprotestors also joined in the general denigration of the national government, the protestors led the way with an absolute drop of 52% ($\gamma = -.42$), resulting in one of the most precipitous movements in all of the analyses carried out for this volume. A reverse image of this pattern occurs with respect to the level in which the respondents had the least confidence. In 1965 the two groups were almost equally unlikely to cite the national government as the least trustworthy, whereas by 1973 the demonstrators were much more likely to give the worst marks to the national government (54% vs. 26%). Again it is important to recollect that these 1973 ratings came well after most of the disruptive activities had occurred. Leveling-off effects would have had time to set in. Despite this, the demonstrators remained profoundly less enthusiastic about the national government than did other college graduates. Having pressed their claims on what they saw as the villain, the demonstrators were even more reluctant to restore the national government to its former preeminent position.

A final set of indicators supporting the generation-unit hypothesis comes from questions used only in 1973. Several retrospective questions about the Vietnam War were asked. One ran, "Do you think we did the right thing in getting into the fighting in Vietnam, or should we have stayed out?" Sixty-four percent of the nonprotestors compared with 91% of the protestors said we should have stayed out. Another question was, "Did our participation in the Vietnam War cause you to change any of your views about the United States?" Whereas some 55% of the nonprotestors said that it had, the same was true of 85% of the protestors. Responses to the follow-up question of how their views had changed were overwhelmingly in a negative vein.

Attempts to capture an individual's past attitudes through such questions are notoriously inept. Two considerations can be raised in the present case. First, the findings are fully consistent with those based on before-and-after comparisons wherein the protestors showed more net change. Second, if the protestors had entered the period as relatively less enthusiastic about the U.S. government, then they should have reported less (or at least no more) change of heart than did the nonprotestors. Finally, the existence of the large contrast in 1973 offers an additional indication that the demonstrators had constructed a different political history of the period than their less demonstrative classmates. Fully of a piece with this rendition is the fact that two-thirds of the demonstrators versus one-third of the nondemonstrators subscribed to the proposition that "a change in our whole form of government is needed to solve the problems facing our country."

As a final installment in this story of differential decay in the trust placed in government we may introduce the questions dealing with external efficacy, asked of the youthful respondents only in 1973. We have previously treated the external efficacy index as an indicator of political resources, and it is clear that for substantial elements it does serve that function. But there are grounds for treating it as an indicator of support or trust in the government, for the statements reference the government's responsiveness and concern about people like the respondent.

In light of what we have already observed, we should expect the protestors to be *less* efficacious than nonprotestors, an expectation borne out by the results ($\gamma = -.29$). This modest difference must be placed against the ordinary notion that the more participative people come from the ranks of the more efficacious, especially those participants who perform the more difficult, demanding acts. That is precisely what we found with respect to internal efficacy, as noted above. The positive relationship between protesting and internal efficacy ($\gamma = .33$) is almost equal in magnitude to the negative relationship for external efficacy. Incidentally, this contrasting set of findings for a criterion group such as protestors provides additional support for the contention that the traditional efficacy items contain at least two separate dimensions.[15] Our main point, however, is that we have here another firm indicator that the protestors' summary evaluations of governmental responsiveness put them once more at odds with the nonprotestors.

ACADEMIC MILIEU AND LEVELS OF ACTIVITY

The college graduates' eight-year trends differ markedly according to whether they were involved in the protest movement. As we stated initially, we are not attempting to demonstrate that being a part of the movement caused these differential patterns in any strict sense. Yet we do want to know if the difference between the two groups is simply masking the play of other likely influences. Many of the possible elements of spuriousness have already been suppressed due to the inherent homogeneity of the college graduates as a whole. But large within-group differences certainly remain, some of which could be accounting for the apparent impact of protest behavior. In the first

[15] Philip E. Converse, "Change in the American Electorate," in Angus Campbell and Philip E. Converse, *On the Human Meaning of Social Change* (New York: Russell Sage, 1972); George I. Balch, "Multiple Indicators in Survey Research: The Concept 'Sense of Political Efficacy,'" *Political Methodology*, 1 (Spring 1974), 1-43; and J. Miller McPherson, Susan Welch, and Cal Clark, "The Stability and Reliability of Political Efficacy," *American Political Science Review*, 71 (June 1975), 509-21.

part of this section we take up variations in the academic milieu, an oft-cited determinant of protest phenomena. Another set of differences occurs among the protestors themselves. One of the most prominently mentioned is that between the frequent, intense participants and the one-time, episodic participants. A test of the thesis that protesting makes a difference lies in whether there are predictable variations according to level of protest intensity. That is the theme of the second part of this section. Both parts respond to the challenge that the differences between protestors and nonprotestors are artifactual rather than real.

Academic Milieu

We cited at the outset of our discussion three important academic corollaries of unconventional behavior among the college graduates. Social science majors, students attending colleges in the 10,000 and larger range, and those matriculating at private, nondenominational schools were considerably more likely to have been protestors. That being the case, it would be prudent to make certain that it is not these characteristics that are linked to the observed changes, rather than the presence of protest activity. That is, we want to make sure that the patterns uncovered are not simply the result of the fact that protestors had different majors and attended different sorts of schools.

A straightforward way of doing this is to compare demonstrators and nondemonstrators within each of these classifications. If the two groups continue to exhibit different traits, we can rule out several plausible rival hypotheses. This procedure will also alert us to variations in the relationships according to academic characteristics. A major shortcoming in this approach is that the number of cases available for analysis is quite low, thus requiring very sizeable relationships in order to attain statistical significance. Consequently we will pay more than customary attention to the patterning of results.

We will confine the presentation to attitudes, preferences, and evaluations of governmental performance, since milieu seems to be more consequential in these areas than in those of attentiveness and resources. Turning first to party preference and voting behavior, we find a similar overall pattern within each of the classifications (Table 11.2). At the earlier time points protestors tended to be less Republican than nonprotestors, though not overwhelmingly so. By 1973 the cleavage between the two groups had become extremely pronounced. College major and type of school may have been facilitating or catalytic devices in the partisan swings over time, but it seems that having been involved in the protest world itself seriously retarded Republican voting and identification.

TABLE 11.2: Comparison of Protestors and Nonprotestors, by Academic Milieu[a] (College Graduates)

	Social Science Majors				School Size ≥10,000				Private Colleges			
	Nonprot.	Prot.		Correlation (γ)	Nonprot.	Prot.		Correlation (γ)	Nonprot.	Prot.		Correlation (γ)
Party identification 0 (Dem) - 6 (Rep)												
1965	2.92	2.39	-.53	-.14	3.10	2.39	-.71	-.18	3.64	2.78	-.86	-.29
1973	2.72	1.64	-1.08	-.44	2.72	1.57	-1.15	-.43	3.00	1.70	-1.30	-.56
	-.20	-.75			-.38	-.82			-.64	-1.08		
Presidential preference (% Rep)												
1964	44	21	-23	-.48	38	18	-20	-.48	40	19	-21	-.47
1968	53	22	-31	-.66	57	18	-39	-.80	52	19	-33	-.75
1972	67	15	-52	-.84	61	17	-44	-.76	57	27	-30	-.56
School prayers (% anti)												
1965	27	32	+05	.19	26	36	+10	.13	38	46	+08	.15
1973	50	68	+18	.28	49	70	+21	.42	39	72	+33	.60
	+27	+36			+23	+34			+01	+26		
School integration (% pro)												
1965	61	68	+07	.16	64	72	+08	.19	68	89	+21	.54
1973	65	95	+30	.84	56	77	+21	.48	41	77	+36	.59
	+04	+27			-08	+05			-27	-12		

TABLE 11.2 (cont.)

	Social Science Majors			School Size ≥10,000			Private Colleges			
	Nonprot.	Prot.	Correlation (γ)	Nonprot.	Prot.	Correlation (γ)	Nonprot.	Prot.		Correlation (γ)
Civic tolerance 1 (Low) - 4 (High)										
1965	3.08	3.27	.16	3.05	3.20	.13	3.50	3.25	-.30	-.37
1973	3.66	3.89	.57	3.60	3.89	.69	3.78	3.85	+.07	.34
	+.58	+.62		+.55	+.69		+.28	+.65		
Gov't level most trusted (% nat'l.)										
1965	85	79	-.20	86	89	.11	92	92	0	.02
1973	62	42	-.38	65	35	-.57	48	33	-15	-.29
	-23	-37		-21	-54		-44	-59		
Political trust 1 (Low) - 6 (High)										
1965	4.56	4.55	.08	4.62	5.02	.28	4.22	4.50	+.38	.15
1973	2.98	2.16	-.48	2.95	2.16	-.43	2.52	2.29	-.23	-.04
	-1.58	-2.39		-1.67	-2.86		-1.70	-2.11		
Gov't attentiveness to public opinion 1 (Low) - 5 (High)										
1965	3.60	4.05	.32	3.98	4.02	.08	3.72	4.23	+.51	.39
1973	3.37	2.71	-.54	3.23	2.73	-.36	3.08	3.00	-.08	-.06
	-.23	-1.34		-.75	-1.29		-.64	-1.23		
External political efficacy 1 (Low) - 5 (High)										
1973	2.64	2.36	-.33	2.51	2.20	-.43	2.58	2.52	-.06	-.04

a Maximum N's for the table categories are as follows: Social Science Majors = 44 nonprotestors, 50 protestors; School Size ≥10,000 = 61 nonprotestors, 46 protestors; Private Colleges = 25 nonprotestors, 27 protestors.

A parallel finding emerges for the three indicators of issue preferences for which we have over-time materials. In 1965 the two groups were, with one exception among liberal arts students, scarcely distinguishable in their attitudes about school integration and prayers in the public schools. What difference there was consisted of the eventual protestors being more liberal. Eight years produced a remarkable shift. Despite the meager N's involved, five of the six relationships are significant at the $\leq.02$ level. By the same token, the associations undergo a radical change for the civic tolerance index among social science majors and those who attended large schools. Only among those going to private schools is the 1973 relationship insignificant, and here it is interesting to note that in 1965 the *nonprotestors* were substantially more tolerant. Protestors caught up with the nonprotestors in the interim.

Our findings for the entire group of college graduates also hold in the domain of governmental evaluations. As of 1965 the protestors and nonprotestors did not differ in a statistically significant sense in terms of the level of government they most trusted. Both groups shared in the dramatic drop in confidence accorded the national government, but the decline was much sharper among the protestors. The same development occurs with respect to the political trust measure. Positive relationships in 1965 became negative ones eight years later. Again, however, the pattern among those going to private schools, while in the hypothesized direction, is not as accentuated. The single item dealing with the attentiveness of government to ordinary people exhibits the same diachronic pattern. Regardless of milieu, protestors more often saw the government as attentive in 1965, but less frequently so in 1973. Finally, using external efficacy scores as an indicator of governmental responsiveness, we see that in 1973 the protestors, aside from those in the liberal arts colleges, were much less positive than were the nonprotestors.

On balance we have found that the portrayal of demonstrators and nondemonstrators based on the full complement of college graduates has its sequel within three critical subgroups. The progressively accelerating differences between the two are not spurious ones due to the differential collegiate environments or courses of study being pursued. Having said that, it is nevertheless apparent that the overall pattern was less well reproduced within the private school category. These students more often started off with fewer differences between them (though partisanship proved to be an exception) and also wound up less differentiated. Recruitment from a more homogeneous environment and a collegiate experience in a more intimate and homogeneous setting probably account for this singularity. By the same token, alterations tended to be most marked among students in the larger universities. Greater heterogeneity, more conflictual campuses, and greater polarization helped drive a wedge between the demonstrators and nondemonstrators.[16]

Another method for evaluating the discriminatory power of having been a protestor assesses the relative role of protest behavior as compared with the other variables we have been using. Each of the attitudes and evaluations being treated became the dependent variable in a multiple regression analysis. In addition to the protest variable, the regressor variables included the 1965 analogue of the dependent variable, race, and three dummy variables representing whether the student was a social science major, had attended a school with a student body of $\geq 10,000$, and whether the school was private and nondenominational.[17] Our aim here is not to build an all-inclusive model for testing the direct and indirect effects of protest on attitudes and evaluations. Rather, it is to establish whether protesting continues to make a contribution to the 1973 scores once a number of prominent threats are taken into account.

Does having been a demonstrator continue to make a difference? To answer this question four items of information are presented in Table 11.3—the multiple correlation (R) for the equations, the unstandardized (b) and standardized (β) regression coefficients for the protest variable, and the rank order of the protest variable (based on the magnitude of the β's) as one of several predictors. In evaluating the multiple R it should be borne in mind that we are dealing with a restricted, more homogeneous set of people than if we included all of the youth sample. For some of the variables the variance has already been reduced by having dropped the non-college graduates.

Regardless of which attitude or evaluation is considered, protest behavior makes a substantial and statistically significant contribution. Somewhat surprisingly, it is the strongest predictor of the four measures denoting trust in federal government, stronger even than the 1965 scores on these same measures. Moreover, having attended a large or private school typically fails to make any meaningful contribution to the 1973 scores. Having been a social science major is significantly related to about one-half of the measures, but in no instance does that relationship eradicate the independent effects of protest activity. Whatever contribution protesting makes is not due to the hidden workings of these various corollaries of protest.

[16] For a discussion of the relationship between college size and protest activity see Joseph W. Scott and Mohamed El-Assel, "Multiversity, University Size, University Quality and Student Protest," *American Sociological Review*, 34 (October 1969), 202-209.

[17] For the equations involving the 1968 and 1972 presidential preference, the reported preference for the immediate past presidential election was also included.

TABLE 11.3: Effects of Protesting on Political Orientations,
with Other Factors Controlled (College Graduates)

	R	b	β	Rank[a]
Party identification	.55	.21[b]	.25	2
1968 Presidential preference (Rep)	.51	−.07	−.23	2
1972 Presidential preference (Rep)	.64	−.08	−.28	2
School prayers (anti)	.40	.17*	.16	2
School integration (pro)	.35	.12*	.14	2
Civil tolerance	.33	.05	.17	2
Level of gov't most confidence in (nat'l scored high)	.27	−.07	−.25	1
Level of gov't least confidence in (nat'l scored high)	.34	.09	.33	1
Political trust	.41	−.21	−.28	1
External efficacy	.25	−.06*	−.14	1

[a] Based on the magnitudes of the β's.
[b] Unless otherwise indicated, all coefficients are significant at the .001 level.
* Significant at .01-.02.

As a final check on whether the protest variable was simply masking the effects of some associated factors, we reran the regressions, incorporating all of the youth sample. Because we were no longer physically separating out the college graduates, education was added as an independent variable. Without exception, having been a demonstrator continued to be substantially related to each of the attitudinal and evaluational measures, all of the relationships being significant at the .01 level. These results supply yet another confirmation of the contention that the protestors emerged as a distinctive generation-unit, that there was something inherent in being a part of the protest movement that ultimately differentiated them from other members of the class of 1965.

The Intensity Principle

There is another way in which we may test the proposition that the results associated with having been a demonstrator point toward the development of a generation-unit. This method will also help support the theory that a public, unconventional enactment of a privately held political viewpoint provides a powerful reinforcement effect. What we will do is divide the demonstrators into those who reported only one specific activity ($N = 59$) versus those who engaged in a multiple number of activities ($N = 59$).[18] We will refer to this division as indi-

[18] Because of ambiguous or incomplete information regarding the circumstances and timing of the protest activities, the total N here of 118 is lower than the N of 129 used previously.

cating the intensity of the behavioral experience and as the degree of commitment to the movement. Other things being equal, those individuals who engage repeatedly in a dramatic act such as public protest should receive more reinforcement and strengthening of the underlying ideology than those who do it only once. If the constellation of experiences surrounding protest behavior really has played a part in separating the protestors from nonprotestors over the eight-year period of our study, then those having shared in that experience most completely should set themselves even further apart from the nondemonstrators. Our ability to make such comparisons is hampered by the presence of ceiling and floor effects. That is, protestors as a whole sometimes virtually exhausted the extremes of our various measures, so that we cannot sort out the effects of intensity. For example, on the civic tolerance measure almost nine in ten of all protestors had the highest possible score. However, we have enough illustrations to test the soundness of our argument.

There are plentiful signs that intensity is consequential even in the areas of political attentiveness and resources. One very persuasive piece of evidence appears in the domain of political salience at the primary group level. As high school seniors the less intense protestors reported a slightly higher rate of political discussion in their families than did the frequent protestors—51% vs. 48% describing this as occurring several times a week. (Frequent protestors did report talking politics more with friends—44% vs. 31% saying several times a week.) Using a parallel measure in 1973, that of political conversations with one's spouse, we find a marked shift. Some 59% of the intense protestors report talking politics "very often" with their spouses compared with 32% of the less intense ($\gamma = .48$).

Other evidence points toward a shifting relationship according to level of activity. Whereas the less intense had expressed considerably more interest in public affairs at the verbal level in 1965 ($-.49$), by 1973 the two groups differed much less ($-.18$). Similarly, the relationship between intensity and internal efficacy shifted from a negative one ($-.26$) to a slightly positive one ($.12$). While the ratio of active to allegiant portrayals of the model citizen went from 2.01 to 5.16 among the less active, it jumped from 2.37 to 7.35 among the more vigorous. Finally, the two groups differed in terms of the frequency with which they engaged in "conventional" activities in the 1965-1973 period. The more committed outperformed the less committed by wide margins on all of the seven activities listed in Figure 11.3 (above). Thus just as the demonstrators differentiated themselves from the nondemonstrators, the more engaged demonstrators tended to become relatively more involved and participative than the less engaged.

To the degree that behavior strengthens the pull toward or away from attitude objects, we should also discover intensity effects in the domain of preferences and evaluations. Results with respect to partisanship provide the firmest support for this proposition. At the beginning of the period the less intense protestors were the more Democratic. Counting as Democrats all those who identified outright with the party or were Independents leaning that way, some 74% of the less intense versus 59% of the more intense could be classified as Democratic partisans. Eight years later, the figure for the less intense remained exactly the same, whereas there had been an 18% rise (to 77%) among the more intense.

Turning to voting preferences, the outcomes are equally convincing. Figure 11.9 contains the reported Republican preferences for three presidential contests. For comparative purposes the display also contains the balance of the college graduates, i.e., the nondemonstrators. The movements here are nothing short of spectacular. We have already shown that the gulf between nondemonstrators and demonstrators as a whole expanded sharply across time. What this further break-

FIGURE 11.9: Republican Preference in Presidential Elections, by Level of Protest Activity (College Graduates)

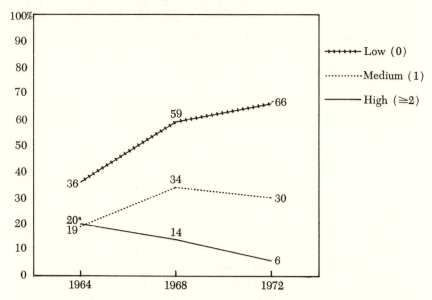

ª The average of the medium- and high-level protestors is 1% lower than the percentage reported in Figure 11.5 for all protestors due to 11 cases being dropped in constructing the intensity variable.

down shows is the degree to which manifest commitment to the movement widened that breach even further. Beginning with essentially no difference in the 1964 contest, a gap between the more and less intense also increased as the political drama was played out. The strong activists proceeded on a course directly opposite that of the nonprotestors, so that by 1972 there was a 60% difference in their support of Richard Nixon.

It would be difficult to disregard the probable impact of protest intensity in evaluating these results in the partisanship domain. Richard Nixon became the electoral symbol of much that the most avid participants in the movement detested about American public life. His departure from the active scene may have served subsequently to bring the more intense and less intense closer together in voting inclinations. Nevertheless, the act of voting almost unanimously against Nixon can only have served to hasten and intensify the swing of the more committed protestors to an identification with the Democratic party. To the extent that party identification represents more of a long-term, enduring psychological attachment, the switch observed among the intense demonstrators is eloquent testimony to the probable enduring effects of protest activity.

Although rather fragmentary, the results in the area of public policy preferences also support the contention that those most involved in the protest movement underwent more change in their orientations. Civil rights is the only issue area that meets the conditions of saliency across the eight-year stretch, the availability of good indicators at each time point, and the absence of ceiling effects. Despite the slippage of civil rights on the political agenda and the frequent conflicts in strategy between those focusing primarily on the antiwar movement and those stressing the civil rights campaign, there is little doubt that much was shared between the two movements. Our question is whether the intense activists, most of whom had demonstrated against the war rather than against racial discrimination, were so caught up in the antiwar movement that they began to render relatively less moral support to civil rights than did those not so involved in the antiwar cause.

Two findings speak directly to the question. Even in 1965 the intense protestors more strongly favored school integration—81% compared with 69% for the less intense. The figures for the intense remained identical in 1973 but dropped slightly among the less intense. Coupled with shifts in the other response categories this meant that the overall relationship grew from $\gamma = .23$ to .34. A second finding parallels this one. In 1965 the less intense white protestors were a shade more likely to claim that they had black friends—49% vs. 42% for the more intense. By 1973 the relationship was reversed, with 64% of the more intense compared with 57% of the less intense professing to have black friends. Thus the more committed white demonstrators scored a net gain of 14% in relation to the less committed.

Notwithstanding the vicissitudes of the civil rights movement during the late sixties and early seventies, the most demonstrative of the student protestors continued to render it and its objects of concern high absolute and relative support. Instead of displacing a moral commitment to improving the lot of blacks, intense engagement in the protest movement abetted it. This outcome is all the more impressive in light of the declining salience of the civil rights struggle.

The effects of intensity on group evaluations are not confined to the domain of race. Prominent among the targets of the protest movement were the giant corporations, which were accused of profiting immensely from the war and of being a central part of the so-called establishment. More than one confrontation erupted over the efforts of large corporations to recruit on the campus. We have previously recounted the enormous decline in favorable ratings accorded big business over the life of our study, a decline especially noticeable among the college educated (Chapter 8).

What can be added to this account is that whereas the demonstrators and nondemonstrators differed by only a shade in 1965, the ensuing decline was more drastic among the demonstrators; and within the latter group the drop was even more precipitous among the most involved. By 1973 the mean thermometer ratings of big business on the 0-100° scale were as follows: nondemonstrators, 44; moderate demonstrators, 38; and frequent demonstrators, 25. These differences are all very large in an absolute sense. The low mark accorded big business by the very committed is one of the very lowest registered for *any* group about which they were asked, being overtaken only by the rating of 23 given to the military. The gap between the less and more vociferous protestors is also one of the largest encountered.

Finally, we can address the question of whether frequency of behavior accompanied a differential movement in the widespread decline in approval accorded governmental institutions. Despite the intuitively sound proposition that more frequent displays directed against an object should lead to greater negative evaluations of that object, our findings on this score are not overwhelming. In part we are caught by ceiling and floor effects. Political trust of the national government had descended from almost universally high readings to nearly equal low readings among all protestors. Further differentiation is difficult within our measurement framework.

Three suggestive findings are on hand, however. It will be recalled that protestors and nonprotestors reversed themselves on the degree to which they felt the government paid attention to public opinion. Not surprisingly, that switch was most pronounced among the intense participants. In 1965 they had been only marginally more likely than the less intense to deny the government's attentiveness ($\gamma = .14$). This difference stretched out considerably in the interim ($\gamma = .33$). A second suggestive finding comes in the area of citizenship norms. If we take declarations of allegiant behavior as signs of positive affect, then the more active protestors underwent a greater loss of affect. Among the less intense the drop in the proportion giving any allegiant description was 24%; among the more intense it was 33%. Finally, we also found variations in the area of external efficacy, an area that we argued previously is in part an indicator of system responsiveness. Although the differences are very modest, by 1973 the more intense felt less efficacious in this respect than did the less intense ($\gamma = -.17$).

Overall, the degree of protest commitment as indexed by frequency of participation apparently supplied a boost that often carried the intense activists beyond the degree and type of changes experienced by their less intense fellows. In addition to illustrating how behavior can strengthen and solidify political attitudes and evaluations, our findings also support the thesis that the chain of events associated with protesting—and not some hidden factors—facilitated and abetted the generally expanding gap between demonstrators and nondemonstrators among these college graduates. Materials to be presented in the following section will strengthen that interpretation.

Protestors and the Politics of the 1970s

Relying almost exclusively on indicators for which we had repeated observations, we have demonstrated the growing dissimilarity between protestors and nonprotestors. With only occasional exceptions this trend applied to attitudes and evaluations as well as to political attentiveness and resources, and apparently to other forms of political participation as well. As we have acknowledged at several points in our presentation, however, our replicated indicators of attitudes and evaluations are deficient on two counts. In the first place, we have relatively few of them, so that the range is limited. A second point is that new issues and personalities had entered the political scene by 1973, a large number of which could scarcely have been contemplated eight years previously. To determine the relative ideological standing of yesteryear's protestors in the likely context of post-Vietnam politics, we need to employ measures available only from the 1973 soundings.

Our procedures here will follow in general the lines pursued earlier. The primary way in which the confounding effects of education will be handled is by restricting our analysis in large part to the set of college graduates. Again, this will provide us with a relatively pure set of respondents on several counts. Since we have reason to believe that degree of protest activity is important, we will again divide the demonstrators into one-time versus multiple-time participants. A brief look will be directed to possible erosion effects by dividing the protestors into recent versus more distant participants. As one check on our assessments via these methods we will also employ a multivariate analysis of the entire youth sample. Three types of attitudinal indicators will be used: self-locations on the seven-point issue scales, ratings of groups and individuals on the feeling thermometer, and appraisals of differential group influence in American politics.

Issue Positions and Group Evaluations

Any doubts as to the basic policy divisions between the participants and nonparticipants in the protest movement should be erased by the figures in Table 11.4. Without exception there is a wide gulf between the two, as summarized by the gamma coefficients (fourth column). This is true of the six specific issues, as well as of the two of a more global nature—whether there should be some changes in the American form of government, and the individual's location on the political liberalism-conservatism dimension. While the differences are large across the

TABLE 11.4: Self-Location on Public Policy Issues, by Level of Protest Activity (College Graduates)

	Number of Protest Activities			Correlation (γ)	
	Low (0)	Medium (1)	High ($\geq$2)	Low vs. medium and high	Medium vs. high
Gov't guarantee jobs	3.58[a]	4.61	5.32	.53	.34
Busing for integration	2.90	3.88	4.96	.58	.34
Gov't help minorities	4.34	4.98	5.74	.44	.37
Protect rights of accused	4.55	5.32	5.83	.45	.27
Legalize marijuana	4.46	5.59	6.46	.58	.49
Equality for women	5.53	6.02	6.64	.47	.55
Change form of gov't	3.72	4.51	5.17	.42	.30
Conservative-liberal self-placement	4.10	5.21	5.54	.64	.28

[a] Entries are mean scores on the 1-7 point scales; the higher the score the more liberal the response.

board, it is significant that they are as strong on the new issues of sexual equality and the legalization of marijuana. These are symptomatic of the life-style, non-bread and butter issues that formed so much a part of the new politics. Nor did such issues fade away as the Vietnam War and Watergate receded and as economic stress developed in the late 1970s. The new values espoused by the demonstrators are clearly manifested in the striking differences shown here.

Equally compelling are the gaps between the more intensely and less intensely involved demonstrators. As revealed in a comparison of the mean scores and also in the summary coefficients (last column), there is not as much distance according to level of engagement as there is between demonstrators and nondemonstrators as a whole. But it must be recalled that we are now dealing with a matter of shade rather than color. Whether the attitudinal differences by level of intensity preceded, followed, or accompanied the differential levels of protest intensity is difficult to sort out, but in one sense is not the major point anyway. What is important is that these highly committed activists of the protest era carried with them into the 1970s and their adulthood a set of political views that stamped them as the epitome of a generation-unit.

Another area in which sizeable differences emerge is that of group evaluations. Collectivities tended to be identified rather indiscriminately as friends or enemies during the protest era. Some of the passion directed toward certain groups has probably subsided even since the time of our 1973 observations; and some groups that were practically household words during the height of the movement have all but faded from everyday vocabulary. Other groups, or at least the qualities with which they were invested, have persisted and continue to be symbols of deep cleavages in the polity. Thermometer ratings of six of the groups asked about in 1973 are presented in Figure 11.10. To highlight the polarities involved we have selected three groups widely perceived to be conservative and three held to be liberal.

Our threefold classification yields impressive variations. Demonstrators as a whole are much less generous than nondemonstrators about the conservative groupings and much more generous with respect to the liberal bodies. And the high-level demonstrators exceed the mid-level ones in the expected directions, though the distance between the two is much shorter vis-à-vis the liberal targets. An interesting feature of the pattern is that the nonprotestors give their highest marks to policemen and, by a huge margin, their lowest to radical students. These two groups were often physically and symbolically at odds with each other; it is manifest where the sympathies of onlookers lay even in the twilight of the movement.

Figure 11.10: Evaluations of Political Groups, by Level of Protest Activity[a] (College Graduates)

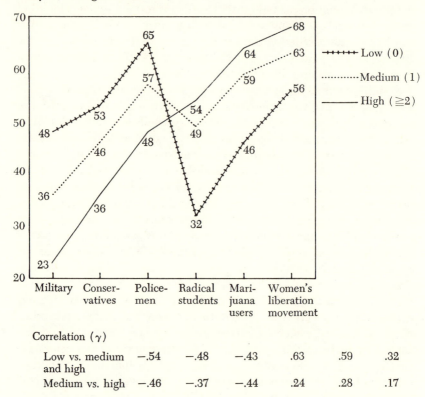

Correlation (γ)

	Military	Conservatives	Policemen	Radical students	Marijuana users	Women's liberation movement
Low vs. medium and high	−.54	−.48	−.43	.63	.59	.32
Medium vs. high	−.46	−.37	−.44	.24	.28	.17

[a] Entries are scores on the 0-100° thermometer; the higher the score the more favorable the evaluation.

By contrast the protestors have a much more favorable view of radical students, with the result that the largest dissimilarity emerges here. Of course, higher rankings by the protestors are a form of self-validation, since at least some of them undoubtedly labeled themselves in that very way during the movement. Many protestors, however, viewed themselves as acting fully in the American tradition, and others dissociated themselves from such fringe elements as the Weathermen. Because of the disapprobation attached to the term radical, the ratings applied to radical students even by our intense protestors are lower than might be expected.

In any event, the larger message is apparent enough: protestors had sorted themselves out from other college graduates within their cohort, and frequent protestors made themselves particularly distinctive.

Particular groups might rise and fall in the future, but it seems highly likely that the general configuration portrayed here will persist for some time. These differential evaluations seem to be rooted and reinforced in the differential historical experiences of what we can now more confidently call generation-units.

Images of groups can be used in another way to illustrate the political cleavages within this cohort. A common part of the protest rhetoric was the call for a redistribution of power and influence in American society. The student protestors were neither the first nor the last to voice such calls, but they were exceptional in that they, as a privileged class not yet fully of age politically, were making such claims on behalf of relatively powerless groups as well as on their own behalf. We took advantage of this concern with the redistribution of power to ask whether the youths perceived various groups in American society as having too much influence, about the right amount of influence, or not enough influence.[19] Results bearing on six such groups are presented in Figure 11.11. These groups would usually be bracketed under the label of the less powerful, even though some of them are numerically quite large.

That the protestors more frequently saw all of these collectivities as having too little influence comes as no surprise. With the possible exception of intellectuals, they are all a standard part of the shopping list of groups seen as being discriminated against and needing more clout. Two features stand out. One is the magnitude of the perceived inequities across such a wide spectrum. Although the demonstrators have their favorite underdogs, the absolute proportions perceiving all six groups as too weak are impressive. A second feature is the degree to which the three levels of protestors differentiate themselves. Each movement along the protest measure brings a very decided jump in calls for more influence. Significantly, these jumps are just as noticeable for "newer" groups such as women and young people as for the older, more traditional have-nots of blacks and the poor.

Lest it be thought that these results reflect a positivity bias among the protestors, it should be noted that judgments about conservative groups tend to be a mirror image of those just presented. Here the standard is whether the groups are perceived as having too much influence. Three examples will illustrate the point. Beliefs that the Republicans have too much influence ranged from 25% among the non-

[19] The exact wording was: "Some people think that certain groups have too much influence in American life, while other people feel that certain groups don't have as much influence as they deserve. On this card are three statements about how much influence a group might have. For each group I read to you, just tell me the number of the statement that best says how you feel."

FIGURE 11.11: Groups with Too Little Influence, by Level of Protest
Activity (College Graduates)

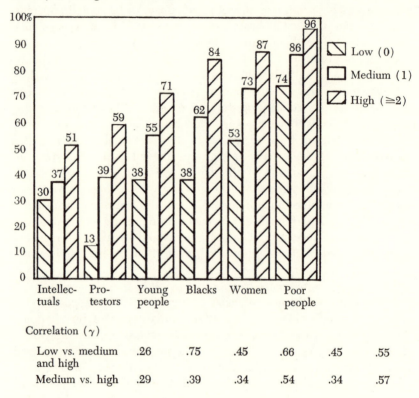

Correlation (γ)						
Low vs. medium and high	.26	.75	.45	.66	.45	.55
Medium vs. high	.29	.39	.34	.54	.34	.57

protestors to 40% and 56% of the less and more intense protestors, respectively. Corresponding figures with respect to Southerners were 12%,
24%, and 35%. Finally, even though big business was almost universally
perceived by all these college graduates as having too much influence,
there was the customary progression from 87% to 91% to 96%.

Taking all these results into account, it is abundantly clear that the
contemporary issue positions, group evaluations, and influence assessments of protestors as a whole diverge markedly from those who were
not caught up in the movement. And degree of commitment or involvement, as represented by repeated behavioral acts, is faithfully
reproduced in the visible attitudinal differences within the ranks of
the protestors themselves. As with the over-time materials, we performed the same analysis within three key strata known to be heavily
populated with protestors, viz., social science majors, students at large
universities, and students at private liberal arts colleges. The pattern

for college graduates as a whole proved to be very robust within these critical subcategories also. Sharp differences continued to characterize the protestors and nonprotestors.

A true test of a generation-unit is whether its view of the world will persist in the face of a changing personal and political environment. Admittedly, our youthful protestors are still relatively close in calendar time to their protest era. Future developments may bring them closer to their generational compatriots. As of their mid-twenties, however, they bore the indelible print of a political ideology fired in the kiln of protest politics.

Erosion Effects

A common palliative offered to those who were upset by the protestors was that time was the great physician, that after leaving the milieu of the campuses and entering the "real world" the dissenters would assume their rightful places as members of the more privileged ranks in society. Not only would their rancorous behavior subside, but the holding of extreme views about the ills and cures of American society would diminish. This life-cycle interpretation was complemented by the historical one: with the disappearance of the Vietnam War the raison d'être of the protest movement would also disappear and with it the perversities of the young. While in some respects these prognoses have been realized, it is equally clear that the residues of the period remain at both the societal and individual levels. The status quo ante did not reappear.

At the individual level we have seen that by 1973 the erstwhile demonstrators had not become indistinguishable from comparably educated individuals in their cohort. Quite the contrary. For this reason, we would infer that whatever erosion effects had set in, they were not sufficient to dampen the differentiation supplied by having been part of the movement. Indeed, one could build a case that this differentiation would increase over time if the two subsets were to develop politically in separate, homogeneous, and reinforcing environments. Nevertheless, there are reasons for suspecting that for many protestors the movement represented a "peak" experience and that the further away in time they move from it the less it will be vitally associated with other political properties. Even among college graduates, to be a demonstrator was to be in the minority. The press of the majority culture would be expected to take its toll with the passage of time.

We can provide a partial test of the erosion effect hypothesis, or its obverse—the recency effect hypothesis. Having obtained the specific years during which the students demonstrated, sat in, or marched, we were able to allocate them into distant versus recent categories. Those who demonstrated before 1970 were placed in the older category, and those who had demonstrated since then were put in the newer category. Those falling into both periods were counted only once, in the new category. This split produces a total of 59 old and 57 recent demonstrators among the college graduates.[20]

There are some biases at work in this division. For example, nonwhites were more likely to have protested earlier, a corollary to the diminishing prominence of civil rights demonstrations as the period wore on. Students further removed from their college days were also disproportionately represented among the distant participants. There is little that can be done about such biases. In the case of nonwhites the impact is small because they comprise but one-tenth of the protestors. As for the bias by proximity to college attendance, that is undoubtedly connected to other factors—some of them completely idiosyncratic—affecting the timing of college attendance. There is no inherent reason why it should be these factors rather than the timing of the protest behavior that would yield whatever differences we might uncover; but there is no good way to untangle these complexities statistically. One potentially crippling bias *not* at work here is that of protest intensity; the correlation between recency and intensity is $\tau_b = .10$.

If erosion effects are at work, the patterns found among demonstrators as a whole should be attenuated among the distant activists and exaggerated among the recent ones. One way of showing this effect is to relate the remoteness of demonstrating to the dependent variables we have been working with. For convenience we will score the recent demonstrators low and the old demonstrators high. All of our dependent variables will be scored to run from conservative or status-quo oriented to liberal or reform oriented. Thus a negative relationship means that the more distant the protest behavior the less liberal or reform oriented the 1973 scores on the various indicators. The greater the magnitude of the negative relationship, the greater the implicit erosion effect. From the opposite side of the same coin, the greater is the recency effect.

Judging only by the sign of the relationships there is some support for the erosion hypothesis. The sign is negative on the six specific issues asked about, using the seven-point scales. The same is true of self-placement on the general liberal-conservative scale, but not so with respect to the question of whether the American form of government should be changed. These correlations (gamma) run from −.18

[20] As with the intensity classification, this one produces a total N lower than 129 due to ambiguous and incomplete details about the specifics of the protest activity.

on protecting minority rights to $-.38$ on the issue of women's equality. Although these relationships are properly signed, they are quite modest for the most part and are dwarfed by those between nonprotestors and protestors as a whole and by those between one-time and frequent protestors. Moreover, only one of the seven relationships reaches statistical significance at the .05 level. Still, we cannot reject erosion out of hand.

If we had found confirmatory evidence in the areas of group evaluations and influence assessments, we would feel more secure about the presence of such effects. Of the six groups evaluated on the thermometer and reported in Figure 11.10 (above), the correlation signs support the erosion hypothesis in only four instances. And for only one of these, the ratings of the women's liberation movement, does the relationship achieve significance at even the .05 level. Taking all the thermometer ratings of groups and personalities into account, it is true that in the great majority of cases the more recent demonstrators are marginally more liberal.

Of the six groups appraised in terms of whether they had the appropriate amount of influence, the sign was "correct" in only three instances and in no case was the relationship large enough to be significant at the .05 level. An examination of the several other groups assessed in this fashion also produced mixed and weak results, with more correct than incorrect signs. On balance there are traces of erosion effects in the area of group evaluations and influence appraisals, but they are modest at best.

What is the meaning of these results for interpreting the impact of the protest experience? It seems reasonably clear that if there is to be decay, it has not yet set in with any force. Certainly for the pre-1970 demonstrators there has been ample time for any immediate deflation. Yet they are nearly as leftward in their thinking as are the more recent participants. Of course most of these college graduates are still very much in the process of settling down, of establishing themselves occupationally, socially, and residentially. Conceivably the environmental press in which most will find themselves will pull them in the direction of their majoritarian, nonprotesting fellows. Fading memories and a failure to "recharge the batteries" may have their effect. Still, one has to be impressed with the apparent staying power of the protest experience. The failure to find appreciable differences by recency of protest activity supports the thesis of unique, enduring generation-unit effects.

A Multivariate Analysis

Coupled with our analysis of the over-time patterns, the more recent, one-time soundings provide a strong basis for claiming that the protest experience symbolized a (re)socializing episode in the political development of these young adults, one that helped stamp them as a generation-unit within the larger generation. Working only with the college graduate stratum, we have established that by their mid-twenties these cohort members could be distinguished by whether they were veterans of the protest movement and by the intensity of their involvement. We have also established that erosion effects, if any, were weak. We need now to step back and consider for a moment the *entire* youth sample from the standpoint of how consequential protesting was in a larger sense. Two purposes will be served by doing this. It will provide a double check on our inference that the protest experience was making a genuine and unique contribution to subsequent political preferences as assayed in 1973. It will also yield an indication of the magnitude of that contribution relative to the contribution of other factors.

To achieve this broader picture we employed a multiple regression analysis of the questions dealing with issues, group evaluations, and influence appraisals. All of these items are associated with the familiar liberal-conservative dimension. Because we do not have 1965 readings of these same items, we used as predictor variables several pre-1973 soundings that were known to have, in virtually all cases, a bivariate relationship with the 1973 items. From the 1965 interviews these measures included opinions on the issues of integrating the schools and the use of prayers in public school; the civic tolerance index, composed of responses to three more abstract, hypothetical statements; party identification; and race. From the 1973 interviews we used educational achievement and the threefold measure of protest activity. Since these two latter measures stand for phenomena that occurred well before the 1973 data gathering, we can say that all seven of the predictor variables are antecedent in time to the measurement of the attitudes and evaluations comprising our dependent variables.

One shortcoming in this procedure is that the protest variable may simply be acting as a surrogate for a more generalized conservative-liberal orientation that was developed or abetted during the eight-year period. That is, the substitution of some other indicator(s) of liberalism might perform the same function as the protest indicator. Because protesting is positively related to virtually every indicator of liberal attitudes that we have employed, this argument cannot be dismissed lightly, especially since one could argue that attitude change or crystallization occurred anterior to protesting. Although we would contend that the many-sided approach used in our analysis supports the thesis of a unique effect from, or association with protesting, it seems prudent to provide still another check.

A very strong testing device is at hand in the form of the respondents' self-placement on the liberalism-conservatism scale. As we saw earlier, protesting is related to scores on that scale, but not so strongly as to present colinearity problems ($r = .33$). Therefore, a second series of regressions was run with the addition of this variable. In some senses this inclusion provides too strong a test because protesting may have pushed people further along toward the liberal end of the scale or the two may have been moving in tandem. Moreover, by including this measure we are introducing a contemporaneous attitude, one that clearly lies within the same dimensional framework as most of the dependent variables in the equations. We are relating attitudes to attitudes in that respect. If the protest variable survives as a significant predictor under these adverse circumstances, our reasoning will be all the more confirmed.

Table 11.5 presents the relevant information under both sets of circumstances. The multiple R is given as a reference point and the unstandardized (b) and standardized coefficients (β) show the contribution of the protest variable with the remaining variables controlled. To provide a crude guideline of the relative importance of protesting, the rank order of the β associated with the protest variable is also shown.

Consider first the results with the global, liberal-conservative measure excluded. Across the three domains of issue positions, group evaluations, and influence assessments the net impact of the protest variable is universally strong and statistically significant. There are variations that could be dealt with more extensively, but for our purposes the general picture is sufficient. Note too the relative place of protesting compared with the other predictors. In sixteen cases it emerges as the most powerful predictor, and in the three other instances it stands second.

Turning to the results based on including scores from the liberal-conservative scale, we find the expected. The rise in the multiple R is primarily a consequence of the fact that we have now introduced another indicator of the kind of attitudes being referenced by the dependent variables. We have also lost some "noise" because those youths not placing themselves on the liberal-conservative continuum (14%) are dropped from the analysis. More relevant for our discussion, the values for the protest variable all decrease in magnitude, some by a good bit, others less so. For the reasons spelled out earlier, this is precisely what should happen. Despite this attrition, fourteen of the nineteen relationships remain significant at the .001 level and all of them at the .05 level. We conclude that having been a demonstrator continues to make a difference even under these stringent statistical conditions.

TABLE 11.5: Effects of Protest Activity Level, with Other Factors Controlled (Entire Youth Sample)

	Excluding liberal-conservative scale				Including liberal-conservative scale			
	R	b	β	Rank[a]	R	b	β	Rank[a]
Issues								
Gov't guarantee jobs	.35	.83[b]	.28	1	.42	.55	.19	2
Busing for integration	.53	.96	.29	1	.57	.72	.22	2
Gov't help minorities	.41	.55	.18	1	.48	.31	.11	5
Protect rights of accused	.27	.49	.15	1	.37	.25*	.08	3
Equality for women	.38	.54	.16	2	.44	.25*	.08	3
Legalize marijuana	.47	1.08	.26	1	.53	.73	.19	3
Change form of gov't	.33	.83	.27	1	.41	.57	.19	2
Group Evaluations								
The military	.46	−10.92	−.24	1	.52	−7.42	−.17	3
Conservatives	.33	−6.67	−.23	1	.55	−2.27*	−.08	2
Policemen	.36	−8.84	−.25	1	.38	−7.23	−.21	1
Radical students	.39	11.01	.30	1	.44	8.65	.25	1
Marijuana users	.39	9.33	.21	1	.44	5.91	.14	3
Women's liberation movement	.27	6.91	.17	1	.35	5.00	.13	2
Influence Assessments								
Intellectuals	.21	.11	.10	2	.24	.08**	.08	5
Young people	.21	.18	.16	1	.28	.11	.11	2
Poor people	.21	.13	.13	1	.24	.09*	.10	2
Blacks	.39	.25	.19	2	.44	.15	.11	4
Women	.35	.19	.19	1	.38	.14	.14	2
Protestors	.42	.39	.30	1	.47	.28	.22	2

[a] Based on the magnitudes of the β's.
[b] Unless otherwise indicated, all coefficients are significant at the .001 level.
* Significant at .01-.02.
** Significant at .04.

In sum, the use of both physical and statistical controls provides supportive evidence for the role of the protest experience. Conservatively, one would say that protesting continues to be associated with attitudes and evaluations under *ceteris paribus* conditions. This is extraordinarily important in a political sense for it suggests an enduring cleavage organized around a set of unique historical experiences. More speculatively, one would say that the protest experience had a hand in shaping and reinforcing subsequent political preferences and assessments. By successively rejecting a number of plausible rival explanations, and by showing variation among the ranks of the protestors, we have developed a case for the unique place of protest in their political coming of age.

Conclusion

At the outset of this chapter we presented a discussion of the concept "generation-unit," and speculated that the cluster of activities, interactions, goals, and values associated with protest behavior would identify the protestors as such. It is now time to take stock of the speculations in light of the findings. In brief, a strong argument can be made that the protestors in fact did emerge as a generation-unit within the high school class of 1965. As expected, the protestors came overwhelmingly from the college population, especially from that portion completing its undergraduate education. Thus they had much in common to begin with in terms of social background and exposure. Yet within this stratum the protestors developed into a distinctive subgroup. Nascent differences in 1965 between them and their nonprotesting peers tended to expand considerably over time, especially in the areas of political preferences and evaluations. In many instances these growing contrasts were sharp. A number of tests helped rule out the likelihood that these divergences simply reflected compositional differences between protestors and nonprotestors. Similarly, there were wide differences between the two groups as of 1973 across a great range of political attributes—even when rather stringent statistical controls were imposed. Adding strength to our contentions about the emergence of a generation-unit were the but faint traces of erosion effects and the magnified consequences accompanying more intense levels of protesting. All things considered, the protest segment of our generation of college graduates seems truly to have been reacting to and coping in unique fashion with the history common to the entire generation.

To appreciate the uniqueness of the protestors it is worthwhile to compare them with another segment of these young adults. Elsewhere we have reported on the effects of military service on the male portion of this cohort.[21] Although there were some residual effects on political

[21] M. Kent Jennings and Gregory B. Markus, "The Effects of Military Service on Political Attitudes: A Panel Study," *American Political Science Review*, 71 (September 1976), 131-47; and "Political Participation and Vietnam Veterans: A Longitudinal Study," in Nancy L. Goldman and David R. Segal (eds.), *The Social Psychology of Military Service* (Beverly Hills, Calif.: Sage, 1976).

attitudes and evaluations and some interesting consequences on the unfolding pattern of political participation, by and large the *political* consequences of having served during the Vietnam War were nonexistent to negligible. Certainly the magnitude of any such relationships is dwarfed by the values obtained in comparing protestors and non-protestors.

At first blush this is a surprising result, for military service during the war would seem to provide an ideal setting for the molding of a generation-unit. More prosaically, serving in the war should have generated some clear political repercussions at the individual level. After all, the servicemen were subjected to unique experiences, they were readily identified by others as undergoing different sorts of experiences, and there was much (enforced) personal contact among them. It is true, of course, that the political beliefs and practices of many individual servicemen were modified by military service. Similarly, it is true that some organizational life with political characteristics emerged around the status and problems associated with the plight of Vietnam veterans. Nevertheless, in the broad view the political orientations of veterans were only marginally distinguishable from those of nonveterans by 1973.

It is not difficult to sort out the reasons for the contrasts between the strong effects associated with protest behavior and the minor effects associated with military service. Perhaps the fundamental factor is the differential basis of recruitment into the two groups. Aside from instances of extreme social pressure, we may assume that becoming a protestor was a voluntary, willful act. Quite the opposite prevailed in the case of military service. Some 35% of the men were conscripted and the bulk of the "volunteers" maintained that they pre-empted the draft by volunteering instead. A number of consequences flow from this differential recruitment process. Servicemen constituted a much more heterogeneous lot than did protestors, in terms of both social and political backgrounds.[22] Whereas male protestors had already diverged somewhat from nonprotestors as early as 1965, the same could scarcely be said about military versus nonmilitary youths. A generation-unit typically shares many pre-formation characteristics; clearly the protestors met this criterion much more fully than did the servicemen.

[22] Despite the widely held view that college students by and large escaped the service during the war, the facts are otherwise. Within our own sample, for instance, approximately one-half of the college-going males wound up in active service compared with about three-fifths of those not going beyond high school. In a related vein, the proportions of whites and nonwhites entering the military were nearly identical. See also Michael Useem, *Conscription, Protest, and Social Conflict* (New York: Wiley, 1973), 91-99.

This differential base was also crucial in terms of interaction with the immediate environment in which the two groups found themselves. Latent protestors on campuses found ready primary and secondary group support and a general climate of opinion that facilitated their personal interaction and organized behavior. The comparison with the military is vivid. Given the initial social and political heterogeneity, the response of servicemen to contemporary political history and to the military as a semitotal institution was understandably varied, poorly crystallized, and closely monitored by superiors. Finally, the fact that protesting carried its own political raison d'être whereas military service was most often a personal act with few or no political overtones constitutes a singular difference. In the former case there was a strong, policy-oriented motivation, though the personal stakes for potential recruits were by no means negligible. (The contrast with World War II or even the Korean War is instructive, however.) For those entering the service there is little indication of a political motive such as saving the world for democracy or protecting Southeast Asians from the hands of oppressors.

Overall, then, the set of conditions accompanying protest behavior was highly conducive to the emergence of what can be loosely termed a generation-unit. But the comparison with servicemen shows that it is not simply the exposure to a common set of experiences that determines whether a generation-unit will emerge. In Mannheim's terms, the servicemen experienced the "same concrete historical" problems, but it is not apparent that they worked up the materials of their common experiences in *politically* distinguishable ways or with different outcomes that would set them apart from other members of their generation. By contrast, the protestors responded to the political-historical environment in a singular fashion, one that appears to have the potential of enduring effects.

CHAPTER TWELVE

Conclusion:
Interpretation of a Half-Empty Glass

T HROUGHOUT this work our focus has been on the twin concepts of stability and change. Even a cursory glance at our results, however, leads to a perplexing observation: both change and stability abound. What, then, are we to conclude—merely that adults are subject to both or simply that sometimes one predominates and sometimes the other? In one sense this is exactly what we can conclude. In any given era with any large and diverse population, moderate stability is likely to characterize most of the population on most political attributes. Pockets of instability will exist, both in the sense of some individuals changing rapidly and of some characteristics being transformed more rapidly than others, but on the whole we would predict mid-range stability levels.

There is, however, a further conclusion to be drawn—namely, that the *potential* for change in adulthood is great throughout the population. Though this potential will often not be realized, its existence carries a number of important implications about ordinary and extraordinary political life. After setting the stage by reviewing the evidence of change and stability, we will consider some of these implications.

EVIDENCE OF CHANGE

Of the many pieces of evidence indicative of change, probably the most significant is the frequency with which members of the parental generation altered their attitudes and behaviors. Fluctuations among the young were to be expected. The young are always regarded as more flexible due to their more limited life experiences. This is equally true of political and nonpolitical domains. In addition, the historical era under study was one in which young adults had reasons to pay unusual attention to politics and to take part in political affairs at a premium rate. Therefore it was not too surprising that the high school graduates of 1965 bore a different cast by the year 1973.

More striking was the labileness observed among the parents. Older adults have to a large extent been viewed as being beyond the stage at which transformations in the political and personal landscapes have a major impact. They have already made whatever adjustments are needed in their lives, having gone through many of the transitions demarcating the significant phases of pre-adult and adult life. Even the unattentive have had to come to grips with many political realities and options in the course of 25-30 years of adulthood. By the time one of their children graduates from high school, they have perhaps even had to deal with the challenges to their values brought about by their own offspring. Putting all of this together, the fact that the parents were far from highly stable during the panel years is significant. Nor does the fact that parents were almost uniformly less variable than the young adults diminish the importance of this observation. As anticipated, adults in their forties and fifties are less subject to fluctuations than are new adults; but even the middle-aged are responsive to changes in their personal and political worlds.

A second strand of evidence supporting a view of changeability is that change was apparent at both the individual and aggregate levels. At the individual level, fluctuations were apparent in an abundance of low over-time correlations and gross stability figures. When one considers that we spoke of "substantial" persistence as a correlation of .3 or higher, and that low to moderate persistence occurred despite this minimal base, the malleability of the population stands out. Lifelong openness was the term used to describe this condition. If only individual-level movement existed, however, with fluctuations simply canceling each other in the aggregate, we might well claim that in one significant sense of the term no change had taken place at all—especially if the switchers did not differ systematically from the standpatters. At least it would be difficult to argue that movement occurred in response to alterations in the political and social environment. Additionally, unreliability of the measures would be a most formidable rival hypothesis in the case of equal change in both directions. But on several crucial topics—political trust, school integration, partisanship among the youths, etc.—change was predominantly in one direction. Therefore, not only did many individuals undergo change between 1965 and 1973, but so too did each generation as a whole. Life-cycle, generational, and period effects could be detected in varying and mixed quantities in these aggregate transformations.

Nor was individual change without systematic consequences in terms of group differences. It seemed to be uniformly the case that group contrasts detectable in 1965 grew into wider gaps over the ensuing eight years. Especially compelling was the growing cleavage between protestors and nonprotestors among the college educated, because this expansion supported Mannheim's formulation of generation-unit members responding in like fashion to contemporary political events. Similarly, the frequently increasing gaps among educational strata, males and females, and females by gender roles in the youth sample were all indicative of meaningful aggregate movements.

Even what we have summarized so far would be unimpressive if confined to one or two items in the shopping basket of indicators at our disposal. But over-time variability was not narrowly restricted by subject matter. Not that the rate of change was uniform across all areas. A rather sizeable gap exists between the relative constancy of factual political knowledge and the extreme plasticity displayed on the political trust index. Yet by and large, obvious stability could not be said to characterize entire components of the political or nonpolitical self.

Party identification is typically cited as the major attribute which is almost invariant over time. And in a relative sense this is true. Among both generations the 1965-1973 correlation was higher than that for almost all other attributes, a striking commentary indeed. The aggregate distribution of parents on the three-way categorization was virtually indistinguishable in the two years. Even on this prime example of stability, however, movement was of significant proportions, especially among the young. And while most of the movement was across the partisan-independent boundary, we speculated that interparty movement could also be quite frequent when the times were supportive of party allegiance rather than party independence.

A similar point can be made about the most stable nonpolitical trait. Belief in the divinity of the Bible varied less than most other political or nonpolitical attributes, with turnover coefficients much like those for party identification. This is understandable given the meaning attached to religious convictions, with their extraworldly as well as this-world implications. Yet a quarter of the parents and fully half of the youths who said in the first interview that the Bible is "God's Word and all it says is true" concluded in the second interview that the Bible was "written by men inspired by God but it contains some human errors."

The main point, however, is not the limited degree of continuity even at its extreme, but the fact that significant amounts of instability occurred everywhere—in people's involvement in politics, in their resources and participation, in their preferences and attitudes, and in comparable nonpolitical domains. Though instability is itself variable, it seems like a common rather than an unusual characteristic of adult political behavior and attitudes. Consequently, the other evidence of change from our panel analysis should be accorded that much more significance.

In a similar vein, the observed change pervades various segments of the population. Most significant, perhaps, was our conclusion regarding the effects of schooling. Whereas previous work, by its emphasis on the imputed influence of higher education, might lead one to think that post-high-school change is concentrated among those who go to college, our results showed equal amounts of individual variability at all levels of future training. Nor was aggregate change restricted to one educational group. Differences between educational strata continued to grow as individuals moved through early adulthood, but not as a consequence of one stratum being more fluid than the other. At the parental level, also, there was no concentration of change among the well educated.

When individual turnover rates and aggregate movement were examined in other population categories, nowhere were there major groups immune to change. Sources of change were also variable insofar as we could identify them. Period effects, for example, were some times felt more strongly by one or the other racial group or by one sex. But even when alteration was less in one segment, it tended to be counterbalanced by greater variation elsewhere. Thus, just as change was spread across the variety of political and nonpolitical attributes, it was likewise distributed throughout an array of population clusters.

Certain intergenerational comparisons also bolster a far-reaching interpretation of the evidence of change. Our very first report of the 1965 wave emphasized the absence of high agreement between parents and their own children. We recognized, however, that we might have tapped young people at the time they were least apt or willing to acknowledge and display parental values and behavioral modes. If so, subsequent developments might bring the young people more in line with their parents' views, taking them full circle, as it were, into positions where intergenerational continuity was high. The 1973 results pointed out with a vengeance that this simply did not occur. In virtually every comparison of the parent-offspring pairs, youths had become less like their parents than they were as high school seniors as well as less like what their parents had become in the intermediate years. Rather than regenerating parent-child continuity, later development heightened within-family discontinuity.

Aggregate comparisons were not so indicative of intergenerational discordance. In fact, convergence seemed a rather frequent phenomenon. Historical effects often combined with life-course development to produce this convergence. But there were some attitudes—most notably, partisanship and opinions on certain public policy questions—on which parents and youths had moved apart over the eight years. And in the nonwhite portion of the population, intergenerational discontinuity was the norm rather than the exception. At the very least, such results suggest that aggregate similarity across generations is far from assured.

All of these results taken together suggest that, rather than being unusual, change is a characteristic pattern of the adult years. The change is often orderly, resulting from transitions through the life cycle or from reactions to political events and personalities. It is also nonuniform, being considerably more common in early than in middle adulthood. And, while our data are only from one period, both the frequency and locus of change are undoubtedly variable across time. The important point, however, is how frequent and widespread change is among adults. While the particulars would vary for other populations of adults (i.e., other than high school graduates and their parents) and for other times, changeability and adaptability to alterations in one's political surroundings are a key feature of adult political life.

EVIDENCE OF STABILITY

As is typical, results are not all one-sided. Just as there is considerable evidence of change in the adults we studied so also there are indications of stability and continuity. One indication is the simple but powerful fact that virtually all of the over-time correlations were greater than zero. Even in the most extreme cases at our disposal—e.g., youths' answers to unstructured, open-ended questions—there was some carryover from their responses as high school seniors to those as adults in their mid-twenties. The same is true of concordance between parents and their offspring. Despite the drop in correlational magnitudes between 1965 and 1973, a positive link always exists in the later year. Weak though some of these correlations are, they do not support an interpretation of a turning away from parents or even the milder statement that youths develop completely independent of parental attributes.

More important than simple directionality, of course, is the magnitude or degree of similarity over time and across generations. Many of the over-time correlations were in the .30-.50 range, which we interpreted as showing strong continuity. In a few notable instances—e.g., partisanship among the parents—the statistic was over .60. In general, the results can be interpreted as showing that after a period of shifting and twisting as young adults, individuals settle into some modes that are rather stable. Parent-offspring congruence suffers as a result of the elastic quality of the young. But even these correlations were over .25 in a number of cases.

Besides the magnitudes of the relationships, however, we noted several points that suggest that the turnover correlations underestimated true stability. In a few cases the gross stability percentages alerted us to the exaggerated effects of a small number of cases on the correlation. The most extreme example was on the issue involving "anti-church speeches," in which the correlation was very meager in spite of the fact that over four-fifths of the young people gave identical answers in both interviews. Question unreliability was another factor that depressed the statistical stability. As we noted repeatedly, true stability is somewhat above what the turnover figures show because of the unreliability introduced by less than perfect measurement techniques. Finally, we must recall the historical period during which our interviews took place. If behavior and attitudes were no more transformed during this period than what we observed, then they must be much more stable during less stormy periods. Taken as a whole, the examination of individual-level stability reveals several sources of support for a lifelong persistence argument.

This evidence of stability draws on individual-level data. If we look at aggregate results instead, there are additional indications of continuity. Much has been made of the enormous decline in political trust throughout the 1960s and 1970s. One reason for this emphasis is that few other shifts came close to matching this one in magnitude. Even when individual turnover was quite high, many of the changes were "cross-cutting," simply canceling each other out at the aggregate level. An illustrative case is newspaper reading. Gross stability was only about 50% for each generation, but the proportion reporting that they read newspapers daily changed by no more than a few percentage points. In one instance noted for dramatic aggregate shifts—resulting in a generation-unit of college student protestors—erosion effects could not be entirely ruled out.

Intergenerationally, aggregate results tended to bring parents and youths in line with each other even though pair correlations were declining. Movement on the part of the young people often fit a life-cycle model, so that their "adult" responses of 1973 more closely matched their parents' answers than did their "adolescent" responses of 1965. This was particularly true in the areas of involvement, resources, and participation. Another factor drawing the generations together was their common response to political forces prevailing in this period. If only one generation had grown more cynical, for example, generational differences would have tended to increase (as happened on party identification). Instead, with both generations responding to political and social forces, the net result was often greater overall agreement between parents and offspring by 1973.

A different kind of continuity was also preserved at the aggregate level. Some standard demographic differences, such as those between males and females and between better and less educated adults, were maintained despite the amount of individual discontinuity. In fact, the changes between 1965 and 1973 tended to highlight educational and gender differences, making the new generation of adults more like the old in this respect. Slackening racial contrasts indicate that traditional demographic differences are not immutable. Still, the fact that racial differences did not wither away and that sex contrasts hardly abated at all—both in the face of enormous, relevant political forces—suggests the potency of these divisions. Continuity in this sense is most unlikely to be disrupted in normal times.

Finally, we recall the useful addition of the 1973 cohort of high school seniors. Evidence from these students suggested that the 1965 senior class may have been a mild deviant case. The apparent generation gap in the late 1960s may have been a product of a rather unusual set of attitudes and behavior on the part of new and emerging adults. After that period, and presumably before it as well, aggregate parent-adolescent similarities would have been greater. Thus, part of the discontinuity observed was a function of the timing of the original study.

In sum, the evidence on the stability side of the ledger is also quite compelling, especially if we think of stability as more than individual continuity. If, in a period as tempestuous as any in the past several decades, profiles of the two generations were not so very different at the beginning and end of the panel years, and if the generations did not differ from one another by all that much, one might argue that continuity rather than change will most often characterize adult populations. Absolute stasis will not be found, and there will always be a few examples of rapidly changing individuals and ideas, but this accounting of the evidence might indicate that stability is the key to understanding adult political behavior and attitudes.

INTERPRETATION: THE EVER-PRESENT POTENTIAL FOR CHANGE

We have now laid out the evidence of both stability and change. Is the evidence on one side more conclusive than that of the other? Even if the evidence is more favorable to one side, can we ignore the other side? And if the answer to either of these questions is "No, we cannot conclude that only stability or that only change is the proper description of our results," then what do we conclude? We seem to have the classic, frustrating situation of the half-empty, half-full glass.

As we noted at the outset, we think our results mean much more than this. We interpret the results to mean that there is an enormous potential for change in adult populations which has been largely unrecognized. It is as if the frequent aggregate stability of adult attitudes and the persistence of demographic divisions in the population —along with the technical difficulties of obtaining data from individuals over time—have blinded researchers to the possibility that adults can and occasionally do change radically.

For a time, some researchers were convinced that development of political attitudes crystallized prior to late adolescence. When that position became untenable it became fashionable to believe that development and change continued through early adulthood. While precise limits were rarely asserted, it seemed to be commonly assumed that rigidity had set in at least by age 30. We are now taking issue with even that limitation on adult changeability. Without denying that young adults change more frequently than older persons, and that the likelihood of change is less as one gets older, we argue that older adults are far from intractable.

Approximately equal amounts of change across age groups may be especially likely at the aggregate rather than the individual level. New adults have to react to a variety of new features in their lives—higher education, the military, new friendships, full-time jobs, marriage, children, and so on. Since these factors affect young people in a number of ways depending on an individual's background, on what combination of these factors affect him or her, and on their timing, we should anticipate a certain amount of flip-flopping in both directions on political issues and on some aspects of involvement and participation. Crisscrossing changes will always lower individual-level stability, but may cancel each other out at the aggregate level, leaving overall distributions relatively undisturbed. Among older adults, external changes are somewhat less frequent and abrupt, suggesting that unpredictable, individual-level change is less frequent. Therefore, individual turnover rates will be higher for young people than for parents, but aggregate stability may be quite similar.

In contrast to these life-cycle factors, period effects brought about by changes in the political, economic, and social environment act more in concert on all ages, resulting in changes predominantly in one direction. Depending on the issue or behavior in question, period-induced changes may be as great or greater among older individuals. We should not be surprised, then, to find instances in which individual turnover is noticeably greater among youths and yet aggregate change is virtually equal (e.g., political interest and magazine reading) or greater among parents (e.g., radio listening). Among our issue questions, none showed equal amounts of aggregate change among parents and youths, but the result on the question of school integration is suggestive. We found aggregate changes of 21% and 14% among youths and parents, respectively, but with the individual-level correlation for parents (.32) more than twice that for youths (.15).

It does not necessarily follow, of course, that period effects touch everyone as deeply and—a key point—at the same time. There are undoubtedly leading elements, such as college students on opposition to the Vietnam War, blacks on civil rights, women on abortion rights, and so on. So our tendency to find relatively uniform effects across population divisions and across generations to a certain extent reflects diffusion from initiating groups to the rest of the population. Nevertheless, period effects—in contrast to what seems to happen with life-cycle effects—tend to appear as uniform impacts across age categories in the form of aggregate shifts.

In addition to explicating differences in rates of change, consideration of the sources and kinds of variability suggests a more accurate characterization of change *processes* during the adult life cycle. Change among young adults is likely to be more predictable than that among older adults because the former are responding to a cluster of age-related phenomena. Young adults are confronted by a whole set of new stimuli in a very short span of years. To the extent that individuals react to these phenomena in politically relevant ways, and to the degree that the reactions are at all similar, it lends a certain uniformity to the development we observe in young adulthood. Among older adults the changes are less likely to be so patterned. Even though many adults ultimately have common experiences, such as the leave-taking of the youngest child, these occur over a wider range of ages and are not concentrated with other experiences to the same degree as in young adulthood. As a consequence, changes in mature adults are less likely to fit a simple pattern.

This view of the adult period meshes well with our earlier characterization of the socialization process. Our previous focus was almost entirely on pre-adults, although their degree of similarity with the preceding generation was a major concern. In summarizing that work, we described the socialization process as one of inertia and happenstance. By inertia we meant that:

> There is always some tendency for the upcoming generation to be like the preceding one. This is the passing on of orientations by family, school, and other institutions of the extant culture. . . . In the absence of forces deflecting them [i.e., children] in one direction or another, the inertia of this early period [childhood] sustains them through the turbulence and growth of adolescence and they go on as adults to develop into a fair resemblance of the older generation.[1]

[1] M. Kent Jennings and Richard G. Niemi, *The Political Character of Adolescence* (Princeton: Princeton University Press, 1974), 333.

Things do not always work out so smoothly, however, and this is where happenstance enters:

> Sometimes . . . highly significant events occur prior to or with the advent of political maturity. Such events may be cataclysmic and manifestly political . . . or they may be politically relevant and slower moving. . . . Under the press of such circumstances young people in particular can be deflected out of the channels in which their previous development has been rooted.[2]

We are now refining this notion by observing that much the same description applies to the entire life span. Not only is there a tendency for a new generation to be like the preceding one, but there is a tendency within each generation to maintain attitudes and patterns of behavior once they are established. But just as major political events occurring prior to the advent of maturity can deflect a new generation from the paths set down by the previous one, events can shake up existing generations, including the older members of those generations. Indeed, it would be surprising if events as momentous as the war in Vietnam did not impinge on mature adults' political views.[3]

The major point in all of this is not so much the nature of change but the fact that older adults can and do change, and that they change in response to developments in their personal and social environments. We would even go so far as to say that sharp breaks with the past— perhaps even support for radical changes in the form of government— can occur among older adults. Such extreme discontinuities are, of course, rare. But such rapid social change as evidenced, for example, by changing feelings toward and treatment of minority groups in the United States, could hardly have come about without transformations that characterized much of the adult population. Similarly, shifts of attitudes in the 1970s about the size of government and toward governmental spending could hardly have occurred as quickly as they did without opinion changes on the part of many established adults. In general, rapid political change would be nearly impossible if older adults were unyielding. As it is, the young may be the most malleable (with pre-adults even more so), and the impetus for many social movements may be found among the young. But were it not for the sensitivity of older adults to their shifting environment, changes in

---

[2] Ibid.

[3] Markus analyzed changes in party identification and political trust using the same data set upon which this book is based. He concluded that opposition to the Vietnam War led directly to increased political cynicism in both generations. See Gregory B. Markus, "The Political Environment and the Dynamics of Public Attitudes: A Panel Study," *American Journal of Political Science*, 23 (May 1979), 338-59.

political attitudes and behavior would surely occur at a more glacial pace.

This characterization of adults as having an ever-present potential for change has important implications. Most importantly, it gives a different perspective to the role of early political socialization. It has often been suggested that the attitudes and behavior learned earliest are likely to be persistent because they are the most thoroughly internalized. Considerable force is needed to deflect thought and habit out of their early pathways. Our view also suggests that early learning is likely to persist, but there are important breaks with the "internalization" theory.

We believe that the reason for stability of political views and behavior is not that they are so deeply ingrained, but that the political orientations of most individuals are simply not challenged very frequently. It is well known that politics in the conventional sense is not salient for most people on a day-to-day basis. Personal features of their lives —especially friends, families, work, and entertainment—take precedence. This yields the inertia of which we spoke. Politics often does not penetrate the layers of individuals' personal interests, And even when it does, basic beliefs are typically not called into question. Instead, people are concerned about specific policies or applications of policies; more fundamental matters about the nature of the polity are not raised. Therefore, since politics is most often a peripheral concern, change typically comes about rather slowly; because the questions raised are seldom about the foundations of the political system, basic political beliefs are most likely not to shift.

Our view also differs from the internalization theory in suggesting that change is not so unlikely if political values and practices are in fact challenged. Since early learning (or later learning) is not thoroughly ingrained, people are quite susceptible to challenges to what they have learned. As noted, this is most often observable as shifts in attitudes on specific policy matters. Less frequently it is seen in altered views of the scope of governmental activities generally. And occasionally it is noted in changing beliefs about the nature of desirable or "appropriate" political norms, rules of the game, and the constitutional order. Older adults are typically more integrated into existing social and political structures and therefore have more at stake than young people in any changes to that structure. Consequently, it usually takes a stronger challenge to present circumstances or contemporary beliefs to alter their current attitudes and behavior. Even older adults, however, are susceptible. The supposed internalization of norms and values over the long period from early childhood to middle and late adulthood is not sufficient to immunize individuals against self-doubt and development brought about by changing circumstances and innovative thinking.

From this view of early socialization one can derive the conclusion that even frequent reinforcement of political ideas will often be insufficient to prevent the infusion of new beliefs or values. As much as particular modes of participation, general feelings about the role of government, and occasionally even specific policy preferences are reinforced through the schools and through adult rituals and personal interaction, they can still be altered by political events and by changing political circumstances. Reinforcement no doubt slows the process of change, but it does not stop it. Attesting most vividly to the impact of events and circumstances was the emergence of our college student protestors as a subgroup undergoing profound change during the study period.

Perhaps the most important implication of all this is the emphasis it places on political leadership. If individuals—especially middle-aged and older adults—are less rigid or fixed in their beliefs and practices than has been thought, then the quality of political leadership takes on added importance. It is political leaders, after all, who are likely to provide the challenges that stir people out of the inertia that otherwise characterizes them. More importantly, they are called upon to determine the new direction that political ideas will take. Citizens are willing to change with the times, and occasionally demand change. But the possible directions of change are many. The task of political leadership is to channel developments in ways that prove to be satisfactory.

This does not mean that sharp breaks with the past need be frequent. Indeed, the real genius of political leadership may be in stimulating enough small changes that radical transformations are rarely felt to be necessary. Our contribution is to suggest just how receptive adult populations are to new political ways. Far from being immovable by virtue of having internalized early learning, individuals remain flexible well into adulthood, perhaps even throughout adult life. Political leaders must realize that this flexibility exists and understand the responsibility it entails as they constantly determine and redetermine not simple preferences on current policy matters, but the nature of the political system itself.

Data Sources

The Samples

Table A.1 presents in summary form the various data bases used in this study. Because all of the bases have a common origin in the 1965 sample of high school seniors, it will be useful to describe briefly the nature of the 1965 sample design, as presented earlier.[1]

The students selected for this study were a probability sample of second semester seniors in public and private high schools of the coterminous United States in the spring of 1965. To meet the study requirement that seniors would have been enrolled in classes taught by the social studies teachers of grades 10-12 in the sample schools, new schools opening after September 1963 were excluded from the study population. In order to provide efficient use of field resources, schools with senior classes of less than nine members were also excluded.

The probability selection of schools progressed through several stages. In the first stage an area probability sample of Standard Metropolitan Statistical Areas (SMSA's) and of the remaining United States counties was selected with probabilities proportional to total population of the SMSA's and counties. Thus the 12 largest metropolitan areas, 32 other SMSA's, and 30 non-SMSA's were designated as sample areas. These 74 primary sampling units (psu's) are those selected for the Survey Research Center's national sample of dwellings.

A subselection of central cities and of suburban areas was made from the 12 largest metropolitan areas. In the remaining sample psu's, a subselection of counties was made in those cases where the psu contained more than one county. In all cases probabilities of selection were in proportion to population, and controls were maintained by geographical region, SMSA classification of the psu's, and enrollments in public and in private secondary schools.

The sampling frame of schools for each psu (county, city, or suburban area) was compiled from school lists obtained through an anonymous national organization and several published lists of schools. Estimates of senior class enrollments were calculated on the basis of these sources.

---

[1] The following paragraphs are basically excerpted from our earlier report, M. Kent Jennings and Richard G. Niemi, *The Political Character of Adolescence* (Princeton: Princeton University Press, 1974), 337-38, 340-41.

TABLE A.1: Summary of Field Work and Data Sources

Primary Respondents	Youth		Parent	
	N	%	N	%
Completed interviews	1119	67.0	1118	71.6
Completed mailback questionnaires	229	13.7	61	3.9
Total number of panel respondents	1348	80.8	1179	75.5
Refusal, unavailable	142	8.5	204	13.1
Unable to locate	141	8.4	99	6.3
Ill, outside country	15	0.9	26	1.7
Deceased	23	1.4	54	3.4
Original 1965 completed interviews	1669	100.0	1562[a]	100.0
			107 (No 1965	
			—— interview)	
			1669	
Total number of offspring-parent pairs in both waves: 1063				
Secondary Respondents (Spouses)[b]				
Completed questionnaire	566	73.1	671	72.0
Noncooperation	178	26.9	261	28.0
Total number of spouses	744	100.0	932	100.0

Replicated Sample of High School Senior Classes	No. of Schools	No. of Students
Completed self-administered questionnaires in 1965[c]	77	20,674
Completed self-administered questionnaires in 1973	85	16,929

[a] Excludes the 430 cases where respondent was other half of a mother-father pair.
[b] Of those primary respondents *interviewed*. These data were not used in this volume.
[c] The *school* response rate was 79% in 1965, and 88% in 1973.

After these steps the actual selection of schools was based on a probability proportionate to the size of the senior class. From the sampling frame 98 schools were selected at the rate of one school for each estimated 26,000 seniors. Of the 98 sample schools, 12 were unable to cooperate. Because of initial refusals, an additional thirteen schools were selected. Each substitute school matched the original selection, insofar as possible, with respect to geographic location, type of psu, expected number of seniors, type of school system (public or nonpublic), and curriculum (general or technical). Altogether 97 of the 111 schools (87 percent) were included in the study.[2]

[2] A full report on school response characteristics is provided in M. Kent Jennings

To satisfy the requirements for an eventual sample of approximately 1,700 students, 18 seniors were to be selected from each sample school. When permission to enter a sample school was granted, the total number of seniors was obtained. Because the original estimates of senior class sizes were unavoidably imprecise (no recent lists covered all senior classes), the number of selected seniors varied from 15 to 21 per school, to correct for the original estimates. Individual students were selected by taking a systematic random sample from an up-to-date class list provided by the school. The response rate was 99% and the total N was 1,669.

As sampling instructions were prepared for the probability selection of seniors from each sample school, a probability sample of parents was also designated. Within each school, interviewers were instructed to interview the fathers of one-third of the seniors, the mothers of one-third, and both parents of the remaining one-third of the seniors. Each student would then be represented by at least one parent and one-third (ideally) by two. The specific designation of mother, father, or both parent interviews was predetermined; interviewers were permitted no personal choice in the selection. However, in the interest of obtaining family-level information in those cases where the designated parent was deceased or otherwise absent from home (e.g., divorced or overseas) during the entire study period, an interview was attempted with the other parent or parent surrogate. In practice under 10 percent of the interviews assumed this provisional form. The response rate was 93% and the total N was 1,992; of this total there were 430 mother-father pairs.

In the 1973 follow-up an effort was made to recontact all of the youth sample and all of the parent sample where only one parent had been interviewed. Random selections of one parent were made in the 430 instances where both mother and father had been originally interviewed. Other details about the 1973 data gathering are presented in Chapter 1 and Table A.1.

Comparing Panel and Non-Panel Respondents

The possibility of respondent bias in most panel studies is a very real one due to the attrition usually experienced between successive periods of data gathering. At issue is whether the individuals not retained in the panel depart in some systematic way from those who are retained. In some respects the answer to that question can never be fully satisfactory because information about most characteristics of the lost cases is obviously not available at the subsequent observation

and Lawrence E. Fox, "The Conduct of Socio-Political Research in Schools: Problems and Strategies of Access," *The School Review*, 76 (December 1968), 428-44.

points. In lieu of such information, a common approach is to compare the two groups at a time point when full information is available for both. If systematic differences are not present, it is typically assumed that the reasons for attrition are not related to the major variables of concern. It follows that the panel respondents are viewed as being representative of the original pool of respondents.

Given the high response rate for each of our samples we know that the degree of overall bias is limited. Nevertheless, it is well within the realm of the possibility that the nonpanelists and panelists could vary in some systematic, consequential ways. Such a possibility is some-what more likely for the younger than for the older generation due to the highly mobile character of the former. To check on such possibili-ties we made comparisons for most of the major variables used in this volume that were available for 1965. There were scarcely any differ-ences in the parental sample aside from a modestly lower representa-tion in the panel of males, Northeasterners, and inhabitants of large metropolitan areas. Political differences were almost unobservable. For example, analysis of variance results consistently yielded eta coeffi-cients in the .00 to .05 range, which is, to say, of no real consequence.

As anticipated, contrasts were more evident in the youth sample. Tables A.2-A.4 present the relevant information. Compared with those not retained, the panel respondents as of 1965 were more often female, white, from smaller environs, academically better and more ambi-tious, from more privileged backgrounds, more interested in and knowledgeable about politics, more trusting of the government and of people in general, and more conservative in the partisan domain, but about as liberal or more so on public policy issues. Another way of putting this is to say that we were a bit less successful in retaining the "have-less" portion of the original sample. This was due in large part to an inability to track people with these characteristics rather than to a higher refusal rate. In any event, most of these differences— race and educational aspirations being the major exceptions—are in the trivial range. Moreover, the fact that panel members outnumber non-panel members by a 4 to 1 margin dampens even further whatever bias might be at work in the panel attrition.

Comparison of 1965 Data from Personal Interviews and Mass-Administered Questionnaires

Information from questionnaires administered en masse to members of the 1965 senior classes was utilized in Chapter 7. It was argued there that occasional discrepancies between the results based on these questionnaires and those from the personal interviews of 1965 were in part a consequence of instrument effects. More specifically we hypoth-

TABLE A.2: Background Comparisons of Panel and Non-Panel Respondents from the 1965 Youth Survey

	Max. N =	Panel Respondents (1348)	Non-Panel Respondents (321)	Total (1669)
Sex				
Males		50%	57%	52%
Females		50	43	48
		$(\tau_b = -.05)$		
Race				
White		92	77	89
Nonwhite		8	23	11
		$(\tau_b = .18)$		
Region				
Northeast		23	25	24
Midwest		30	28	30
South		28	32	29
West		18	15	18
Residence				
Non-SMSA's		39	31	37
Other SMSA's		38	31	37
12 largest SMSA's		23	38	26
		$(\tau_b = .11)$[a]		
Grade average				
A		8	6	8
B		47	35	44
C or lower		45	59	48
		$(\tau_b = .11)$[a]		
Educational plans				
Continue, very sure		59	44	56
Continue, less than very sure		25	31	26
Stop or not sure		16	25	18
		$(\tau_b = .12)$[a]		
Parent's education				
Some college or more		22	21	22
High school graduate		38	29	36
Less than high school		40	50	42
		$(\tau_b = .06)$[a]		
Church attendance				
Never		2	4	3
Few times a year		14	14	14
Once or twice/month		18	20	18
Almost every week		66	62	65
		$(\tau_b = -.03)$		

[a] Based on full distributions.

TABLE A.3: Sociopolitical Comparisons of Panel and Non-Panel
Respondents from the 1965 Youth Survey

Max. N =	Panel Respondents (1348)	Non-Panel Respondents (321)	Total (1669)	Correlation (eta)
School political activities				
1 (Low) - 5 (High)	2.94	2.60	2.87	.08
Interest in public affairs				
1 (Low) - 4 (High)	3.25	3.09	3.22	.08
Anticipated political activity				
1 (Low) - 3 (High)	1.93	1.88	1.92	.03
Cosmopolitanism				
1 (Low) - 7 (High)	5.24	5.22	5.24	.00
Internal political efficacy[a]				
1 (Low) - 3 (High)	2.20	2.05	2.17	.08
Political knowledge[a]				
1 (Low) - 7 (High)	4.79	4.26	4.69	.12
Recognition and understanding of party differences				
1 (Low) - 5 (High)	2.71	2.56	2.68	.04
Political trust[a]				
1 (Low) - 6 (High)	4.25	4.17	4.23	.03
Civic tolerance[a]				
1 (Low) - 4 (High)	2.62	2.49	2.59	.06
Social trust[a]				
1 (Low) - 4 (High)	3.06	2.76	3.00	.11
Self-confidence[a]				
1 (Low) - 4 (High)	3.03	2.81	2.99	.09
Opinion strength[a]				
1 (Low) - 4 (High)	2.63	2.63	2.63	.00

[a] This index or scale is based on the original 1965 scoring techniques, which differ somewhat from those subsequently developed for panel analysis. See ICPSR Student-Parent Socialization Study Codebook for the original scoring.

esized that the personal interview setting was more likely to evoke socially desirable responses.

A more precise test of that explanation is possible due to the fact that about two-thirds ($N = 1,012$) of the personal interviewees also subsequently completed the mass-administered questionnaire a few weeks after the personal interview. In principle we should be able to compare the personal interview responses of these students with their questionnaire responses and then determine if instrument effects are at work. At least two factors complicate any easy interpretations. First, the two-thirds could deviate in some way from the one-third that was only interviewed. Second, it is possible that contamination effects oc-

TABLE A.4: Comparisons of Partisan and Issue Positions of Panel and Non-Panel Respondents from the 1965 Youth Survey

	Panel Respondents (1348)	Non-Panel Respondents (321)	Total (1669)
Max. N =			
Party identification			
Strong Democrat	17	26	19
Weak Democrat	24	26	24
Independent Democrat	15	12	15
Independent	13	15	13
Independent Republican	8	8	8
Weak Republican	14	9	13
Strong Republican	9	4	8
	$(\tau_b=-.10)$		
1964 Presidential preference			
Johnson	72	81	74
Goldwater	28	19	26
	$(\tau_b=-.08)$		
School integration			
Oppose	21	17	21
Depends	10	9	9
Favor	69	74	70
	$(\tau_b=.04)$		
School prayers			
Favor	29	35	30
Depends	4	4	4
Oppose	67	60	66
	$(\tau_b=-.05)$		

curred, that the responses to the mass-administered questionnaires were affected by the recent exposure to the personal interview. Our interpretation, therefore, must be guarded. Given below are the results for questions for which social desirability was hypothesized to have been a consideration or for which the differences between the youth panel figures and the youth cohort figures reported in Chapter 7 were especially large.

The comparisons reported in Table A.5 tend to support our suppositions about the role of socially desirable behavior in the interview setting. Students were less openly critical about both school and governmental figures when supplying views in the more personal setting of the interview. Similarly, they presented themselves as a bit more successful, proper, politically alert, and efficacious; and they displayed as much or more civic tolerance. Most of these differences, fortunately, are not large, and most are in accordance with our hypothesis that in-

TABLE A.5: Comparisons of Personal Interviews and Mass-Administered Questionnaires from Same Respondents, 1965 Youth

	Personal Interviews	Mass-Administered Questionnaires
Max. N =	(1012)	(1012)
Academic and Social		
Teachers unfair to R (yes)	32%	39%
Administrators unfair to R (yes)	10	16
Student behavior too restricted (agree)	48	76
Student run school affairs (a good deal)	54	47
Grade average (A and B)	54	46
Church attendance (weekly)	66	62
Most people try to be (fair)	77	65
Political		
Courses increased interest in politics (a lot)	54	48
Follow public affairs (most of the time)	41	39
Anticipated political role (very active)	15	12
Government beyond understanding (disagree)	40	33
Voting only way (disagree)	66	66
Government interested in public opinion (a lot)	46	44
Government people crooked (hardly any)	30	22
Government waste money (not very much)	21	14
Trust government do right (always)	43	44
People running government (smart)	85	85
Government run (for benefit of all)	86	81
Allow Communist to hold office (agree)	36	36
Allow speeches against religion (agree)	87	85
All countries should have American system (disagree)	50	48

strument effects lead to at least some portion of the modest discrepancies between the 1965 youth panel and the 1965 youth cohort data.

Personal Interviews Compared with Mailback Questionnaires in 1973

Only 55% ($N = 61$) of the 1973 parental respondents supplied data via a mailback, self-administered questionnaire rather than through a personal interview. Any consequences arising from instrument effects, falsification, or "real" differences between mailback and interviewed respondents would be negligible. However, the 17% ($N = 229$) figure in the younger generation cannot be dispensed with so easily. If differences do exist between the two types of respondents we cannot be sure whether they are due to the form of data gathering or to underlying contrasts between the two groups—though for some hard indicators such as sex or race one can rather safely rule out instrument effects. If differences are trivial to nonexistent, then it seems likely that the two groups are basically the same barring some strange interaction effects between mode of data gathering and personal characteristics of the respondents.

A finding of no meaningful differences would be the preferred one here because the mailback instrument was a considerably shortened version of the personal interview schedule. If trivial differences are the rule on the variables common to both sets of respondents, then we would conclude that the personal interviewees do not differ systematically from the mailback respondents and that the findings based on variables associated only with the personal interviewees would likely be true of the mailback respondents also. To gauge the degree of similarity between the two sets of respondents we compared the two groups across a range of variables employed in the analysis (Tables A.6 and A.7).

TABLE A.6: Selected Comparisons of Personal Interviews and Mailback Questionnaires, from 1973 Youth Survey

Max. N =	Personal Interviews (1119)	Mailback Questionnaires (229)	Total (1348)
Sex			
Males	48%	58%	50%
Females	52	42	50
	$(\tau_b = -.07)$		
Race			
White	90	95	91
Nonwhite	10	5	9
	$(\tau_b = -.07)$		
Region			
Northeast	24	23	23
Midwest	31	27	30
South	28	30	28
West	18	20	18
Education			
High school graduate	39	26	36
Some college	32	31	32
College graduate	30	43	32
	$(\tau_b = .11)$		
Planning to move			
No	68	54	66
Yes	32	46	34
	$(\tau_b = .11)$		

TABLE A.6 (cont.)

Max. N =	Personal Interviews (1119)	Mailback Questionnaires (229)	Total (1348)
Party identification			
Strong Democrat	9	12	9
Weak Democrat	25	22	25
Independent	48	42	47
Weak Republican	12	17	12
Strong Republican	6	8	6
	$(\tau_b=.03)$		
1972 presidential preference			
Nixon	62	59	61
McGovern	38	41	39
	$(\tau_b=.02)$		
School integration			
Oppose	34	46	36
Depends	18	4	16
Favor	48	50	49
	$(\tau_b=.04)$		
School prayers			
Favor	64	68	65
Depends	3	2	3
Oppose	33	31	32
	$(\tau_b=-.02)$		
Interpretation of Bible			
Irrelevant today	3	1	3
Not inspired by God	9	12	10
Some human error	59	59	59
God's Word	29	27	29
	$(\tau_b=-.02)$		

It is apparent that the two groups are remarkably similar in most respects, though there is a pattern to the results. Personal interviewees were a bit more likely to be female, nonwhite, less well-educated, less politically interested and participative, less politically and personally self-confident, more politically trusting and less personally trusting, less politically cosmopolitan, and less politically liberal. Yet these are, with two or three exceptions, exceedingly small differences. Perhaps the major way the two groups differ is simply in terms of geographical rootedness, as indicated by the difference on whether they were planning a move in the future. On balance, however, the two groups are quite proximate to each other. Thus we would conclude that the findings associated only with the personal interviewees are not distorted in any meaningful way due to the relevant questions not being utilized in the mailback version.

TABLE A.7: Comparisons of Indexes Based on Personal Interviews
and Mailback Questionnaires from 1973 Youth

Max. N =	Personal Interviews (1119)	Mailback Questionnaires (229)	Total (1348)	Correlation (eta)
Interest in public affairs				
1 (Low) - 4 (High)	3.27	3.38	3.29	.05
Cosmopolitanism				
1 (Low) - 7 (High)	4.82	5.12	4.88	.07
Internal efficacy				
1 (Low) - 3 (High)	1.96	2.04	1.98	.04
Political trust				
1 (Low) - 6 (High)	3.04	2.86	3.01	.05
Political activity				
1 (Low) - 9 (High)	2.06	2.33	2.11	.05
Civic tolerance				
1 (Low) - 6 (High)	3.26	3.29	3.26	.01
Political self-placement				
1 (Liberal) - 7 (Conservative)	3.81	3.85	3.81	.01
Personal trust				
1 (Low) - 7 (High)	4.52	5.00	4.60	.08
Self-confidence				
1 (Low) - 7 (High)	4.88	5.36	4.96	.10

Description of Basic Measures
and Their Distributions for Youths and Parents,
1965 and 1973

A DESCRIPTION is provided here of most of the major political and nonpolitical variables used in the analysis. (Those fully described in the text are omitted here.) They are given in the approximate order in which they are introduced in Chapters 2 and 3. Marginals are for all respondents who were in both waves of the panel, including those who completed a mailback questionnaire in 1973 (see Appendix A). All questions were identical for youths and parents. Missing data ("don't know" and "not ascertained") have been deleted. This represents only a small number of cases, except in those instances where the relevant questions were omitted from the mailback questionnaires.

Several of the measures are based on multiple items. A decision was made to determine the scalability of these items by factor analysis, in contrast to Guttman scaling, which was the primary procedure used in 1965. This was done in part because of the numerous questions that have been raised about the appropriateness of the Guttman model and about the usual goodness of fit measures.[1] The factor analysis consisted of a principal component's analysis for each sample separately. Typically, the loadings were very similar across samples and across time, which gives added confidence that the scales are meaningful.

Scale scoring was done by means of a simple additive combination of responses.[2] This procedure was chosen for three reasons. First, factor scores are likely to vary from sample to sample, making cross-sample comparisons somewhat problematic. Major changes in the dimensional patterning of a set of items is certainly a matter of substantial interest, but minor variations in factor scores are likely to be a source of annoyance, and nothing more. Second, the scale scores resulting from an

[1] On the appropriateness of the Guttman model, see e.g., Jim Nunnally, *Psychometric Theory* (New York: McGraw-Hill, 1967). On goodness of fit, see e.g., John P. Robinson, "Toward a More Appropriate Use of Guttman Scaling," *Public Opinion Quarterly*, 37 (Summer 1973), 260-67.

[2] We are grateful to Gregory B. Markus for carrying out this work and for supplying the supporting rationale. Further elaboration concerning several of the scales discussed here can be found in his "Continuity, Change, and the Political Self: A Model of Political Socialization" (unpublished Ph.D. dissertation, University of Michigan, 1975).

additive approach are more readily interpretable than those based on factor scores. Third, where a relatively small number of items that do not differ greatly in their relative contributions to a traditional factor score are concerned, scales based on factor scores and on additive scoring are likely to correlate highly anyway.[3] As an extreme example, the correlation between the two versions of the political trust scales for the youths in 1965 was .995. (Each was also highly related to the corresponding Guttman scale: .823 for the factor scale score and .817 for the additive score.) A large number of other comparisons convinced us that little was to be lost and much to be gained by employing the additive combination technique. This approach was used to build scales for the 1965 responses as well as for those from 1973. Thus throughout this book a variable is measured, scaled, and scored identically, whether it is from 1965 or from 1973.

All variables are presented below in such a way that "low" to "high" runs from top to bottom. Similarly, words which connote "negative" responses (no, nonvoting, oppose, irrelevant, etc.) are at the left and top end. In addition to the marginals and percentage bases, the following presentation also contains the means and standard deviations for measures (including several ordinal-level, single-item variables) that are displayed as means for the sake of economy, especially in Chapters 8-11. This will facilitate comparisons of subsample and whole-sample central tendencies.

1. Good Citizenship
"People have different ideas about what being a good citizen means. We're interested in what you think. Tell me how you would describe a good citizen in this country—that is, what things about a person are most important in showing that one ["he" in 1965] is a good citizen?"

Up to four responses were coded in order of mention, using a code of approximately fifty categories. New codes were created in 1973 for responses which had not occurred in 1965; however, all categories from 1965 were retained, and the same major headings were used in both time periods. For purposes of analysis we have recoded responses into major categories as illustrated in various chapters, especially 2, 5, and 11. Specific responses included in each category are given elsewhere.[4]

2. Interest in Public Affairs
"Some people seem to think about what's going on in government most of the time, whether there's an election going on or not. Others

[3] See, e.g., Douglas A. Hibbs, Jr., *Mass Political Violence* (New York: Wiley, 1973), 7-17.
[4] Jennings and Niemi, *Political Character of Adolescence*, p. 121. For 1965, see also the ICPSR Student-Parent Socialization Study Codebook.

aren't that interested. Would you say you follow what's going on in government most of the time, some of the time, only now and then, or hardly at all?"

Follow Public Affairs	Youths		Parents	
	1965	1973	1965	1973
Hardly at all	2%	3%	7%	5%
Only now and then	13	12	13	12
Some of the time	43	37	30	29
Most of the time	42	48	50	55
	100%	100%	100%	100%
	(1348)	(1347)	(1178)	(1174)
Mean (1 = low, 4 = high)	3.25	3.29	3.22	3.34
St. dev.	.75	.80	.93	.86

3. Media Usage

"We're interested in finding out whether people ordinarily pay much attention to current events, public affairs and politics. Take newspapers, for instance—Do you read about *public affairs* and *politics* in any newspapers? (If yes) How often do you read newspaper articles about public affairs and politics—Almost daily, two or three times a week, three or four times a month, or a few times a year?"

Read Newspapers	Youths		Parents	
	1965	1973	1965	1973
Not at all[a]	15%	17%	16%	20%
3-4 times a month	6	8	4	4
2-3 times a week	32	27	16	16
Almost daily	46	48	64	60
	99%	100%	100%	100%
	(1344)	(1339)	(1174)	(1172)
Mean (1 = low, 5 = high)	3.95	3.90	4.12	3.98
St. dev.	1.37	1.42	1.45	1.55

[a] Includes a small number of respondents who said "a few times a year." They are given a value of "2" in calculating the mean scores.

"How about television—do you watch any programs about public affairs, politics and the news on television? (If yes) About how often do you watch such programs—Almost daily, two or three times a week, three or four times a month, or a few times a year?"

Watch Television	Youths		Parents	
	1965	1973	1965	1973
Not at all[a]	14%	10%	10%	9%
3-4 times a month	17	12	9	7
2-3 times a week	32	21	19	17
Almost daily	37	57	62	67
	100%	100%	100%	100%
	(1344)	(1342)	(1165)	(1177)
Mean (1 = low, 5 = high)	3.80	4.17	4.25	4.35
St. dev.	1.29	1.83	1.21	1.16

[a] Includes a small number of respondents who said "a few times a year." They are given a value of "2" in calculating the mean scores.

"How about radio— do you listen to any programs about public affairs, politics, and the news on the radio? (If yes) How often do you listen to them on radio—Almost daily, two or three times a week, three or four times a month, or a few times a year?"

Listen to Radio	Youths		Parents	
	1965	1973	1965	1973
Not at all[a]	36%	43%	35%	48%
3-4 times a month	6	8	4	5
2-3 times a week	15	12	11	10
Almost daily	43	36	50	36
	100%	99%	100%	99%
	(1342)	(1345)	(1176)	(1179)
Mean (1 = low, 5 = high)	3.31	3.00	3.42	2.88
St. dev.	1.78	1.79	1.81	1.85

[a] Includes a small number of respondents who said "a few times a year." They are given a value of "2" in calculating the mean scores.

"Finally, how about magazines—do you read about public affairs and politics in any magazines? (If yes) Are there any magazines that you read pretty regularly about public affairs and politics?"

Read Magazines	Youths		Parents	
	1965	1973	1965	1973
Do not read	33%	42%	41%	50%
Read, but not regularly	10	12	4	7
Read regularly	57	46	54	43
	100%	100%	99%	100%
	(1346)	(1346)	(1179)	(1176)
Mean (1 = low, 3 = high)	2.24	2.04	2.13	1.92
St. dev.	.92	.94	.97	.96

4. Cosmopolitanism

This scale was based on a rank ordering of the level of public affairs from the one in which the respondent was most interested to the one in which he or she was least interested. N's are slightly lower because the ranking was not obtained for those who followed public affairs "hardly at all" (see 1 above), on the grounds that a ranking for these respondents would be relatively meaningless. The question sequence was as follows:

"Which one do you follow *most closely*—international affairs, national affairs, state affairs, or local affairs? Which do you follow *least closely* [interviewer reads the three remaining levels]? Of the other two [interviewer reads the two remaining levels] which one do you follow most closely?" With the first, second and fourth ranks thus determined, the residual level occupies the third rank.

A seven-point ranking from least to most cosmopolitan was obtained by use of the unfolding technique developed by Coombs. Each of the possible rank orders is assigned to one of the seven levels, with the least cosmopolitan category being the single ranking local-state-national-international, and the most cosmopolitan category being the single ranking international-national-state-local. Incomplete orderings were dropped from the analysis. A complete description of the scaling procedure is given elsewhere.[5]

[5] M. Kent Jennings, "Preadult Orientations to Multiple Systems of Government," *Midwest Journal of Political Science*, 11 (August 1967), 291-317.

Cosmopolitanism	Youths		Parents	
	1965	1973	1965	1973
Least 1	4%	5%	9%	10%
2	3	5	9	11
3	5	7	10	10
4	17	21	24	27
5	18	17	19	18
6	34	35	22	18
Most 7	20	9	7	6
	101%	99%	100%	100%
	(1212)	(1196)	(941)	(939)
Mean (1 = low, 7 = high)	5.24	4.88	4.30	4.08
St. dev.	1.51	1.55	1.70	1.71

5. Internal Political Efficacy

Analysis of both samples and times confirms Balch's conclusion that there is a conceptual distinction between "internal" and "external" political efficacy.[6] This result, coupled with the fact that only the two in-

Internal Efficacy	Youths		Parents	
	1965	1973	1965	1973
Low (agree to both statements)[a]	21%	27%	39%	46%
Medium (agree with one, disagree with other statement)	47	49	40	39
High (disagree with both statements)[a]	31	24	21	15
	99%	100%	100%	100%
	(1340)	(1336)	(1169)	(1161)
Mean (1 = low, 3 = high)	2.10	1.98	1.82	1.69
St. dev.	.72	.72	.75	.72

[a] A few respondents (less than 1 percent) said "it depends." They were arbitrarily coded low if they agreed with the other item and high if they disagreed with the other item.

[6] George Balch, "Multiple Indicators and Survey Research: The Sense of 'Political Efficacy,'" Political Methodology, 1 (Spring 1974), 1-43.

ternal items were asked of the student sample in 1965, leads us to use an index based on only these two statements. Cases with missing data were dropped. The statements were included in a series of agree/disagree items:

"Voting is the only way that people like my mother and father can have any say about how the government runs things" (1965 youths).

"Voting is the only way that people like me can have any say about how the government runs things" (1965 parents; all samples in 1973).

"Sometimes politics and government seem so complicated that a person like me can't really understand what's going on."

6. External Political Efficacy

The same scoring procedures were used as with the internal efficacy measure.

"I don't think public officials care much what people like me think."

"People like me don't have any say about what the government does" ("People like my family," 1965 youths).

External Efficacy	Youths		Parents	
	1965	1973	1965	1973
Low (agree with both statements)	—[a]	20%	13%	23%
Medium (agree with one, disagree with the other)	—	26	25	27
High (disagree with both)	—	54	62	50
		100%	100%	100%
		(1108)	(1154)	(1085)
Mean (1 = low, 3 = high)		2.33	2.49	2.28
St. dev.		.79	.71	.81

[a] Not asked of youths in 1965.

7. Recognition and Understanding of Liberal-Conservative Dimension

This index, developed by Converse, is based on a series of questions about whether one party is more conservative or more liberal than the other.[7] General definitions of the categories, from no understanding to a broad understanding, respectively, are given in Table 2.8.

[7] Philip E. Converse. "The Nature of Belief Systems in Mass Publics," in David E. Apter (ed.), *Ideology and Discontent* (New York: Free Press, 1964).

1. "Do you think there are any important differences in what the Republicans and Democrats stand for? (If yes) 2. What are they? (Asked of all) 3. Would you say that either of one of the parties is more conservative or liberal than the other? (If yes to Q.3) 4. Which party is more conservative? 5. What do you have in mind when you say that the ———— are more conservative than the ————? (If No or DK to Q.3) Do you think that people generally consider the Democrats or the Republicans more conservative or wouldn't you want to guess about that? (If party named) What do you have in mind when you say that the ———— are more conservative than the ————?"

There has been considerable discussion in recent years of new political dimensions or of realignments on the old dimensions. However, elections preceding both waves of our panel—1964 and 1972—involved only the two major parties (in contrast to 1968 in which George Wallace considerably muddied liberal-conservative placements) and involved candidates widely identified in ideological terms (Goldwater as a conservative or a reactionary and McGovern as a liberal or radical). Therefore, use of this measure seems appropriate.

The relevant marginals and means are displayed in Figure 5.8. Standard deviations for youths are 1.63 for 1965 and 1.56 for 1973; corresponding figures for parents are 1.55 and 1.54.

8. Political Knowledge

An index representing the number of correct responses to six factual items. Incorrect and "don't know" responses were treated the same way

Number Correct	Youths		Parents	
	1965	1973	1965	1973
0	2%	1%	1%	1%
1	7	6	4	4
2	16	15	13	15
3	23	25	27	26
4	22	22	26	22
5	19	16	17	18
6	12	15	13	14
	101%	100%	101%	100%
	(1344)	(1093)[a]	(1158)	(1088)[a]
Mean (number correct)	3.61	3.69	3.73	3.72
St. dev.	1.51	1.50	1.39	1.44

[a] Not asked of 1973 mailback questionnaire respondents.

in the scoring. Cases with any missing data (not ascertained) were dropped.

"About how many years does a U.S. senator serve?"

"Marshal Tito is a leader in what country?"

"Do you happen to know about how many members there are on the U.S. Supreme Court?"

"Who is the governor of (name of this state) now?"

"During World War II, which nation had a great many concentration camps for Jews?"

"Do you happen to remember whether President Franklin Delano Roosevelt was a Republican or a Democrat? (If necessary): Which?"

9. Party Identification

"Generally speaking, do you usually think of yourself as a *Republican*, a *Democrat*, an independent, or what? (If Republican or Democrat) Would you call yourself a *strong* (R) (D) or a *not very strong* (R) (D)? (If Independent) Do you think of yourself as closer to the *Republican* or *Democratic* party?"

The marginals for the seven-way measure are presented in Figure 6.1. Because the mailback questionnaire elicited the five-way categorization, all reports of the seven-way measure rest exclusively on the personal interview data.

10. Voting

Turnout was determined by the following questions:

"In talking to people about the presidential election last year [1972] between Nixon and McGovern we found that a lot of people weren't able to vote because they weren't registered or they were sick or they just didn't have time. How about you, did you vote or did something keep you from voting?"

"How about the election for Congress in 1970—did you vote for a candidate for Congress that year?"

"Now, in 1968 you remember that Mr. Nixon ran on the Republican ticket against Mr. Humphrey for the Democrats and Mr. Wallace on an Independent ticket. Do you remember for sure whether you voted in that election?"

Turnout figures are reported in Figure 5.10.

The direction of the vote utilized in most of the analysis includes the reported vote for those who did vote and the stated preference of those who did not. Minor party voters are eliminated, except for Wallace voters in 1968.

"If you had been old enough to vote in the election last year between Goldwater and Johnson, who would you have voted for?" (1965 youths).

"Who did you vote for President?" "Who would you have voted for President if you had voted?" (1965 parents).

"Who did you vote for in the presidential election?" "If you had voted in the presidential election, for whom would you have voted?" (1973, about 1972).

"Did you vote for the Republican or Democratic candidate?" (1973, about actual 1972 and 1970 Congressional vote; no preferences obtained for nonvoters).

"Which one did you vote for?" "If you had voted, who would you have voted for?" (1973, about 1968).

Presidential preferences are reported in Figure 6.2.

11. Public Policy Issues

"Some people say that the government in Washington should see to it that white and black [Negro in 1965] children are allowed to go to the same schools. Others claim that this is not the government's business. Have you been concerned enough about this question to favor one side over the other? (If yes) Do you think that the government in Washington should see to it that white and black children go to the same schools or stay out of this area as it is none of its business?"

	Youths		Parents	
School Integration	1965	1973	1965	1973
Oppose	21%	37%	30%	42%
Depends[a]	10	16	12	15
Favor	69	49	58	44
	100%	102%	100%	101%
	(1251)	(1269)	(1075)	(1032)

[a] Volunteered response.

"Some people think it is all right for the public schools to start each day with a prayer. Others feel that religion does not belong in the public schools but should be taken care of by the family and the church. Have you been interested enough about this to favor one side over the other? (If yes) Which do you think—schools should be allowed to start each day with a prayer or religion does not belong in the schools?"

School Prayers	Youths		Parents	
	1965	1973	1965	1973
Oppose	29%	32%	16%	16%
Depends[a]	4	3	5	2
Favor	67	65	79	82
	100%	100%	100%	100%
	(1170)	(1164)	(1097)	(1064)

[a] Volunteered response.

(Agree or disagree)

"If a person wanted to make a speech in this community against churches and religion, he should be allowed to speak."

Anti-Church Speeches	Youths		Parents	
	1965	1973	1965	1973
Oppose	13%	6%	25%	24%
Favor	87	94	75	76
	100%	100%	100%	100%
	(1346)	(1344)	(1166)	(1169)

(Agree or disagree)

"If a Communist were legally elected into some public office around here, the people should allow him to take office."

Communist Holding Office	Youths		Parents	
	1965	1973	1965	1973
Oppose	62%	40%	70%	57%
Favor	37	60	30	43
	99%	100%	100%	100%
	(1344)	(1329)	(1157)	(1152)

12. Things Least Proud of as an American

"What things about this country are you least proud of as an American?"

Coding was similar to that for the "good citizenship" question except that only three responses were coded (due to fewer mentions by the respondents) and the code contained about seventy-five categories.

Again, the 1973 coding categories were expanded to take into account new content. Illustrations of how this variable was used are presented in various chapters, especially, 3, 6, and 10.

13. Political Trust

An index based on five questions. Repeated factor analyses have shown these items to scale very adequately, both for our own samples (loadings in the .45-.60 range) and for nationally representative samples of the electorate.[8] Responses to each item were scored 1 (least trust), 3 (a middle response), or 5 (most trust). Then items were combined to form an index running from 5 (least trusting) to 25 (most trusting). This was in turn collapsed into six categories (5-7, 9-11, 13, 15-17, 19-21, 23-25). Cases with missing data on more than one item were dropped. A value of 3 (middle response) was assigned to the missing data item.

"Do you think that quite a few of the people running the government are dishonest, not very many are, or do you think hardly any of them are dishonest?"

"Do you think that people in the government waste a lot of the money we pay in taxes, waste some of it, or don't waste very much of it?"

"How much of the time do you think you can trust the government in Washington to do what is right—just about always, most of the time, or only some of the time?"

"Do you feel that almost all of the people running the government

		Youths		Parents	
Political Trust		1965	1973	1965	1973
Low	1	2%	14%	9%	17%
	2	6	28	14	24
	3	12	26	18	26
	4	15	10	13	13
	5	44	18	36	17
High	6	22	3	9	4
		101%	99%	99%	101%
		(1306)	(1251)	(1152)	(1129)
Mean (1 = low, 6 = high)		4.58	3.01	3.81	2.99
St. dev.		1.23	1.40	1.50	1.43

[8] See Arthur H. Miller, "Political Issues and Trust in Government: 1964-1970," *American Political Science Review,* 68 (September 1974), 951-72, n. 12.

are smart people who usually know what they are doing, or do you think that quite a few of them don't seem to know what they are doing?"

"Would you say the government is pretty much run by a few big interests looking out for themselves, or that it is run for the benefit of all the people?"

14. Faith and Confidence in Multiple Levels of Government

"We find that people differ in how much faith and confidence they have in various levels of government in this country. In your case, do you have more faith and confidence in the *national* government, the government of this *state*, or in the *local* government around here? Which level do you have the least faith and confidence in—the *national* government, the government of this *state*, or the *local* government around here?" For most purposes responses only to the first question were used in the analysis. The "all equal" and "no level" categories were eliminated from the percentage base. The "local" and "state" categories, in turn, were combined so that most of the analysis uses a national, non-national dichotomous variable.

Most Faith and Confidence	Youths		Parents	
	1965	1973	1965	1973
Local	6%	23%	25%	23%
State	12	18	14	13
National	80	43	53	36
All equal	1	10	7	24
No level		6	1	4
	99%	100%	100%	100%
	(1327)	(1301)	(1108)	(1103)

15. Group Evaluations

"Thermometer" ratings for eight different groups: Southerners, Catholics, blacks (Negroes in 1965), whites, Jews, Protestants, labor unions, big business. Respondents rated each group on a scale from zero (not caring at all for the group) to 100 percent (feeling very favorably toward a group). In 1965 a "don't know" response was coded as a 50. In 1973 this response was coded separately, but for purposes of comparability with 1965 we have recoded it as a 50 for use throughout this book.

	Youths				Parents			
	1965		1973		1965		1973	
Group		St.		St.		St.		St.
Evaluations	Mean	Dev.	Mean	Dev.	Mean	Dev.	Mean	Dev.
Labor Unions	60.0	18.6	52.2	21.4	58.7	24.9	56.0	22.4
Southerners	62.1	22.8	62.3	20.3	65.7	22.9	68.5	18.8
Catholics	69.8	21.2	64.3	18.2	70.0	23.0	69.3	19.4
Big business	62.7	17.1	45.1	19.5	62.9	21.0	55.8	19.8
Jews	63.7	18.7	60.7	16.8	66.2	20.2	66.4	18.7
Whites	82.4	16.1	68.9	18.4	83.0	16.3	77.0	17.0
Protestants	78.6	17.4	67.4	18.4	82.6	16.2	76.5	17.2
Negroes	68.3	21.2	62.2	18.7	66.8	21.5	66.8	18.2

16. Religious Preference

"Is your religious preference Protestant, Roman Catholic, Jewish, or something else? (If Protestant) What church or denomination is that?"

In 1973 a further follow-up question was added: "(If Baptist) Is that Southern Baptist or something else?"

A detailed code of fifty responses was used.

17. Belief about the Bible

"Here are four statements about the Bible and I would like you to tell me which is closest to your own view.

The Bible is God's Word and all it says is true.

The Bible was written by men inspired by God but it contains some human errors.

Interpretations	Youths		Parents	
of the Bible	1965	1973	1965	1973
Irrelevant today	1%	3%	1%	1%
Not inspired by God	4	10	4	7
Some human error	51	59	41	43
God's Word	45	29	54	49
	101%	101%	100%	100%
	(1305)	(1307)	(1156)	(1135)
Mean (1 = irrelevant, 4 = God's Word)	3.39	3.14	3.48	3.39
St. dev.	.60	.69	.63	.68

The Bible is a good book because it was written by wise men but God has nothing to do with it.

The Bible was written by men who lived so long ago that it is worth very little today."

18. Church Attendance

"Would you say you go to (church/synagogue) almost every week, once or twice a month, a few times a year, or never?"

In 1973 the alternative "every week" was inserted. For purposes of comparability, however, that alternative is combined with "almost every week" throughout this book.

Frequency of Attendance	Youths		Parents	
	1965	1973	1965	1973
Never	2%	17%	7%	10%
Few times a year	14	38	25	28
Once or twice a month	18	15	16	15
Almost every week	66	30	52	47
	100%	100%	100%	100%
	(1300)[a]	(1157)[a]	(1144)[a]	(1119)[a]
Mean (1 = low, 4 = high)	3.47	2.59	3.13	2.98
St. dev.	.82	1.08	1.01	1.08

[a] Excludes those with no religious preference (youths: 2% in 1965, 13% in 1973; parents: 2% in 1965, 4% in 1973).

19. Personal Trust

A three-item index. Factor analysis of these items yields quite similar results across all of our samples, with loadings consistently in the .60-.70 range. Responses were coded 1 (least trust), 3 (a middle response—volunteered), or 5 (most trust), and then combined to form an index running from 3 (least trust) to 15 (most trust), which was then recoded to run from 1 to 7. Missing data on more than one item resulted in the case being dropped. A value of 3 (middle response) was assigned to the missing data item.

"Generally speaking, would you say that most people can be trusted or that you can't be too careful in dealing with people?"

"Would you say that most of the time people try to be helpful or that they are mostly looking out for themselves?"

"Do you think most people would try to take advantage of you if they got a chance or would they try to be fair?"

	Youths		Parents	
Trust	1965	1973	1965	1973
Least 1	12%	21%	11%	16%
2	1	1	1	1
3	16	16	12	11
4	1	1	1	1
5	25	21	19	21
6	2	1	2	2
Most 7	43	39	54	48
	100%	100%	100%	100%
	(1335)	(1323)	(1159)	(1155)
Mean (1 = low, 7 = high)	5.06	4.60	5.40	5.06
St. dev.	2.09	2.34	2.08	2.25

20. Personal Efficacy

Two indices of personal efficacy were constructed, each one composed of three items. Factor analysis showed that the two components are distinct across all samples. In each case, the indices were scored in an identical fashion to that used for personal trust.

The first index refers to *opinion strength*:

"When you get into an argument, do you usually get your own way or do you often give in?"

	Youths		Parents	
Opinion Strength	1965	1973	1965	1973
Low 1	9%	10%	14%	15%
2	2	2	5	5
3	21	21	22	25
4	6	5	8	8
5	35	33	28	25
6	9	6	10	8
High 7	18	23	13	14
	100%	100%	100%	100%
	(1337)	(1096)[a]	(1175)	(1110)[a]
Mean (1 = low, 7 = high)	4.54	4.57	4.14	4.03
St. dev.	1.78	1.87	1.87	1.90

[a] Not asked of 1973 mailback questionnaire respondents.

"Some people have strong opinions about a good many things. Other people are more in the middle of the road. What kind of person are you?"

"When you make up your mind about something, is it pretty hard to argue you out of it or do you change your mind pretty easily?"

The second index refers to self confidence:

"Have you usually felt pretty sure your life would work out the way you want it to, or have there been times when you haven't been very sure about it?"

"Do you feel that you are the kind of person who gets more than his share of bad luck or do you feel that you have mostly good luck?"

"When you make plans ahead, do you usually get to carry out things the way you expected, or do things usually come up to make you change your plans?"

Self-Confidence	Youths 1965	1973	Parents 1965	1973
Low 1	5%	6%	5%	7%
2	3	1	5	3
3	20	20	19	15
4	4	2	7	6
5	39	35	31	32
6	2	1	4	4
High 7	28	34	28	33
	101%	99%	99%	100%
	(1333)	(1301)	(1176)	(1174)
Mean (1 = low, 7 = high)	4.88	4.96	4.78	4.99
St. dev.	1.71	1.83	1.80	1.83

Abeles, Ronald P., 8n
Aberbach, Joel D., 307n, 313n
Abramson, Paul, 49n, 308n, 315n, 323n
Achen, Christopher H., 54n
age: and youth-parent similarity, 89,
    100, 110-12. See also life cycle effects
aggregate level change: importance of,
    5-6; models of, 117-24
Alexander, Joseph, 77n, 80n, 82n
Allerbeck, Klaus R., 44n, 77n
Allport, Floyd H., 166n
Almond, Gabriel, 230n, 279n
Altbach, Philip G., 7n, 22n, 122n, 331n,
    345n
Andersen, Kristi, 54n, 282n, 294, 303
Apter, David, 37n, 52n, 141n
Astin, Alexander W., 232n, 236n, 237n,
    263n

Bachman, Jerald G., 233n, 236n, 242n,
    257n, 262n, 351n
Bailey, J. P., Jr., 233n
Bailey, Kenneth D., 75n, 192n
Balch, George I., 36n, 354n, 408
Baltes, Paul B., 8n, 78n, 192n
Barnes, Samuel H., 44n, 77n, 344n
Beck, Paul Allen, 44n, 46n, 76n, 77n,
    148n, 151n, 155n
belief systems, see liberal-conservative
    recognition
Bengtson, Vern L., 21n, 77n, 116n,
    345n
Bennett, Stephen E., 54n
Bennett, W. Lance, 54n
Bible, see fundamentalism
big business, ratings of: aggregate level
    change, 177-81; generational com-
    parisons, 177-81; individual level
    stability, 66-67; youth-parent similar-
    ity, 96-97. See also group evaluations
    under education; protestors; race; sex.
Binstock, Robert, 21n
Bishop, George F., 54n
blacks, ratings of: aggregate level
    change, 177-81; individual level sta-
    bility, 66-67; influence of, 369-70,
    376; generational comparisons, 177-
    81; youth-parent similarity, 96-97.
    See also race; group evaluations un-
    der education; protestors; race; sex.

Blalock, Hubert M., 24n
Blau, Peter M., 235n
Block, Jack, 22n
Bradburn, Norman M., 198n
Braungart, Richard G., 341n
Brim, Orville, 21n
Brookes, Marilyn, 23n, 228n
Bullock, Charles S., III, 307n
Butler, David, 122n

Campbell, Angus, 35n, 230n, 279n,
    285n, 307n, 354n
Campbell, Bruce, 77n
candidate preferences: aggregate level
    change, 155-56; cohorts of '65 and
    '73, 206-207; generational compari-
    sons, 156; individual level stability,
    52-54; youth-parent similarity, 90-93.
    See also candidate preferences under
    education; protestors; race; sex.
Cannell, Charles F., 198n
Caporaso, James A., 192n
Carmines, Edward, 71n
Carter, Jimmy, 326
Catholics, ratings of: aggregate level
    change, 177-81; generational com-
    parisons, 177-81; individual level sta-
    bility, 66-67; youth-parent similarity,
    96-97, 103. See also religion; group
    evaluations under education; protes-
    tors; race; sex.
Chaffee, Steven H., 22n, 32n
Chandler, Robert, 333n
change form of government, 366, 376;
    generational comparisons, 162
change, see aggregate level change; in-
    dividual level change. See also
    specific issues
children, effects of: on parents, 299-
    300; on youths, 295-98
church attendance: aggregate level
    change, 183-85; cohorts of '65 and
    '73, 217; generational comparison,
    183-85; individual level stability, 69-
    70; youth-parent similarity, 98-99.
    See also church attendance under
    education; race; sex.
citizenship norms: aggregate level
    change, 124-26, 135-36; cohorts of
    '65 and '73, 224-25; generational

citizenship norms (*cont.*)
    comparisons, 125; individual level
    stability, 26-27, 35-36; youth-parent
    similarity, 83-84. *See also* citizenship
    norms *under* education; protestors;
    race.
Citrin, Jack, 172n
civic tolerance, 348, 350
Clark, Cal, 354n
Cohen, Roberta S., 279n, 308n
cohort effects, *see* generational effects
Cole, Richard L., 70n
Coleman, James S., 236n
college, *see* education
Communists in office issue: aggregate
    level change, 157-61; generational
    comparisons, 157-61; individual-level
    stability, 56-61; cohorts of '65 and
    '73, 208-10; youth-parent similarity,
    93-95. *See also* public policy issues
    under education; protestors; race; sex.
compositional factors, 123-24
conceptual sophistication, *see* liberal-
    conservative recognition
Connell, R. W., 78n, 81n
conservative-liberal scale, *see* liberal-
    conservative recognition
conservatives, ratings of, 368, 376
Converse, Jean M., 198n
Converse, Philip E., 25n, 37n, 48n, 52n,
    54n, 56n, 57n, 66n, 72n, 123n, 141n,
    154n, 230n, 257n, 279n, 286n, 354n,
    410n
cosmopolitanism: aggregate level
    change, 126-28; cohorts of '65 and
    '73, 200-203; generational compari-
    sons, 127; individual level stability,
    29-30; youth-parent similarity, 83-84.
    See also cosmopolitanism *under* edu-
    cation; protestors; race; sex.
Crockett, Harry J., 160n, 230n, 287n
Cutler, Neal E., 21n, 74n, 129n
Cutler, Stephen J., 160n

Dalton, Russell J., 77n
Danowski, James, 129n
Davies, James C., 20n
Democratic party, *see* liberal-conserva-
    tive recognition; partisanship
Dennis, Jack, 23n, 81n, 138n, 173n,
    280n
discussion of politics: aggregate level
    change, 133-34; cohorts of '65 and
    '73, 224; generational comparisons,
    133; individual level stability, 33-34
Duncan, Otis Dudley, 235n

Easton, David, 280n
Eckland, Bruce K., 233n
education: achieved levels of, 235; and
    aggregate level change, 124; and
    candidate preferences, 255-56; and
    church attendance, 264-66; and citi-
    zenship norms, 247-48; and cosmo-
    politanism, 242-46; and discussion of
    politics, 242-46; and fundamental-
    ism, 263-66; and government
    levels, 262; and group evaluations,
    262-63; and individual rates of
    change, 237-41; and liberal-conserva-
    tive recognition, 248-49; media atten-
    tion, 242-46; and opinions about teen-
    agers, 265-67; and partisanship, 255;
    and personal efficiency, 264-66; and
    personal trust, 265-66; and political
    efficacy, 248-50; and political interest,
    242-46; and political knowledge, 248-
    49; and political participation, 250-
    54; and political trust, 261-62; and
    public policy issues, 257-61; and re-
    ligious affiliation, 263; and turnout,
    250-51; and youth-parent similarity,
    89
Eisenhower, Dwight D., 7
El-Assel, Mohamed, 359n
Elder, Glen H., Jr., 22n
employment, effects of: on youths, 295;
    on parents, 301-303
Erikson, Erik H., 7, 8n
erosion effects on protest activity,
    371-73

Farah, Barbara, 279n
Featherman, David L., 235n
Feldman, Kenneth A., 232n, 236n,
    237n
Fendrich, James M., 116n, 341n
Feuer, Lewis S., 122n, 331n
Fields, James M., 166n
Fishel, Jeffrey, 173n
Flacks, Richard, 116n, 237n, 345n
Flora, Cornelia B., 294
Foner, Anne, 21n, 118n, 157n
Fox, Lawrence E., 395n
Friedrich, Elaine Ader, 316n, 321n,
    323n
fundamentalism: aggregate level
    change, 183-84; generational compar-
    isons, 183; individual level stability,
    69; youth-parent similarity, 98-99,
    107. *See also* fundamentalism *under*
    education; race; sex.

Gallup, George, 182n, 217n
gender roles: defined, 271. *See also* children, effects of; employment, effects of; marriage, effects of; sex differences
generation gap, 115-16, 122, 186-88, 220-22, 227-29, 386; subjective perceptions and, 161-66; among nonwhites, 307, 315, 322, 324-25, 327, 329
generation, political, 6-7
generation unit: defined, 331-33; protestors as, 371, 373-79
generational effects, 5-6n, 21, 75, 118-23, 190-97; and compositional factors, 123-24
Gergen, Kenneth J., 20n, 71n
Glenn, Norval D., 21n, 123n, 126n
Goel, M. L., 230n
Goldman, Nancy L., 377n
Goldwater, Barry, 255, 348, 411, 413
good citizen, *see* citizenship norms
Goslin, David A., 78n
government levels, evaluations of: aggregate level change, 175-76; cohorts of '65 and '73, 215-16; generational comparisons, 175; individual level stability, 65. *See also* government levels *under* education; protestors; race.
Grassmuck, Sherri, 279n
Greely, Andrew M., 22n
Greenstein, Fred I., 19n, 25n, 54n, 138n, 173n, 272n, 279n
Grimes, Michael, 126n
Gurin, Gerald, 35n
Gustafsson, Gunnel, 77n

Harris, Louis, 286n
Hatchett, Shirley, 307n
Hauser, Robert M., 235n
Hentoff, Nat, 327n
Hess, Robert D., 23n, 272n, 279n, 286n
Hibbs, Douglas A., Jr., 405n
Himmelfarb, Milton, 327n
Himmelweit, Hilde T., 22n
Hirsch, Paul M., 129n
historical effects, *see* period effects
Hoskin, Marilyn Brookes, 19n. *See also* Brookes
Humphrey, Hubert, 412
Hyman, Herbert H., 122n, 230n, 261n, 272n

individual level change: importance of, 4-5
inertia: and political change, 388-90

Inglehart, Ronald, 22n, 122n
integration of schools issue: aggregate level change, 157-61; generational comparisons, 157-61; individual level stability, 56-61; in 1965 and related issues in 1973, 60-61; youth-parent similarity, 93-95, 105. *See also* public policy issues *under* education; protestors; race; sex.
issue opinions, *see specific issues*

Jaquette, Jane S., 282n
Jennings, M. Kent, 4n, 26n, 28n, 37n, 44n, 46n, 49n, 77n, 78n, 81n, 82n, 93n, 104n, 111n, 127n, 135n, 148n, 151n, 174n, 223n, 279n, 282n, 294, 312n, 351n, 377n, 388n, 393n, 394n, 405n, 408n
Jews, ratings of: aggregate level change, 177-81; generational comparisons, 177-81; individual level stability, 66-67; youth-parent similarity, 96-97, 107. *See also* religion; group evaluations *under* education; protestors; race; sex.
Johnson, Lyndon, 207, 347, 413
Johnson, Marilyn, 21n, 118n, 157n
Johnston, Jerome, 233n, 236n, 242n, 257n, 262n
Joslyn, Richard, 78n, 79n, 80n, 81
Jukam, Thomas O., 25n

Kaase, Max, 44n, 77n, 344n
Kagen, Jerome, 71n, 78n, 82n
Kahn, Robert L., 198n
Kasschau, Patricia L., 345n
Kaufman, Robert L., 160n
Kennedy, John F., 7
King, Martin Luther, Jr., 306
Kirkpatrick, Jeanne, 294
Kline, F. Gerald, 129n
Knutson, Jeanne H., 20n
Koenig, Kathryn E., 237n
Kubota, Akira, 77n

labor unions, ratings of: aggregate level change, 177-81; generational comparisons, 177-81; individual level stability, 66-67; youth-parent similarity, 96-97. *See also* group evaluations *under* education; protestors; race; sex.
Lamare, James, 257n
Lambert, T. Allen, 7n
Lane, Robert E., 70n, 71n
Lansing, Marjorie, 282n
Laufer, Robert S., 7n, 22n, 122n, 331n, 345n

least proud attributes: individual level
stability, 62-63; youth-parent similarity, 95-96
Lee, Marcia Manning, 294
Levitin, Teresa E., 117n
liberal-conservative recognition: aggregate level change, 139-41; generational comparisons, 141; individual
level stability, 37-39; youth-parent
similarity, 86-87, 108. *See also* liberal-conservative recognition *under*
education; protestors; race; sex.
liberal-conservative self-placement: and
protestors, 366-67; youth-parent
similarity, 103, 105, 162. *See also*
liberal-conservative recognition
life-cycle effects: 5-6n, 75, 380-81; and
aggregate change, 118-23, 188, 192-
97, 227; models of, 20-21; sex and,
272-74; youth-parent agreement,
81-82, 98, 102, 113-14
lifelong openness model, 20, 74-75, 113,
380-84, 386-91
lifelong persistence model, 20-21, 74-
75, 385-86
Lipset, Seymour Martin, 327n
Livson, Norman, 78n
Lynn, Naomi B., 294

McClosky, Herbert, 230n
McGlen, Nancy E., 282n, 294
McGovern, George, 116, 207, 411-12
McPherson, J. Miller, 354n
Mankoff, Milton, 116n, 345n
Mannheim, Karl, 7, 22n, 122n, 331,
333, 341n, 381
Marcus, George E., 160n, 350n
marijuana, legalization of: generational
comparisons, 162, 222; and protestors, 366, 376; youth-parent similarity, 102, 105
marijuana users, 222; ratings of, 368,
372
Markus, Gregory B., 57n, 70n, 71n, 75n,
90n, 101, 282n, 351n, 377n, 389n,
404n
marriage: effects of, 295; frequency
among youths, 294-95; and youth-
parent similarity, 109-12
Massey, Joseph, 77n
measurement error, 73-74
media attention: aggregate level
change, 129-33; cohorts of '65 and
'73, 200-201; generational comparisons, 129-33; individual level stability, 30-32; youth-parent similarity,

83-85. *See also* media attention *under*
education; protestors; race; sex.
Medsker, Leland L., 237n
Merelman, Richard M., 280n
Merton, Robert K., 166n
methods effects, 335-40
Meyer, John W., 231-32, 269n
Milbrath, Lester, 230n
military, ratings of, 368, 376
military service: effects of, 377-79
Miller, Arthur H., 62n, 172n, 323n,
324n, 415n
Miller, Peter V., 129n
Miller, Warren E., 35n, 117n, 230n,
257n, 279n
Monroe, Alan D., 286n
Moss, Howard, 71n, 82n
Muller, Edward N., 25n

Nader, Ralph, 103
Newcomb, Theodore M., 22n, 232n,
236n, 237n
Nie, Norman H., 54n, 117n, 126n, 139n,
230n, 316n
Niemi, Richard G., 4n, 20n, 23n, 26n,
37n, 48n, 49n, 77n, 80n, 81n, 82n,
93n, 104n, 111n, 127n, 135n, 155n,
174n, 223n, 228n, 312n, 388n, 393n,
405n
Nixon, Richard, 104, 156, 171, 255-56,
347, 348, 412
Noelle-Newmann, Elisabeth, 166n
Nunn, Clyde Z., 160n, 230n, 287n
Nunnally, Jim, 404n

O'Gorman, Hubert, 166n
Oldenick, Robert W., 54n
O'Malley, Patrick M., 233n, 236n,
242n, 257n, 262n
opinion strength, *see* personal efficacy
Oppenheim, Karen Mason, 123n
Orum, Amy W., 279n
Orum, Anthony, 279n, 280n, 308n

parent-youth similarity, *see specific issues*, youth-parent similarity
participation, political: aggregate level
change, 148-51; and high school participation, 46; index of, 45-46; individual level stability, 41-47; youth-
parent similarity, 86-89, 110-11. *See
also* protestors; political participation
under education; protestors; race;
sex.
partisanship: and aggregate change,

152-55; cohorts of '65 and '73, 205-207; generational comparisons, 154; individual level stability, 48-52; youth-parent similarity, 90-93, 108. *See also* partisanship *under* education; protestors; race; sex.

party identification, *see* partisanship

period effects: and aggregate change, 118-23, 188, 192-97

persistence, individual-level: education and, 25, 237-41; measurement of, 23-25; models of, 19-22; and protestors, 338; race and, 308-10; sex and, 275; summarized, 73-75

personal efficacy: aggregate level change, 185-86; cohorts of '65 and '73, 218-21; generational comparisons, 186; individual level stability, 71-72; youth-parent similarity, 99. *See also* personal efficacy *under* education; race, sex.

personal trust: aggregate level change, 185-86; cohorts of '65 and '73, 218-19; generational comparisons, 186; individual level stability, 71-72; youth-parent similarity, 99. *See also* personal trust *under* education; race; sex.

Petrocik, John R., 117n, 139n

Piereson, James, 160n, 350n

police, fairness of, 105; ratings of, 367-68, 376

policy preferences: 1965 preferences and related issue preferences in 1973, 60-61, 104-105; object change vs. evaluation change, 54-55, 58-60. *See also* public policy issues *under* education; protestors; race; sex.

political cynicism, *see* political trust

political efficacy: aggregate level change, 137-38; cohorts of '65 and '73, 203-205; generational comparisons, 37-38; individual level stability, 36-37; youth-parent similarity, 86. *See also* political efficacy *under* education; protestors; race; sex.

political knowledge: aggregate level change, 141-46; generational comparisons, 141-42; individual level stability, 39-41; youth-parent similarity, 86-87. *See also* political knowledge *under* education; race; sex.

political interest: aggregate level change, 126, 128; cohorts of '65 and '73, 199-201; generational comparisons, 126; individual level stability,

28-29; youth-parent similarity, 83-84. *See also* political interest *under* education; protestors; race; sex.

political trust: aggregate level change, 172-74; cohorts of '65 and '73, 210-14; generational comparisons, 173-74; individual level stability, 64-65; youth-parent similarity, 95-96, 106. *See also* political trust *under* education; protestors; race; sex.

Polsby, Nelson W., 19n, 25n, 54n

prayers in school issue: aggregate level change, 157-61; generational comparisons, 157-61; individual level stability, 56-61; youth-parent similarity, 93-95, 105, 107

pre-adult socialization, 23

Protestants, ratings of: aggregate level change, 177-81; generational comparisons, 177-81; individual level stability, 66-67; youth-parent similarity, 96-97. *See also* religion; group evaluations *under* education; protestors; race; sex.

protestors: and candidate preferences, 344-48, 355-56, 360, 362-63; and citizenship norms, 339-42, 361, 365; cosmopolitanism, 339; defined, 333-37, 360-61; and discussion of politics, 339, 361; and government levels, 352-53, 357-58, 360; and group evaluations, 364, 367-70, 373-76; and individual rates of change, 338; and level of education, 335-36; and liberal-conservative recognition, 339-41; and media usage, 339-41; and partisanship, 344-48, 355-56, 360, 362-63; and political efficacy, 354, 357-58, 360-61, 365; and political interest, 339-41; and political participation, 343-44; and political trust, 349-52, 357-58, 360, 364; and public policy issues, 348-49, 356-58, 360, 363-64, 366-67, 372-76; and race, 335; and turnout, 344; and Vietnam, 353, 371

Rabinowitz, George, 20n

race: and candidate preferences, 318; and church attendance, 327-28; and citizenship norms, 311-14; and cohorts of '65 and '73, 329-30; and cosmopolitanism, 311-12; and education levels, 315, 317, 319; and fundamentalism, 327-28; government levels, 323; and group evaluations, 325-27; and individual rates of

race (*cont.*)
change, 308-10; and least proud attributes, 169; and liberal-conservative recognition, 312-14; and media usage, 310-12; and partisanship, 318-20; and personal efficacy, 328-29; and personal trust, 328-29; and political efficacy, 313-14; and political interest, 310-12; and political knowledge, 312-14; and political participation, 308, 316-18; and political trust, 323-24; and public policy issues, 320-22; and turnout, 315-16. *See also* integration of schools
racial problems: least proud of, 168-69
radical students, ratings of: youth-parent similarity, 103, 367-68, 376
Radler, D. H., 287n
Ransford, H. Edward, 345n
recognition and understanding of liberal-conservative dimension, *see* liberal-conservative recognition
Reed, John Shelton, 230n, 261n
Reich, Charles A., 116n
religious affiliation: aggregate level change, 182-84; cohorts of '65 and '73, 215; and education, 263; generational comparisons, 182; individual level stability, 68; and sex, 291-92; youth-parent agreement, 98-99. *See also* fundamentalism; speeches against church issue
Remmers, H. H., 287n
Renshon, Stanley Allen, 19n, 20n, 32n, 71n, 75n, 76n
Republican party, *see* liberal-conservative recognition
response set, 198
reverse socialization, 82, 100-101
Riley, Matilda White, 8n, 21n, 118n, 157n
Robinson, John P., 404n
Rodgers, Harrell R., Jr., 307n
Roos, Leslie L., 192n
Roosevelt, Franklin, 6, 41, 146, 412
Rosenau, Norah, 20n
Rosenberg, Milton J., 286n
Rosenmayr, Leopold, 44n, 77n
Ross, R. Danforth, 77n, 80n, 82n
Rozak, Theodore, 116n
Rusk, Jerrold G., 257n

salience of politics, *see* political interest
Sapiro, Virginia, 272n, 293n
Schaie, K. Warner, 8n, 78n, 192n
Schuman, Howard, 166n 198n, 307n
Schwartz, David C., 20n, 322n

Schwartz, Sandra Kenyon, 20n, 75n, 322n
Scott, Joseph W., 359n
Searing, Donald, 20n
Sears, David O., 19, 54n, 293n, 307n
Segal, David R., 377n
self-confidence, *see* personal efficacy
sex differences: and candidate preferences, 284-85; and church attendance, 291-92; cohorts of '65 and '73, 303-304; and cosmopolitanism, 277-78; distinguished from gender roles, 271; and fundamentalism, 291-92; group evaluations, 289-90; and individual rates of change, 275; and liberal-conservative recognition, 280-81; and media attention, 278-79; and partisanship, 284-86; and personal efficacy, 291-92; and personal trust, 291-92; and political efficacy, 280-81; and political interest, 276-77; and political knowledge, 280-81; and political participation, 282-83; and political trust, 289-90; and public policy issues, 286-88; and religious affiliation, 291-92; and turnout, 282-83; and youth-parent similarity, 110-12. *See also* children, effects of; employment, effects of; gender role; marriage, effects of
sex equality issue, 366, 376; generational comparisons, 162; and protestors, 367-68, 373, 376; youth-parent similarity, 103
Shanah, Ethel, 21n
Shingles, Richard D., 80n
Sigel, Roberta S., 19n, 22n, 228n, 285n
southerners, ratings of: aggregate level change, 177-81; generational comparisons, 177-81; individual level stability, 66-67; youth-parent similarity, 96-97. *See also* group evaluations *under* education; protestors; race; sex.
Spaeth, Joe L., 22n
speeches against church issue: aggregate level change, 157-61; cohorts of '65 and '73, 208-10; generational comparisons, 157-61; individual level stability, 56-61; youth-parent similarity, 93-95, 105. *See also* public policy issues *under* education; protestors; race; sex.
Steinem, Gloria, 103
Stimson, James, 54n
Stokes, Donald, 122n, 230n, 279n
Stouffer, Samuel A., 230n, 287

Sudman, Seymour, 198n
Sullivan, John L., 160n, 350n
superpatriotism issue: cohorts of '65 and '73, 208-10
Swift, Betty, 22n

Tedin, Kent L., 77n, 82n, 93n
teenagers, opinions about: aggregate level change, 186-87; individual level stability, 72
television commentators, influence of: youth-parent similarity, 103
Tipton, Leonard P., 23n
Tito, Marshal, 41, 412
Torney, Judith V., 23n, 272n, 279n, 286n
Trent, James W., 237n
Tuchfarber, Alfred J., 54n
Tufte, Edward R., 54n
turnout, voting: aggregate level change, 147-48; generational comparisons, 147; individual level stability, 42-44; youth-parent similarity, 86-87. See also candidate preferences; turnout under education; protestors; race; sex.

Ullman, Matthew, 20n, 71n
Useem, Michael, 378n

Vaillancourt, Pauline, 23n
Vaughter, Reesa M., 271n
Verba, Sidney, 117n, 126n, 139n, 230n, 279n, 286n, 316n
Vietnam War: and political generations, 203-10; and protestors, 331, 334-35, 353, 365, 371; youth-parent similarity, 103, 105
voting, see candidate preferences; turnout

Walker, Jack L., 307n
Wallace, George, 156, 256, 411-12
Ward, L. Scott, 23n
Ward, Robert E., 77n
Warwick, Donald, 237n
Watergate: and political trust, 211, 226, 367
Weisberg, Herbert F., 24, 48n, 155n
Weissberg, Robert, 78n, 79n, 80n, 81
Welch, Susan, 282n, 294, 354n
welfare, influence of: youth-parent similarity, 103
Wheeler, Stanton, 21n
whites, ratings of: aggregate level change, 177-81; generational comparisons, 177-81; individual level stability, 66-67; youth-parent similarity, 96-97. See also blacks; race; group evaluations under education; protestors; race; sex.
Williams, J. Allen, 160n, 230n, 287n
Wilson, Thomas P., 24n
Wolfe, Arthur C., 257n
women, equality of: see sex equality issue
women's influence, 288, 369-70, 376
women's liberation movement, ratings of, 288, 368, 376
Wright, Charles R., 230n, 261n
Wright, Gerald, 20n

Yankelovich, Daniel, 115n, 210n, 253n, 257n, 333n

Library of Congress Cataloging in Publication Data

Jennings, M Kent.
    Generations and politics.

    Includes index.
    1.   Public opinion—United States—Longitudinal
studies.   2.   Political socialization—United States—
Longitudinal studies.   3.   Conflict of generations—
Longitudinal studies.   I.   Niemi, Richard G., joint
author.   II.   Title.
HN90.P8J46   306.8'7   80-8555
    ISBN 0-691-07626-X
    ISBN 0-691-02201-1 (pbk.)

M. Kent Jennings is Professor of Political Science and Program
Director of the Institute for Social Research at the University of
Michigan. Richard G. Niemi is Professor of Political Science at
the University of Rochester. They are the authors of *The Political Character of Adolescence* (Princeton).